WORKING-CLASS IMAGES OF SOCIETY

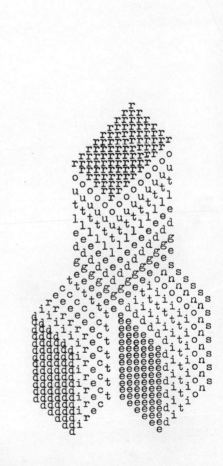

WORKING-CLASS IMAGES OF SOCIETY

edited by
MARTIN BULMER

ROUTLEDGE DIRECT EDITIONS

ROUTLEDGE & KEGAN PAUL
London and Boston

in association with the
SOCIAL SCIENCE RESEARCH COUNCIL

First published in 1975
by Routledge & Kegan Paul Ltd
Broadway House, 68-74 Carter Lane
London EC4V 5EL and
9 Park Street,
Boston, Mass. 02108, USA
Typed by Betty R. Ozzard
Printed and bound in Great Britain
by Unwin Brothers Limited,
The Gresham Press, Old Woking, Surrey
A member of the Staples Printing Group
© Routledge & Kegan Paul Ltd 1975

ISBN 0 7100 8308 4

CONTENTS

v

FOREWORD

The study of working-class social imagery is a field which was
established early in the development of British sociology.   The
idea of a conference which would bring together a variety of more
recent research and theory on the subject originated with Mr Martin
Bulmer, and was recommended for support by the Sociology and Social
Administration Committee of the Social Science Research Council
(SSRC).   The conference took place at Durham in September 1972,
and this edition of the papers has been prepared by Mr Bulmer, to
whom all credit is due.   It does not necessarily represent any
agreed view of the SSRC's Sociology and Social Administration
Committee or of the Council itself.   Grants made by the SSRC for
studies connected with working-class social imagery are referred
to in the Preface.

Jeremy Mitchell

Secretary, Social Science Research Council

PREFACE

The papers on working-class social imagery appearing in this
volume were originally presented to the SSRC Conference on The
Occupational Community of the Traditional Worker (referred to in
Mr Mitchell's Foreword), which was held at Van Mildert College,
Durham from 25 to 27 September 1972.   The subject of the conference
was recent and current British research on social imagery and
subjective perceptions of social stratification among those in
'traditional' working-class occupations.   Professor David Lockwood's
article entitled Sources of Variation in Working-Class Images of
Society (first published in the 'Sociological Review', vol.14, no.3,
November 1966, pp.249-67 and reproduced by permission) provided the
thematic focus of the conference.

The papers which follow are divided into four groups.   In Part
One is reprinted Lockwood's 1966 paper, containing the influential
ideal types of the 'proletarian traditional worker' and the 'deferential traditional worker'.   This paper is the starting point for
all the others in the symposium.   It is preceded by a short
Introduction setting the article and the debates around it in a
broader sociological context.

Part Two contains six papers reporting the results of empirical
research on manual workers' perceptions of the class structure.
Two of these papers - by Moore on coal-miners and Cousins and Brown
on shipbuilding workers - are concerned with occupations which
Lockwood linked to the existence of 'traditional proletarian' images
of the class structure.   Three of these papers - Bell and Newby on
agricultural workers, Martin and Fryer on textile workers, and
Batstone on workers in small firms in Banbury - are concerned with
occupations or work 'milieux' which Lockwood linked to the existence
of 'traditional deferential' images of the class structure.   The
sixth paper, by Blackburn and Mann, analyses the results of a survey
conducted among a sample of non-skilled manual workers in a range of
industries in the town of Peterborough, and examines the genesis and
nature of workers' social imagery from a rather different standpoint.

In Part Three are several papers considering more general
theoretical and methodological issues.   As an introduction, the
editor discusses a number of methodological problems associated with
the study of class imagery.   This is followed by a paper by Willener

(a pioneer of the study of class imagery in the 1950s) in which he
makes several valuable distinctions between different types of
imagery, and raises questions about the contexts of research and
action in which imagery is elicited.   Davis and Cousins direct
attention to the historical dimension (with what state of affairs
is the social imagery of contemporary 'traditional' and 'affluent'
workers being compared?) and to the status of ideal-type analysis.
Both Salaman and Allcorn and Marsh discuss from different stand-
points the status of the concept 'occupational community', which
Lockwood identified as supporting in particular 'traditional
proletarian' imagery of the class structure.

In Part Four Lockwood comments on the preceding papers in the
light of the original article, and replies to his critics.   This
is followed by a comment by Westergaard on radical class consciousness, and a postscript by Lockwood on the radical worker which
rounds off the symposium.

In the Bibliography, which includes all items referred to in the
text, the opportunity has been taken to include other material not
referred to by contributors.   The coverage is selective, relating
mainly to the period since 1950.   Some items contain reports of
empirical research, others are more theoretical, a few are personal
documents.   There are few references to material on the 'new'
working class, since the symposium is concerned primarily with the
'traditional' worker.   Most of the items relate to Britain or the
USA.   These lacunae underline the highly selective character of
the Bibliography.

The intellectual background to the conference is sketched in the
Introduction, but one relevant point should be mentioned here.
Since the publication of Lockwood's article in 1966, the Social
Science Research Council had supported and continued to support a
number of sociological projects in this area, and it seemed worthwhile to try to draw some of the threads of this research on
working-class social imagery together at a conference without
waiting for its eventual publication.   Five of the eleven papers
in Parts Two and Three of this volume arise from research projects
funded by the Sociology and Social Administration Committee of
SSRC.   The research grants in question are:

R.S. Moore	The effects of Methodism on social and political structures of mining communities.	(HR 425)
R.K. Brown	Orientation to work and industrial behaviour of shipbuilding workers on Tyneside.	(HR 260)
Dr R Martin	Unemployment and labour mobility: a case study.	(HR 443)
Dr R.M. Blackburn	Social and industrial determinants of workers' attitudes.	(HR 600)
Dr D.H. Allcorn	Constraints, choice and chance: social stratification and work.	(HR 599)

In addition, a sizeable number of other participants attending the
conference were or still are engaged upon research into aspects of
social stratification with SSRC support.   It should also be borne
in mind that the manuscript was completed in the summer of 1973.

The pleasant task remains for the editor to acknowledge the

assistance of those who helped to make the present volume possible.
I should like to thank all those who participated in the Durham
conference for their interest and co-operation. This applies
particularly to those who gave papers and also to I.C. Cannon,
J.E.T. Eldridge, Miss I. Emmett, G.K. Ingham, W.G. Runciman and
R.C. Taylor, who acted as discussants to the papers. I am
grateful also to Mrs Jean Floud (then Chairman) and to the other
members of the SSRC Committee on Sociology and Social Administration,
who agreed to sponsor the conference, and to the committee's secretary, Stella Shaw, for smoothing the way administratively. Robert
Moore, Colin Bell and particularly my colleague Richard Brown
provided encouragement and advice about whom to invite to give
papers at the early stages. Mrs June Wallis has provided most
expert and exemplary secretarial assistance throughout the prepara-
tions for the conference and for the book. Finally, I should like
to thank David Lockwood for putting up with it all so good-humour-
edly.

Martin Bulmer

CONTRIBUTORS

D.H. ALLCORN is Senior Lecturer in Sociology at the University of Kent at Canterbury.

ERIC BATSTONE is Research Fellow in the Industrial Relations Research Unit of the Social Science Research Council at the University of Warwick.

COLIN BELL is Professor of Sociology at the University of New South Wales, Australia.

R.M. BLACKBURN is Senior Research Officer in Sociology in the Department of Applied Economics, University of Cambridge, and Fellow of Clare College.

RICHARD BROWN is Reader in Sociology at the University of Durham.

MARTIN BULMER was until recently Lecturer in Sociology at the University of Durham.

JIM COUSINS is Senior Research Fellow in Sociology at the University of Durham.

R.L. DAVIS is Research Fellow, North Tyneside Community Development Project, Newcastle-on-Tyne Polytechnic.

R.H. FRYER is Lecturer in Sociology at the University of Warwick.

DAVID LOCKWOOD is Professor of Sociology at the University of Essex. He is currently a member of the Social Science Research Council and Chairman of its Committee on Sociology and Social Administration.

MICHAEL MANN is Senior Lecturer in Sociology at the University of Essex.

C.M. MARSH, until her death, was Lecturer in Sociology at the University of Kent at Canterbury.

RODERICK MARTIN is Lecturer in Sociology at the University of Oxford and Fellow of Trinity College.

ROBERT S. MOORE is Reader in Sociology at the University of Aberdeen.

HOWARD NEWBY is Lecturer in Sociology at the University of Essex.

GRAEME SALAMAN is Lecturer in Sociology at the Open University.

J.H. WESTERGAARD is Professor of Sociological Studies at the University of Sheffield.   Until recently he was a member of the SSRC Committee on Sociology and Social Administration.

ALFRED WILLENER is Professor of Sociology and Director of the Institute of Mass Communications Research at the University of Lausanne, Switzerland.

Part one

INTRODUCTION

Chapter 1

INTRODUCTION

Martin Bulmer

> The word 'class', to be sure, only appears relatively rarely in
> the responses on a variety of subjects.   The illusion of certain
> intellectuals, that everyone talks, or should talk, in terms of a
> theory of society, must be abandoned.   But nevertheless the
> replies on diverse themes - success, wealth, inequalities, etc. -
> show quite unambiguously that people do refer (using everyday
> language) to 'society' and to stratification.
>
> Willener, 1957, p.214

At least since Marx distinguished between 'Klasse an sich' and
'Klasse für sich', the nature of men's perceptions of society,
social inequality, social stratification and social class have been
of central philosophical, political and (more recently) sociological
concern.   In a stratified industrial society, how do members of
different social strata come to form, to develop and to hold, images
or mental representations of that structure? How do men come to
perceive and evaluate a world in which marked objective inequalities
of class and status exist?   What is the relationship between such
objective differences as exist in terms of income, wealth, life
chances, labour market situation, work situation or education, and
subjective perceptions of the system of social stratification in
industrial society?   What is the nature of industrial man's
'Weltanschauung'?   Such questions are of course of interest not
only to academic sociologists.   They relate in a direct sense to
social, political and philosophical questions about the nature of
the most desirable, equitable and just form or forms of social
organisation.   The studies of sources of variation in working-class
images of society which follow connect with these broad concerns,
but are primarily social scientific in their conception and execution.   That is to say, the primary purpose of the research reported
here has been to enlarge our knowledge and understanding of the
system of stratification in contemporary Britain, not to provide the
basis for philosophical or political prescriptions or refutations.
(1)
    A second theme underlying this research, of a more specifically
sociological nature, is the problem of the relationship between the
objective social situation of individuals and groups, and their own

subjective perception of that situation.   Given the possibility of
constructing sociological accounts of the social world from both an
objective and subjective standpoint, what is the relationship
between the objective and the subjective? (2)   The tension between
social structures and social meanings has been present in sociological work ever since Durkheim enjoined us to 'consider social facts
as things' and Max Weber directed our attention to the 'subjectively meaningful' nature of social action.   As a recent restatement
of some of the central theoretical problems of sociology emphasises,
this dualism is complementary.   'Society does indeed possess
objective facticity.   And society is indeed built up by activity
that expresses subjective meaning.   It is precisely the dual
character of society in terms of objective facticity and subjective
meaning that makes its reality sui generis ...' (Berger and
Luckmann, 1966, p.30).   The theoretical importance of work on class
imagery lies in its embodiment of this complementarity in the
approach, and indeed in the reciprocity which Lockwood sought to
establish between particular features of social structure and
particular distinctive patterns of class imagery.

Yet arguably the synthesis of complementary elements, and to some
extent the demonstration of a necessary connection of a reciprocal
kind between structure and meaning, remains problematic.   It is
probably no accident that Lockwood chose to develop his argument in
1966 by the use of ideal types, for the study of class imagery is
fraught with difficult methodological problems.   The papers in this
volume illustrate the extreme complexity of the inter-relationships
between objective class situation and perceptions of that situation.
The clarity provided by an approach via ideal types is all the more
welcome because many current social issues of industrial relations,
wages policy, and the organisation of workplace and workpeople turn
on how workers interpret and act upon their objective social
situation. (3)

These theoretical and methodological issues were one of the
principal sources for the idea of holding a conference based upon
Lockwood's article.   To secure as cohesive and integrated a
programme as possible, contributors were asked in advance to pay
particular attention to the relationship between the empirical
evidence about particular occupational groups and the theoretical
formulation of the sociological ideal types of 'proletarian
traditional worker' and 'deferential traditional worker' and their
underlying work and community structures.   The value of the 1966
article lies not least in drawing together strands from both
theoretical and empirical sources to provide a new theoretical
perspective on working-class social imagery, in turn stimulating
further empirical research.

Apart from these theoretical issues, one of the main stimuli to
research on class imagery has undoubtedly been a normative one, the
desire to understand the nature and progress of working-class
industrial and political action, particularly of a radical kind.
Too direct a political significance should not, however, be read
into the research reported here.   Indeed it should be made clear
that this symposium is not a commentary upon the conservative or
radical political potential of the English working class.   This is
not to deny wider philosophical, ethical and social significance to

the papers here.   To read, however, direct political significance
into the Lockwood article of 1966 and the research which it
stimulated is probably unwarranted.

A distinction should be maintained, moreover, between the study
of images of society and of stratification, and the study of political and industrial class consciousness.   The two are not unrelated,
but it would be a mistake to equate them with each other.   The
importance of this distinction between social imagery and class
consciousness may be seen by considering the main characteristics
of the latter.   Class consciousness may be said to exist when
(following Goldthorpe (1970a, pp.327-8), three characteristics are
present:
1 A sharp awareness of being in a similar situation to other
   workers and hence of having interests in common.
2 The sharing of a definition of these interests as basically in
   conflict with the interests of another class.
3 The perception of class conflicts as pervading all social
   relationships and containing within them the germs of a future
   social order.

As both the opening quotation by Willener and several of the
papers in this volume suggest, there is an apparent absence on the
part of some manual workers of direct reference to social class
when questioned in an interview situation.   In some cases, too,
when a model of the stratification system is elicited by questioning,
this is not found to correspond to the antagonistic conflict model
implicit in the above definition of class consciousness.   Yet people
who have difficulty in using the concept of class, or who deny its
validity altogether, may nevertheless have the clearest conception
of social inequality in a more general sense;   a focus upon class
consciousness may lead to this being overlooked.   The postulation
of, or search for, class consciousness (either manifest or latent)
presupposes its articulation in a coherent ideological form.   Yet
an important feature of images is that they may be fragmentary,
ambiguous or uncertain.   How far they cohere to form unitary
images is open to question.   So is the extent to which they are
underlain by a unitary ideology of a coherent kind which could be
written down.

Moreover, the articulation of sentiments of class antagonism and
the sharing of a definition of common interests as basically in
conflict with the interests of another class both require the
development of an organisational context for their effective
expression.   The collective political and industrial organisation
and articulation of class sentiment is a main feature of class
consciousness (cf. Banks,1970, Chapter 8).

> To study ... class consciousness ... is to study the factors
> affecting ... sense of identification with, or alienation from,
> the working class.   More precisely, such a study should aim at
> an understanding of the relationship of the ... worker to the
> trade union movement, the main vehicle of working-class
> consciousness. (Lockwood, 1958, p.13).

By its very nature, the study of social imagery focuses upon the
unorganised and often diffuse representations of social structure
held by members of particular occupational groups.   The relationship between unorganised images and organised consciousness is

complex and ramified, and the one should not be assimilated to the other, any more than varieties of religious belief on the one hand, and church doctrine on the other, should be treated as identical. Moreover, to insist upon the overriding political significance of the work upon social imagery is surely an oversimplification, for classes and status groups may be regarded as manifestations of what Durkheim called a society's 'moral classification of men and things', which is ultimately a 'religious' phenomenon (Lockwood, 1971, p.71).

In short, the relationship between social imagery and class consciousness is problematic.   Although the existence of certain images of society may be regarded as underlying collective class action, there is no automatic connection between men's views of the stratification system and of the social hierarchy, and the con- sequences of those views for voting behaviour, strike action, or other manifestations of collective solidarity of a class-based kind. In the papers which follow, different views are taken of the possible relationship between social imagery and class consciousness. This is highlighted in the concluding part, where Lockwood and Westergaard disagree as to whether a viable distinction may be maintained between them.   Caution, therefore, is advisable before identifying the one with the other.   On the other hand, they are not unconnected.

The study of images of society and images of stratification thus stands somewhat apart from classical studies of class consciousness, and it may be useful to sketch the intellectual antecedents and milieu of the Lockwood article and the subsequent research stemming from it.   Any such sketch is exceedingly tentative given the difficulties of writing intellectual history, and the influences identified do not necessarily provide an exhuastive account.   The intellectual antecedents of the research reported here can be traced to three main sources: certain general developments in sociological theory, a series of empirical studies of subjective aspects of social class, and continuing debate among sociologists interested in theories of stratification.

The general theoretical importance of the work on stratification of Karl Marx and Max Weber is self-evident, apparent in all the papers which follow, and needs no recapitulation.   More recently, the importance of theories of purposive social action (or action frames of reference) in influencing research into the structural correlates of class imagery can hardly be doubted.   The origins of the modern critique of positivism in sociology, marked by the publication of Talcott Parsons's 'The Structure of Social Action' in 1937, have been elegantly sketched by H.S. Hughes (1959).   The work reported here is very clearly influenced by a voluntaristic theory of action in this tradition, although the extent to which it has entailed a critique of positivism in its methods of research may be questioned.   The tradition, of course, is hardly homogeneous. Different sociologists emphasise the influence of the rediscovery of the writings of the early Marx, the importance of Max Weber's methodological writings, the fertile influence of pragmatist philosophy upon empirical research in the USA, or the European significance of existentialist and phenomenological philosophy. The theoretical convergence lies in the central emphasis upon the interpretation of social action as it appears from the point of view of the social actor.   This emphasis on the objective importance of actors' subjective interpretations, though posing many method-ological problems, has broadened and enriched sociology to the point where explanations of social action conceived purely in terms of social structure are criticised as inadequate by many sociologists. The interest of the present volume lies in the interrelations which it seeks to explore or demonstrate between structure and subjective meaning.   Moreover, although there would be differences in the emphases given to different elements in the theory of action, Parsons's (1937) formulation points to the central theoretical concern, the 'normative orientation' of the actor.   In his choice of alternative means to desired ends, there is a 'normative' orientation to action.   Within the area of control of the actor, the means employed must in some sense be subject to the influence of this independent determinative selective factor.   A knowledge of this is necessary for the understanding of concrete courses of action.   'The discrimination of various possible modes of normative orientation is one of the most important questions with which this study will be confronted' (Parsons, 1937, p.45).

It would be misleading and procrustean to suggest that all or even some of the work on class imagery presented here stems directly from Parsons, but his early work remains the single most important contribution to the development of an action frame of reference. Even those who would maintain quite distinct and in parts opposing theoretical viewpoints within the general tradition (cf. Schutz, 1967; Berger and Pullberg, 1965; J.D. Douglas (ed.), 1971) confront similar general problems in attempting to account for the nature of meaningful subjective aspects of concrete social action.

A notable weakness of many of these general theoretical formula-tions, however, is an indifference to the empirical and procedural aspects of the action frame of reference.   While at a general methodological level the positivist - anti-positivist battle rages (not only against structuralists, but between proponents of different versions of the action frame of reference), much less attention has been paid to the very considerable practical problems of operationalising action or 'verstehen' approaches to the study of social reality.   This state of procedural uncertainty is discussed further in Part Three, but at this point it justifies looking more closely at the empirical researches which preceded and influenced the publication of Lockwood's 1966 article.

The background to the work on class imagery lies at one remove in empirical research attempting to investigate consciousness of class.   One of the earlier attempts to do this was that of Geiger (1949), in a little-known monograph. (See also Geiger, 1969, pp.8-14.) A better-known study, notable for the amount of criticism which it attracted, was Centers's social psychological study (1949) trying to link interest-group theory to the class identification of the individual.   Apart from methodological and technical weaknesses, the study treated the whole problem at too elementary a level, regarding answers to highly simplistic survey questions as an adequate basis for theoretical work.   Later work of a more reliable kind, carried out in Britain, has thrown some light on subjective class identification.   Studies by F.M. Martin (1954), W.G. Runciman (1966), M. Kahan et al. (1966), and D. Butler and D. Stokes (1969)

have shown that most people are prepared to assign themselves to a
particular social class, in response to open-ended interview
questions.   The majority of respondents, moreover, distinguish
between a middle and working class, although the proportions
identifying with each vary.   This evidence from studies of 'self-
rated class' is, however, hardly conclusive, and requires filling
out and explaining.   One important attempt to do this - by
Runciman - has used reference-group theory and attempted to show
the social referents of self-rating in terms of a range of
variables.

The work on class imagery drawn on by Lockwood in 1966 had,
however, a somewhat different emphasis.   Although starting from a
consideration of 'subjective social class', it was concerned to
explore in more detail the meaning of class identification, and the
complex mental representations which underlay simple answers to
straightforward interview questions.   In a sense the research
sought to go beyond the sociologist's operational measures of class
(in terms of manual/non-manual work, or middle- or working-class
identification) to investigate the models of class structure with
which social actors operated, and the ramifications and wider
social linkages which might account for such models being held.
Particularly influential were the studies of social class published
in Britain by Bott and Hoggart in the late 1950s, and several other
studies of working-class social imagery and its theoretical
significance which appeared about the same time (Willener, 1957;
Popitz et al., 1957; Andrieux and Lignon, 1960; Dahrendorf, 1959).

Like the studies of 'self-rated class', these studies also
provided convincing evidence that actors did hold mental
representations of the class structure which could be elicited
spontaneously - that is, the sociologist did not interpose notions
of 'class' prior to their being offered.   The model held, of course,
was not a uniform one;   nor, however, was there infinite variation.
As Willener observed, certain kinds of answers recurred in such a
way that one could group them together into types.   In fact, the
groupings of categories emerged 'almost entirely of itself' from
this analysis (Willener, 1957, p.213).   As an example of the kind of
results produced by this research, two tables are reproduced from
the work of Willener and Popitz et al. respectively. (Tables 1.1 and
1.2).

These typologies, developed in the course of earlier empirical
research, may be compared with those produced by the empirical
studies reported in this volume;   they also relate indirectly to the
typology proposed by Lockwood in 1966, although it must be
emphasised that the 1966 typology was an ideal type, not intended in
any sense as a concrete description of reality.   Several of the
studies cited sought not only to document the nature of people's
concepts of class and their models of the class structure, but to
identify the processes by which these concepts and models were
developed.   Particularly important in this regard is the work of
Elizabeth Bott on 'Family and Social Network', first published in
1957.

Lockwood has acknowledged the influence upon him of Bott's work,
and the central propositions of the 1966 article may be directly
related in their form to the kind of methodological standpoint taken

TABLE 1.1 Types of 'classes'

Definition of classes in terms of:	%
1 Socio-economic categories	22
2 Socio-professional categories	21
3 Dependence: dichotomy between workers and those of independent means	20
4 Power and/or property: classes (class struggle)	10
5 Social prestige: strata	21
6 Political categories	4
various: manual/non-manual workers	4
workers/intellectuals/capitalists	2
Non-response to question (of which 12% were 'no, there are no classes')	18
n =	550

Source: Willener, 1957, p.159.
Notes: (a) The question asked was: 'Do you think that there are social classes in our society?' (Yes - 88%, No - 10%, Don't know - 2%.) 'If yes, what are they?'
(b) In the table above some responses are counted more than once. The percentages do not therefore add up to 100%.

by Bott.   In particular, her sixth chapter on Norms and Ideology: the Concept of Class sought to relate images of the class structure to the social environment and situation of particular actors who held those images.   Bott argued that the effective social environment of a family is its network of friends, neighbours, relatives and particular social institutions.   People base their notions of social class upon their own pattern of social relationships.

The hypothesis advanced here is that when an individual talks about class, he is trying to say something, in a symbolic form, about his experiences of power and prestige in his actual membership groups and social experiences both past and present. (Bott, 1957, p.163).

This illuminating attempt to link the world-views of individuals and married couples to their actual membership groups and social relationships past and present bore unexpected theoretical fruit when applied in a different substantive context.   Thus the family and community underpinnings of images of social class, which Bott pointed to, were recognised and embodied in the construction of the ideal types in the 1966 article, in generalisations of much broader scope.   The principle of explaining social imagery in terms of the patterns of social relationships constituting social structure was explicitly followed.

The ideal types were, however, also grounded in occupational as well as family and community characteristics, and for an indication of the sources of this inspiration one must look to industrial

TABLE 1.2   Proportion of the total number of respondents
             corresponding to each type

Type	Total no. of respondents	%	% of types 1-6 only
1 Type one (static order)	60	10	14
2 Type two (progressive order)	150	25	34
3 Type three (dichotomy as collective fate)	150	25	34
4 Type four (dichotomy as individual conflict)	60	10	14
5 Type five (reform of the social order)	12	2	3
6 Type six (class warfare)	6	1	1
7 No image of society	120	20	
8 Records of insufficient quality	12	2	
9 Intermediate cases - excluded	30	5	
	600	100	100

Source: Popitz et al., 1969, p.321, (translation of 1957).

sociology, in particular certain tendencies among industrial
sociologists to look toward the influence of non-work factors in
explaining industrial attitudes and behaviour.   If Bott's sixth
chapter provided the 'Leitmotiv' at the interactional level, Robert
Blauner's concept of the 'occupational community', put forward in
his essay Work Satisfaction and Industrial Trends in Modern Society
(1960), provides the key to the institutional analysis of class
imagery.   This concept was developed in the course of an article
seeking to explain gross differences in work attitudes between
different occupations and industries.   In the course of this,
Blauner identified the central importance of non-work, community
features of social structure impinging upon work and industrial
experience.   In the 'occupational community', the social relations
of work and the social relations of leisure-time overlap, people
tend to talk 'shop' in their leisure-time, and the status system of
work tends to determine prestige in the local community.   The
existence of 'occupational communities' as key elements in
explaining work attitudes is taken up by Lockwood and generalised
in the explanation of social imagery.   By identifying the community
linkages of certain occupations and relating these in a systematic
way to variations in class imagery, a breakthrough was achieved in
bringing together the study of social stratification, industrial

sociology and the local community.   The establishment of this
linkage underlies the influence of the 1966 article.

A further source for the 1966 article was provided by studies of
voting behaviour which attempted to explain why such a relatively
large proportion of the English working class votes for the
Conservative party.   The work of R. Samuel (1960), M. Abrams (1961),
R.T. McKenzie and A. Silver (1964), and W.G. Runciman (1966)
provided the main sources, together with Stacey's study of Banbury
(1960) and an article by Plowman and others (1962), for the
construction of the ideal type of the 'deferential traditionalist'.
The connections between the study of class imagery and political
behaviour were underlined in 1967 when Frank Parkin published an
illuminating article on working-class Conservatives and their
relation to national political culture (Parkin, 1967).

The influence of a comparatively small number of empirical
studies, together with one or two more speculative essays, has laid
the basis for a quite substantial body of research into the social
determinants of class imagery. (4)   Indeed, one of the sources of
the idea of holding the Durham conference came from the observation
of the considerable influence which Lockwood's article had upon a
number of colleagues working in the field of social stratification,
to some extent independently of the impact by 'The Affluent Worker'
series.   However, the work reported in this volume can hardly be
considered apart from the volumes in 'The Affluent Worker' series
(Goldthorpe et al., 1968a, 1968b, 1969), produced by a team of which
Lockwood was a senior member.   Indeed, Lockwood has said in an
understatement that the 1966 article represented an extended footnote to Chapter 5 of Volume 3 of 'The Affluent Worker'.   If only
because the 1966 article is more theoretically refined than the
ideal type in that chapter, this claim must be questioned.   The
substantive difference in emphasis between 'The Affluent Worker'
and the research reported and discussed here is also evident.
Contributors were specifically asked to direct their attention to
the traditional worker, and away from the 'embourgeoisement' thesis
and the debate on the 'new' working class.   In at least two
respects, however, 'The Affluent Worker' series is important for the
present symposium.   Substantively, that research had implicit in it
a comparison between the 'affluent' worker and a previous or
alternative status, that of the 'traditional' worker, most fully
developed in theoretical terms in Lockwood's 1966 article.   Moreover
the treatment of class imagery in the third volume provided a model
for some of those reporting on their research here.   Like the
earlier research of Willener and Popitz et al., the authors found
considerable variation in the class imagery of their respondents.
Table 1.3 and Figure 1.1 present a distillation of the results of
this research, which is fully reported in Chapter 5 of 'The Affluent
Worker in the Class Structure'.   It is included here for purposes
of comparison when reading the later empirical papers.

At the theoretical level, 'The Affluent Worker' remains the
'locus classicus' of the study of industrial attitudes and behaviour
in terms of orientation to work or an action frame of reference, as
a special case of its development in sociology as a whole.   It
should be located, however, among a body of work sharing a similar
general approach to industrial sociology.   Although again these

TABLE 1.3   Images of class structure

	N	%
Approximate 'power' model - i.e. two major classes, differentiated in terms of possession and non-possession of power and authority	10	4
Approximate 'prestige' model - i.e. three or more classes, differentiated in terms of aspects of life-style, social background or acceptance	19	8
Approximate 'money' model - i.e. one large central class plus one or more residual or elite classes differentiated in terms of wealth, income and consumption standards	124	54
Other images not approximating above models	59	26
No communicable image	17	7
Totals	229	99

Source: Goldthorpe et al., 1969, p.150.

intellectual origins are very diverse, the importance of the younger Marx, Max Weber and Talcott Parsons is pre-eminent.   In empirical research, early work by Dubin, Roy and Gouldner in the USA, Lupton and Cunnison in Britain (influenced by the Manchester School of social anthropology), and Touraine and Willener in France may be regarded as having adopted a similar (i.e. sociology of labour) approach.   The sociology of work developed by Everett Hughes and his associates is a linked phenomenon, as Salaman's paper in this volume suggests.   More recent statements of an action frame of reference approach have appeared by Goldthorpe (1966), Silverman (1968, 1970), Fox (1971), Eldridge (1971a) and Hyman (1972).   Brown (1973) provides a sympathetic critique, Daniel (1969, 1971) a more acidulous one.

The theoretical standpoint from which 'The Affluent Worker' was written is therefore integrated into a whole current of sociological research which it might be interesting (although this is not our purpose) to describe and analyse further.   As it does exemplify particularly clearly the methodological approach followed by several of the contributors to this symposium, it may be useful to mention briefly the origins and main features of the approach.   As Goldthorpe has indicated (Goldthorpe, 1970b), the adoption of an action frame of reference occurred in the course of the Luton research, when the initial 'technological implications' approach guiding the research proved inadequate.   Having failed to find, as expected, marked dissimilarity between those in different occupational groups - such as semi-skilled assemblers, process workers and machine operators - in their relationships with work-mates, supervisors, employers and unions, the research team began to

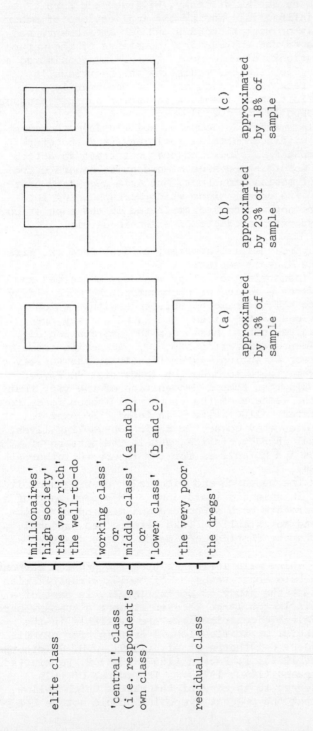

elite class { 'millionaires'
              'high society'
              'the very rich'
              'the well-to-do'

'central' class   { 'working class'
(i.e. respondent's   or
own class)   'middle class' (a and b)
                        or
                    'lower class' (b and c)

residual class { 'the very poor'
                 'the dregs'

(a) approximated by 13% of sample

(b) approximated by 23% of sample

(c) approximated by 18% of sample

FIGURE 1.1 'Money' models of class (a breakdown of responses in the third category in Table 1.3)

Source: Goldthorpe et al., 1969, p.148

look for other explanatory principles.

Prompted both by the thinking of various colleagues (in my own case, contributions by Dubin, Wilensky, Willener and Karpik were particularly influential) and by the implications of other of our data (notably on work histories and job attachment) we arrived at the idea of the explanatory importance of the nature of workers' orientations to employment, this being considered as a factor influencing job choice, mediating the individual's experience of work tasks and roles, and thus necessarily influencing his definition of the work situation and his conduct within it (Goldthorpe 1970b, p.200).

Lockwood's 1966 article was not, of course, written from the same standpoint of debates within industrial sociology, and therefore differs somewhat in emphasis. Lockwood does not treat an action frame of reference as something outside of and quite separate from an analysis in terms of social structure, but as a necessary part of such an analysis. The orientations which workers bring into industrial settings are not randomly distributed in the population, but are themselves systematic products of extra-industrial structures.

The congruence of approaches is, however, evident from the first volume in 'The Affluent Worker' series:

We believe that in industrial sociology what may be termed an action frame of reference could, with advantage, be more widely adopted; that is to say, a frame of reference within which actors' own definitions of the situations in which they are engaged are taken as an initial basis for the explanation of their social behaviour and relationships.... An action frame of reference would direct attention systematically to the variety of meanings which work may come to have for industrial employees. And this in turn would then compel recognition of the fact that in modern society the members of the industrial labour force form a highly-differentiated collectivity - in terms, for example, of the positions and roles they occupy in their non-working lives, in their sub-cultural characteristics, and in the pattern of their life histories and objectives for the future (Goldthorpe et al., 1968a, p.184).

Lockwood's article and the research and discussion drawing upon it do not therefore exist in splendid isolation. They form part of a larger concern to interrelate both structure and meaning in socio-logical explanation, and to establish links between occupational, community and family characteristics and images of the class structure.

More generally, the third main influence upon the present current of work - continuing debate about theories of social stratification - reinforces the point that the study of social imagery is part of a wider discussion. This is too large to even attempt a summary here. Fortunately, several valuable contributions are available in the recent literature on social stratification in Britain, for example by A. Giddens (1973), J.H. Goldthorpe et al. (1969), J.H. Goldthorpe (1972a), M. Mann (1970, 1973), F. Parkin (1967, 1971) F. Parkin (ed.) (1974) and J.H. Westergaard (1970, 1972). The course of this continuing debate, referred to in many of the papers which follow, underlines the point that the present symposium should not be read in isolation, but as part of a substantial and continuing body of work, both theoretical and substantive, into the nature of perceptions of social class in contemporary Britain.

NOTES

1 I am grateful to Richard Brown, Jim Cousins, David Lockwood and Alfred Willener for comments on an earlier draft of this paper.
2 This dichotomy involves considerable over-simplification, since what is regarded as 'objective' may contain subjective elements. The study of social status or prestige, for example, involves the objective measurement of prestige positions using scales which are based upon social judgments and hence on 'subjective' data.
3 The 'objective social situation' includes, of course, subjective elements, most notably the residue of past subjective inter-pretations (and action upon those interpretations) which survive into the present to become part of the 'objective' situation. The concept of 'tradition' embodies just such a dualism.
4 And a much smaller body of work into the relationship between social imagery and political and industrial action in crisis situations (e.g. Willener, 1970).

Chapter 2

SOURCES OF VARIATION IN WORKING-CLASS IMAGES OF SOCIETY

David Lockwood

For the most part men visualise the class structure of their society from the vantage points of their own particular milieux, and their perceptions of the larger society will vary according to their experiences of social inequality in the smaller societies in which they live out their daily lives. (1)   This assumption that the individual's social consciousness is to a large extent influenced by his immediate social context has already proved its usefulness in the study of 'images of society' and it has been stated most clearly by Bott, who writes:

> People do have direct experience of distinctions of power and prestige in their places of work, among their colleagues, in schools, and in their relationships with friends, neighbours, and relatives.   In other words, the ingredients, the raw materials, of class ideology are located in the individual's various primary social experiences, rather than in his position in a socio-economic category.   The hypothesis advanced here is that when an individual talks about class he is trying to say something, in a symbolic form, about his experiences of power and prestige in his actual membership groups and social relationships both past and present (Bott, 1957, p.163).

Working from very similar premises, several quite independent investigations have suggested that there seem to be two broad ways in which individuals conceptualise class structure: 'power' or 'conflict' or 'dichotomous' models on the one hand; and 'prestige' or 'status' or 'hierarchical' models on the other.   Further it has been proposed that the social ideology of the working class tends to take the form of a power model whereas that of the middle class approximates the hierarchical model.   Although some of these studies have noted variations in social imagery within the working class, they have concentrated chiefly on explaining the variations between the classes.   Thus the power or dichotomous ideology of the working class and the hierarchical ideology of the middle class have been accounted for primarily in terms of difference in the industrial life chances and life experiences of manual and non-manual employees. (See Bott, 1957; Oeser and Hammond, 1954; Popitz et al., 1957; Willener, 1957; Hoggart, 1957; Kornhauser et al., 1956; Andrieux and Lignon, 1960). (2)

   While the similarity of the findings of these various investigations is very striking, it is also quite clear from other studies
that the industrial and community milieux of manual workers exhibit
a very considerable diversity and it would be strange if there were
no correspondingly marked variations in the images of society held
by different sections of the working class.   Indeed, on the basis
of existing research, it is possible to delineate at least three
different types of workers and to infer that the work and community
relationships by which they are differentiated from one another may
also generate very different forms of social consciousness.   The
three types are as follows: first, the traditional worker of the
'proletarian' variety whose image of society will take the form of
a power model; second, the other variety of traditional worker,
the 'deferential', whose perception of social inequality will be one
of status hierarchy; and, third, the 'privatised' worker, whose
social consciousness will most nearly approximate what may be called
a 'pecuniary' model of society. (3)
   The 'traditional worker' is, of course, a sociological rather
than an historical concept; a concept relating to workers who are
located in particular kinds of work situations and community
structures rather than one purporting to give a description of the
working class as a whole at some particular point of time.   Moreover, the concept encompasses not only the most radical and class
conscious segment of the working class (the proletarian worker) but
also its most socially acquiescent and conservative elements (the
deferential worker).   Yet, distinct as the two traditionalists are
from one another in social and political outlook, they do share
several characteristics which make them traditionalists and thus
distinguish them from the privatised worker.   It would seem best,
then, to begin with an account of the work and community structures
underlying proletarian and deferential traditionalism. (4)
   The most highly developed forms of proletarian traditionalism
seem to be associated with industries such as mining, docking, and
shipbuilding; industries which tend to concentrate workers together
in solidary communities and to isolate them from the influences of
the wider society. (5)   Workers in such industries usually have a
high degree of job involvement and strong attachments to primary
work groups that possess a considerable autonomy from technical and
supervisory constraints (Blauner, 1960, p.343 ff).   Pride in doing
'men's work' and a strong sense of shared occupational experiences
make for feelings of fraternity and comradeship which are expressed
through a distinctive occupational culture.   These primary groups
of workmates not only provide the elementary units of more extensive
class loyalties but work associations also carry over into leisure
activities, so that workers in these industries usually participate
in what are called 'occupational communities'. (6)   Workmates are
normally leisure-time companions, often neighbours, and not
infrequently kinsmen.   The existence of such closely knit cliques
of friends, workmates, neighbours and relatives is the hallmark of
the traditional working-class community.   The values expressed
through these social networks emphasise mutual aid in everyday life
and the obligation to join in the gregarious pattern of leisure,
which itself demands the expenditure of time, money and energy in a
public and present-oriented conviviality and eschews individual

striving 'to be different'.   As a form of social life, this
communal sociability has a ritualistic quality, creating a high
moral density and reinforcing sentiments of belongingness to a work-
dominated collectivity.   The isolated and endogamous nature of the
community, its predominantly one-class population, and low rates of
geographical and social mobility all tend to make it an inward-
looking society and to accentuate the sense of cohesion that springs
from shared work experiences. (7)

Shaped by occupational solidarities and communal sociability the
proletarian social consciousness is centred on an awareness of 'us'
in contradistinction to 'them' who are not a part of 'us'.   'Them'
are bosses, managers, white-collar workers and, ultimately, the
public authorities of the larger society.   Yet even though these
outsiders are remote from the community, their power to influence it
is well understood; and those within the community are more
conscious of this power because it comes from the outside.   Hence
the dominant model of society held by the proletarian traditionalist
is most likely to be a dichotomous or two-valued power model.
Thinking in terms of two classes standing in a relationship of
opposition is a natural consequence of being a member of a closely
integrated industrial community with well defined boundaries and a
distinctive style of life.   It may well be, as Popitz has argued,
that the propensity to hold a dichotomous social imagery is a
general one among industrial workers in large establishments:
certainly the social divisions of the workplace, the feeling of
being subject to a distant and incomprehensible authority, and the
inconsiderable chances of escaping from manual wage-earning employment are all conducive to the formation of such an ideology (Popitz
et al., 1957, p.237 ff).   But it is probable that this image of
society is fully developed only among those workers whose sense of
the industrial hiatus is strengthened by their awareness of forming
a quite separate community.   Moreover, to anticipate the subsequent
discussion, it would seem that the tendency to adopt a power model
of society is most evident among workers who have a high degree of
job involvement and strong ties with their fellow workers.   In
other kinds of work situations, where these factors are absent, or
nearly so, the whole significance of the workplace as a determinant
of a dichotomous class ideology is correspondingly reduced.

Our knowledge of the second variety of traditional worker is
rather skimpy and results mainly from the efforts that have been
made to track down that elusive political animal, the 'deferential
voter'. (8)   It may be assumed, however, that the model of society
held by the deferential worker is a prestige or hierarchical, rather
than a power or dichotomous model.   In fact, given that people who
think of social divisions in terms of status or prestige usually
distinguish higher and lower strata as well as status equals, his
model is likely to be at least a trichotomous one (Bott, 1957,
p.176).   Further, the deferential worker does not identify himself
with his superiors or strive to reach their status;   he defers to
them socially as well as politically.   His recognition of authentic
leadership is based on his belief in the intrinsic qualities of an
ascriptive elite who exercise leadership paternalistically in the
pursuit of 'national' as opposed to 'sectional' or 'class' interests.
But how refined his image of the status hierarchy really is, or how

exactly he perceives his own position in it, is not known.   It is
merely suggested that he has a conception of a higher and unapproachable status group of leaders, his 'betters', the people who 'know
how to run things', those whose performance is guaranteed by
'breeding'; and that he himself claims to be nothing grander than
'working class'.   However, given these elements, it is possible to
go a little further and to draw the not unreasonable, but wholly
speculative, conclusion that the deferential worker thinks in terms
of at least a four-fold division of society.   Since he thinks in
terms of 'genuine' or 'natural' leaders in both a local and a
national context, it is likely that he thinks also of 'spurious'
leaders and, by implication, of 'misguided' followers.   Spurious
leaders are those who aspire to leadership, and indeed from time to
time acquire it, without possessing the requisite qualities.   They
may have achieved wealth, power and position, but they lack the
hereditary or quasi-hereditary credentials which the deferential
worker recognises as the true marks of legitimacy. (9)   Misguided
followers are those, broadly in the same layer of society as himself,
who refuse to acknowledge the objects of his deference, and who aid
and abet the spurious leaders in usurping authority. (10)   If the
deferential worker has an image of society as a status hierarchy,
then the existence of 'undeferential' workers is almost a necessary
condition for the protection of his own sense of self-esteem.
There are few instances of lower status groups who both accept the
legitimacy of the status hierarchy and fail to discover groups with
an even lower status than their own.
    Whatever niceties of status differentiation enter into the
ideology of the deferential traditionalist, it would seem that he
does hold a hierarchical model of some kind, and it would seem worthwhile exploring the hypothesis that such a model of society will be
the product of very special work and community relationships.   Here,
studies of the deferential voter do not take us very far.   The
findings that these voters are more likely than non-deferentials to
be elderly, to be women, to have low incomes and to come from rural
areas are demographic facts relating to the properties of individuals rather than facts relating to the properties of the social
systems in which these individuals are located (Abrams, 1961, p.42;
Samuel, 1960, p.11; McKenzie and Silver, 1964, p.199).   Nor is it
to be assumed that all deferential voters will be deferential
traditionalists.   The latter, like proletarian traditionalists,
must be thought of as an extreme type, characterised by a combination of social roles which, taken together, are most likely to
lead to a hierarchical social imagery.
    The typical work role of the deferential traditionalist will be
one that brings him into direct association with his employer or
other middle-class influentials and hinders him from forming strong
attachments to workers in a similar market situation to his own.
These work conditions are most clearly present in the sorts of
occupations that are to be found in small towns and rural areas,
although they are by no means entirely absent in larger urban
centres.   Workers in various kinds of service occupations, in non-
(or rather pre-) industrial craft jobs, those working in small-scale
'family enterprises', and in agricultural employment, are workers
who are most exposed to paternalistic forms of industrial

authority. (11)   The essence of this work situation is that relationship between employer and worker is personal and particularistic.   The worker has a unique position in a functional job hierarchy and he is tied to his employer by a 'special relationship' between them and not only by considerations of economic gain.

In the making of the deferential traditionalist certain features of community life will also play an important part in fixing and sharpening the sense of hierarchy that he acquires in his role as worker.   Small, relatively isolated and economically autonomous communities, particularly those with well differentiated occupational structures and stable populations, provide the most favourable settings for the existence of 'local status systems'.   The key characteristic of such systems is that the allocation of status takes place through 'interactional' rather than through 'attributional' mechanisms. (12)   The boundaries of the several status groups making up the local system are maintained by various means of social acceptance and rejection in both formal and informal association.   People do not judge one another from a distance and attribute status on the basis of a few, readily observable criteria, such as the amount of an individual's material possessions.   Status groups (or rather the cliques of which they are constituted) are membership as well as reference groups.   Through close acquaintance, people have a detailed knowledge of each other's personal qualities and can apply relatively complex criteria in deciding who is worthy of membership of a particular status group.   There is also widespread consensus about the rank order of status groups in the community, so that lower strata regard their lowly position less as an injustice than as a necessary, acceptable, and even desirable part in a natural system of inequality.   Local status systems, therefore, operate to give the individual a very definite sense of position in a hierarchy of prestige, in which each 'knows his place' and recognises the status prerogatives of those above and below him. For the deferential traditionalist, such a system of status has the function of placing his work orientations in a wider social context. The persons who exercise authority over him at his place of work may not be the same persons who stand at the apex of the local status system, but the structural principles of the two social orders are homological;   and from neither set of relationships does he learn to question the appropriateness of his exchange of deference for paternalism.

Although in terms of social imagery and political outlook the proletarian and deferential traditionalists are far removed from one another, they nevertheless do have some characteristics in common. They are first of all traditionalists in the sense that both types are to be found in industries and communities which, to an ever-increasing extent, are backwaters of national industrial and urban development.   The sorts of industries which employ deferential and proletarian workers are declining relatively to more modern industries in which large-batch or mass-production techniques are more and more the major modes of production.   Again, the small isolated country town, or the mining village, or the working-class enclave, such as is represented by the dockworkers' community, are gradually becoming linked with, or absorbed into, larger urban concentrations and with an increased amount of voluntary and involuntary residen-

tial mobility of the labour force the close link between place of
work and community is being broken down.

They are also traditionalists in the sense that their horizons
of expectations do not extend much beyond the boundaries of the
communities in which they live and of which they are, so to speak,
'founding members'.   This again is largely a product of the social
isolation and social stability of both the deferential and proletarian communities.   Workers in such environments are as unlikely to
change their patterns of consumption as they are their political
loyalties, because in both cases they are encapsulated in social
systems which provide them with few alternative conceptions of what
is possible, desirable, and legitimate.

Finally, and perhaps most significantly, the work and community
relationships of traditional workers involve them in mutually reinforcing systems of interpersonal influence.   The effect of group
membership on class ideology will, of course, vary depending on the
type of traditional worker under consideration.   In the case of the
deferential worker, his role in a paternalistic authority structure
at work and his position in a local status system in the community
both predispose him to think of society in terms of hierarchy.   In
the case of the proletarian traditionalist, his membership of the
work gang and his participation in the system of communal sociability lead to a conception of a 'class-divided' society.   But
although the effects of group membership are very different in the
two cases, both the deferential and the proletarian traditionalists
are highly integrated into their respective local societies;   and
this means that their attitudes and behaviour are to a large extent
influenced and controlled by means of direct face-to-face encounters.
In this way, they experience a sense of belonging to actual social
groups which are marked off from other groups by boundaries that are
maintained through social interaction.   This consciousness of
definite social placement in turn affects their perception of the
class structure.   Whether their models of society are basically
hierarchical or basically dichotomous, the fact that traditional
workers have a strong sense of group membership means that they will
tend to see 'strata' or 'classes' as active social formations and
not merely as amorphous aggregates of individuals.   In this respect,
the social consciousness of the traditional worker differs markedly
from that of the privatised worker, whose model of society is shaped
by work and community relationships which do not convey, to the same
extent, an awareness of group affiliation.

The social environment of the privatised worker is conducive to
the development of what may be called a 'pecuniary' model of society.
The essential feature of this ideology is that class divisions are
seen mainly in terms of differences in income and material possessions.   Naturally, there will be few individuals who think of class
divisions in purely pecuniary terms.   But the social consciousness
of many individuals in the 'new working class' may be closer to this
pecuniary model of society than to either of the two types of social
imagery previously discussed. (13)   Basically, the pecuniary model
of society is an ideological reflection of work attachments that are
instrumental and of community relationships that are privatised
(Dubin, 1956, p.135; Argyris, 1957, especially Chapter 4; Blauner,
1960).   It is a model which is only possible when social relation-

ships that might provide prototypical experiences for the construction of ideas of conflicting power classes, or of hierarchically interdependent status groups, are either absent or devoid of
their significance.

The work situation of the privatised worker is such that his
involvement in the job and his attachments to the enterprise and to
his fellow workers are slight.   Numerous studies have provided us
with the generalisation that workers employed in large factories
with mass-production technologies and doing jobs which are highly
specialised, repetitive, and lacking in autonomy, are workers for
whom, in Dubin's words, 'work and the workplace are not central
life interests' and for whom work is viewed 'as a means to an end -
a way of acquiring income for life in the community'. (14)   Under
these conditions, work is a deprivation which is performed mainly
for extrinsic rewards;   and 'money-mindedness', the calculative
exchange of labour power for maximum pay, is the predominant motive
for remaining in the job.   Frequently isolated from their workmates
by the constraints of technology, and seeking no close relationships
in a work situation that is viewed in purely instrumental terms,
such 'alienated' workers do not form cohesive groups inside the
factory and they are not prone to form occupational communities
outside the factory.   Their main attitude to work is that of its
being a necessary evil;   and given this orientation they have no
desire to carry over into their leisure-time the atmosphere and
associations of work (Blauner, 1960, p.351).   In all these
respects - the low involvement in the job itself, the lack of
cohesive work groups, the absence of occupational communities -
privatised workers differ significantly from the traditional worker,
and more especially from the proletarian traditionalist.   Relative
to the latter, the privatised worker finds himself in a work
situation that is socially isolating and, to a large extent,
socially meaningless;   a situation in which the dominant relationship is the cash-nexus.   But, although he is 'alienated' labour,
he is unlikely to possess a strongly developed class consciousness
because his involvement in work is too low to allow for strong
feelings of any kind, except perhaps the desire to escape from it
altogether.   He is neither deeply involved with his workmates, nor
deeply antagonistic to his employer;   on the whole his attitude to
both more nearly approximates one of indifference. (15)

These tendencies of the work life are reinforced and accentuated
by a certain form of community life which is increasingly representative of the new working class, namely, the social structure of the
council, or the private, low-cost housing estate. (16)   From the
present point of view, the most salient feature of these estates is
that they bring together a population of strangers, who have little
in common, save that they have all experienced residential mobility
and that most of them gain their livelihood from some kind of
manual labour.   In such communities, social life is very different
from the communal sociability of the traditional working-class
community.   Unrelated by the ascriptive ties of kinship, long-
standing neighbourliness and shared work experiences, and lacking
also the facility for readily creating middle-class patterns of
sociability, workers on the estates tend to live a socially isolated,
home-centred existence.   Such conditions favour the emergence of

attributional rather than interactional status systems. Whereas
in the traditional proletarian community status is allocated (or
more precisely made indeterminate) through the individual's participation in several overlapping cliques, the status order of the
housing estate is based on conspicuous consumption, by means of
which people judge their social standing relative to others without
usually associating with them in formal or informal leisure-time
activities. The low housing density of the estate, its lack of
recreational amenities, the uprootedness of its inhabitants and
their limited capacities for creating new styles of sociability
produce a society in which residents are only superficially
acquainted and associated with those who live around them. The
attributional nature of the status ranking that arises from this
situation in turn induces an acquisitiveness and a sensitivity to
competitive consumption that are quite alien to the communal
sociability of proletarian traditionalism.

The work and community settings just described are the breeding
grounds of the privatised worker, and his socially isolated
existence not only predisposes, but also enables, him to adopt a
pecuniary model of class structure. In the first place, he is
strongly motivated to view social relationships in pecuniary terms.
Lacking close primary group ties inside and outside the work
situation, at work he is wage-oriented and in the community
consumption-oriented. Just as money wages become of salient
importance in attaching him to his work role, so, too, consumer
durables are of primary significance in mediating his status with
his neighbours. This pattern of motivation is neither natural nor
accidental. If the privatised worker is more of an economic man
than the proletarian or the deferential traditionalist, it is
because his environment conspires to make him so. (17) Second,
however, the work and community relationships that foster this
pecuniary outlook are unlikely to give the individual a feeling
of definite social location through membership of either a status
group or a class fraternity. The privatised worker may be a trade
unionist and he may live in a community where status is reckoned by
material possessions; but from neither of these sources will he
derive more than a rudimentary awareness of belonging to a cohesive
group and hence of the social distance between such groups.

By contrast with the proletarian traditionalist, the privatised
worker will tend to join and support his trade union for instrumental rather than class solidaristic reasons. Given his materialistic, home-centred aspirations, the trade union for him is less
the symbolic expression of an affective attachment to a working
class community than a utilitarian association for achieving his
private goal of a rising standard of living. Lacking the class
consciousness which the proletarian traditionalist acquires from
his involvement in solidary work groups and communal sociability,
the privatised worker expects his union to devote itself exclusively to bettering the economic position of his own job category
rather than to dissipate any of its resources in pursuing the more
distant political objective of changing the wider society. As far
as he is concerned, the trade union is a 'service organisation',
not part of a social movement; and, far from his union membership
providing him with a consciousness of class, his orientation to

trade unionism reflects precisely his lack of such a sentiment.

By contrast with the deferential traditionalist, the privatised worker is unlikely to be made aware of a system of status groups arranged in a stable hierarchy of prestige.   His neighbours on the estate are mostly manual wage-earners like himself, socially undistinguished from one another save by marginal differences in their ownership of consumer durables.   This means that whatever status distinction arises from the competition to possess these goods is inherently unstable and too superficial to be the source of a sense of unbridgeable social distance.   Moreover, in so far as status groups fail to coalesce, the pattern of sociability in the community will remain privatised and there will be small opportunity for the individual to experience personal acceptance by his status equals or personal rejection by his status superiors. Hence, in the typically attributional status system of the housing estate, the worker will not learn to perceive status as a phenomenon that manifests itself in group relationships.

The daily social encounters of the privatised worker do not, therefore, lead him to think of a society divided up into either a hierarchy of status groups or an opposition of class.   His model of society is one in which individuals are associated with, and dis-sociated from one another less by any type of social exchange than by the magnitude of their incomes and possessions.

Before going on to outline the elements of this pecuniary model of society, it may be useful to summarise the argument thus far by two tables (Tables 2.1 and 2.2) which differentiate proletarian, deferential, and privatised workers in terms of work and community variables.   The meanings of the terms used to describe these variables should now be evident from the foregoing discussion.

TABLE 2.1   Work situation

	Involvement in job	Interaction and identification with workmates	Interaction and identification with employers
Middle-class (18)	+	+	+
Deferential	+	-	+
Proletarian	+	+	-
Privatised	-	-	-

The social isolation of the privatised worker reflects itself in his ideology of a 'de-socialised' class structure. (19)   The single, overwhelmingly important, and the most spontaneously conceived criterion of class division is money, and the possessions, both material and immaterial, that money can buy.   From this point of view, for example, education is not thought of as a status-confer-ring characteristic, but rather simply as a good that money can buy and as a possession that enables one to earn more money.   In general, power and status are not regarded as significant sources of class division or social hierarchy.   Power is not understood as the power of one man over another, but rather as the power of a man to

TABLE 2.2   Community structure

	Interactional status system	Occupational community	Occupational differentiation
Middle-class	+	+	+
Deferential	+	-	+
Proletarian	+	+	-
Privatised	-	-	-

acquire things: as purchasing power.   Status is not seen in terms of the association of status equals sharing a similar style of life. If status is thought of at all it is in terms of a standard of living, which all who have the means can readily acquire.   It may not be easy to acquire the income requisite to a certain standard of living and hence qualify for membership in a more affluent class; but given the income there are no other barriers to mobility.

Within this pecuniary universe, the privatised worker tends to see himself as a member of a vast income class which contains virtually the great mass of the population.   This class may be called 'the working class' or 'the middle class'.   Whatever it is called, it is a collection of 'ordinary people' who 'work for a living' and those who belong to it include the majority of manual and non-manual employees.   They are united with one another, not by having exactly the same incomes, but by not having so much or so little income that their standard of living places them completely beyond the upper or lower horizons.   A minority of persons in the society have either so much wealth or such an impoverished existence that they lie outside the central class.   They are the very rich and the very poor.   Since the main criterion of class membership is money, the lower and, especially, the upper limits of the central class are hard to define, and are consequently defined arbitrarily or regarded as indeterminate. (20)   In general the 'upper' or 'higher' or 'rich' class is not perceived as wielding power or deserving of respect.   It is simply a vague category of 'all those up there' who have incomes and possessions and a standard of life that are completely beyond the bounds of possibility as far as the ordinary worker is concerned. (21)   The rich, however, are different from the rest only in the sense of Hemingway's rejoinder to Scott Fitzgerald: that they have much more money. (22)

Finally, the central class with which the privatised worker identifies himself is seen as a relatively new phenomenon, brought about by the incorporation of the old middle class into the new 'working class', or, alternatively, by the incorporation of the old working class into the new 'middle class'.   Whether the end result of the change is seen as a 'working class' or a 'middle class', its identity is basically an economic one; people are assigned to this central class because they have roughly similar levels of income and possessions.   Because the convergence of the 'old' working and middle classes is seen in essentially economic terms, the desig- nation of the new central class as 'middle' or 'working' would seem to be largely a matter of how the change is perceived as having taken place rather than an expression of a status or class consciousness. (23)   Indeed, the logic of a purely pecuniary model of society leads to neither class consciousness nor status consciousness but to commodity consciousness.   Class and status models entail a perception of social groups whose boundaries are identifiable by acts of power and deference.   But the pecuniary universe is one in which inequalities are not expressed through social relationships at all.   Income and possessions may be the marks of persons, but unlike power and status they do not involve persons in relationships of inequality with one another.   Inequalities take on an extrinsic and quantitative, rather than an intrinsic and qualitative form.   In fact, compared with power and prestige, money is not inherently a divider of persons at all; it is a common denominator, of which one may have more or less without its thereby necessarily making a difference to the kind of person one is.

In so far as the privatised worker thinks in terms of the pecuniary model, he has, of course, a somewhat distorted view of the class structure.   All available evidence indicates that the amount of informal social interaction between the lower-middle and upper working classes is very small and that, in this sense at least, class boundaries are still quite distinct.   The privatised worker's idea of a vast central class, differentiated only by marginal differences in income and possessions, is not, therefore, an accurate sociological picture.   At the same time, it must be noted that the boundary between the middle and working classes is probably maintained as much by work and residential segregation as by personal exclusion.   Thus, from this point of view, the mechanisms of class dissociation operate in a way which is not entirely incompatible with an image of a 'de-socialised' class structure.

There is, finally, no suggestion that the pecuniary model of society is to be thought of as a direct product of working-class affluence. (24)   The pecuniary model is an outcome of the social rather than the economic situation of the privatised worker; and he is only able to hold such a theory of society in so far as this social environment supports such an interpretation.   His relative privatisation, his lack of a sense of class cohesion and his isolation from any system of hierarchical social status are the conditions under which he can view his society simply in pecuniary terms.

A purely pecuniary ideology is, of course, just as much of a limiting case as a purely class or purely status model of society. But it may be that it is at least as relevant as the other two in understanding the social and political outlook of the increasingly large section of the working class that is emerging from traditionalism. (25)

NOTES

1 This paper was originally given as a lecture at the University of Göttingen in February, 1966, and was first published in the 'Sociological Review', vol.14, no.3, November 1966, pp.249-67. It is reproduced here by permission.
2 Ralf Dahrendorf was the first to draw attention to the similar-

ity of the conclusions of Popitz, Willener, and Hoggart (Dahrendorf, 1959, pp.280-9).

3 On the traditional and privatised working class see Lockwood (1960) and Goldthorpe and Lockwood (1963).   The present paper may be regarded as an extension of these earlier statements and in particular as an elaboration of one major element in the normative dimension of 'class'.   John Goldthorpe and I have worked together so closely on the wider problem of which this paper is a part that I find it difficult to say where my thoughts end and his begin.   Although he may not fully agree with my interpretation, the present essay draws much from a paper of his entitled Attitudes and Behaviour of Car Assembly Workers, which will be published shortly in the 'British Journal of Sociology' (Goldthorpe, 1966).

4 Work and community relations do not, of course, exhaust the range of variables which may affect the formation of models of society.   In particular, the experience of social mobility (in the present context, downward mobility) is most likely to have the effect of predisposing a worker towards a hierarchical, rather than a class model.   This is so for two reasons: first, because the experience of social mobility makes a person more sensitive to the fact of hierarchical social distance;   and second because the downwardly mobile worker is likely to have been socialised into a set of values ordered around a concept of status hierarchy.   However, the number of socially mobile persons in any particular section of the working class will be determined to a large extent by the self-same factors that shape their work and community relationships, i.e., by the industrial and occupational structure of a particular locale.

5 The first to draw attention to this phenomenon in a systematic way were C. Kerr and A. Siegel (1954).   See also, for example, University of Liverpool (1954) and Dennis et al. (1956).

6 The defining characteristics of an occupational community are: (1) Workers in their off-hours socialise more with persons in their own line of work than with a cross-section of occupational types;   (2) Workers 'talk shop' in their off-hours;   (3) The occupation is the reference group;   its standards of behaviour, its system of status and rank, guide conduct (Blauner, 1960, p.351).

7 The one-industry town with its dominant occupational community would seem to produce the most distinctive form of proletarian traditionalism.   But, given a relatively isolated community with a stable and preponderantly working-class population, a quite high degree of proletarian traditionalism is perfectly compatible with industrial diversification.   Indeed, industrial diversification may promote the stability of the population by allowing a man to change his work without leaving the locality.

8 For an exposition of the political philosophy to which he is held to respond, see S.M. Beer (1965).   For a preliminary report on the investigation by R.T. McKenzie and A. Silver, see idem, 1964.   See also Samuel (1960), Abrams (1961), Runciman (1966, Chapter 9).   Probably the best description of the deferential traditionalist and his social context is by Stacey (1960).   See also the highly instructive paper by Plowman et al. (1962).

9   See Stacey (1960, pp.159-60) on the tensions between the traditional and non-traditional segments of Banbury.

10 'They support the parties of their "social betters" while insisting on their own position at the bottom of the social ladder. Compared with their neighbours, they are not interested in a party which stands for the ordinary working class and which aims to raise the standard of living of ordinary people' (Abrams, 1961, p.42).

11 See the account of 'traditional' firms in Stacey (1960, pp.27-8) and the discussion of paternalism in Lockwood (1958, pp.78-81, and 141-9).   A more fully developed system - 'patriarchalism' - is portrayed by Solomon B. Levine (1958, pp.36-8) discussing Japan.

12 On the concepts of 'local status systems' and 'interactional' status systems, see Plowman et al. (1962, especially pp.186-95). The distinction between interactional and attributional status systems is also made by M. Young and P. Willmott when they contrast the 'face-to-face' relationships of Bethnal Green with the 'window-to-window' relationships of Greenleigh. (See Young and Willmott, 1957, especially pp.134-5.)   The perception of status groups as interactional groups is basic to the fully developed status or hierarchical model of society as E. Bott makes clear when she writes that: 'status was not conceived in relative terms as a continuum.   Each class was given a specific subculture' and 'each category differed from others in subculture and prestige' so that 'individuals in one class, if they happened to meet, might associate with one another as equals in informal interaction' (Bott, 1957, pp.176-7).

13 See Goldthorpe and Lockwood (1963, pp.149-54) for a discussion of these two terms.

14 The general theme is quite old.   See, for example, Karl Marx on The Power of Money in Bourgeois Society, 'Economic and Philosophical Manuscripts of 1844'.   A more recent Marxist interpretation which concentrates on the work situation is that by Andre Gorz (1965, especially pp.348-9).

15 On the significance of intensity, as opposed to direction, of involvement, see Etzioni (1961, p.9).

16 Some of the abundant literature on this topic is summarised in Klein (1965, vol.II, Chapter 5).

17 It is of course possible that, in addition, a process of 'self-selection' occurs, so that those workers who are more instrumental in their work orientations and less well integrated into their local communities than other workers are more likely to enter and remain in the jobs and communities of the kind described.

18 Since this paper concentrates on manual workers, only the briefest comments on the position of the middle-class employee are called for.   Here 'middle class' refers to the administrative, managerial, technical and professional white-collar group (i.e., excluding lower grade clerical employees, who in many respects are similar to the privatised worker, as well as entrepreneurs).   This group is included in the paradigm partly because their presence gives it a certain pleasing symmetry; but also because the same variables that are used to differ-

entiate the three types of manual worker would also appear to be
relevant in analysing the social situation of non-manual
employees.   From the paradigm, it can be seen why the white-
collar employee is predisposed to hold a hierarchical model of
society.   What cannot be seen is why his hierarchical ideology
differs from that of the deferential worker.   This is because
a variable relating to chances and expectations of upward
mobility is not included in the table, which, since it was
designed to show differences within the manual group, implicitly
assigns a low and constant value to this variable.   It is also
quite obvious from the work of Prandy that there is much more
variation in the work situation of the white-collar employee
than is suggested by the above scheme (see Prandy, 1965).   The
characterisation of the middle-class employee in terms of
community variables is likewise undoubtedly something of an
oversimplification.   However, even as it stands, the following
points can be made in defence of the present scheme.   First,
there is ample evidence that middle-class employees of the kind
in question do find their work intrinsically more rewarding and
are more highly involved in their jobs than most industrial
workers.   Second, because their working relationships usually
bring them into close contact with higher management and administration as well as with small groups of workers of their own
rank, they are likely to identify themselves with both 'the
firm' and their colleagues.   Third, because of their high job
involvement, they are likely to form occupational communities;
and this tendency should be more pronounced the more they are
geographically mobile and thus the more they are dependent on
friendships acquired through their occupational roles.   Fourth,
middle-class employees are likely to live in occupationally
mixed communities.   Simply because there are relatively so few
men in the middle ranges of white-collar employment, it is
almost inevitable that their neighbours will include small-
scale entrepreneurs, independent professionals, lower grade
clerical and sales employees, and perhaps even highly paid
manual workers.   Finally, white-collar employees are likely to
be involved in interactional status systems.   Whether social
visiting, or membership of and participation in voluntary
associations is taken as a measure of communal (and hence
status) interaction, the middle classes rank so much higher
than the privatised working class that the difference is
qualitative.

19   In singling out the basic features of this model of society I
have been influenced by my reading of the responses to an open-
ended question on class which was part of the interview
schedule used in a study of a sample of affluent workers.   I
should stress, however, that the responses to this particular
question have not yet been systematically analysed and that the
present paper can in no way be regarded as a description of the
findings of this part of the study.   For an account of the
study, see Goldthorpe et al., (1967).   (For a full account of
this part of 'The Affluent Worker' research, published subsequently, see Goldthorpe et al., 1969, Chapter 5).

20   To take two examples from our own study: First, a man who has

a conception of a two-fold class system, the 'rich' and the 'middle class'. 'Q - What is the main thing that decides which class someone's in? A - Money.   Q - Just money?   A - If you've got an income coming in, say £5,000 a year, that brings you a rich person; if you've got an income of £1-2,000 or just under, you're middle-class'. (034)   Second, a man who holds a two-class model, and calls his classes the 'higher class' and the 'working class'.   'Q - What's the one main thing that decides which class a person's in?   A - Money.   The more money a person has the better he can live.   Q - Where does the working class end and the higher class begin?   A - The more money you have, the higher you get - but there isn't an end to the working class.   Q - Are there any other differences between classes?   A - No, it's just the money'. (035)

21 This tendency of persons in socially ambiguous positions to enlarge their own class and to relegate the remainder of the population indiscriminately to the periphery is well known. 'Some people who placed themselves in the "working class" made differences within it but lumped together everyone else as "the rich".   The more remote the people of another class, the less opportunity there is for checking fantasy against fact so that the individual can see in such people what he wants to see' (Bott, 1957, p.165).   'The earnings of these suburbanites permit some of them to call themselves "middle class" but the framework of hierarchy of class that is meaningful to these workers is not a conceptual framework that applies to society as a whole, but one that is limited to what is possible for them ... there is a tendency to lump together as "way up there" everyone whose income is greater than the upper limit of what is possible for them ... to be "middle class", then, probably means to them not what sociologists mean by middle class, but rather the middle of the working class ... the "upper" middle class, white-collar worlds of engineers, junior executives, professionals and would-be professionals are completely beyond their ken; this latter milieu is alien to them beyond their limits of possibility' (Berger, 1960, pp.85, 89).

22 This is, of course, an extreme position.   In fact, deviations from a purely materialistic interpretation of class structure are likely to occur in both an ascriptive and moralistic direction.   Thus, the 'rich' class may be seen as containing persons whose wealth is inherited and/or undeserved ('The idle rich').   Similarly, the 'very poor' may be seen as containing persons who are lacking in ability and/or lacking in motivation to raise themselves ('poor character').

23 If the pecuniary model of society appears to resemble the 'sociology' of class that is frequently purveyed via mass media ('We're all middle-class nowadays' or 'We're all workers now-adays'), the reason for this may very well be that the privatised worker is more likely to be reached by mass commun-ication and more readily influenced by its message.   Because of his relative social isolation, he may be more exposed to impersonal influence; and, given his affluence and privatis-ation, the view that class differences are on the wane is a plausible one for him to maintain.

24   Renate Mayntz, in her study of social class in Euskirchen, notes
     the contrary tendency: for income models to increase in
     importance, the lower the income of the respondent, and suggests
     that this is so because at the lower levels 'diese materielle
     Frage ein wichtiges, oft sorgenvolles Problem des taeglichen
     Lebens ist' (Mayntz, 1958, p.99).   This essentially 'ad hoc'
     explanation is not very convincing.   In the absence of privatis-
     ation there is no sociological reason why privation any more
     than affluence should lead to a pecuniary model of society.

25   The related concepts of privatisation, instrumentalism and
     pecuniary ideology are merely intended to serve as points of
     reference for the study of the new working class.   As such, they
     help to specify the conditions affecting the direction of
     working-class politics, and yield the conclusion that this will
     take the form of 'instrumental collectivism'.   Recently, Perry
     Anderson has argued that instrumental collectivism could be the
     basis for the development of a new 'ideological collectivism'
     (a sort of Hegelian synthesis in which the rational elements of
     an otherwise apolitical instrumental collectivism combine with
     the radical elements of an otherwise parochial solidaristic
     collectivism).   The major activating force of this new radical-
     ism could in turn be a sense of relative deprivation arising
     from new aspirations for power and status.   Thus, John
     Westergaard has suggested that working class radicalism could
     have its sources in workers' aspirations for middle class status
     in the community;   and others, including Gorz and Mallet, see
     the work situation as the potential locus of a new radicalism
     stemming from workers' demands for 'control' over production.
     However, in so far as the work and community milieux of the new
     working class generate 'privatisation' and 'instrumentalism',
     neither of these radicalising aspirations is likely to emerge
     and to lead to ideological collectivism.   On the contrary,
     since a privatised style of life is likely to create aspirations
     for higher consumption rather than for higher status, and since
     instrumentalism devalues work save as a means to higher
     consumption, the most probable form of radicalism is that which
     centres on immediate 'shop-floor' demands for maximising
     earnings;   a form of radicalism in its way just as parochial,
     if not more so, than the solidaristic collectivism of the
     traditional worker (see Anderson and Blackburn (eds), 1965,
     pp.108, 265, 317, et seq.).

Part two

EMPIRICAL RESEARCH

Chapter 3

RELIGION AS A SOURCE OF VARIATION IN WORKING-CLASS IMAGES OF SOCIETY

Robert S. Moore

The history of the coal-miners appears to be the history of class struggle. Probably no industry has been marked by such frequent and bitter conflicts as coalmining. The events of 1844, 1893, 1912, 1921, 1926 and perhaps 1974 have passed into the legend of labour history, and their leaders into the calendar of labour saints and martyrs. Certainly no other section of the working class has consistently aroused such venomous hostility amongst the middle and upper classes. Against such hostility the resolution, courage and fortitude of the miners are readily interpretable as expressions of class solidarity. (1)

The conditions of the miner's life are suited to the creation of strong bonds of solidarity. Miners work together in a hazardous and physically isolated occupation. The technical demands of coal-getting and the dangers of the mine make men dependent upon one another in order to earn a living and to ensure the safety of life and limb. Miners and their families live amongst other miners' families in homogenous communities, typically geographically cut off from other communities. In the mining village one finds a distinctive culture centring around the Club and the Union lodge, including pigeon clubs, dog racing, gambling schools, brass bands, sports teams and the Labour party. The cultural distinctiveness and solidarity of the mining community is articulated in various ritual expressions; in the conduct of a miner's funeral, in a village carnival or, on a wider scale, in events such as the Durham Miners' Gala or the Northumberland Miners' Picnic. In these latter celebrations the miners assert their identity and their solidarity as miners, they assert an occupational rather than local solidarity.

We might expect therefore that the miner would have a 'traditional proletarian' image of society. Nearly all the conditions of work and community, set out by Lockwood, are fulfilled. Lockwood seems to suggest that the miner is the traditional proletarian worker par excellence. His model of the traditional proletarian outlook seems to be based very largely on the miner. Lockwood's model of the miner rests upon the Ashton study 'Coal is our Life' (Dennis et al., 1956).

The Ashton study was historically specific, being carried out after the Second World War amongst miners who had recently

experienced the depression, in a period when political and industrial consciousness was heightened by the activities of the post-war
Labour government and the nationalisation of coalmining. This
study has helped to propagate a stereotype of the rough and tough,
hard-drinking, Labour-voting miner. This image of the miner is a
partial image to students of mining history, for in spite of the
struggles of the miner against his master a traditional proletarian
image of society was remarkably slow in developing. Also a
substantial section of the miners were amongst the most 'respectable'
part of the working class.

MINERS' LEADERSHIP IN THE NINETEENTH CENTURY

The early part of the nineteenth century was a period in which the
miners struggled to unionise and suffered crushing defeats in every
attempt. The modern trade unions began to develop around 1870. It
is with the leadership of the 1870 unions that we can begin to outline our objections to the traditional proletarian image of the miner,
before moving on to the empirical data drawn from a study in the
Durham coal-field.

The most striking feature of the union leadership was its
rejection of a class model of society and industrial relations. The
union leaderships were Gladstonian Liberal and non-conformist.
Their economic views were liberal, they believed that the market
operated according to laws that could not be contravened. One
particular expression of these economic views is to be seen in the
adoption of sliding scales which tied wages to the selling price of
coal.

Market relations were not seen as class relations, but as
functional relations governed by the laws of the market and in which
conflicts arose mainly from misunderstanding alone. The unions'
leaderships advocated 'conciliation and peaceful settlements'
(E.W. Evans, 1961, pp.138-9) and were forthright in their rejection
of socialist or class-conflict approaches to industrial conflict.
We will see in our empirical data that both masters and men articulated this functionalist view of industrial relations and that the
masters approved of unions because they thought the unions would
facilitate the effective operation of the market.

The South Wales and Durham miners left the Miners' Federation of
Great Britain in 1889 because they favoured the sliding scale
against the Federation's policy of establishing a wages conciliation
board. The persistence of the Sliding Scale Associations
'suffocated trade unionism in South Wales' (Arnot, 1949, p.61).
Two thirds of the Welsh miners favoured the sliding scale in 1893
and the scale was not abolished until 1902 (E.W. Evans, 1961, p.151).

Abraham ('Mabon'), Bruce, Morgan and Isaac Evans were all
advocates of the sliding scale. They were prominent in religious
life, just as many of the Welsh Agents were preachers (E.W. Evans,
1961, pp.138-9). These old leaders were not replaced until the
Cambrian Combine Strike of 1911 in which the owners' intransigence
discredited the leaders' conciliatory attitude (E.W. Evans, 1961,
p.211).

In Derbyshire Haslam was an advocate of moral force rather than the strike.   He opposed nationalisation of the coal mines and proposed co-operation as an answer to socialism (J.E. Williams, 1962, pp.276, 303).   He and other Derbyshire leaders were Liberal non-conformists and the Derbyshire leadership was prominent in opposing Labour affiliation by the miners' unions (J.E. Williams, 1962, Chapter 12).   Another moderate Derbyshire leader, Harvey, publicly condemned the activities of Hardie and Lansbury during the 1912 Minimum Wage strike.   Haslam opposed the idea of the minimum wage, both as an unrealistic expectation and a breach of market laws (J.E. Williams, 1962, p.416).

The Durham miners were led for much of the early period by John Wilson who was a Primitive Methodist local preacher and a temperance campaigner.   He was also an ardent advocate of conciliation, and rejected views that stressed conflict in industrial relations: 'Throughout the 1890's the sole representative of the Durham mine-workers in Parliament was the pugnacious and sharp-tongued John Wilson, a staunch Liberal and a determined opponent of socialism' (Gregory, 1968, p.69).   He always tried to find a basis for conciliation and see the best in the masters and apparently he failed to see how the sliding scale was being used to depress miners' wages.   Questioned on this by Tom Mann during the Royal Commission on Labour in 1891 Wilson answered, 'I am watchful as most can be mind - I like to look around the corner but I like to go with trust' (Royal Commission on Labour, 1891, Q.614).

Until the early part of this century the miners' leadership 'rejected socialist doctrine and fiercely resented and resisted the concomitant idea of a new and independent working class party' (Gregory, 1968, p.6).   The MFGB was the last of the great unions to affiliate to the Labour party.   Wilson would not accept the party constitution nor the whip.   The Derbyshire leadership accepted with reluctance and reservations (J.E. Williams, 1962, pp.508-9).

Far from being in the van of class politics the miners appear to have been reluctant latecomers.   Furthermore, the affiliation of the miners to the Labour party, far from injecting combative class attitudes into the Labour party had the opposite effect, for Labour had to modify its attitude 'in the face of a large accession of Lib-Lab M.P.'s and their supporters' (J.E. Williams, 1962, p.513) from the mining constituencies.

We are not suggesting that the miners can be judged entirely by the beliefs and activities of their leaders.   None the less, leaders to some extent represent a constituency and can not wholly misrepresent their constituents.   We know that the socialist groups were agitating amongst the miners from the 1890s onwards and with increasing success up until the First World War.   But the old leadership persisted until about 1918.

If Lockwood was wholly correct then we might have expected the miners to have been among the earliest occupational groups to join the Labour party and to bring with them a strong sense of proletar-ian class identity.   Why was this not the case?   We will concen-trate on two reasons:

1 Beyond formal similarities, the actual social experiences of the miner at work and in his community do not conform to Lockwood's expectations.
2 Independently derived beliefs about society may have influenced the miners' interpretation of their social experience.

Plainly, taken together, these two closely related considerations
might lead us to a fundamental reappraisal of Lockwood's methodological assumptions, which seem to include an idea of a relatively
mechanistic and one-way relationship between formal social relations
and social beliefs.

We can examine our two themes by an empirical discussion of a
group of small mining villages in County Durham from 1870-1914, a
period marked by the dominance of the Liberals in politics and in
the local trade unions, and the dominance of John Wilson in both.

LEADERSHIP IN A VILLAGE CONTEXT

The villages studied were small and relatively isolated.   The total
population of the four villages included in the study probably never
exceeded 9,000 persons.   The housing was provided by the coal-
owners.   The managers lived in the villages, slightly apart and in
larger houses.   The deputies and overmen, promoted from amongst the
hewers, lived in slightly larger houses than the miners but situated
at the end of the colliery rows.

The union leadership was non-socialist in 1890 and remained so
until the First World War.   Very early in the history of the union
we find expressions of the organismic view of industrial relations
that we have already seen amongst the national leaders.

In 1879 a local strike leader said at a rally: 'the men had no
interest in damaging the interests of their employers, because the
interests of the employers was the interest of the employed, and the
men regarded it as their bounden duty to study their employers'
interests....' (2)

Bargaining at the place of work was based on pragmatic considerations and mutual trust.   In the words of an old miner: 'X and Y
(President of Lodge and checkweighman respectively) always assumed
that management spoke in good faith; they were more sympathetic to
management's position....   Z (a later militant) never believed a
word management said.'   Conduct was in terms of what MacIntyre has
called the 'secondary virtues': 'a pragmatic approach to problems,
fair-play, tolerance and gift for compromise, and fairness'
(MacIntyre, 1967, p.24).   The reasonableness of the union leadership is shown in company reports and press comment on the 1892
strike: 'We have had no trouble with the workmen during the year,
they all conducted themselves very well during the twelve weeks of
the County strike.'   'The cessation of work has been in a quiet
and orderly fashion.   There were no outbursts, the interchange of
a few friendly words between officials and men being all that was
noticeable.'   In other parts of the county there was considerable
violence, extra police and troops were drafted into the county in
preparation for disorder.   The local union lodges showed a marked
reluctance to strike.   Table 3.1 shows this for 1909 and 1912.

In the earliest period the miners were even more reluctant; the
strike of 1879 was rather forced upon the men when the owners'
association forced the local owners into a unilateral wage reduction.
In 1892 the leaders in the villages were, according to the 'Durham
Chronicle', more disposed to settle with the management than men in
the eastern collieries.   The east coast pits were larger and deeper

TABLE 3.1   Voting figures for selected villages 1909 and 1912

1909 National Strike (Scottish Miners' Wages)

	For strike	Against	% for
National	518,361	62,980	89
Durham County	25,103	2,786	90
Village A	211	88	70.5*
Village B	140	69	67*
Village C	365	41	90

* Significantly different from County vote at P greater than .001

1912 Minimum Wage Strike Ballot

National	445,801	95,919	82.5
Durham County	57,490	28,504	66.5
Village A	124	153	44.5*
Village D	154	68	69

* Village A was one lodge out of six voting against strike in a total of 62 lodges

1912 Minimum Wage Strike: Ballot to Continue

National	244,011	201,013	54.8
Durham County	48,828*	24,511*	66.6
Village A	219	325	40
Village B	141	137	50.5**
Village C	282	103	73
Village D	191	82	70

* 61.5% poll only
** Significantly different from County vote at P greater than .001

Notes: 1   Few such figures are available: it was not normal
          practice to release individual lodge voting figures.
          Although the release of such figures was forbidden by the
          DMA there were leaks to the press from time to time;
          these are the sources for this table.
       2   Village A doubles its voting turn-out to end the 1912
          strike.

than those of the west of the county.   Methodism never gained such
a powerful hold in the mining villages associated with these pits,
although many Methodists from our village migrated to the east coast
in 1926.

Conciliatory leadership continued into the twentieth century
under the leadership (in the largest village) of X (above) who
consciously modelled his style of leadership upon John Wilson, of
whom he was a friend and admirer.   After the affiliation of the
MFGB to the Labour party and during the growth of the local Labour
party, X, with other Methodists, formed a Liberal party (1910).

TABLE 3.2 Methodist participation in village leadership

| Name | Occupation and village | Methodist activity | Union Lodge | Offices held | | | Other |
				Party	Local govt	Co-op	
James Hammel d.1931	Shopkeeper A	P.M. Foundation Trustee. Delegate to Conference		Committee of Young Liberals 1911	Liberal Councillor 1910. Guardian		Chairman of Coronation Committee. Military Service Tribunal 1916
Joseph Harrison d.1910	Shopkeeper A	P.M. Trustee. Circuit Steward			Liberal Councillor. Guardian		President, Flower Show 1901-3. Anti-Education Bill, 1902-5
Isaac Johnson d.1952	Coal Hewer B	Sunday School Teacher. Society and Circuit Steward. Trust Treas.	President and Secretary	Liberal		Committee	
Tom Pearson d.1920	Check-weighman B	P.M. Choir-master	Check-weighman, Secretary etc.	V-President Young Liberals 1911	Councillor Chairman U.D.C. Guardian	Chairman 1894 Committee until 1903	Director of local Building Society. Secretary of Flower Show 1903

Name	Occupation and village	Methodist activity	Offices held				
			Union Lodge	Party	Local govt	Co-op	Other
Robert Barren d.1923	Miners' official D and Durham City	M.N.C. Sunday School Superintendent	Check-weighman, Secretary D.M.A. Exec.	Liberal	Chairman Parish Council	Committee (Village A)	Temperance Work, Education Committee of County Council
Sam Dove killed in pit 1933 or 1934	Hewer and Check-weighman A & D	P.M. Trustee. Christian Endeavour Delegate 1902	Lodge Secretary			Committee (Village B)	Club Committee (led to his leaving chapel)
John Henery	Deputy B	P.M. Trustee		V-President Spennymoor Lib-Lab Association	Liberal Councillor. Guardian (for 23 yrs). Chairman of U.D.C. 1912-1914. Justice of Peace	Committee	Military Service Tribunal

Table continues over

Name	Occupation and village	Methodist activity	Union Lodge	Party	Offices held Local govt	Co-op	Other
Robert McDonald (last heard of c.1926)	Hewer C	P.M. Evangelist Preacher	Secretary Permanent Relief Fund 1903. Check-weighman	Secretary village Liberals and then Ind. Lab. Party			Aged Miners' Homes. Temperance. Peace Movement 1914-
Matthew White d.1932	Hewer B	P.M. Trustee. Circuit Steward. Delegate to Conference 1932	Chairman, President & Lodge Secretary for 32 years	V-President Young Liberals. V-President Spennymoor Lib-Labs 1919. Labour Party 1926	Councillor. Guardian. Justice of Peace	Committee	Many Local Committees esp. connected with Hospital Work
Aron Richardson d.1936	Hewer C & D	P.M. Sunday School Teacher Village B until 1904. Preacher	Lodge Chairman	Liberal and then Labour			

Name	Occupation and village	Methodist activity	Offices held				
			Union Lodge	Party	Local govt	Co-op	Other
William Foster Left 1920s	Coke-burner (Official) A	P.M. Preacher				Delegate C.W.S.	Anti-Education Act 1902. League of Nations. Pacifist. Temperance Work.
J. Johnson	Hewer (?)	P.M.	Treasurer	Committee of Young Liberals	Parish Council 1901		
J. Fitz-patrick	Small runner B	Preacher			Parish Council 1901	Committee 1902-15	
Joseph Stephen-son	Hewer (?) B	P.M. Preacher		Liberal	Councillor. Guardian. County Magistrate		

This was necessary as Labour affiliation had deprived the Liberal party of its normal agent for votes, namely the union chapel leadership.   X's sons report that he was also unrelenting in his opposition to their work on behalf of the Labour party.

Table 3.2 gives an impression of the extent to which the Methodists occupied positions in the union leadership.   This table only gives details of those Methodists of whom we have substantial biographical data.   There were long periods in the village when all the key union posts were held by Methodists.   Village B, for example, had Methodists and checkweighmen from the beginning in the 1870s until the First World War.   Village C had three Methodist checkweighmen in succession holding office from the 1870s until the pit closed in 1926.   Village D had a similar series of checkweighmen, although the Methodist succession appears to have been lost in the 1920s or 1930s.   All of these checkweighmen were, for varying periods, lodge presidents.   In 1913 the president, secretary, treasurer and delegate of the B lodge were Methodists.   In 1917 in lodge A the treasurer, financial secretary and pit inspectors were Methodists.   This apparent dominance of the Methodists had been virtually universal in the earlier years.   It was also a collective exercise of power by Methodism, for all the key figures in the local unions interacted in the chapels and were bound to other Methodists through kinship and common activities.

THE ROLE OF METHODISM

An understanding of Methodism is one of the keys to understanding the nature of the local union leadership.   This can best be explicated by asking two questions: first, how did the Methodist see himself, and second, what was the Methodist's understanding of social and industrial relations?

The Methodist saw himself as a saved man.   This set him apart from the mass of the village population.   In the early days of the villages, social conditions were like those of a frontier town: a high rate of population growth, overcrowding, drunkenness, gambling, and violence.   The Methodist was 'saved' from this either because he was already a Methodist and therefore a non-participant in the ethically suspect activities of the population, or because as a result of evangelisation he had experienced a change in his life-style, which separated him from his old drinking and gambling ways. Methodism was a peculiarly ethical religion with immediate implications for conduct;   the saved man was a new man - upright, honest, sober, trustworthy, and respectable.   The chapel provided an alternative 'gregarious pattern of leisure' for the Methodist: class meeting, prayer meeting, choir, band, lectures, concerts, teas, bazaars, anniversaries, etc.   There was thus some degree of cultural discontinuity between the Methodists and non-Methodists in the community.   It was precisely the qualities that separated the Methodist from his workmates at leisure which made him so acceptable as a candidate for union office.   Research in the village produced numerous anecdotes from miners and their families about the young local preacher who was elected to office on the vote of Club men in preference to their Club friends, because it was felt that a

Methodist could be trusted, especially with money.

The sense of being a saved man, and a man of some ethical
standing, provided something of the basis of trade union morality
also.   According to MacIntyre union morality rests on the view that
a man is 'essentially equal to those who claim superiority to him,
and that in knowing that he is equal to them he has his chief weapon
against them' (MacIntyre, 1967, p.42).   The Methodist could stand
face-to-face with the owner or the managers in a self-assured and
dignified way.   He expected to be respected by the management.

The Methodist's idea of society was partly bound up in the idea
of 'calling'.   The earliest sermon of which we have a record in the
villages was preached in January 1878 on the Parable of the Talents.
The preacher stressed the necessity of men making an active use of
the talents they have been given by God.   Faithful men, according
to this preacher, are active and diligent.   This kind of theme
occurs throughout the period studied.   Preaching based on the
Talents parable also includes, or implies, that man will have to
give account of his use of his talents on the Day of Judgment.   Thus
the Methodist miner was called to be a good miner, but by implication the coal-owner was also called to be a good coal-owner.   Each
has his place in God's plan and the overall social arrangements
between men were not questioned in any fundamental way.   This
clearly fits with notions of the market as a concrete phenomenon
according to the objective laws of which we must all arrange our
economic relations.   The social and economic order is the creation
of a relatively inscrutable God and in this order we have to prove
our Christian temper - not overthrow the order.   None the less the
Methodist was not called to passive acceptance of the social order.
Sermons also stress the need for 'service' to the local community
and to the nation, and papers read at Bible classes and study groups
underline the importance of the task facing Christians in seeking to
improve housing and removing the causes of vice and poverty.   The
means are personal regeneration, education and effort by individuals
and groups.   This was summed up in an undated sermon from the early
years of the century: 'Nothing but Christian service of the kind
which has self-denial for its cornerstone, and activity for its
super-structure will save the world.'   It is only in the 1910s that
some of the preachers began to suggest that there may be social-
structural problems that could not thus be righted.   But as late as
June 1926 a preacher was stressing the importance of individual
rescue work in the slums and back streets.   Social service could be
represented by various forms of activity: working for the temperance movement, encouraging thrift and self-help in one of the local
Co-operative Societies, serving as a lodge official or a local
Councillor.   Methodists expressed their desire to serve the
community in all these ways (as Table 3.2 also shows).   But given
their participation in these activities, in the latter third of the
nineteenth century at least, Methodist union leaders were unlikely
to develop a critical or conflict model of society.   Implicitly
society was viewed as a functioning whole, not as consisting of
contending classes.

It is important to note also that religious views as such did not
have to stand alone to interpret the world to the miner.   The
highly ethical nature of Gladstonian Liberalism, with its concern

for international peace and conciliation, temperance, education and Parliamentary reform, tied the Methodist miners very closely to the Liberal party and hence to the Liberal economic ideas of that party.

THE COAL-OWNERS

The Liberal-Methodist view of class structure would not have stood up if the coal-owners had not in some way conformed to the expectations arising from the Methodist model.   In our villages both the main coal-owners were Liberal non-conformist.   One was a Methodist (Methodist New Connexion), he was a prominent local preacher and famous in non-conformism nationally.   The other owner was a Quaker, and a Liberal MP.   Both supported temperance activities and the expansion of education, both were very generous patrons of the local chapels, giving land, materials, labour and money for the building and maintenance of the chapels.   The crucial questions in our present context are first, how the Methodists viewed the owners and, second, how the owners viewed industrial relations - especially the activities of the unions and union leadership.

It is important to note that the ownership was local or regional and that the mining companies were traditional family firms. Authority was not something that impinged upon the miners from outside, but was exercised by men who lived in the villages, were related to miners in some cases, and who represented an ownership that was local and familiar to the miners.   Lockwood suggests that proletarian social consciousness is based on an awareness of 'Us' as distinct from 'Them', and 'They' were outside the community. This was not the case in the villages, and thus one factor predisposing men towards a dichotomous model of power and authority was not present.

The Methodists held the owners in considerable respect.   Because of their religion the owners were obviously ethically upright men, with whom some of the Methodists might have felt they had more in common than with the 'rougher' elements in the villages.   The owners also supported causes that were important to the Methodists, especially temperance and education.   There were other good reasons for holding the owners in respect; the owners were in a dominant position having destroyed the previous unions in the county.   The Methodist owner had, in fact, been the prime mover in the dispute leading to the 'rocking' strike of 1863-4 which had resulted in the destruction of the immediately previous union (Welbourne, 1923, pp.118, 121).

In spite of this he was none the less held up by Methodists as an example of the possibility of achieving a rags to riches career through diligence and hard work: 'From whence did his wealth arise? ... It was the result of industry - industry combined with frugality, self-denial, economy; sanctified and regulated by the highest principles of genuine religion.'

The Quaker was seen less often locally than the Methodist; but one aged Methodist evangelist asserted that it was an honour to have him visit the village.   The old man added, 'We kept his villages in good order with our Christian work.'

It is important to note that the attitudes of the owners as

outlined were shared by the local management who exercised personal
patronage of chapels and 'good works', in addition to acting as
agents for the owners' benefactions.   Up until the First World War
all but one of the managers were church or chapel men, and regular
attenders at Sunday services - one early manager played the
harmonium in a chapel.

The answer to our first question about the owners is that the
Methodists tended to view them in ethical terms and thus saw the
possibility of some sort of partnership with the owners in the moral
reform of local society.   There was plainly no view of the owners
as 'Them' who were opposed to 'Us', even though in one case there
were very good grounds for seeing the owner as an enemy of the
union.   This should be compared with the ethical discontinuity of
the mining community as seen by the Methodist leaders.   For these
two factors together constitute the basis for a status order that
cuts across any putative class order.   The Methodist-Liberals
(including the union leadership), the owners and managers can be
grouped together in distinction from the rough and unregenerate
miners.

The owners' ideology is a factor that Lockwood does less than
justice to in his original formulation.   It is upon the owners'
beliefs about society and economic relations that the content of a
large part of the social relations at work and in the community
depends.   In addressing our second question, about the owners'
attitude to industrial relations, we find a situation in which
there was a kind of reciprocity between owners and men than inhibit-
ed the development of a class model of society.

PATERNALISM AND CALCULATION

Bendix has shown how at the turn of the eighteenth and nineteenth
centuries entrepreneurs moved away from paternalistic and personal-
istic control of their workers towards more impersonal and calculative modes of control (Bendix, 1963, Chapter 2).   Once control
became calculative the entrepreneurs 'tended to regard the workers
as factors of production, whose costs could be calculated' rather
than as men who were known personally to his employer.   But the
coal-owners in our study seem to have carried the paternalistic
mode of management through to the end of the nineteenth century.

Non-conformist entrepreneurs seem to have been under the
influence of Andrew Ure and this in part accounts for their advocacy
of education and their support of the Sunday School movement.   A
report from one manager to the Quaker owner that the local workmen
were 'religious and industrious' vindicated the contention that
'Godliness is great gain' (Bendix, 1963, p.93).   One of the Quaker
owners almost echoed Ure's assertion that 'animated with a moral
population, our factories will flourish in expanding usefulness'
(Ure, 1835, p.428), when he said that he felt 'that to have a body
of intelligent, sober and well-conducted men must ever tend to the
prosperity of the works.'

The paternalism of the owners took many forms, some we have
already mentioned.   The Quaker distributed free coal to the poor
of various villages, the Methodist gave coal to the poor of his

village in cold winters.   The owners allowed their men to draw
coal from the supplies at bank during strikes.   They built the
local schools, provided Miners' Institutes and a circulating
library, gave sports fields and patronised the colliery bands and
the flower show.

Their attitude to the working class, whilst it may have owed much
to Ure earlier in their anti-union days, had been modified to
conform more to the theories of Samuel Smiles.   Ure believed that
the workers were essentially depraved but that they might respond to
the ministrations of Sunday School and chapel.   The coal-owners
admitted that there was drunkenness and gambling amongst the miners,
but that these were social phenomena that could be overcome through
the work of the temperance organisations, or avoided altogether
through the preventive work of the Sunday Schools.   But they went
beyond such beliefs towards Smiles' position in believing that the
men could be responsible, self-reliant people, capable of independent organisation and co-operation.   Their attitude to the unions
of the 1870s reflect this change of attitude from the days when
they had sought to destroy all attempts at union.   The trade unions
were useful in that 'they pointed out which market gave the best
pay for certain work', according to the Quaker.   But 'when they
began to meddle with prices, that were best regulated by the laws of
supply and demand, then there was great objection to them.'

The Quaker was an ardent advocate of industrial conciliation
(hence his reluctance to reduce wages in 1892) and asserted that a
victory for either side in a dispute would be a disaster - even if
it was the owners who won.

Implicit in the Quaker's statements on trade unions is the view
that the function of trade unions is to facilitate the operation of
the market by providing good communication amongst the men and
between men and owners.   The union also provided a means of conciliation if disputes arose as a result of misunderstanding.   For
example: 'All recent reductions (in wages) had been accomplished
without a single strike, that was something very remarkable in the
process of the feeling between labour and capital.'   The Quaker
denied that there was any opposing interest between owners and
miners: '... he had never admitted, and hoped he never would admit
that there was any opposing interest between the employer and the
employed, at any rate in the coal fields of South Durham (applause).
He might say: "We have lived and loved together through many a
changing year".'(2)   He believed that: 'While the men were
looking out for themselves they would also look at the position of
the employers and the employers would also try while working for
themselves to look at the position of the men, so that employer and
employed might go hand in hand, not only for the benefit of each
other but for the benefit of the community at large.'

From this discussion of the owners and the management of the
collieries we see that whatever the actual relations at the place of
work (and crucially in piece-work bargaining) the Methodist union
leaders and the owners and managers shared a very wide range of
assumptions about economics and morals.   The managers respected the
union leaders in the way that the union leaders expected to be
respected.   They shared a non-conflict, organismic view of industry
in which everyone had his proper function to perform, and which with

goodwill all could fulfil to their mutual benefit.   Underlying
these beliefs was the assumption that the roles that men played at
work and in the community were not merely the functions of an
economic and social system, but God-given roles which had to be
fulfilled as a calling.

The pragmatic and apparently compliant and co-operative attitudes
of the union leadership, their rejection of notions of conflict and
their firm adherence to liberal economics is entirely comprehensible
in these terms.

Thus the Methodist miners had a consistent and coherent set of
ideas about society.   The consistency of such ideas depends on many
factors:

> (They) will vary according to both the personal attributes of
> individuals and the nature of their social relationships and
> experience.   But usually they will be organised into a model,
> the consistency of which will hold up to a certain point - so far,
> one would suggest, as it needs to hold in order to enable the
> individual to 'make sense' of his experience.   Thus, most
> individuals can present a more or less consistent image of the
> class structure for so long as they are not confronted with
> issues to which their models are inadequate (Goldthorpe, 1970a,
> p.335).

We have presented the miners' model of the class structure and have
suggested that in the latter part of the nineteenth century it was
entirely adequate for 'making sense' of his experience at work and
in the community.   It was the operation of factors extrinsic to the
social relations of the village, and largely beyond the control of
anyone in the village that confronted the Methodists with issues to
which their model was inadequate.

THE RISE OF CONFLICT AND CLASS POLITICS

During the last three decades of the nineteenth century coal had
been a relatively prosperous industry and our villages shared in
this prosperity, producing not only coal but, as important by-
products, coke and bricks.   Most of the produce of the villages
went to the iron and steel industry.   By the end of the century the
easy seams were largely worked out, foreign coal was competing with
the Durham export trade and new fuels were beginning to challenge
coal.   The largest cost of production was labour, and management
therefore directed its attention to cutting labour costs.   Meanwhile many companies, including our Quaker company, ceased to be
private family concerns and became public companies, answerable to a
body of shareholders.

The owners' ideology changed also.   Paternalism was replaced by
calculation and patronage was reduced.   By 1907 the chairman of the
company (nephew of the Quaker owner cited above) was saying of the
miners' attempts to resist wage reductions: 'We must put our foot
down if there is an organised attempt on the part of the miners of
the country to place themselves in a privileged position ... and
cost what it may we must see the matter through.'

The new generation of owners were also remote from the villagers
and seemed to have little understanding of the life of the miners.

Older miners still recount examples of the disdainful treatment they received when they met the owners on certain occasions in the villages.   In 1923 one owner complained of the unreasonableness of the miners: 'I cannot understand the great reluctance of the men to work slightly longer hours.... I cannot see why they object so much to working an extra half-hour when they have nothing particular to do with the time.'

Thus the companies and ownership were changing their characters. This was matched by the rise of the Labour party and more vigorous industrial activity on the part of the trade unions generally.   The economic and industrial conflicts of the early part of this century culminated in the very bitter strife of 1912 to 1914, which included the Miners' Minimum Wage strike.

The Liberal party changed too.   Its policies of peace, retrenchment and reform crumbled before the onslaught of the trade unions, women, peers, the Irish problem and the First World War.   The party lost its high ethical tone and was increasingly torn by internal division (see A.J.P. Taylor, 1965, pp.17, 105 and Chapter 8, and Dangerfield, 1936).   The traditional links with nonconformity whilst not disappearing seemed to be losing some of their rationale.

Locally the Labour party made very slow progress in the villages, which were Liberal strongholds.   A nascent branch of the ILP started as a Bible Class but was excluded from use of the chapel. The younger men who were converted to socialism usually also espoused the New Theology of J.R. Campbell and the Higher Criticism of Peake - thus making them doubly suspect to the Methodists and liable to exclusion from preaching.   The Labour party in fact made most progress outside the chapels, recruiting younger men who had not known the days of prosperity and patronage.   The villages (which straddled three Parliamentary constituencies) finally returned Labour MPs in 1922.

The Labour party was not, however, concerned to make traditional proletarians out of a population that showed such a large measure of traditional deferentialism.   It was trying to win votes.   A series of interviews with early Labour organisers, including the Labour electoral agent for the constituency in which most of the villagers voted, showed that Labour in fact compromised with existing social outlooks in order to win votes.

For example the agent (who was a local preacher until 1926) deliberately used Biblical allusions in his speeches.   He persuaded one candidate to give up drinking for the duration of his campaign. A prominent local party organiser made a speech in which he said that his hearers needed guns in order to make a revolution; the agent immediately followed with an impromptu speech on the need to embody the Sermon on the Mount in any party programme (see P. Jones, 1968, p.353n).   He was afraid that the stress on conflict and violence in the first speech might alienate the 'Methodistically inclined' audience.

The union leaders of the 1870s survived into the 1920s and commanded sufficient community support for it to be necessary for Labour to win them over to the party rather than attempting to eliminate them electorally.   A reason for the relative power of the old leadership against the new was that it was based in part on kinship.   The Methodists tended to be endogamous and therefore many

Methodist families were related to one another in multiple ways.
Thus the old leaders as founders of Methodism in the villages were
also the heads of complex lineages.   Their community power was
therefore considerable and not easily overcome by appeals to class
or party loyalty.

When the old leaders did join Labour they filled important
positions (X, for example, remained a Councillor).   According to
accounts from friends and relatives of these men they remained
Liberal whatever their party label.

Notions of class and class politics did not begin to gain real
currency in the villages until the outbreak of unmistakeable and
very bitter class warfare in the 1920s - it was this that finally
brought X into the Labour party in 1926.   All reciprocity
disappeared as barbed wire and policemen were deployed on the
streets of hitherto peaceful villages.   Respectable Methodist
union leaders no longer found management willing to listen to them,
but rather policemen ready to clear them off the street.

Methodist influences declined as the old leadership died.   The
historical link between Methodism, Liberalism and the union was
broken, and with this break the influence of Methodists in politics
and industrial affairs waned.   The tight base of union lodge,
chapel, Co-op and Liberal party sponsorship had been destroyed.
The Labour party emerged as a specifically political institution
and the chapels remained, in effect, as wholly religious organisations.

Another source of the decline of Methodists' influence was that
the social mobility of Methodists and the aspirations of Methodist
parents reduced the recruitment of Methodists into the pits.
Union leadership moved to another group of men with a powerful
community organisation, who had previously been excluded from
office, the Roman Catholics.

Conciliatory attitudes were still expressed by Methodists in
1926.   According to the Primitive Methodist Minister who was in
the village in 1926 and interviewed in 1967: 'Some Methodists
thought the General Strike was inopportune.   They were not against
what lay behind it, but the wrong way of going about it.   They
thought that constitutional methods were preferable, not strikes
and so on.   Some Methodists thought that not all the possibilities
were exhausted.'   Enormous hostilities were aroused in two of the
villages, in one of which the 'blackleg' Miners' (Non-Political)
Union was formed (the first branch in the county) (Garside, 1971,
p.232; J.E. Williams, 1962, Chapter 19, sections III and VII).
A dozen or more union leaders were imprisoned after disturbances
and to this day many men will not speak to blacklegs of the period.
Yet in this village a Methodist said in 1967: 'We often wondered
which side people took in 1926.   But we tried to be Christians and
we agreed to differ.   1926 didn't make much difference in the
chapel.   "Things said" didn't lead to any falling off.   At times,
chapel cemented things together.'   This is a very conciliatory
attitude given the hostilities and bitterness of conflict in the
villages.

At the time of the General Strike there would still have been
many Methodists amongst the miners, for in 1919 the Methodists
regarded about 40 per cent of all colliery households as being

Methodist households (i.e. having one or more member, including children, active in the life of the chapel).   So the views quoted would have been quite common in 1926.

Today many of the miners accept that they were beaten in 1926 and aver that this is a lesson that other unions should note when they consider strike action today.   The old Liberal outlook is still found too; no systematic collection of data was conducted, but amongst the Methodists we found much criticism of the 'Welfare State' and many assertions of the value of hard work and thrift, many spoke of the need for a government that served the national interest and encouraged self-reliance.   A number of Methodists asserted that they would vote Liberal if a candidate was offered locally in an election.

We are not suggesting that there are, or were, no traditional proletarians in the villages or that class consciousness never developed (although the present Labour agent said that he was British first and Labour second because 'I believe in the Royal Family').   We are suggesting that the proletarian outlook is relatively modern.   It is the social and political commentators who have traditional views of the proletariat and their class relations.

THE TRADITIONAL PROLETARIAN?

The discussion so far has suggested that there was, and maybe is, a very substantial part of the mining community that did not develop a traditional proletarian image of society and that we can understand why this was.   Lockwood may have been underwriting a traditional social science view of the proletarian worker.   This is hardly surprising given the material he had to work from.   The Ashton study includes only slight reference to the 'religious' members of the community; were we meant to infer from this that they were not influential (Dennis et al., 1956, pp.169-70)?   But Dennis et al. present no evidence to this effect.

One unfortunate and inaccurate interpretation of Lockwood's model is that workers in industries like shipbuilding and mining do have traditional proletarian images of society.   Lockwood is partly at fault for this misrepresentation because he does not elaborate his argument in sufficient detail.   He recognises that the very traditionalism of the traditional proletarian and deferential worker means that they have much in common in their outlook.   For example, working-class culture can institutionalise a kind of parochialism that can undermine or prevent class solidarity.   What Lockwood does not consider is that these two kinds of worker can be the product of very similar social situations.   He presents polar types of social conditions in which the two types of worker are typically found; he does not examine the implications for the outlook of traditional workers of their social situation including elements of both polar types of situation.   According to Lockwood 'the work and community relationships of traditional workers involve them in mutually re-inforcing systems of interpersonal influence' and that the attitude and behaviour of traditional workers 'are to a large extent influ-enced and controlled by means of direct face-to-face encounters.' We have shown this to be so; but in our mining villages the

employers and managers are included amongst those with whom the
miner has direct face-to-face encounters, and that these were
relations of both dependence and reciprocity.

We have tried to show the coherence of religious, economic and
political beliefs, and we have suggested, like Parkin, that
socialist voting was a form of deviance (Parkin, 1967).   Furthermore, we would suggest that the adoption of a traditional proletarian image of society is also a form of deviance that has to be
explained.   Parkin's explanation of socialist voting is in terms
of deviance from conservatism;   we would need to explain traditional
proletarianism in terms of deviance from Liberal functionalism.   We
have seen that Liberalism and the organismic view of society was
sub-culturally well supported by non-conformity, the Co-operative
movement, the union leadership and ownership and management.   It is
unsurprising that the Labour party had such a difficult struggle to
win votes and institutional support in the community.   Lockwood's
model tends to lead us away from any consideration of the need for,
and nature of this struggle, because from his analysis we expect to
find miners adhering to images of society which would predispose
them to left voting.   Furthermore the social relations of work and
community do not necessarily reinforce one another, in our villages
the tendency was for them to cross-cut one another.   Thus market
conflict was moderated by ethical considerations by the union
leaders, and the logic of exploitation was moderated by paternalism
by the owners and managers.

Lockwood seems to have oversimplified the question of the
relations between work, community and social beliefs.   It is clear
that the miners developed a strong sense of occupational community
(unlike the traditional deferential worker) but this does not mean
that class consciousness emerged from this.   We might suggest,
speculatively, that the miner only developed a consciousness of
market interest.   Market interest is usually equated with class
interest, but we are suggesting that the worker may be conscious of
his interest in an economic situation which he believes includes
not only his fellow workers but his employers and supervisors also.
Members of other occupations might even be seen as rivals, as has
been the case in the shipbuilding industry, for example.   In
defending this kind of market interest the miner confirmed the
social order.   Occupational and market interests were expressed
through the trade unions locally and nationally, and were celebrated
ritually in carnival, gala and picnic.   But a miner representing
his lodge and his village with his banner on the race-course during
the Durham Miners' Gala is not necessarily expressing class consciousness in the classic sense.

An anecdote will illustrate this point.   The above line of
reasoning started when the author was travelling in a train with two
miners in 1967.   The miners were discussing the seamen's strike;
each asserted that it was a communist plot to weaken the economy.
The author joined in this discussion and eventually pointed out that
the seamen had struck for a basic wage very much less than the
miners', for a considerably longer working week.   The main discus-
sant immediately responded, 'Oh well, I don't know much about
politics' and changed the subject of discussion.   The relative lack
of sympathy (and at times outright hostility) for other workers

found amongst the miners suggested that their consciousness of
market position had not yet become consciousness of class position.
We would need to examine the way in which the Labour party has
sought votes through a series of compromises in order to understand
this.

Lockwood did not suggest that miners would be Labour voters, nor
that they would feel a common cause with other sections of the working class, none the less consideration of political outlook and
voting behaviour does, as Parkin suggested, indicate something of
the values generally held by an occupational group.   It might be
assumed from Lockwood that the miners were likely to vote Labour in
a class conscious way, Lockwood does not consider the possibility
that men may have to be converted to a traditional proletarian outlook in certain situations.

Finally Lockwood seems to have underestimated the importance of
ideas as such in forming images of society.   In the first place he
neglects the role of religious and economic ideas in shaping men's
social relations and their interpretations of those social relations.
Second he does not ask whether political parties have a specific
role in deliberately promoting or suppressing certain views of the
social order.   Third he does not discuss the role of managerial
ideologies for the social relations of work.   In this last respect
it seems important to make allowance for the possibility of cases
in which workers and employers share areas of belief about work and
society.

The peculiarly non-socialist nature of the mining unions and the
reluctance of their leaders to accept class models of industrial
relations can be readily understood if the unions and their leaders
represented the kind of constituencies that we have described.   It
is even more remarkable that the Labour party succeeded in winning
the miners.   Perhaps without the intransigence and severity of the
coal-owners' demands upon the miners, the Labour party would have
failed. (3)

NOTES

1 Part of the research on which this paper is based was financed
   by the Social Science Research Council.   I would also like to
   thank Peter McCaffery and Rex Taylor for their critical comments
   on a draft of this paper.
2 This quotation is from the 'Durham Chronicle'.   Unless otherwise cited, all quotations in the text are taken from local newspapers, MSS and unpublished sources, collected in the villages;
   sermon-notes, diaries, etc., and interviews conducted between
   1966 and 1970.
3 A fuller discussion of the themes of this paper is to be found
   in Chapters 6 and 7 of Moore (1974).

Chapter 4

PATTERNS OF PARADOX: SHIPBUILDING WORKERS' IMAGES OF SOCIETY

Jim Cousins and Richard Brown

INTRODUCTION

Sources of Variation in Working-Class Images of Society is undoubt-edly one of the most important contributions to sociology in Britain during the past decade.   It is important to establish this judgment initially because much of what we want to say subsequently in this paper will be critical of Lockwood's presentation, and the form of the renewed 'debate on the working class' which it inaugurated. (1) Indeed, even without any consideration of empirical material, his formulation of three working-class 'images of society' raises a number of problems, especially with regard to 'proletarian tradition-alism' which is our main area of interest.

First, Lockwood's proletariat is very different from Marx's. What classical Marxists saw as the social accompaniments of large-scale machine industry in which labour has the status solely of a commodity, namely rapid occupational formation and dissolution, high rates of mobility, continual changes in industrial location (Lenin, 1967, pp. 550-5), are not found in Lockwood's traditional commun-ities.   Indeed Marx's proletariat would appear to correspond far more closely to Lockwood's 'new', 'privatised', or 'pecuniary worker'. Traditional and proletarian are in a sense contradictory terms when applied to working class consciousness (Westergaard, 1965;   Cousins, 1971).   There is a sense in which Lockwood has inverted this classical Marxist idea of the proletariat.   We hope to show that some of the factors that Lockwood associates with the traditional community - notably the existence of interactional status systems, localised labour markets and high job involvement inhibit prolet-arianism rather than support it.

Second, the term 'traditional' implies, despite disclaimers in Chapter 2, an historical point of reference, a state of affairs from which more recent developments (e.g. the 'privatised' worker) can be seen to flow.   In other words the argument reflects a particular conception of the evolution of industrial society, a conception which does not encompass by any means all recent and contemporary social changes.   Indeed our own work inclines us to think that even those occupational groups which Lockwood specifically points to as providing the basis for a class conscious 'traditional proletariat'

(namely miners, dockworkers and shipbuilders) are historically mis-
represented by such a description.   Lockwood, in common with others,
seriously over-estimates both the homogeneity and the class consciousness of these kinds of worker (Westergaard, 1965).   In particular we would point to competition between settlements, religious
groups, and work gangs in these traditional communities.   This is
compounded in shipbuilding by the existence of crafts (and sometimes
non-crafts) with different places in the work cycle, different
labour markets, payments systems and union organisations.   The
expression of this lack of homogeneity in a long history of rivalry
over demarcation hardly needs to be stressed.

Indeed communities that are isolated and dependent upon a single
employer or a single source of employment are peculiarly disadvantaged in their opposition to these employers.   Workers are quite
likely to identify with the employer and his achievements;   constraints are likely to be exercised by the community on any section
that attempts to rock the boat;   internal struggles over the
allocation of work or the allocation of rewards may break out.
Militancy may take the form of contest over job rights, or demarcation or differentials with other workers, rather than direct
contests with the employer.

The industries where common 'one-class populations' (Lockwood,
Chapter 2) exist generally lack large professional management and
administrative structures.   Indeed it is precisely because they
lack these structures that they are 'one-class'.   But even in these
'one-class' communities intermediate social formations can exist.
The declining industries where mass and batch production technologies are absent are typically managed on a craft administration
basis.   The supervisors are recruited from amongst the workers.
But in the absence of a professional management structure these
supervisors often control job allocation and recruitment as well.
They become powerful figures in their own right.   Precisely because
status systems are 'interactional' and not 'attributional' (Chapter
2) particularistic relationships with the 'gaffers' can become an
important source of favour, security and reward.   In addition, the
traditional industries of mining, dockwork and shipbuilding are, or
were, strongholds of piece-work.   This payments system focuses
industrial conflict on the relationship between 'gaffer' and worker
in the day-to-day struggle for good jobs, better prices, concessions
for special difficulties.   This may seriously dilute the workers'
awareness of an external 'Them'.   Indeed the employer in shipbuilding could often appear to act as arbitrator and conciliator
inside his own yard between foreman and workman.

Thus by the recognition of dependence on the employer and his
agents, sectionalism, internal competition, and particularistic
conflict, the solidarity of the traditional community may be broken
down.   We hope to show that this was the case with the shipbuilding
workers we studied.

Third, a key argument of Lockwood's paper is that 'men visualise
the class structure of their society from the vantage point of their
own particular milieux' and that 'the industrial and community
milieux of manual workers exhibit a very considerable diversity' so
that 'it would be strange if there are no correspondingly marked
variations in the images of society held by different sections of

the working class'.   In terms of this argument Lockwood differen-
tiates his three types of worker, and of social consciousness.

But the argument can be taken further: there may be more than
three types; different aspects of workers' work and community
milieux may predispose them to visualise the class structure in
different, possibly contradictory ways; a social situation which
gives rise to a coherent image of society may well be the exception
rather than the rule; indeed, given that almost all workers are
exposed to the influence of the education system and the mass media,
it would be surprising if their images of society did not reflect
some incorporation of or adaptation to the world views which they
receive by these means.   If therefore neither the social situation
of a particular group of workers nor the interpretations of these
situations are as homogeneous as Lockwood suggests then the way is
opened for apparent contradictions between attitude and behaviour,
and for considerable contextual variation in attitude and behaviour.
We shall try to show that this was the case with shipbuilding
workers.

Our purpose is not to reject the effort at typification that
Lockwood's article represents, but to suggest that the non-homogen-
eous social situation in shipbuilding presents shipbuilding workers
with divergent but rational alternative courses of action and
definitions of the situation.   Within this 'vocabulary' of
strategies individual opinion and collective action may show
considerable confusion at any particular time and veer quite suddenly from one position to another over time.   But the overall number
of strategies of action and interpretation is not unlimited.
Indeed, we shall try to show that a powerful but often latent class-
consciousness is part of the interpretive vocabulary of shipbuilding
workers, though the number of structural contexts where this could
be displayed has hitherto been very limited.

SOURCES OF DIFFERENTIATION AMONGST SHIPBUILDING WORKERS

1 The community and the labour market

Lockwood specifically identified shipbuilding as an industry where
'highly developed forms of proletarian traditionalism' might be
found; he did so because it concentrated workers in isolated and
one-class communities with low rates of geographical and social
mobility (Chapter 2).   The shipbuilding workers of Tyneside with
whom we are concerned in this paper fit in many respects Lockwood's
description.   They are concentrated in a narrow belt of the
Tyneside conurbation consisting of a number of distinctive areas
which are, even now, to some extent physically separated.   In 1961
even after a long period of decline (the north-east coast shipyards
achieved their greatest output as long ago as 1906) more than 10
per cent of the occupied male population of the county boroughs of
Tynemouth and South Shields, more than 20 per cent in Hebburn UDC
and over 35 per cent in Wallsend borough were in shipbuilding or
ship-repairing (Cousins and Brown, 1970, pp.313-29).   Of our sample
only 16 per cent said that none or very few people round them worked

in shipbuilding and only 27 per cent said that there were none or
very few who worked at their particular yard. (2)   The shipbuilding
communities of North and South Shields, however, are based mainly on
ship-repair yards with a greater emphasis on casual employment, and
with an occupational structure with less emphasis on the steelmaking
trades, and they have an association with dockwork, seamen and
fishing.   In contrast the shipbuilding communities further up the
river at Hebburn, Walker and Wallsend are mainly based around shipbuilding yards with a rather different tradition.   Shipbuilding and
ship-repairing are in many ways two distinct industries.

Each community is traditionally associated with a particular
shipyard.   Favouritism based on residence is still firmly felt to
be a factor in employment in an industry and in an area where
unemployment is a major problem.   There is good reason for these
feelings because the 'market' or daily callstand method of recruitment formerly common in the yards encouraged localism.   A chargehand from the former Blyth shipyard a little further up the coast
and now closed told us 'with us it was always keep the Tynies out'.
One Sunderland man employed on the Tyne went to extreme methods
including the forgery of his union card to conceal where he lived.
The closure of a yard can be fatal to the shipyard labour force of
the surrounding community.   The dependence on a particular local
community for employment emerges clearly from the sample of shipbuilding workers at a Wallsend shipyard that we interviewed.   Fifty
per cent had had personal experience of unemployment;   nearly 50 per
cent of those who had had more than one job gave redundancy as their
reason for leaving their last job.   Of the 54 per cent who had not
either started straight from school (23 per cent) or gave no clear
reason as to how they started at the yard (20 per cent), 42 per cent
had made direct approaches to a foreman or had been spoken for by
friends or relatives etc.;   17 per cent had made a direct approach
at the shipyard gates (these approaches were until about 1969
normally referred to the 'Head Foreman' of a trade Department);
only 20 per cent had got a job from the employment exchange (12 per
cent), from the union (2 per cent) or been transferred from other
firms (6 per cent).   This localism in the labour market combined
with unemployment and casual employment made the community a differentiating factor.   Much conversation in the yard centred on
rivalries and unfavourable comparisons between particular communities and served to reinforce these differences.   Men from certain
areas sometimes formed distinct groups, particularly in situations
like post-overtime working, lift sharing or drinking.   Thirty-five
per cent of the employees at the yard came from the borough of
Wallsend itself and were thus able to share to a much greater extent
the social life of the yard.

2   Identification with the job

Our sample of shipbuilding workers did show a high degree of that
identification with the job that Lockwood expected of the traditional worker.   This was confirmed in the observational studies we also
undertook.   Sixty per cent of those who had had more than one job
preferred their present job.   Of those who named qualities of the

job rather than describing tasks, 75 per cent thought factors such as achievement, creativity, ability and importance to production were the most important things about their job.   Sixty-two per cent would prefer no other job in the shipyard, and, of the 38 per cent who did, over a third gave as their reason achievement, creativity, etc.   Sixty per cent did not find work monotonous; 70 per cent were 'always learning something new';   62 per cent claimed to 'try out their own ideas'.   Only 8 per cent thought their work in general 'hardly ever' or 'never' interesting.   We asked shipbuilding workers to compare their job with that of factory workers with the results shown in Table 4.1.

TABLE 4.1   Shipyards compared with factories (per cent)

	Interest	Better pay	Freedom from supervision	Workmates	Freedom of movement
Better	60	56	76	61	74
Worse	12	14	9	2	7

This was supported by a strong craft pride and customs.   Fifty-six per cent said they were never given instructions about how to do a job.   Fifty-four per cent of the craftsmen said they frequently or sometimes used plans.   Seventy-three per cent said they were never told how long to take over a job;   72 per cent claimed their time was never checked.   On the other hand 48 per cent of the craftsmen said their work was frequently checked for quality;   over 80 per cent of the craftsmen said they could not or would not lower their standards of quality.   Paradoxically this high level of identification with the job, and the high value placed on personal skill made it more difficult and not less for workers to oppose their employers in many crucial respects.

It might be supposed that unemployment, which was obviously a considerable common experience in the shipbuilding industry, and in an area where unemployment was above the northern regional, let alone the national, average (North Regional Planning Council, 1970, D6), might be one of the factors making for solidarity and common efforts to control life-chances.   But this was not the case. According to shop stewards' reports not a single group within the shipyard had a last-in first-out rule;   only one operated an automatic overtime ban when local unemployment in that trade reached a stipulated number.   Few shop stewards were aware of apprentice-ship ratios.

Despite the relatively high local unemployment levels, of our sample only 15 per cent had not worked overtime the previous week; 77 per cent normally worked 4 hours overtime or more;   45 per cent worked 8 hours or more overtime.   One can see that the factors Lockwood sees as combining to produce class consciousness often conflict with one another in an industry where there are often deadlines to be met or bad weather to be compensated for, and workers may be inspired by a genuine identification with the job. Similarly shop stewards made few attempts to work overtime rotas.

'It's the job that's worked not the man' was the frequent reason
given.   Yet of those who thought that it was the foremen who
decided overtime, 41 per cent felt it was distributed unfairly.
     In the same way as solidarity with workmates conflicted with
identification with the job over overtime the same occurred over
job security.   Shop stewards commonly accepted redundancies that
followed from the cycle of shipbuilding work and also largely
accepted that management could select men to be paid off on the
basis of personal assessment of work quality.   In this way identification with the job, the craft ethic and the particularistic
relations with foremen prevented rather than supported solidaristic
responses to problems of unemployment and job security (Brown et al.,
1972).

3 Status system and the labour market

We have pointed out elsewhere (Brown et al., 1972) the historical
and technological reasons why occupations were highly differentiated
in shipbuilding.   We have also presented evidence for the existence
of a clear occupational hierarchy amongst shipyard workers.   This
in itself is an indication that 'attributional status systems' were
present amongst shipyard workers.   But within the trade group,
interactional status systems of a kind highly relevant to the
functioning of the labour market could, and did, exist.   The foreman was the traditional recruiter of labour in the shipyards through
the market system.   Favouritism was constantly alleged in observation at the yard though it emerged much less strongly in interviews.   Even in the yard the foremen tended to have their own
squads who were rewarded by overtime-bearing jobs, extra allowances,
etc.   In the past personal reputation and particularistic relationships with foremen were considered to be critical in getting jobs.
Of those who felt their job was secure over 25 per cent still gave
those two reasons despite specific job security agreements that had
been introduced.
     This in itself led to considerable differences in the labour
market strategy pursued by shipbuilding workers.   Some, to use yard
terminology, became 'floaters' or 'cowboys' moving round the shipyards, or in the case of some trades, outside them, chasing work or
money.   Others stayed in the yards where they were known and tried
to build up reputation and particularistic contacts.   Every yard
and most trade groups in a yard had a set of these men - sometimes
known as 'royals'.   These men would be the last to be paid off in
a situation of shortage of work and regarding themselves as being
'in the squad' would wait to be invited to return to work when it
restarted.   A study of unemployment in North Shields (Sinfield,
1970) revealed that skilled shipyard workers often took no steps to
jobhunt when unemployed.   They simply waited to be recalled.   These
differences were shown in our sample, and were reflected in workers'
attitudes to labour market strategy.   The changes in advice dependent on age in Table 4.3 are more drastic than the percentage
figures suggest.   Of 107 who recommended staying in a firm and
working for promotion for a young man, only 55 still recommended it
for an older man.   Of 92 who advocated moving around for a young

TABLE 4.2 Employers and industries since apprenticeship (skilled workers only)

	Employers	Industries
	%	%
One	37	49
Two	}32{	27
Three		14
Four/Five	17	10
Six plus	14	1
N	193	193

TABLE 4.3   Labour market strategies

	Advice given to a younger man	Changed advice given to older men
	%	%
Stay in the same firm and work for promotion	48	38
Stay in firm conditional on pay or security	-	8
Get in with a good squad of workers and stick with them	15	19
Move around trying different jobs	35	6
Find a secure job or good firm	-	6
Get in with the foreman - he'll look after you	1	9
DK/NA	1	14
N	266	266

man only 7 still recommended it for an older man.

These differences in experience and attitude reflected themselves in conflicts in the work situation. Shop stewards often expressed disapproval of the overtime-hunting and more militant 'cowboys'. In several disputes that occurred over bonus in one trade that was observed particularly closely a small group of 'cowboys' was held to be responsible.

These divisions amongst the workers (which are also suggested in an early observation study of a Clydeside shipyard coppersmiths'

shop (Stokes, 1949))often showed up a firm and foreman-based
deference which resulted in the reverse of proletarian class-
consciousness.   It is precisely in the one-industry isolated communities that Lockwood refers to that workers are least able to
show consistent independence of or opposition to their employers.
The heavy concentration of shipbuilding workers round a limited
number of Tyneside shipyards shows these difficulties very clearly.
The control over employment, earnings (by overtime, allowances and
job allocation) and promotion exercised by the employers' principal
agent, the foreman, made a proletarian strategy very difficult
particularly when the workers also showed a genuine commitment to
the work and accepted the exigencies that justified bouts of overtime and semi-casual employment.   The policy of autonomy suggested
by a third of our respondents was seen as possible only for the
younger man who could accept its risks.

4   Identification with workmates

The source of differentiation at work that prevented occupational
solidarities arising was in the differences between craft groups and
between craft and non-craft groups.   The shipbuilding worker is
thus differentiated not merely into different crafts with, often,
different unions, different labour markets, different positions
within the cycle of shipyard work from keel-laying to outfitting,
but also vertically between the craftsmen, semi-skilled service
workers and labourers serving the craftsmen directly as mates.   The
social life of the yard is largely determined by these differences.
And it is precisely on the interconnection between work and sociability that Lockwood places such stress in developing his exposition
of the proletarian situation.   This structuring of yard social life
round craft groups takes place despite the similar community background of the men and the work situation where occupations were
generally mixed and supervision could not be very close.   Indeed,
while 61 per cent of the sample claimed to talk regularly to workers
of other occupational groups, this might in the context be thought
a low figure.   Further, the work group itself remained occupationally exclusive even if other occupations were working in the same
general location.   Contacts with other occupations were often confined to servicing work, such as drilling, burning or welding.
Only in certain steelmaking situations were these contacts so permanent and continuous as to create a multi-occupation workgroup.
Most work groups changed their service worker several times a day
and indeed this was a general cause of inter-occupational resentment rather than a source of solidarity.
    It might be argued that work group composition is independent of
the workers' will.   But information about workers' dinner and tea
groups also suggests that the various occupations remain largely
distinct.   Indeed 43 per cent ate their dinners either in cabins
or shops belonging to their occupation, or in the steel sheds; 16
per cent went home to dinner.   Only 23 per cent ate in the yard
canteen and even fewer visited local cafes, pubs or clubs (6 per
cent) where occupations were liable to be mixed.   Thus, multi-
occupationality in voluntary social situations seems, if anything,

TABLE 4.4   Contacts with other occupations at work

	Work group composition	Dinner group	Tea group
	%	%	%
Alone	26	14	24
Single occupation	33	44	48
Occupation plus unskilled 'mate'	16	11	15
Multi-occupation	24	15	13
Not applicable	1	16	-
N	266	266	266

slightly less than in involuntary social situations.   This kind of occupational differentiation is not what Lockwood suggests as likely in the proletarian situation.   Nor can this be dismissed as a sign of the emergence of a new working class.   There is no reason to think that occupational differentiation has been increasing at the expense of wider 'proletarian' solidarities.   Occupational differentiation has been with shipbuilding since the industry began and is expressed in the form of a complex history of demarcation (Webb, 1920; Roberts, 1967) and craft unionism.   Indeed occupational differentiation is now diminishing; and signs of wider proletarian solidarity are only now beginning to appear.

The shipyard was regarded as a good place for finding friends by 84 per cent of the sample; when asked what they liked about ship-yard work about 23 per cent mentioned sociability as their first reason; and nearly 75 per cent of those who had served an apprenticeship claimed still to be in touch with men they had 'served their time with'.   But these statements derive their meaning from the existence of distinct craft occupations.

Before turning to consider to what extent either shipbuilding workers as such or specific occupations within the industry can be said to form 'occupational communities', there are two further kinds of differences to mention, those within occupational groups and those between occupational groups which cause them to be in actual conflict.   Traditional payments systems are the cause of considerable differences of both kinds.   The steelmaking trades organised by the Boilermakers' Society traditionally worked 'on piece', generally in squads.   The piece-work prices were some-times based on standard lists, but often were not (Robertson, 1960).   This had the effect of fragmenting wage negotiations on to the squad rather than the occupational group.   Personal bar-gaining ability thus played a considerable part in earnings. 'People call it craftsmanship', said one plater in another yard, 'but it's more the ability to bully, fight and cajole.'   'I do believe', said a shed manager referring to one well known plater, 'that when he got short he booked the bloody shed in.'   This payments system had been substantially altered by the widespread

use of 'lieu' rates but it was clear from observation where the
system survived and from recollections of where it has operated
that personal reputation, rivalry and favouritism were its accompaniments.   Poor workers were often weeded out of squads by the
workers themselves; and it was not unknown for craftsmen effectively to act as employers over their labourers.

This piece-work system was the cause of the superior earnings of
steelworkers in the shipyard and, as such, was much resented by the
non-piece-working outfitting trades.   Of the sample as a whole 51
per cent felt the pay for their job compared with others was too
low; the figures were 39 per cent amongst boilermakers but 58 per
cent amongst fitting-out tradesmen.   Forty-eight per cent thought
pay differentials between trades were too big; 27 per cent of
boilermakers, but 66 per cent of the fitting out tradesmen.   The
boilermakers' history of piece-work made them find incentive payments schemes and productivity bargaining much more acceptable.
Seventy-seven per cent of boilermakers, but only 49 per cent of
outfitting workers thought bonus schemes a good idea.   Twenty-six
per cent of outfitters but only 17 per cent of boilermakers were
hostile to productivity bargaining.

Another factor which tended to differentiate workers was the
distinction between 'shop' and 'ship' men.   The shopmen were
thought to be in better conditions and were commonly older than the
shipmen.   In some trades movement between shop and ship was very
much less flexible than others which tended to create a separateness
between the groups.   When asked whether they felt any workers had
worse conditions than others, of those that named an occupation 43
per cent (93 of 219) specified a location.   Of these 93 all but one
specified outside or ship workers as having worse conditions.

It might be thought that their distinctive working conditions
would be an important source of unity among shipyard workers.
Shipbuilding is, in fact, one of the most dangerous industries to
work in outside coalmining and fishing.   Eighty-two per cent of our
sample thought that management could do more to make conditions safe.
There is a local custom that all workers in the trade group affected
and sometimes all workers in the yard affected down tools for a day
when a death occurs in the yards - the only occasion when all
workers in the yard go on strike as the result of shopfloor-level
initiative.   Yet 94 per cent of the sample also agreed with the
statement that workers were their own worst enemies with regard to
safety.   Thus the shared danger of shipyard work seemed not to be
quite the source of solidarity that it might have been.

The day to day problem of safety in the shipyards did bring
particular groups of workers into sharp conflict notably over such
issues as poor and inadequate staging, noise, fumes and sparks from
burning and welding, and the accidental dropping of tools and
materials on to men working below.   Here is an example drawn from
the observational material (which has been little used in this
paper):

The plumber chargehand has seen the platers' helper lowering
supports down a tank.   'They're ignorant. One twist more round
that rail and there's a danger of rope burn.'   The platers'
helpers are lowering the plate down using the rope straining
against the edge of the hold rather than a crane.   The drillers'

pipes are also going down into the tank.   There's a Swinburne
(plumbing contractor - hostility between them and yard plumbers)
pipe going down too and they're using the crane which is holding
up John (a plumber), in other words there is complete confusion
from several different people trying to gain access through the
same hole at the same time.   The 'Con Man' (plumber's labourer)
goes up and finds the bolt for a hanger in the Swinburne's store.
John takes it.   They are too long, brass, etc.   'It's our turn
now.'   Other people have stopped using it long enough for the
five men, if they include Bob (plumber's labourer) as well to
help, to go down below.   The drillers won't move their pipe out
of the way for the plumbers to push their pipe in.   The drillers'
pipe of course is flexible, more like a cable.   John is furious
with them.   The craneman makes too rapid a move with the pipe,
and the huge pipe which contains an off-set so that it's a very
cumbersome shape, lurches right on to the staging.   The Swinburne's men two levels of staging down shout up in alarm critical
of Swan's men.   They shout back to the craneman's guider above.
Arthur (a plumber) remarks: 'If we fall we fall on somebody, the
bottom's full.   There are blacksmiths, welders, platers, burners
and fitters down there.'   Certainly fumes are rising out of the
pump room from a variety of different forms of gear.   Once again
it's not just a question of lowering the pipe in.   It has to be
moved along once it gets down to the right level which again
needs a second block to hold it while it's getting off the crane
on to the next block.   The craneman lurches it up five feet by
mistake.   Crash, it hits the staging above it.   The staging
trembles where the men are standing.   John says 'My heart's in
my mouth now.'   A staging bracket nearly goes.   The movement
of the staging means that the staging is irregularly put down.
The staging here has bracket extension arms in use which makes
it weaker.   The pipe is slightly twisted so that one hanger is
not on right.   John puts himself in charge and goes up and down
re-bolting it on to the hangers.   The 'Con Man' just holds the
blocks which annoys Nick (a plumber's labourer) who is reluctant
to give him a sweet when the time comes to hand them round.   He
was working on his own bolting on the hangers lower down.

5   The occupational community

It now remains to consider whether, as Lockwood suggests, shipbuilding workers form an 'occupational community' (see also Brown
et al., 1973).   There are three main elements in Lockwood's conception of the occupational community: the size of the work-based
social group; the extension of the work-based social group into
non-work situations; and the non-home-centred 'public and present-
oriented conviviality' of this social life (Chapter 2).   The occupational community brings the worker 'under the social control of
his fellows' (Lockwood, 1960, p.257) and thus promotes solidarity
and collective identity.
     Social groups in the shipyard are not only occupationally
distinct but also small in size.   Only 23 per cent had met dinner
group associates outside the yard; and only 28 per cent tea group

TABLE 4.5 Size of sociable groupings at work

	Size of work group	Size of dinner group	Size of tea group	Size of group of friends
	%	%	%	%
One	26 (i.e. alone)	14 (i.e. alone)	24 (i.e. alone)	24 (i.e. no friends)
Two	24	18	26	18
Three	15	11	11	12
Four	10	14	14	10
Five	6	13	5	6
Six	4	5	6	15
Seven	5	12	5	8
Eight +	9	1	–	8
N	266	266	266	266

associates.   On the other hand 58 per cent met workplace friends
outside the yard.   But when asked to describe their friends in
general only 33 per cent of the 655 friends we were given details
of were from the shipbuilding industry.   Half our sample thought
shipyard workers tight-knit but only 13 per cent were prepared to
state a definite preference for the company of shipyard workers.

Of the nature of the social life of shipyard workers it can be
said that while it was oriented to the pub and club outside the home
there was a considerable emphasis on home activities, and on home
entertaining.   Even in visits to the pub and club segregation of
the sexes was not as overwhelming as the ideal type of 'traditional
proletarian' social life might have led one to expect; a third of
those who went to the pub in the week before the interview, and two-
fifths of those who went to the club, were accompanied by their
wives.   Of our sample 60 per cent said they never went drinking
after work with workmates and 43 per cent said they were not members
of a workingmen's club.   Home and family thus seem to be quite as
important as work in creating patterns of social life, though these
patterns are considerably varied.

We would not dispute that there is a distinctive style of social
life on Tyneside though this is hard to quantify.   What we would
question is whether it is confined to any specific industrial basis,
or whether it could be seen as a web of social controls round shipbuilding workers.   One could go further and see in this style of
life not the product or workplace social relations but rather a set
of values to which traditional shipyard life with its particular
favouritisms, its occupational distinctions and skill hierarchies
should be contrasted.   In this sense the democratic style of social
relations represents a latent potential which the very real sources
of differentiation to which we have pointed largely frustrate.   This
lack of homogeneity and latent proletarianism are also features of

THE DIVERSITY OF 'IMAGES OF SOCIETY'

To classify the 'images of society' or 'images of the class
structure' which are being used by respondents in interviews is
difficult.   The problem is not eased when respondents appear to
have given many very varied answers to questions about classes and
class differences, and when one cannot assume that each respondent
has one image of society which provides a point of reference no
matter what the question.
    The most immediate impression of the replies of the shipbuilding
workers is of the great diversity of their views (see also Popitz
et al., 1969; Goldthorpe et al., 1969; Bott, 1957).   Excluding
twelve respondents who were unable or unwilling to give any clues as
to how they viewed the class structure of their own society, it is
possible to distinguish fourteen basic patterns of response varying
from those who declared that everyone was a member of the same
'class' to one worker who was prepared to distinguish and rank six
separate 'classes'.   These fourteen different patterns, which we
classified solely in terms of the number, arrangement and relative
size of the classes distinguished, could be further subdivided in
terms of the types of people' seen as constituting each group, the
respondent's own self-ranking, the criteria used to differentiate
classes, and so on. (3)
    In attempting to summarise these varied patterns in the replies
to questions about 'class' - and most of them were only given by a
small number of respondents - we have emphasised initially two
factors: the number and more particularly the types of grouping
distinguished, and the respondent's own self ranking within such a
hierarchy.   We have paid relatively little attention to the descriptive labels used (they tend to be the conventional ones -
'upper', 'middle', 'working', 'lower' and so on, often used in
different, sometimes apparently illogical, ways), but as the second
stage in the analysis have attempted to characterise the classes
distinguished in terms of the actual social groups the respondents
saw as constituting each class.
    If those who gave no answer (12 replies) or said everybody was
in the same class (7) are excluded, five basic patterns can be
distinguished and these are illustrated diagrammatically in Fig.4.1.
    A third of all respondents (89) distinguished two groups, the
class to which they, and by inference or explicitly, most other
people (and certainly all workers) belonged, and a relatively much
smaller group containing people like employers, directors, top
managers ('bosses'), the 'rich' and/or some other similar 'elite'
group (Type A - see Table 4.6).   Nearly as many, 29 per cent (78),
also conceived of their own class position as a member of a large
grouping to which, by inference or explicitly, most people belonged,
but were prepared to distinguish two or three relatively small
superior groups (Type B).
    The third type of pattern (Type C), held by 18 per cent (47) of
the sample, was one in which the respondents also saw themselves as
members of a large class at the bottom of the hierarchy, but in
addition distinguished a relatively large superior class of white-
collar workers and foremen, or well paid and/or skilled workers, as
well as, in the majority of cases (42 out of 48), enumerating one,
two or three 'elite' groups.

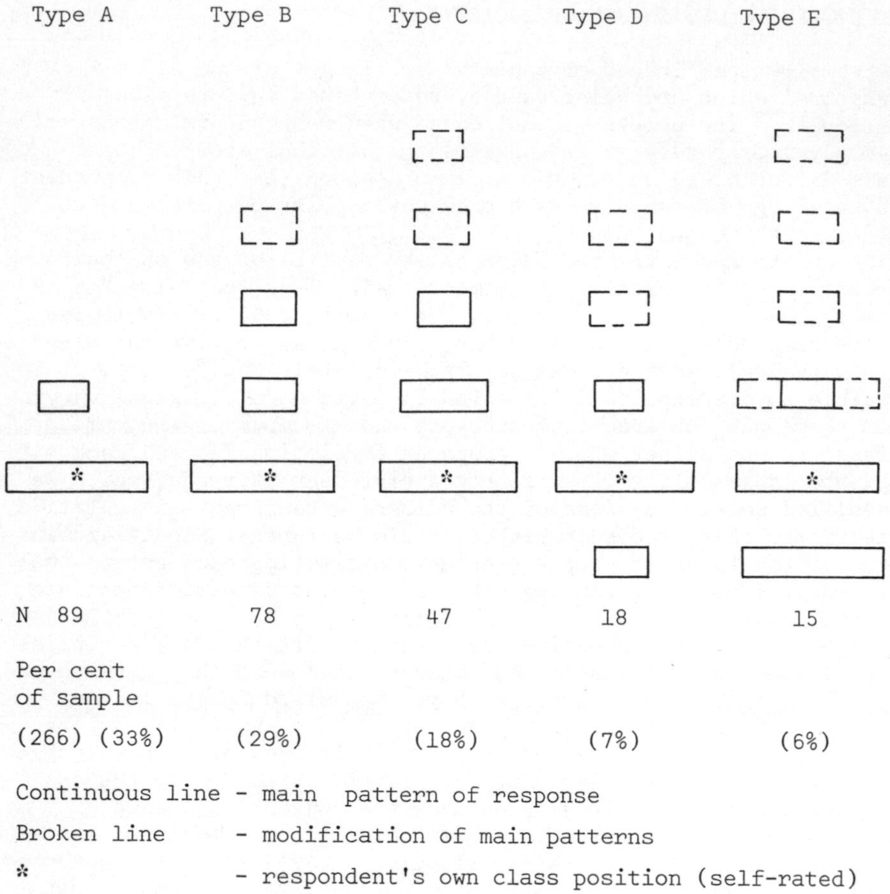

| | Type A | Type B | Type C | Type D | Type E |

N   89   78   47   18   15

Per cent
of sample

(266) (33%)   (29%)   (18%)   (7%)   (6%)

Continuous line - main pattern of response

Broken line   - modification of main patterns

*   - respondent's own class position (self-rated)

FIGURE 4.1 'Images' of the class structure

    The remainder of our respondents saw themselves as members of
some sort of class in an intermediate position in the hierarchy,
with groups above and below them.   They can be subdivided into the
7 per cent (18) who only distinguished a relatively small inferior
group (of pensioners, those on social security, etc.) (Type D);
and the 6 per cent (15) who appear to distinguish a relatively large
inferior class of non-skilled workers, which might also include 'the
poor', the unemployed and so on (Type E).   In almost all cases of
both these types one, two, three or (in one case) four smaller
'elite' groups superior to themselves were listed, but in only one
case was a larger superior class of white-collar and similar workers
referred to.
    The factors which are used to distinguish between 'classes' are
particularly important because it can be argued that they greatly
affect the interpretation to be placed on any classification of
'images of society'.   Thus, in the case of 'The Affluent Worker'

TABLE 4.6   Types of class structure and composition of classes

	A %	B %	C %	D %	E %	Total** %
ELITE GROUP(S)						
Bosses	39	60	42	39	53	46
Rich	36	30	32	39	40	33
Nobs	16	44	23	33	27	27
Professionals	8	41	12	39	40	25*
Small business	5	37	5	6	20	19*
Managers	7	23	6	6	20	13*
'Snobs'	11	12	5	-	7	10*
LARGE SUPERIOR CLASS						
White-collar			76		7	15
Well-off workers			19			4
Professionals			24			
Managers			4			see
Business			6			above
'Snobs'			4			
OWN CLASS						
Workers	67	80	87	67	80	79
Workers and White-collar	8	12	-	11	13	8
'Ordinary folk' &c.	14	6	11	17	-	12
Poor	6	1	6	5	7	3
INFERIOR CLASS						
Labourers and non-skilled					100	6
Poor etc				33	7	4
Unemployables etc				66		6
N	89	78	47	18	15	254
% of sample	(33)	(29)	(18)	(7)	(6)	(93)

*   Including references under 'Large Superior Class'.
** In this and Tables 4.8, 4.9, 4.10 and 4.11 the percentages in
    the total column relate to all those who replied including the
    seven respondents who stated that there was only one class.

study it was suggested that the emphasis on money as a determinant
of 'class' was crucially important, enabling the majority of respondents (many of whom appeared to have had a picture of the class
structure not unlike those we have just described) to be classified
as having a pecuniary model of the class structure.   Equally,
however, this interpretation is very difficult to make, and apparently different criteria may be used in answer to different
questions in different contexts.   In her re-examination of some

of 'The Affluent Worker' data, for example, Platt (1971, p.417) has
written:

it seemed evident during the interviews that respondents answer-
ing the class question frequently did not make, or did not grasp,
the distinction between determinants and correlates of class;
thus the reference to money could mean only that it was a con-
veniently observable, and easily conceptualisable, correlate of
class differences rather than being seen as their fundamental
cause.

Our own data are open to such alternative interpretations.   In
considering the answers we are unable to differentiate clearly
between 'determinants' and 'correlates' of class and suspect that
most of our respondents did not do so.   We would, however, argue
that references to income, property, wealth, standard of living and
so on should only be judged with great caution as indicating a
'money model' of the class structure, and appear more likely to
indicate a convenient way of referring briefly to the whole range
of social differences of which 'money' is the symbol.

Thus although more than four-fifths of the sample referred to
'money' as a criterion for distinguishing between classes - by far
the most frequently mentioned item - only a fifth did not also make
reference to one or more other criteria (Table 4.7).   Of these a
person's definition of themselves, or of others, as belonging to a

TABLE 4.7   Main criteria used to distinguish 'classes'

	A	B	C	D	E	Total
N	89	78	47	18	15	247
	%	%	%	%	%	%
CRITERIA MENTIONED						
Money, possessions, standard of living	83	81	85	100	100	84
(only money)	(24)	(13)	(12)	(26)	(20)	(18)
Self definition, snobbery	40	49	32	28	33	41
Behaviour, style of life, dress, etc.	20	39	21	33	27	27
Education	21	33	23	11	53	26
Social standing	18	30	30	22	47	26
Background, birth, breeding	17	35	19	11	27	23
Work, job, position	16	19	28	22	33	21
Being friendly, sociable	18	22	19	22	13	19
Ability, brains	8	13	8	11	7	9
Area of residence	5	6	11	6	20	7

different 'class' was the most frequently mentioned item, but there
were a considerable number of references to differences in 'objective' social characteristics like education, job or position at work,
style of life, and birth and early upbringing ('breeding').   A few
of our respondents clearly did have a pecuniary model of society,
and others may have done so but 75 to 80 per cent of them saw differences in income, standard of living and so on as being explicitly
associated with other differences.

It is notable that there are very few references to 'power',
although those answers classified as referring to aspects of the
work situation did include some in which giving or receiving orders
was a criterion.   On the other hand the frequent references to
'bosses' indicate that such considerations were relevant for these
workers.   Such apparent discrepancies reinforce the need for
caution in interpreting replies and lend weight, it can be argued,
to the possibility that 'money' can be seen as a symptom or a
correlate of class differences determined by other means.

TABLE 4.8   'Do you think it is possible to move from one class to
another?'

	A %	B %	C %	D %	E %	Total %
Yes	51	65	64	67	100	62
No	44	30	34	28	-	33
Don't know, etc.	5	5	2	5	-	5
N	89	78	47	18	15	254

With regard to mobility between classes, the majority of the sample
regarded mobility as possible.   This was so even in the case of
those (Type A) who distinguish only two classes - an 'elite' and the
rest - though the proportion was greater for those with more complex
models of class structure.   In many cases such mobility was,
however, seen as contingent upon more or less exceptional circumstances (e.g. winning the pools), and fewer desired mobility for
themselves than regarded it as theoretically possible (33 per cent
as compared with 62 per cent).

Certain general points can be made about these replies.   In the
first place only a third of those interviewed appeared to have a
two-class model of society (Type A), which has been regarded as the
typical 'traditional proletarian' response.   Indeed, not all these
respondents can be considered as having a 'power model' of the class
structure.   This category includes three, if not more, different
types of reply: those who do see society in 'us' and 'them' terms;
those who have a 'money' model of society of the type described by
Goldthorpe (1970a) in which most people are seen as belonging to a
large central class with only a small residual elite group;   and
those, perhaps particularly older and/or less skilled workers, who
had no very clearly articulated 'image of society' but in an interview situation were prepared to make the minimum distinction of two
groups.

On the other hand, it is notable that the great majority (80 per cent) saw themselves as occupying a position in the lowest class they distinguished.   Their view of the world was one which saw the class structure of their society from the bottom upwards (cf. Brown and Brannen, 1970).   The emphasis on the association of self with the bottom class is reinforced by the fact that their description of this 'class' was as a class of 'workers', or 'everyday people', 'ordinary folk', and so on, though in a few cases it explicitly included white-collar and similar workers (8 per cent), and in more cases did so by inference.

Third, although in a number of cases classes were categorised in broad, and rather meaningless, general terms - 'upper' and 'lower', the 'rich' and the 'poor' - in many more identifiable social groups were referred to (see Table 4.6).   Indeed a number of replies reflected very closely either the immediate experience of the respondents as in the case of 'managers, foremen, workers', or reflected such direct experience supplemented by ideas about the world gained through the mass media - the rich 'with titles' or 'who don't work'.   Given these references to identifiable social groups it is notable that nearly half of all those responding referred to an upper 'class' of 'bosses' (and some others referred to managers). This fact, combined with the self ranking of most respondents in the lowest 'class', does give support for the view that an underlying 'proletarian' dichotomous 'image of society' is held by many ship-building workers.   This sort of interpretation of their replies is reinforced by the fact that so few clearly distinguished a conventional middle, or lower-middle 'class' of white-collar workers, and a number explicitly included such groups as 'workers'.

Even if in broad terms one can describe these workers' 'images of society' as being 'proletarian' in the sense in which that term is used by Lockwood, they are not however a simple division into 'us' and 'them'.   They reflect fairly sophisticated and realistic awareness of the world around them; and as we shall see they are not always associated with the 'proletarian' views which might be expected on other matters, nor with a highly developed 'class consciousness'.

In addition there are indications that many respondents did not have one 'image of society' which provided a constant point of reference, but apparently used different conceptions of the world in different contexts.   This point, to which we shall return, is most simply illustrated by considering the choices made from three statements presented at the end of the interview (see Table 4.9 C). Thus half of those (Types C and E) who appeared in answer to other questions to distinguish at least two substantial 'classes' endorsed the view that everybody belonged to the same class, and only 38 per cent of those with a two class model of society (Type A) endorsed such a statement.

TABLE 4.9 Types of 'images of society' and class statements

Here are four sets of statements.   Would you read the first set carefully, then tell me which of the statements you agree with most (and continuing through each set)

	Types	A	B	C	D	E	Total
	N	89	78	47	18	15	254
		%	%	%	%	%	%
A Anybody can get to the top if they have the ability and are prepared to work hard.		69	74	70	44	67	69
Some people are born to rule: ordinary people cannot hope to become bosses.		8	9	19	28	20	13
Basically the people at the top are no better than anyone else, but try not to give the ordinary man a chance.		19	15	11	22	13	16
B A man's working life is like a ladder which he climbs up from rung to rung until he reaches the top.		32	35	45	39	53	37
If a man has a steady job and a good wage, he should be content.		60	63	53	56	40	59
C In Britain today there are basically two main classes, bosses and workers, and these classes have opposing interests.		38	36	28	39	33	35
Most people in Britain today belong to the same class: the only important difference is how much money they earn.		48	41	51	50	47	47
There are several classes in Britain today: the upper classes run the country and industry, and this is as it should be.		8	18	19	6	7	14
D What happens to you depends a lot on luck, otherwise you have to learn to put up with things.		19	17	28	11	13	19
You can get ahead if you have ability and initiative and are prepared to work hard.		78	82	72	83	87	79

ATTITUDES TO MANAGEMENT AND INDUSTRIAL RELATIONS

Although more or less 'proletarian' images of society appeared to
predominate in the replies given to questions about 'class', answers
to attitudinal questions were by no means straightforwardly solidaristic or highly class conscious.   For example, nearly half thought
industrial relations in their firm 'good' (and almost all the rest
thought them 'moderate') (see Table 4.10);   three-quarters felt that
strike action was unjustified before procedure was exhausted,
although the great majority of them considered the procedure too
slow;   only 36 per cent wished their union to be affiliated to the
Labour party, though twice as many paid the political levy.   On the
other hand there is evidence in the answers for considerable diversity of opinion and outlook.   Very few of the questions received a
pattern of replies overwhelmingly one way or the other.   Even where
there were definite majority viewpoints, there were substantial
minorities;   and the proportions change in ways which suggest a
diversity of viewpoints rather than a few simple ones.   Thus whereas 62 per cent rated Swan Hunter a good firm to work for, only 44
per cent stated that industrial relations there were good, fewer
felt that management had favourable attitudes towards the men, and
66 per cent thought the firm could afford to pay more in wages.

There is also evidence for the point made by both Parkin (1971,
p.95) and Mann (1970, pp.432-6) that replies to abstract questions
may reflect the dominant ideology whereas questions with more
concrete reference may be answered in an apparently contradictory
way which reflects more closely the day to day interest of the
respondents.   This can be illustrated by comparing the answers to
questions about strikes: only 5 per cent expressed the general
view that strikes achieved anything (though others saw them as
reluctantly necessary), but more than half of those with experience
of being on strike approved of that strike.   One might add that
when strikes do happen in shipbuilding, everybody involved stops
work and there is no need for pickets.

The relationships between the types of 'images of society' which
we have distinguished so far and the replies to such attitudinal
questions are complex but not random.   The pattern of replies
(Table 4.10) shows very few instances where the holders of any
particular type of 'image of society' are markedly different from
the average for all respondents.   This is particularly the case
with the larger groupings (Types A, B, and C) which suggests that,
as has already been argued in the case of Type A respondents, each
of these patterns of response may cover several different 'images
of society' which we have so far been unable to disentangle.   If
this is so, it reflects again the diversity of responses, for in
answer to the attitude questions themselves there are in most cases
considerable differences of opinion even though they cannot be
related straightforwardly to 'images of the class structure'.

If the smaller groupings (Types D and E) are considered first
some tendencies are observable which, even though they are not very
significant statistically, do allow a meaningful picture to be
suggested.   Those with a Type E 'image of society' can be the most
clearly characterised as a type of 'instrumental collectivist' or
'right-wing militant';   collectivism in the context of particular

TABLE 4.10   Types of 'images of society' and attitudes to the firm, management, industrial relations and trade unions

Type	A	B	C	D	E	Total
N	89 %	78 %	47 %	18 %	15 %	254
A firm is like a football team? Agree, and like this at Swan Hunter's	55	54	43	83	33	53
Disagree	13	17	23	6	33	18
Management attitudes towards men are favourable	34	40	41	44	43	38
Top management attitudes to men are favourable	34	41	49	35	36	40
Shipbuilding's bad industrial relations record is justified	41	47	46	19	40	42
Industrial relations at Swan Hunter's are good	52	41	33	56	33	44
Strikes don't achieve anything	75	68	70	72	53	70
Main purposes of a trade union are:						
'solidaristic'	21	27	39	29	14	26
'instrumental'	44	40	37	24	50	40
'as spokesman'	24	21	22	29	36	24
Membership of a trade union should be compulsory	81	87	83	78	93	84
There should be one union for all shipbuilding workers	64	60	69	78	57	64
Trade unions should be affiliated to the Labour party	36	41	43	39	27	38
Voted Labour in 1966	80	86	84	82	62	82
Labour 'regular'	57	45	47	59	23	49

industrial relations issues is combined with a tendency to agree with the much more individualistic views about the possibility of mobility between classes.

Those with Type D 'images of society' appear to have a relatively traditional respectable working class outlook. They are most likely to feel that their firm is like a football team and that management attitudes towards the men are favourable; but on the other hand they are least likely to view trade unions in instrumental terms, and they provide the highest proportion of Labour 'regulars'.

Those respondents who appeared to have Type C 'images of society'

formed a somewhat larger category and came closer to a 'traditional
proletarian' position; they might be termed the most solidaristic.
Their conception of the purposes of a trade union is the most
'solidaristic', and they agree the most strongly with the view that
trade unions should be affiliated with the Labour party, though
support for the Labour party is only average.

Those categorised as having Type A and Type B 'images of society'
differ least of all from each other and from the average of all
replies; this reflects the size and presumed heterogeneity of these
groupings.   In so far as there are differences Type A (the two-
class model) tends to be associated with a less militant set of
attitudes than Type B (three- and four-class models), even though
Type A are the least likely to feel that management have favourable
attitudes towards the men.   Type A might be described as the more
'passive', or even 'apathetic', with the highest proportion of those
stating that strikes don't achieve anything; those with Type B
'images of society' include the highest proportion of Labour 'voters'
and tend to take a less satisfied position.

SOCIAL CHARACTERISTICS AND TYPES OF 'IMAGES OF SOCIETY'

In discussing above the ways in which the shipbuilding labour force
has been differentiated we have placed emphasis on occupational and
occupation linked differences, and especially experiences of and
present position in the labour market.   Some support for this
emphasis is provided by attempts to relate the five types of 'images
of society' to some data about the social characteristics of the
sample.   As in the case of attitudes to the firm and to industrial
relations the trends are not significant statistically but do
provide some sort of meaningful picture, although it is again easier
to characterise the smaller than the larger categories.

TABLE 4.11   Types of 'images of society' and social characteristics

Types	A	B	C	D	E	Total
N	89	78	47	18	15	254
	%	%	%	%	%	
AGE						
16 - 30 Young	25	28	34	11	40	28
31 - 45 Young middle	28	24	32	39	26	28
46 - 60 Old middle	37	35	26	33	13	33
61+ Old	10	13	9	17	20	12
OCCUPATION						
Boilermaker trades	31	44	47	33	73	40
Outfitting trades	40	33	38	45	27	38
Semi-skilled	13	9	9	11	0	10
Un-skilled	15	14	6	11	0	12

Types	A	B	C	D	E	Total
N	89	78	47	18	15	254
	%	%	%	%	%	

LABOUR MARKET

	A	B	C	D	E	Total
Unemployment - never	48	42	40	56	80	47
- very short term	23	24	32	17	7	24
- longer term	29	33	28	28	13	29
Redundant or paid-off in previous job	56	53	45	36	22	50
Number of jobs - 2-3	29	26	32	22	27	28
4-5	22	20	30	28	20	24
6-9	31	35	26	33	33	31
10+	17	20	13	17	20	17
Number of employers - 1-3	59	46	59	47	39	53
Number of industries - 1-2	55	46	60	53	43	52
Employed outside shipbuilding, repairing and maring engineering	51	48	44	50	67	50
Only worked for one firm in shipbuilding, etc.	43	44	45	39	46	44
Length of service with present employer						
- 10 or more	47	48	41	45	36	45
- 3 or less	34	32	35	39	40	34

SOCIAL RELATIONS AT WORK

	A	B	C	D	E	Total
Work group - Works alone	31	30	26	33	7	28
- Pair	25	18	28	33	33	25
- 3-5	26	38	27	28	33	30
- 6 or more	18	15	19	6	27	18
Work group composition						
- same occupation	38	27	32	33	47	33
- mixed occupations	32	44	43	28	47	39
Friends at work - none	26	26	24	33	0	25
- one	19	18	15	11	27	18
- 2 or more	55	56	61	56	73	57
Has friends at work with different occupations	30	32	43	50	60	36
Works with none of friends at work	20	31	36	33	17	27
Meets none of friends at work outside	27	21	29	36	31	26

Table continued over

Types	A	B	C	D	E	Total
N	89	78	47	18	15	254
	%	%	%	%	%	%

WAGES

	A	B	C	D	E	Total
Earnings - 'below average'	32	23	19	18	20	25
- 'average'	49	58	62	71	40	56
- 'above average'	15	8	17	6	27	13
Not available	3	10	2	6	13	6

RESIDENCE

	A	B	C	D	E	Total
Live in Wallsend	36	30	43	33	7	35
Housing - owner-occupier	26	10	21	17	27	20
- council tenant	54	53	55	28	60	52
- private tenant	21	37	23	56	13	28
Lived all life in one place	47	53	57	61	40	51
Have lived outside north-east (Northumberland and Durham)	11	14	13	17	7	13

The 15 workers who appeared to have Type E 'images of society' were younger than average, and all skilled, predominantly in the steel trades (see Table 4.11).   Their pattern of work experience seems to have been one of more frequent than average job changes (especially in view of their ages), employment outside the ship-building and related industries, and little experience of being unemployed or made redundant.   In terms of both attitudes (militant instrumental collectivist with 'prestige' models of the class structure) and social characteristics this group of young skilled men can be likened to the mobile 'cowboys' described earlier in the paper who are able to exploit the labour market to their own ends.

The 18 men with Type D 'images of society' were older, and included both skilled and unskilled men, with the highest proportion of outfitting tradesmen.   Their labour market experience was not very different from average, except that they too had less experience of unemployment and redundancy, and they have moved around quite a lot.   These men were older and more stable than Type E, but also the most apparently socially isolated at work.

The 47 men with Type C 'images of society' were predominantly young or middle-aged, with fewer non-skilled than average.   They had the lowest proportion with no experience of unemployment, but in terms of labour market experiences (numbers of jobs, employers and industries) they were the most stable, and the most likely never to have worked outside shipbuilding and related industries.

The social characteristics of the workers with Type A and Type B 'images of society' approximated more closely to each other and to those of the sample as a whole.   Both categories included slightly more older than younger men, and more non-skilled men, especially Type A.   In terms of labour market experience both groups were more likely than others to have been made redundant in their previous jobs, but Type B differs from Type A and from the average in being

slightly more mobile as between jobs, firms and industries.   It is
not possible to characterise either group very precisely.   As we
saw when considering their attitudes, it seems likely that these two
categories are too large and heterogeneous;   it is possible, but not
certain, that further sub-division in terms of attitudes or images
of society could produce groups which were more clearly differentiated in terms of social characteristics.

This account of the 'images of society' of shipbuilding workers
has been characterised more by paradox - or perhaps confusion - than
pattern.   We hope that in due course it may be possible to present
a more polished analysis of these data.   Nevertheless, even in their
present form we feel that the data we have outlined justify us in
making the following concluding points about the social perspectives
of the sample:

1   There is considerable diversity of social perspectives among ship-
    building workers and neither their models of the class structure
    of their society nor their attitudes to a variety of industrial
    and political topics can be characterised as straightforwardly
    'proletarian'.   The ideal type traditional proletarian worker is
    rarely found in its extreme form.
2   There is, however, sufficient evidence to justify the claim that
    these workers show a 'latent proletarianism';   the great majority
    of them see themselves as members of the lowest 'working' class
    in society and as distinguished particularly from those with
    authority in industry and society, from the titled and landed,
    and from the rich;   on the other hand the line between manual
    and white-collar workers was not at all strongly emphasised.
3   It is possible to suggest certain elements of structure in the
    great variety of responses to questions related to 'images of
    society', but such structuring is not especially pronounced or
    clear-cut.
4   There is some evidence to suggest that questions at different
    levels of abstraction were answered in terms of different and
    often incompatible frames of reference;   and that shipbuilding
    workers do not all have one unambiguous 'image of society' which
    is relevant whatever the context of speech or action.
5   One cannot assume any automatic link between 'images of the class
    structure' and attitudes to industrial relations topics; relative
    'militancy' may be associated with individualistic attitudes to
    personal careers and mobility, and a 'prestige' model of the
    class structure;   'solidaristic' support for the Labour movement
    with a consensus model of the firm.
6   In the case of certain categories (Type E and possibly C and D)
    there do appear to be links between the social characteristics of
    shipbuilding workers and their social perspectives and 'images of
    society';   in particular labour market strategies and experiences
    and work situations appear to be important, although of course
    the degree of choice of strategy available within the labour
    market is greater for some workers (young and more skilled?) than
    for others.

Our argument therefore is both that the social situation of
workers in a traditional industry and their images of society are
more varied than has been allowed for;   and that the links between
social context and social consciousness are looser than has been

suggested, that workers faced by similar market and work situations
may interpret them differently and have some choice as to the strategies they may pursue.   This is not to reject the basic proposition
of Bott, Lockwood and others, but to suggest that it demands both
the specification of a much wider range of typical possibilities and
the introduction of a greater element of indeterminacy into the
assumed relationship of social context and social consciousness.

CURRENT DEVELOPMENTS AND FUTURE TRENDS IN SHIPBUILDING

As we noted in the Introduction, the concept of the traditional
worker (proletarian and deferential) has been used to provide support
for arguments about historical developments in the working class.
Although the final volume of 'The Affluent Worker' series does
emphasise the need for openness in suggesting likely future trends,
nevertheless there has been a tendency in studies of 'embourgeoisement' to contrast the affluent worker, however characterised, with
the stereotypical traditional worker and to suggest that the former
is in some respects prototypical.   We would argue that the pattern
of current developments in the shipbuilding industry is open to the
opposite interpretation.   Those features of the social situation
of shipbuilding workers which encourage non-proletarian, and sometimes outrightly deferential, patterns of action and social interpretation we see as diminishing in influence;   the features which
might encourage proletarian action and interpretation seem to be
growing correspondingly stronger.   Accordingly we are forced to
disagree with the core of the revisionist argument;   shipbuilding
workers may in the future be much more proletarian rather than much
less.
   Some very factors that Lockwood points to as buttressing proletarianism we see as sources of differentiation and division.   We
would tend to see the traditional working class community, along
with Mann (1970) and Parkin (1971), as a source of social stability
rather than proletarian radicalism.   Unlike Mann and Parkin, however, we do not see the source of stability in the split between
radicalism of the working-class community and adherence to dominant
values at the societal level.   Our own studies of shipyard appren-
tices incline us to think, for example, that 'school values' are
modified relatively quickly (Brown, 1973).   We see the source of
stability as primarily arising out of differentiations occurring
within the working-class community itself.   If, as we suggest, the
sources of differentiation are diminishing, then it is possible that
the power of dominant value systems to control the articulation of
proletarian radicalism at the societal level may be much reduced.
   During the past ten years or so there have been changes in the
shipbuilding industry which have considerably reduced the differentiation of the workforce.   These changes (discussed in more detail
in Brown et al., 1972) can be seen to be largely the consequence of
deliberate attempts to modernise the industry in the face of
increasing world competition, and include the following:
1 The amalgamation of trade unions.
2 The introduction of standardised schemes of apprentice training
   under the aegis of the Shipbuilding Industry Training Board with

an emphasis on common elements in the training of all craftsmen.
3 The creation of shipbuilding consortia (as proposed by the Geddes
   Report) bringing several, previously independent, yards under
   unified management.
4 As a consequence of this the tendency to specialise as between
   yards in a group, so that each yard would normally build a
   smaller range of types of ship, and therefore have less diversity
   of work tasks and work situations.
5 As a further consequence, the negotiation of common terms and
   conditions of employment for all yards in the group, and of
   'productivity agreements' in which higher rates of pay were
   secured in return for mobility of labour between yards, and flexibility and interchangeability between trades. In particular,
   the agreements replaced the multifarious and complex pay systems
   with uniform pay scales for the membership of each union, and
   reduced the significance of craft differences.
6 As a consequence of the need to negotiate agreements at the level
   of the whole consortium the creation and/or strengthening of
   negotiating committees of shop stewards and full-time union
   officials within each yard and for the whole consortium.
These changes have meant that increasingly shipbuilding workers
on Tyneside - and elsewhere - have both come to share common market
and work situations, and to be aware that they did so. Particularism in relations between management and men is increasingly giving
way to universalism - in larger and necessarily more bureaucratic
organisations. Because of the need, in management's view, to
secure mobility of labour between jobs and yards a deliberate
attempt has been made to break down demarcation lines and to secure
greater all round flexibility in the use of labour. But this can
only be achieved at the cost of creating a much more homogeneous
and potentially unified work force. Shipbuilding workers now more
nearly share the same market situation and have fewer chances to
pursue particular individual strategies in their pursuit of pay and
security; collective action against a common employer is the most
obvious possibility for them. They are now more likely to experience the same range of work situations - and to have fewer, if any,
chances of escaping from deprivations and grievances in one yard
under one employer by going to another employer; collective action
is again the most obvious strategy. If men's social consciousness
is influenced by their immediate social context; and if we are
right in stressing the importance of the market and work situations
as influencing consciousness, then, one must expect 'proletarian'
social perspectives to increase in importance. Whether the logic
of the situation will work out in this way must remain uncertain,
but the 'modernisation' of a traditional industry may indeed have
produced for the first time the conditions in which a 'proletariat'
can emerge.

NOTES

1 This paper is based on work done as part of a research project
   entitled 'Orientation to Work and Industrial Behaviour of Shipbuilding Workers on Tyneside' which was carried out between

1968 and 1970 in the Department of Sociology and Social Administration, University of Durham, and supported by grants from
the Social Science Research Council.   Interviewing, observation
and other fieldwork were carried out in the Wallsend and Neptune
Yards of the Swan Hunter Group.   The members of the research
team, in addition to the authors, were Mr Peter Brannen and Mr
Michael Samphier.   Preparation of this paper was assisted by a
further grant from the SSRC.   A full report of the research is
in preparation.
We are grateful to all those who made the research possible, and
would also like to express thanks to Mrs Sheila Ramsay for her
work coding interview data, and especially to Mr John Reed for
invaluable assistance with computer programming and data analysis.

2   During the course of the investigation a stratified random sample
of 266 shipbuilding workers from the Wallsend Yard were interviewed in their homes.   Unless otherwise stated references in
the text are to this sample.

3   For details of the questions used see Jim Cousins and Richard
Brown, Patterns of Paradox - shipbuilding workers' images of
society, 'Working Papers in Sociology No.4', Department of
Sociology and Social Administration, University of Durham, 1972,
pp.39-40.

Chapter 5

THE SOURCES OF VARIATION IN AGRICULTURAL WORKERS' IMAGES OF SOCIETY

Colin Bell and Howard Newby

David Lockwood's paper was an imaginative attempt to summarise existing research on the meaning systems of the working class and to develop typologies of the sources of variation in working-class images of society. Since the value of these typologies is essentially a heuristic one, it would be inappropriate to criticise them on the grounds that in each and every case they do not coincide with empirical reality. Our object is to develop Lockwood's typologies by examining some of his assumptions concerning both the identification of sections of the working class with certain occupational groups and the homogeneity of 'community' structures. In other words we wish to relate variations in class imagery within a particular occupational group - in this case agricultural workers, by relating them to differing work and locality relationships. (1)

Agricultural workers are 'deferential traditionalists' in Lockwood's terms and indeed most commentators regard them as deferential workers par excellence. Hitherto, however, our knowledge of deferential workers has been, as Lockwood himself pointed out, rather meagre. His material was almost entirely culled from research into working-class Conservative voting behaviour and the first study of Banbury. As a result, much of his analysis was 'wholly speculative' (Chapter 2). Unfortunately this dearth to material on deferential traditionalists remains; as Kavanagh has recently put it, 'At present there is a theory of deference in search of data' (Kavanagh, 1971, p.360). Further rural community studies have appeared since Plowman et al.'s (1962) summary paper which were not incorporated by Lockwood into his characterisation of agricultural workers as typical of those whose 'system of status has the function of placing his work orientations in a wider social content' (Chapter 2). In addition, 'a variable army of scholars has seized on the deferential component' (Kavanagh, 1971, p.333) of English political culture. So before developing an analysis of the varying social situations of agricultural workers we will outline the contribution of recently published material.

FURTHER EMPIRICAL STUDIES

Although there has been something of a hiatus in British locality
studies since the publication of Plowman et al.'s (1962) paper,
those that have appeared have been significant contributions towards
broadening the basis of our understanding of rural social relationships.   Williams's (1963) study of Ashworthy is an important
corrective to the prevalent view of the static, unchanging countryside, but its location in an area where there is an absence of hired
agricultural workers and its concentration on kinship reduces its
relevance to the concerns of this paper.   The belated publication
of Littlejohn's (1963) study of the upland parish of Westrigg,
though also set in the Highland Zone, was important in that for the
first time in a rural locality study the social relationships in the
parish were analysed in terms of class rather than status.   The
presence of a large proportion of hired workers enabled an analysis
to be undertaken of class cultures rather than one, inherently
consensual, rural culture, from which much of the typification of
the deferential traditionalism of rural workers derives.   Littlejohn
therefore undermined prevailing notions of local social stratification in rural areas, but Frankenberg's plea for research into
'capitalist organised business farming areas of Britain' (Frankenberg, 1966, p.252), principally in eastern and southern England,
remains as yet unanswered.   Pahl's (1965) study of the metropolitan
fringe in Hertfordshire was in such an area, but does not deal to
any great degree with agricultural workers.   However, this omission
is in itself significant in showing the changes that have occurred
in the social structure of many rural settlements.   By placing
agricultural workers in a residual category of rural dwellers,
imprisoned by spatial and economic constraints, he is emphasising
the breakdown of the former agrarian local social system until only
a small minority may both work and live locally.   This has led to
considerable changes in the type of local status systems.   It is
apparent that both these changes in the local status system and
those variations which can occur in social stratification in rural
areas must be incorporated into any analysis which seeks to understand the variations in social imagery of agricultural workers.

DEFERENCE

Before doing so, however, it is necessary to consider again the
concept of deference.   The term's usage has become so elastic
(Kavanagh, 1971; Jessop, 1971) that this is essential if we are to
investigate the social milieux in which agricultural workers are
likely to be deferential traditionalists.   Kavanagh has outlined
the myriad meanings that the concept has assumed 'in the literature
describing and analysing the popular political attitudes, and those
aspects of the political system, including stability, which it has
been used to explain' (Kavanagh, 1971, p.333).   He argues that in
this context deference 'has attained the status of a stereotype and
that it is applied to such variegated and sometimes conflicting data
that it has outlived its usefulness as a term in academic currency'
(Kavanagh, 1971, p.333).   We would accept Kavanagh's arguments in

the limited context in which they are applied, but feel that the
concept is of use in explaining certain kinds of social relationships.   The first problem is to decide whether deference is a form
of behaviour or a set of attitudes.   We would argue that it is the
latter since many acts of 'deferential' behaviour like bowing,
curtseying, saluting, touching the forelock, etc., take on a ritualistic form, emptied of all meaning, or may be enforced by sanctions
surrounding the role of the individual concerned which make explanations of his behaviour in terms of 'deference' redundant (Goffman,
1956).   We would agree with Shils that deference must be 'an
element in a relationship between the person deferred to and the
deferent person.   Deference towards another person is an attitude...
Acts of deference judgements are evaluative classifications of self
and other' (Shils, 1968, p.116).   However, we would disagree with
Shils that deference is equivalent to status - quite apart from the
unnecessary confusion of using both terms, we are not convinced that
individuals defer only to those of higher status.   Individuals
frequently defer to those of lower status in role-specific situations where particular forms of expertise are required.   For
instance, in a rural context an upper-class individual will
frequently defer to his servants where they possess a particular
expertise - in the cultivation of the garden, for instance.   This
may seem irrelevant to the explanation of behaviour in other social
contexts, but possibly no less so than attitudes towards the
monarchy, House of Lords, etc., and other indices employed by
investigating academics for large sections of the working class
(Westergaard, 1970).   In the analysis of social systems we would
prefer to reserve, following Parkin, the use of the term 'deference'
to individuals who endorse a moral order which legitimises their own
political, material and social subordination (Parkin, 1971, p.84).
It is the commitment to such a moral order which we shall understand
by the use of the term deference.
    The particular social-structural configurations under which such
a commitment obtains have never been fully explored in Britain,
though studies of Banbury and Glossop (Stacey, 1960; Birch, 1959)
contain a number of insights which could be explored further.   The
relative proximity of those who are powerless to the incumbents of
powerful roles is one aspect that has been taken up by Lockwood,
yet he does not altogether make clear the mechanisms whereby
'interaction with' leads to 'identification with' those in superordinate positions (Chapter 2).   We may however make some comparisons with other social systems where such mechanisms have been
investigated - for instance, patron-client relationships in peasant
societies and relationships between slaveholders and slaves in the
Deep South and the Carribean in the nineteenth century.

PATRONAGE IN PEASANT AND SLAVEHOLDING SOCIETIES

Numerous studies of peasant societies have emphasised the importance of patron-client relationships where the impersonal, universalistic social system of the state impinges upon the face-to-face
particularistic social system of the locality (e.g. Kenny, 1960;
Foster, 1963; Campbell, 1964; Pitt-Rivers, 1961).   Patronage is

the means through which the local social system is linked to the
wider national society.   It is clearly a mechanism that reduces the
degree of conflict between the locality and the bureaucratic state
administration for individuals are integrated piecemeal into the
wider society along lines of personal obligation and not through
membership of a large corporate group capable of attempting resistance to the power of the state (Galtung, 1971).   As Pitt-Rivers has
put it, 'the tension between the state and the community is balanced
in the system of patronage' (Pitt-Rivers, 1961, p.155).   Through
this social institution an individual may convert an impersonal
ephemeral relationship with the powerful into a permanent and
personal set of relationships which can be manipulated more easily.
Relationships between patrons and clients are therefore asymmetrical
but dyadic, informally contracted and multi-purpose.   As Campbell
points out:

> The initial motive is utilitarian, protection and assistance on
> the side of the client, political power and social prestige on
> the part of the patron.   But when such a relationship endures
> for any length of time it takes on a strong moral quality.   The
> patron feels obliged to assist and take a general interest in all
> the client's affairs, and in doing so he is able both to sense
> his superiority and approve his own compassionate generosity.
> The client is conscious of a duty to support his patron politic-
> ally ... and to give free expression to his feelings of gratitude
> and indebtedness (Campbell, 1964, p.259).

This exchange of deference for patronage from the 'big house' is a
relationship that characterised many English agricultural villages
during the nineteenth and early twentieth centuries (Thompson, 1963).
It partly resulted from the isolation of the village and the political powerlessness of its inhabitants, but perhaps the most important
areas of patronage lay in the labour (and, therefore, housing)
market.   A local landowner could hold a near monopoly over the
purchase of labour.   The daughters of villagers were found 'suitable positions' in other large households through the good offices
of the local landlord.   Sons would also be placed on local farms by
word being passed 'along the grapevine'.   Although a great deal of
patronage disappeared with the sale of the large estates it still
persists in the labour market.   Most farmers recruit their labour
through the use of informal contacts: those regarded unfavourably
find it difficult to obtain employment.   There is an incentive,
therefore, to conform to the image of the 'good worker' - which will
include deferential behaviour towards his employer.

   Those American historians who have attempted to understand the
dynamics of the slaveholding system in the Deep South have also
sought to do so by explaining the development of a 'slavish' personality (i.e. deference), rather than by simply sketching the system
of constraints which surrounded the slaves and which ensured their
obedience.   Elkins, for example, has drawn analogies with total
institutions, particularly the concentration camp, in order to
demonstrate the emergence of a deferential personality - 'Sambo'.
He explains this emergence by Freudian theories of infantile
regression, Sullivan's theory of 'significant others' and role
theory (Elkins, 1968, pp.116-33).   Genovese has criticised Elkins
on the grounds that he failed 'to discover the conditions under

which the personality pattern could be inverted and a seemingly
docile slave could suddenly turn fierce....   His thesis ... is
objectionable ... because it proves too much and encompasses more
forms of behaviour than can usefully be merged under a single rubric'
(Genovese, 1971, p.98).   Genovese prefers to understand the dynamics of the slavish personality by inherent contradictions of the
system of authority under slavery:

> We do not need an elaborate psychological theory to help us
> understand the emergence of the slaveholder as a father figure.
> As the source of all privileges, gifts and necessaries, he loomed
> as a great benefactor, even when he simultaneously functioned as
> a great oppressor.   Slaves, forced into dependence on their
> master, viewed him with awe and identified their interests and
> even their wills with his (Genovese, 1971, p.92).

Slaveholders required some kind of servility and feelings of infer-
iority in their slaves, if only because this ensured the long-term
survival of the slaveholding system.   From this sprang two potentially conflicting acts of relationships: 'the patriarchalism of
the plantation community, and the commercial and capitalistic
exploitation demanded by the exigencies of the world market'
(Genovese, 1970, p.98).   As a social system the slave plantation
was therefore shot through with contradictions, and whilst Genovese
does not deny the value of Elkins' insights into the generation of
deferential attitudes, he argues that the sporadic outbreaks of
rebellion are too significant to be discussed as deviant cases: 'If
the basic personality pattern arose from the nature of the regime,
so did the deviant patterns' (Genovese, 1971, p.93).   The explanations of these divergent patterns lie in the 'broad belt of
indeterminacy between playing a role and becoming the role you
always play' which were allowed by the contradictions of the slaveholding system.   In order to make these insights more relevant to
our present concern we need only draw a few analogies.   Elkins's
and Genovese's work enable us to understand the processes by which
interaction of the powerless with the powerful becomes identification of the powerless with the powerful.   But also we must be
careful not to always impute from deferential behaviour deferential
attitudes.   To use examples from our own society, Goffman has
described to degree of 'impression management' which can occur while
an individual is 'on stage' (Goffman, 1956, 1969).   Once the role
constraints are removed 'off stage', true indications of individuals'
attitudes and values may emerge.   Here we may think of servants'
behaviour 'below stairs', or in a rural content the whole gamut of
behaviour - poaching, rick-burning, cattle-maiming, etc., - that was
part of the rural underworld of the agricultural village during the
nineteenth and early twentieth century.   These attitudes only
briefly emerged from the everyday rituals of deferential behaviour,
but were undoubtedly responsible for the great nineteenth century
'explosions' of rural unrest that spontaneously broke out in the
Captain Swing riots (Hobsbawm and Rude, 1970) and the outbreak of
trade unionism led by Joseph Arch (Dunabin, 1963; Horn, 1971),
which so surprised those in authority at the time.

AGRICULTURAL WORKERS IN THE CLASS STRUCTURE

One of us has described elsewhere the developing trends in the
social situation of agricultural workers (Newby, 1972b).   We may
merely note here that it was pointed out that the market situation
of agricultural workers is becoming one of increasing powerlessness
compared with other members of the working class, as evinced by the
ever increasing gap in relative earnings between agricultural
workers and those in other industries.   Part of this increasing
powerlessness is due to the rising proportion of farm workers living
in tied cottages - from 34.3 per cent in 1948 to 52.8 per cent in
1970.   Meanwhile technological advances which have allowed a steady
diminution in the agricultural labour force, so that the number of
workers per farm is now less than two (Heath and Whitby, 1970).
Many agricultural workers have therefore been brought into increasing
proximity with their employers.   In addition, agricultural depopulation has resulted in widespread changes in who lived in many
villages.   Any analysis of the variations in images of society and
of meaning-systems among agricultural workers must take account of
these changes.

THE LOCAL SOCIAL SYSTEM OF AGRICULTURAL WORKERS

We begin our analysis with an outline of a typology of the local
social systems in which agricultural workers can be found.   There
are two key defining parameters: 'size' and 'location' which act on
the third, 'proportion of agricultural workers'.
Size   The size of the population in the local social system is
important due to its effect of role differentiation on the social
division of labour.   The degree of role differentiation clearly
affects the 'density' of the individual's social network and this in
turn will affect the criteria by which status is allocated (Plowman
et al., 1962;   Bell and Newby, 1972).   It will also affect the
degree of social interaction between individuals in different
positions in the class structure.
Location has three components:
1 Proximity to urban settlement - the distance from the nearest
   commercial or industrial centre will to a large extent decide
   the proportion of inhabitants who live but do not work in the
   locality.   We may include here not only commuters but retired
   urbanites and weekend cottagers.   A number of studies have
   shown how this influx of an urban-oriented population will
   alter the local status system by introducing length of residence
   as a criterion of high status.   Hence a rift can appear between
   long-established 'locals' and newly arrived 'immigrants' (Pahl,
   1968, Elias and Scotson, 1965).
2 Type of farming activity - the geographical location of a rural
   settlement is the main determinant of the type of farming
   activity that is carried out there, and is likely to be increasingly so as improved methods of transport allow soil conditions
   rather than proximity to urban markets to be the deciding factor
   (Gasson, 1966).   Caird's famous distinction between the cereal
   areas of east and south-east England and the grassland areas of
   the north and west is still very significant.   The bulk of the

agricultural labour force is in the arable areas, whereas in the north and west hired workers are relatively few and far between and mainly consist of farmers' kin awaiting their inheritance. It is in this area, as we pointed out above, where most British rural community studies have been situated, and it is in this area where there are very few agricultural workers - at least in comparison with East Anglia.

3   Proportion of agricultural workers - this is a result of the combination of the community's proximity to urban settlement and the type of farming activity carried out in the area.   It may be noted that even in the most geographically rural areas this proportion may be surprisingly low - possibly no more than 50 per cent of the economically active males may be sufficient to render a village genuinely 'agricultural'.   This is a result of the trades and minor industries which service the agricultural population and whose fortunes and outlook are intimately bound up in agriculture, but which are not classified as 'agricultural' as far as employment statistics are concerned.   These character- istics are, of course, related to each other.

THE LOCAL SOCIAL SITUATION OF AGRICULTURAL WORKERS

Size and location are then the key defining parameters of rural local social systems.   Within these social systems are broadly three kinds of personal local social situation in which agricultural workers can be found:

1   The occupational community.
2   The encapsulated community.
3   The farm as a community.

While we do not like the term 'community' here we feel that in the interest of parsimonious communication its use here can be condoned as it probably adequately connotes what we mean.   It should be understood though that 'community' here is a shorthand term for a particular type of local social situation which will be described in more detail below.   No evaluative overtones should be attached to our usage.   This division will be elaborated and illus- trated from existing studies of rural communities and by using data currently being gathered in East Anglia.

1   The occupational community

This was and is found predominantly in eastern and south-eastern England, particularly East Anglia.   Rural occupational communities tend to be fairly large in rural terms since they are nucleated and provide a pool of labour for surrounding farms, but they are small enough in urban terms to provide interactional status systems;   a parish population of between 250 and 750 would appear to be the statistical norm.   The dwellings of the workers tend to be separated from those of their employers which will be scattered around the periphery of the village on the farmer's own holding of land - a settlement pattern that results from enclosure, which in East Anglia dates from Saxon times.

   This ecological pattern is reflected in the pattern of social
relationships in the local social system.   The social network of an
agricultural worker consists predominantly of other agricultural
workers.   Farmers do have a position in the social network of most
farm workers, but the content of the relationship is entirely
different, since relationships with farmers are relationships with
authority.   The authority of farmers in the local social system is
confirmed by their multiple occupancy of authoritarian roles - they
are not only employers but also magistrates, councillors, landlords
and school governors.   This gives farmers as a group, and occasionally individual farmers, considerable power in the local social
system against which agricultural workers are powerless.   Almost by
definition in a rural area they have a near monopoly over employment
opportunities.   In addition, however, they have control of the
entire housing stock that is within the reach of farm workers - both
tied housing and council housing.   The constraints which surround
the agricultural worker (Newby, 1972b) have resulted in some rural
villages bearing many of the characteristics that Lockwood has noted
of other occupational communities of miners, fishermen, dockers and
shipbuilders - concentration, isolation, high degree of job involvement, strong attachment of primary groups counterposed to 'them' in
positions of authority (Lockwood, Chapter 2).   The existence of
such occupational communities in the countryside suggests an
immediate reason why not all agricultural workers are 'deferential
traditionalists'.   Here agricultural workers 'in their off-hours
socialize more with persons in their own line of work than with a
cross-section of occupational types', they '"talk shop" in their
off-hours'; and 'the occupation is the reference group; its
standards of behaviour, its system of status and rank guide conduct'
(Blauner, 1960, p.343).
   Since no sociological study of such a community has been carried
out, appropriate illustrative material is generally lacking.   However, because such occupational communities were largely typical of
rural villages in lowland areas during the nineteenth and early
twentieth century, some impressions can be gained from historical
sources.   Evans, for example, has collected a good deal of mostly
oral material from rural inhabitants who had lived through a period
when 'most of the villages in East Anglia, whether ancient or comparatively modern, were communities organised for a particular work'
(Evans, 1969, p.135;   see also Evans, 1956, 1960, 1966 and 1970).
In such villages there occurred the characteristic patterns of
social interaction in leisure hours noted by Lockwood - social networks consist of other agricultural workers and prestige is allocated by skill at work:

> So great was the interest in ploughing a well-finished stretch
> with mathematically straight furrows, or in the faultless
> drilling of a seed-bed and so keen was the rivalry between
> various horsemen that, even after they had spent most of an
> autumn day ploughing an acre or so in the field, they would
> spend the rest of it ploughing the land over once again in the
> cosiness of the inn bar.   And on a Sunday morning they walked
> round the parish inspecting their neighbours' week of ploughing
> to see if it measured up to the high claims that had been made
> for it during the detailed preliminary examination at the four-
> ale bar (Evans, 1970, p.64; see also Kitchen, 1940 and Kendall,
> 1944).

The occupational and communal solidarities of the occupational community has undoubtedly fostered a more radical social imagery among the inhabitants than that generally regarded as typical of agricultural workers.   The rural areas of East Anglia are notable for high density of agricultural trade union membership (Dunabin, 1968; Groves, 1948), and disproportionately high Labour voting behaviour (Blondel, 1963, pp.63-4).   However, the occupational community is in danger of becoming a historical anachronism faced by the twin threats of creeping urbanisation and the steadily falling number of workers required on farms.   It continues only in those areas isolated by bad roads from urban centres and where recent expansion of certain branches of agriculture - notably pigs and poultry - have slowed labour outflows.

2   The encapsulated community

This is the result of the urbanisation of the rural occupational community.   As employment opportunities in agriculture decline due to increasing mechanisation, agricultural workers are forced to seek employment in towns where there are not only expanding employment opportunities but a higher standard of living (Bellerby, 1956; Saville, 1957).   In many areas, however, rural depopulation has been assuaged by urban commuters who are either attracted to a rural environment by their image of the Good Life, or pushed there by housing markets.   The effects of this influx of individuals with largely alien life-styles has been documented by Pahl's work on commuter villages in the 'metropolitan fringe' around London (Pahl, 1965, 1968, 1970).   As Pahl shows, the majority of the newcomers are middle-class with considerable difference in life-styles to the locals.   This has considerable effect on local amenities, in some cases (like education) resulting in an improvement, in others a marked deterioration (such as rural transport).   The greatest conflict, however, probably results from the stereotyped expectations held by the newcomers of what the village should consist of - both in terms of appearance and behaviour.   Because they hold an idealised 'village in the mind' they fiercely object to the provision of additional housing, particularly council house estates which will be detrimental to the 'character' of the village, but which are a necessity for locals who have been priced out of the private housing market by precisely that group which protests against new housing developments - a row of cottages that once housed four agricultural workers' families being converted into one house for a retired or commuting member of the bourgeoisie is not unusual.   This conflict is overlaid by the expectations of the locals' behaviour.   Because they have been attracted by an idealised urban image of village life they like to see a few pet farm workers around the place to help define the village situation - 'props on the rustic stage' as Pahl has called them (Pahl, 1968, p.274).   The paternalism of the newcomers demands a deferential response from local workers, but this is frequently withheld on the grounds that they lack traditional authority.
   The manual worker responds to this situation by excluding the immigrant as a 'stranger' or 'foreigner' simply because non-

acceptance on the basis of length of residence is one of the few
ways in which the established working class can allocate or with-
hold prestige (Pahl, 1968, p.275).
From the viewpoint of the agricultural worker, we may refer to this
process, following Mayer (1968) as encapsulation.   The social network of the locals forms a separate and dense network, encapsulated
within the total local social system.   Depending upon the extent of
urbanisation and the morphology of the local housing market, this
social encapsulation may be accompanied by a physical encapsulation -
the locals living on a council housing estate in one part of the
village with its own leisure amenities, particularly a pub, and the
newcomers living in private housing in the remainder.   Interaction
between the two groups may be limited to certain symbolic occasions,
such as the parish meeting or the village fete, but there may be a
number of gatekeepers between the two - such as domestic cleaners,
small tradesmen, gardeners - whose influence may be of considerable
importance in defining the locals' image of the newcomers.
     The social network of agricultural workers will continue to
consist predominantly of other agricultural workers, though proximity to an urban area may increase the number of locals in the
network who have been attracted to higher-paid industrial employment in the town.   The relationships with farmers tends to change,
however.   Multiple role-occupancy by farmers tends to be reduced
as enthusiastic newcomers take over local associations and become
local councillors.   Farmers are also locals - farm workers often
feel they are understood more by farmers than by the newcomers, who
have little understanding of agriculture and of the nature of their
skills.   Farmers therefore take on the role of employers only -
and as such become more closely integrated with the workers into a
local, agricultural social network than hitherto.

3   The farm as a community

This is a result of urbanisation in a rural village where there is
no suitable housing for agricultural workers.   Agricultural workers
are the lowest-paid group covered by the DEP's six-monthly earnings
surveys, and they lack the resources to compete for house purchase
with middle-class newcomers.   The current (Summer 1972) minimum
wage in agriculture is £16.20 for a 42-hour week.   In September
1971 average earnings in agriculture were £20.46 for a 47.9-hour
week compared with average industrial earnings of £30.93 for 45.7
hours.   These figures include allowance for payments in kind.   In
villages where there are no council houses agricultural workers are
therefore forced to seek housing in tied cottages which are sited
predominantly on the surrounding farms.   Indeed, even council house
rents are onerous to farm workers in areas where the minimum wage
laid down by the Agricultural Wages Board is prevalent.   Many
agricultural workers cannot afford, therefore, to turn down the
chance of a tied cottage, and as their earnings have fallen further
behind average industrial earnings over the years (Newby, 1972a) so
an increasing proportion have moved into tied housing.
     On the farm the worker is both physically and socially isolated
from the remainder of the parish.   The average number of workers

per farm in Great Britain is 1.8 - therefore the average social network of the agricultural worker in such a community situation will
consist of three households: his own, his farmer's and the household of a fellow worker.   The degree of social interaction in this
community situation between farmer and worker is considerably
greater than in the other situations described above.   Role differentiation is lacking; the farmer is not only an employer but a
friend and neighbour.   Assuming an average size of farm, it is in
this kind of situation that an agricultural worker will describe the
relationships at work not so much as a 'team' but as a 'family'.
Indeed the division in his time between 'home' and 'work' will
virtually cease, particularly if he handles stock.   By constantly
'popping in and out' to tend to animals' needs, particularly when
they breed, his actual hours worked may bear little relation to his
contract hours, or to those for which he is paid.   On the other
hand, his employer, realising this, will frequently allow time off
during 'working hours' to suit the worker's requirements - this may
consist of anything from borrowing the farm Land Rover to go
shopping to having a complete day off to attend a local agricultural
show.   The worker's contact with the local village will be
perfunctory and often limited to occasional visits for shopping and
the use of other amenities.   Whilst elsewhere the increasing
home-centredness of affluent workers has been noted (Lockwood,
Chapter 2), here it seems that the relative impoverishment of farm
workers compared with other local inhabitants has resulted in an
increasing tendency to 'farm-centredness'.

THE WORK SITUATION OF AGRICULTURAL WORKERS

In general we may note that the work situation of the agricultural
worker is one that, compared with industrial workers, involves a
much greater degree of social interaction with his employer and,
because they work predominantly on their own, a much lesser degree
of interaction with fellow workers (Newby, 1972a, b).   Because the
diminution of the labour force is at present outpacing the amalgamation of farm holdings these trends have been exacerbated over the
years.   However, the structure of farming enterprises is polarising
and so average figures can be misleading.   The amalgamation of
holdings is creating extremely large farms, both in terms of acreage
and labour force.   These farms have a bureaucratic structure
similar to many factories and with increasing cases of separation of
ownership and control.   There is little or no contact between the
owner of the farm and the workers, and control of the labour force
is subject to a code of formal rules and regulations.   Day-to-day
supervision is in the hands of chargehands or foremen, who may
institute contact with workers through morning 'assemblies' or by
the use of personal two-way radios fitted to tractor cabs.   In the
other direction, however, farms that have not amalgamated have over
the years drastically reduced their labour force due to mechanisation, and may even have dispensed with hired labour altogether.
Here employer-employee relationships will be on a particularistic,
face-to-face, 'gaffer-to-man' basis.   Farmer and worker will see
each other several times a day, probably sharing break-times and

even working alongside each other on certain jobs that demand it.
As the labour force has declined farmer and worker have been brought
closer together and all the trappings of impersonal bureaucratic
administration will have been removed.   A number of studies have
demonstrated the 'size effect' on a worker's identification with the
goals of his firm (Gouldner, 1954; Ingham, 1970; Cleland, 1955).
We may therefore expect the work situation of the agricultural
worker to considerably influence the types of meaning-system which
he would otherwise derive from his local social situation.

Before outlining the various class images which are derived from
the inter-relationships of local social and work situations, it is
first necessary to point out two mitigating factors which may
distort the effects of these situations on certain issues concerning
social inequality that may confront agricultural workers.

THE PERSONAL RELATIONSHIP BETWEEN FARMER AND WORKER

The personal nature of the relationship between farmer and worker
can be maintained on all but the very biggest farms.   Because this
relationship is a personal one and because in many cases there is no
division between ownership and control, costs, and most importantly
labour costs, are seen by the worker to come directly from the
farmer's pocket.   But conversely the worker's contribution to the
profitability of the farm and his contribution to the maintenance of
his employer's life-style is also highly visible, particularly as
the farmer lives on the workplace and the worker therefore often
enters his home, something few factory workers can boast of.   The
contributions of an economic system which allows a disproportionate
distribution of rewards for similar amounts of work are therefore
often apparent: farm workers cycling in to work from their council
houses will pass their employer's pink-washed Georgian farmhouse
with the Jaguars parked on the gravel drive and the maid calling
the children in off the lawn.   These contradictions tend to result
in bitter conflict on certain occasions, notably tied cottage
evictions.   The bitterness generated by the abuses of the tied
cottage system is not wholly attributable to the system itself - a
similar system operates in other industries without generating the
same hostility - but because they flagrantly breach the normative
system built up by perhaps years of face-to-face relationships.
Thus, such a social organisation is likely to lead to greater
harmony between farmer and worker, but where it is flouted, the
resulting conflict is likely to be all the more bitter precisely
because the relationship is a personal one.   But on the whole
these contradictions are mitigated by the face-to-face interaction
of farmer and worker.   The result is often that, as Blythe points
out, 'This prosperity is more wondered at than resented by the
worker who, if he is middle-aged, might remark "When I went to work
along o' him afore the war, he hadn't got two ha'pennies to rub
together"' (Blythe, 1969, p.81). As long as the farmer conforms
to the worker's image of 'the good farmer' it seems that employer-
employee relationships will remain harmonious, however great the
disparities of income and life-style.   The set of expectations
which comprise 'the good farmer' appear to depend on two sets of

factors: whether he is a 'local' or a 'newcomer' and whether he is
a 'working farmer' or an 'office farmer' (see Figure 5.1).

	Local	Newcomer
Working	1	2
Office	3	4

FIGURE 5.1

1 'Local-working' farmers have life-styles almost indistinguish-
able from their workers.   They often speak in the same local
accents, and there are kin links between them.   There seems to be
a tendency for them to be tenants, rather than owner-occupiers,
though why this should be so is not altogether clear.   A 'good'
farmer here is one who works as hard if not harder than the worker
himself, who leads by example and is capable of showing the worker
how to do any job on the farm.
2 'Newcomer-working' farmers tend to be owner-occupiers who have
entered farming for the non-economic rewards of the job.   They
include a number of retired army officers, stockbrokers and merchant
bankers often attracted by the farmhouse rather than the land.
Their life-styles are upper-middle-class and cosmopolitan.   The
'good' farmer here is one who pays a little 'over the odds' but who
has no 'side' - who will not 'talk down' to his workers and who is
prepared to 'muck in'.
3 The 'local-office' farmer frequently takes on the persona of the
'squire'.   His power may have declined, but his status remains.
The 'good' farmer here is one who is not economically instrumental,
who shows a paternalistic concern for the wider personal affairs of
his labour force and the area as a whole.   He is one who provides
his workers with frequent individual acts of concern - small gifts
on birthdays or at Christmas, periodic gifts of farm produce and
who provides 'treats' like harvest suppers, days out at a show, etc.
4 'Newcomer-entrepreneurs' are economically instrumental and make
no pretence of paternalism - indeed they are frequently very
scathing about those in cell 3.   Their relationship with their
workers is purely a contractual one.   The 'good' farmer here is one
who pays good wages, who leaves his workers to get on with the job
on their own without interference (in direct contradiction to cell
2 where an admired quality is the ability to be always there) and
who is technically a competent farmer using bigger and better
machinery and advanced methods of husbandry.
    In each case the greater the conformity of the employer to the
appropriate image of the 'good farmer', the greater is the possibility of the contradictions of the situation being contained and
conflict avoided.   This may inspire sufficient personal loyalty on
the part of agricultural workers to inhibit across-the-board praise
or condemnation of 'bosses' or 'farmers' as an undifferentiated
group - particularism overrides universalism.

THE 'INDUSTRIAL'/AGRICULTURAL DIVISION

The second mitigating factor to be taken into account is the degree
to which lateral identities of interest are possible with other
groups of workers.   Here we may draw out the conflicts that can
arise between agricultural workers and factory workers.   'The shadow
of an immense urban majority falls across the interests of agricultural workers as well as those of farmers and landowners' (Self and
Storing, 1962, p.176).   Factory workers demand a cheap food policy,
but as far as agricultural workers are concerned this entails the
depressions of their wage-levels.   Agricultural workers cannot raise
their earnings by strike action (Newby, 1972a), but factory workers,
already perceived as earning astronomically high wages, are
constantly going to strike to obtain more and put up the price of
manufactured goods to boot.   Farm workers often feel, therefore,
that they have more in common with farmers than with workers in
industry.   Cutting across any hierarchial image of society there is
always this awareness of inter-industrial differences which modify
any identification of interest.

THE SOURCES OF SOCIAL IMAGERY

Bearing in mind these mitigating factors, the agricultural worker's
image of society can be explained by referring to the nature of his
local social situation and his work situation (see Figure 5.2).

		WORK SITUATION	
		Non-bureaucratic	Bureaucratic
	Farm	1	2
LOCAL SOCIAL SITUATION	Encapsulated community	3	4
	Occupational community	5	6

FIGURE 5.2

In only two cells do the two structural situations reinforce the
agricultural workers' images of society.   In cell 1 there is a
tendency for deferential images to prevail, in the sense in which
the term is defined above.   In cell 6 agricultural workers tend to
hold 'radical' meaning-systems (Parkin, 1971).   In cells 2, 3, 4
and 5 there may be a certain amount of what Parkin would call
'accommodation' (Parkin, 1971, pp.97-102), though we would prefer to
use the term 'ambivalence'.   Our own research has shown that
workers in these situations hold a multiplicity of class images or
meaning-systems from which they will draw upon the one most appropriate to explain a particular situation with which they are confronted.   (Illustrative material can be found in Bell and Newby,
1973).

The ambivalence of class imagery is probably not confined to agricultural workers. We would wish to know how far this ambivalence is characteristic of other working class groups. Recent research (e.g. Goldthorpe et al., 1969) has always been sufficiently flexible to cast any light on the extent to which ambivalent class images are held, although a greater awareness of pragmatism as an aspect of working class consciousness is occasionally apparent (Converse, 1964; Mann, 1970). It seems likely that here, as elsewhere (Lane and Roberts, 1971), situational factors do not produce unexpected and apparently unforeseen aspects of behaviour by generating attitudes which hold for all workers in all situations, but rather create conditions in which certain interpretations of the situation become more influential and on the basis of which individual workers will act accordingly. We feel that in this context an approach similar to ours is relevant, not just for agricultural workers in rural areas but for other groups within the working class.

NOTE

1 A fuller version of this paper has appeared in the 'Sociological Review',vol.21, no.2, May 1973, pp.229-53. This condensed version is reproduced here by permission. The argument contained in the paper has not been changed. What has been omitted from the paper originally given at the conference are some introductory remarks on the nature of 'community' and on meaning systems; and some preliminary illustrative material on social images held by agricultural workers as well as some additional references and asides in footnotes. In April 1973 the SSRC awarded the authors a research grant for a study entitled 'Capitalist Farmers in the Class Structure' (HR.2364).

Chapter 6

THE DEFERENTIAL WORKER?

Roderick Martin and R.H. Fryer

As David Lockwood commented in the paper which provides the motif for this conference, discussion of the class imagery of the traditional deferential British worker is largely speculative. When he wrote his paper, in 1965, the only empirical evidence available on the deferential worker comprised a section of a community study and some preliminary findings from a survey of political attitudes (Stacey, 1960; McKenzie and Silver, 1964). Little has changed since 1965, and little has been published about deferential traditionalists, although there has been significant empirical research into the relatively sympathetic 'proletarian traditionalists', and papers have appeared on dockers, ship-builders, navvies, and printers (Hill, 1972; Brown and Brannen, 1970; Sykes, 1969; Cannon, 1967). The purpose of this paper is to present some evidence on the relevant social attitudes of a sample of manual and non-manual workers, gathered during a case study of redundancy, and to speculate about the significance of the evidence for Lockwood's original characterisation of the deferential traditionalist (see Martin and Fryer, 1973, for an account of the research of which the present paper is a by-product: the research was carried out in a community we have called Casterton, and respondents were workers who had been employed at Casterton Mills). Lockwood's original characterisation of the deferential world view is substantially vindicated; the hypotheses about the structural determinants of deference are not.

DIMENSIONS OF DEFERENCE

By deference we mean commitment by lower social groups to a moral order which legitimates their own subordination. This commitment is symbolised by the acceptance of a distinctive world view, and by appropriate behaviour. (Although we do not discuss behaviour in the present paper we do not agree with Bell and Newby that behaviour is irrelevant. Ritual behaviour, far from being 'emptied of all meaning', symbolises the actor's normative commitment). Legitimation may be based upon fear of the consequences of rejecting the moral order, calculation of the rewards to be derived from acceptance, belief in the inherent virtue of acceptance, or, most probably, a combination of all three.   But it is the acceptance of a specific world view, not the reasons for its acceptance, which constitutes the defining characteristic of deference.   In this we disagree with Bell and Newby, who appear to believe that commitment based upon fear of the consequences of the rejection of such commitment should be excluded from consideration.   But the reasons for commitment can only be established after research;   and the distinction between commitment through fear and commitment as an end in itself is difficult to draw.   Research which begins with the distinction between voluntary and enforced commitment is likely to be in difficulties before it is off the ground.

As a measure of deference we constructed a crude index, based upon six questions tapping some of the major issues mentioned by Lockwood.   The questions used covered attitudes towards the class structure, towards authority within the industrial enterprise, and towards trade unions.   The six questions are given here, followed by an explanation of how the index was constructed.

Question One   '(i)   In Britain today there are basically two main classes, bosses and workers.

(ii)   Most people in Britain today belong to the same class.

(iii)   There are several classes in Britain.

Which statement comes closest to your opinion?

Please say if none of the alternatives comes close to your opinion.'

Deferential workers were expected to agree with (iii), representing a belief in an 'hierarchical', 'at least trichotomous', image of the class structure (Lockwood, Chapter 2).

Question Two   '(i)   Working-class people have got to stick together and stand up for each other.

(ii)   Working-class people should strike out on their own.   It's no good being held back by the rest.

Which statement comes closest to your opinion?

Please say if none of the alternatives comes close to your opinion.'

Deferential workers were expected to agree with (ii), indicating a preference for individualism and reluctance to form 'strong attachments to workers in a similar market situation' (Lockwood, Chapter 2).

Question Three   'Do you think it is a good idea to have a system like that, I mean with hourly paid and monthly staff?'   (Asked after a discussion of the difference between hourly paid and monthly staff at the plant.)

Replies were interpreted as indicating attitudes towards the differential distribution of rewards in society, as experienced directly in the employment situation: deferential workers regard differential rewards, and consequently their own low status, as 'less an injustice than as a necessary, accepted, and even desirable part in a natural system of inequality' (Lockwood, Chapter 2).

Question Four   'Some people are born to be bosses, ordinary people cannot hope to become bosses.   Do you agree or disagree?'

Deferentials were expected to agree, showing a belief in 'the

intrinsic qualities of an ascriptive elite' (Lockwood, Chapter 2).
Question Five   'Obedience and respect for authority are the
                     most important characteristics of the good
                     worker.   Do you agree or disagree?'
Deferentials were expected to agree, indicating '(exposure) to
paternalistic forms of industrial authority' (Lockwood, Chapter 2).
Question Six   'Trade unions, shop stewards, and other workers'
                     representatives only introduce trouble into the
                     co-operation between management and workers.
                     Do you agree or disagree?'
Deferentials were expected to agree, indicating a belief in (or
preference for?) personal relationships between employers and
workers, without the intervention of intermediaries or collectivities: 'the essence of the work situation is that the relationship
between employer and worker is personal' (Lockwood, Chapter 2).
    The index of deference did not discriminate sharply between the
deferentials and the non-deferential: the relevant total scores
were distributed normally (see Table 6.1).

TABLE 6.1

	0	1	2	3	4	5	6	Total
N	2	21	50	77	38	17	3	207
%	1.0	10.1	24.2	37.2	18.4	8.2	1.0	100.1

Respondents were divided into three groups for further analysis:
the non-deferential, 35.3 per cent, with scores 0, 1 and 2; the
ambivalent, 37.2 per cent, with a score of 3; and the deferential,
27.6 per cent, with scores of 4, 5 or 6.   The results of this
preliminary analysis are shown in Tables 6.2 to 6.7, which relate to
Questions 1 - 6 in the text (Table 6.2 to Question One, etc.).   As
the six tables show, there were consistent correlations between
scores on the overall index and responses to the individual questions
which composed the index.

TABLE 6.2   Deference and beliefs re class structure

	Non-deferential %	Ambivalent %	Deferential %	All %
Two classes	28.6	18.2	8.8	19.1
All same class	21.4	6.5	3.5	10.8
Several classes	48.6	75.3	87.7	69.6
Other	1.4	-	-	0.5
Total	100.0	100.0	100.0	100.0
N	70	77	57	204

TABLE 6.3   Deference and solidarity

	Non-deferential %	Ambivalent %	Deferential %	All %
Stick together	39.7	33.8	12.3	30.0
Strike out on own	42.5	57.1	84.2	59.4
Other	17.8	9.1	3.5	10.6
Total	100.0	100.0	100.0	100.0
N	73	77	57	207

TABLE 6.4   Deference and equity of distinction between hourly paid and monthly paid staff

	Non-deferential %	Ambivalent %	Deferential %	All %
(a) Fair	9.6	26.0	61.4	30.0
(b) Unfair	38.4	29.9	17.5	29.5
(c) Never considered it	24.7	20.8	5.3	17.9
(d) Other	27.4	23.4	15.8	22.7
Total	100.1	100.1	100.0	100.1
N	73	77	57	207

TABLE 6.5   Deference and ascriptive elite

	Non-deferential %	Ambivalent %	Deferential %	All %
Agree	19.2	53.2	73.7	46.9
Disagree	72.6	45.5	22.8	48.8
Other	8.2	1.3	3.5	4.3
Total	100.0	100.0	100.0	100.0
N	73	77	57	207

TABLE 6.6   Deference and belief in obedience

	Non-deferential %	Ambivalent %	Deferential %	All %
Agree	35.2	70.1	78.9	60.4
Disagree	49.3	23.4	17.5	30.9
Other	15.1	6.5	3.5	8.7
Total	99.6	100.0	99.9	100.0
N	73	77	57	207

TABLE 6.7   Deference and attitudes towards trade unions

	Non-deferential %	Ambivalent %	Deferential %	All %
Agree	12.3	18.2	50.9	25.1
Disagree	80.8	70.1	43.9	66.7
Other	6.8	11.7	5.3	8.2
Total	99.9	100.0	100.1	100.0
N	73	77	57	207

CORRELATES OF DEFERENCE

The deferential, the ambivalent, and the non-deferential each
possessed distinctive sets of attitudes towards social mobility,
work, commitment to the firm, management and trade unionism.   The
deferential minority overwhelmingly believed in hierarchy, individualism, commitment to the firm, and acceptance of managerial
authority.   Their view of the class structure was largely shared
by the ambivalent, who also saw the class system as a pyramid of
individuals.   But the ambivalent were less willing than the deferentials to endorse the hierarchy within the plant.   The non-deferentials shared the individualism of the other two groups, but showed
less accommodating attitudes towards authority.   We examine these
correlates of deference in detail below.

   There is an ambiguity in conventional analyses of deference over
the significance of social mobility.   On the one hand, references
to an 'ascriptive elite', and to the reluctance of the deferential
worker to strive to equal his superiors, may indicate that deferential workers reject the legitimacy of striving for social mobility,
regarding it as a presumptuous incursion upon established superiors
(Lockwood, Chapter 2).   On the other hand, the ideology of the
elite stresses the open-ness of society, and the possibility of
social mobility for workers with the necessary ability and energy.

Moreover, the repudiation of collective attempts at betterment may
be expected to result in individual efforts.   The majority of
workers interviewed believed in the possibility of social mobility;
but deferential workers were more likely than others to do so
(Table 6.8)

TABLE 6.8   Deference and belief in open society*

	Non-deferential %	Ambivalent %	Deferential %	All %
Society open	52.1	51.9	66.7	56.0
Opportunities closed	43.8	42.9	31.2	40.1
Other	4.1	5.2	1.8	3.9
Total	100.0	100.0	99.7	100.0
N	73	77	57	207

* The question asked was: 'Anybody can get to the top if they have
   got ability and are prepared to work hard.   Do you agree or
   disagree?'

It is especially surprising that deferential workers should believe
that the route to the top is open to those with ability and a
willingness to work hard for the deferential tended to be older than
other groups and were unlikely to make any further occupational
progress (if, indeed, they had ever made any occupational progress
at all).

The significance of the association between deference and the
belief in the openness of society may be ambiguous.   But three
further questions concerned with attitudes towards work, loyalty,
and obedience, indicated unequivocal support for Lockwood's
characterisation.   The majority of all workers interviewed gave
'deferential' replies, but the deferential workers were more likely
than others to do so.   An overall majority of respondents believed
in the desirability of a job (even if it was not financially
necessary), in loyalty, and in the need to accept managerial authority;   but the deferential were more committed, more loyal and more
conforming than the non-deferential - as Tables 6.9, 6.10 and 6.11
show.

Casterton Mills workers thus showed many of the attitudes
characteristic of the deferential worker.   However, when attention
is focused more closely upon relations between employer and employee
the symmetry of the pattern disintegrates: there was widespread
consciousness of conflict, amongst the deferential as well as the
non-deferential.   Hence the majority of workers, including a
majority of deferential workers, believed that management was only
concerned with profits, not with the general good of the firm, or
with the national interest (Table 6.12).

TABLE 6.9   Deference and work*

	Non-deferential %	Ambivalent %	Deferential %	All %
Agree	27.4	29.9	22.8	27.1
Disagree	64.4	67.5	75.4	68.6
Other	8.2	2.6	1.8	4.3
Total	100.0	100.0	100.0	100.0
N	73	77	57	207

* The question asked was: 'If you have enough money without working there is no reason for having a job.   Do you agree or disagree?'

TABLE 6.10   Deference and loyalty*

	Non-deferential %	Ambivalent %	Deferential %	All %
Agree	46.6	55.8	57.9	53.1
Disagree	21.9	9.1	5.3	12.6
Other/Missing	31.5	35.1	36.8	34.3
Total	100.0	100.0	100.0	100.0
N	73	77	57	207

* The question asked was: 'The good employee is loyal to his firm even if it means putting himself out.   Do you agree or disagree?'

TABLE 6.11   Deference and managerial authority*

	Non-deferential %	Ambivalent %	Deferential %	All %
Agree	46.6	54.5	57.9	52.7
Disagree	26.0	14.3	8.8	16.9
Other/Missing	27.4	31.2	33.3	30.4
Total	100.0	100.0	100.0	100.0
N	73	77	57	207

* The question asked was: 'Managers are there to give orders and workers who are under them should obey.   Do you agree or disagree?'

TABLE 6.12   Deference and perception of management concerns*

	Non-deferential %	Ambivalent %	Deferential %	All %
Management interested in:				
(a) Profits only	64.8	63.0	56.4	61.9
(b) Firm and workers	13.0	16.7	15.4	15.0
(c) Firm and national interest	-	9.3	12.8	6.8
(d) Other	22.2	11.1	15.4	16.3
Total	100.0	100.1	100.0	100.0
N	54	54	39	147**

*   '(a) Management are only interested in profits.
     (b) Management are interested in the good of the firm and all
         workers.
     (c) Management are interested in the good of the firm and the
         country.
     Which statement comes closest to your opinion? Please say if
     none of the statements come close to your opinion.'
** A number of respondents were given a short questionnaire, which
     excluded this and the following question, because they were un-
     able to spare the time (because of shifts and other obligations)
     to answer the full questionnaire.

When workers were asked directly whether they thought that the
interests of management and workers were the same or opposed 48.7
per cent of all workers thought that they were opposed, including
47.4 per cent of the deferential (Table 6.13).   The deferential
were, however, more likely than the non-deferential or the ambivalent to regard the interests of management and workers as the same:
50.0 per cent compared with 39.3 per cent and 34.5 per cent
respectively.

Nearly half of the deferential workers at Casterton Mills
regarded the interests of management and workers as opposed, and
over half viewed management as solely concerned with profits.
Attitudes towards trade unionism were also different from those
expected of the classically deferential worker.   A slight majority
of all workers were members of trade unions at the Mills (51.7 per
cent):   43.8 per cent of the non-deferential, 61.0 per cent of the
ambivalent, and 49.1 per cent of the deferential.   But such membership was a function of job requirements, rather than social attitude;
craftsmen were union members, whilst process workers were usually
not.   As Table 6.14 shows, there was no association between deference and a negative attitude towards trade union membership.

TABLE 6.13   Deference and perception of management/worker interests*

	Non-deferential %	Ambivalent %	Deferential %	All %
Opposed	51.8	46.6	47.4	48.7
Same	39.3	34.5	50.0	40.1
Mixed/depends	8.9	19.0	2.6	11.2
Total	100.0	100.1	100.0	100.0
N	56	58	38	152

* 'Some people say that the interests of management and workers are opposed, others that they are one and the same.   What do you think?'

TABLE 6.14   Deference and trade union membership*

	Non-deferential %	Ambivalent %	Deferential %	All %
Solidarity	27.4	32.9	26.3	29.1
Wages and conditions	43.8	40.8	49.1	44.2
No need to join	12.3	10.5	12.3	11.7
Other	16.4	15.8	12.3	15.0
Total	99.9	100.0	100.0	100.0
N	73	76	57	206

* '(a) Every worker should join a trade union because workers should stick together.
  (b) It doesn't really matter whether you join a trade union or not.
  (c) There is only one reason for joining a trade union and that is to improve wages and conditions.
  Please choose the statement which comes closest to your opinion. Please say if none of the statements come close to your opinion.'

Only 11.7 per cent of all respondents believed that it did not matter whether one joined a trade union or not, including 12.3 per cent of the deferential.   The only difference between the deferential and the others was a slight tendency for the deferential to give instrumental rather than solidaristic explanations for union membership: 49.1 per cent instrumental, compared with 43.8 per cent for non-deferential and 40.8 per cent for the ambivalent.

The majority of Casterton Mills workers believed that union membership mattered, and were also prepared to countenance strike action.   As Table 6.15 shows, only a minority believed that you should never go on strike.

TABLE 6.15   Deference and justification for strikes*

	Non-deferential %	Ambivalent %	Deferential %	All %
Wages and conditions	22.4	12.0	27.3	19.8
Number of reasons (incl.solidarity)	53.7	54.7	38.2	49.7
Should never strike	14.9	28.0	29.1	23.9
Other	9.0	5.3	5.1	6.6
Total	100.0	100.0	99.7	100.0
N	67	75	55	197

* '(a) The main reasons for going on strike are to get more money or better conditions.
   (b) You should never go on strike.
   (c) There are several reasons for going on strike: for instance in support of other unions and members, to get more money, to get 100 per cent membership, to protect your job, to get a grievance settled quickly.
   Please choose the statement which comes closest to your opinion.
   Please say if none of the statements come close to your opinion.'

Although there was an overall readiness to contemplate strike action, the deferential, the ambivalent, and the non-deferential groups revealed different patterns of responses on strikes.   A significant minority of the deferential (29.1 per cent) were against all strikes, and of those who were willing to support strikes the majority emphasised narrowly instrumental justifications.   Nearly as many of the ambivalent as of the deferential said that one should never strike, but they were more ready to support strikes for a variety of reasons than any other group.   Very few of the non-deferential were against all strikes, but they were more narrowly instrumental than the ambivalent in their justification for strike action.   In short, the majority of deferential workers were not against strikes: but only a minority were willing to countenance strike action when their immediate economic interests were not directly involved.
     In summary, it is possible to characterise three groups of workers at Casterton Mills: the deferential, the ambivalent, and the non-deferential.   The deferential minority overwhelmingly tended to believe in hierarchy, individualism, commitment to the firm, and acceptance of managerial authority.   However, this minority did not correspond completely to Lockwood's hypothesised deferential traditionalist, for most of them also believed that management was concerned only with making profits, almost half believed that the interests of management and workers were opposed, and a majority supported trade unionism and even strike action.   The

difference between the Casterton Mills deferentials and those
depicted by Lockwood lay in attitudes towards industrial relations
and trade unionism, subjects relatively neglected by Lockwood in the
section of his paper dealing with the deferential traditionalist,
and of course areas in which recent experience of redundancy may be
expected to have affected attitudes.

The second group, the ambivalent, were equally balanced between
deference and non-deference: their general attitudes towards the
class structure tended towards the deferential, whilst their attitudes towards management and employer/employee relations tended
towards the non-deferential.   Hence a large majority believed that
there were more than two social classes in contemporary Britain, and
that obedience to authority was a primary requirement in a good
worker;   a narrow majority believed that bosses were born, and a
similar number that workers should strike out on their own.   But
very few of the ambivalent accepted the justice of the marked
distinction between 'works' and 'staff' which had existed at the
Mills, or believed that trade unions caused trouble.

The non-deferential tended to reject the view that bosses were
born and not made, and nearly all believed that union membership was
necessary.   But the non-deferential were not proletarian traditionalists (and we have carefully avoided using the term 'proletarian
traditionalist' throughout the paper).   Only a minority believed
that workers should stick together, and only a minority believed
that there were only two social classes in Britain: there was no
tendency for those who believed that workers should stick together
to also believe in a dichotomous model of the class structure.
Although only a small minority believed that the distinction between
the hourly paid and the monthly staff was justified (9.6 per cent)
only 38.4 per cent regarded it as positively unfair: the remainder
either answered the question in terms of administrative convenience -
monthly payment would cause problems for family budgeting - or had
not thought about the subject.   It is not surprising that the non-
deferentials, with their rejection of authority and individualism,
tended to be young.

There is thus evident confirmation, in general terms, for
Lockwood's view that specific attitudes towards the class structure,
towards individual opportunities, and towards managerial authority
correlate with each other, and form distinctive patterns, which can
with only slight exaggeration be called images of society.   More
specifically, workers who were exposed to a paternalistic form of
industrial authority at Casterton Mills were likely to believe that
such authority was 'natural', to conceive of the class structure as
multi-layered, and to believe that individuals with the necessary
ability could 'get ahead'.   This pattern of beliefs could legitim-
ately be described as deferential.

However, it is easy to exaggerate the coherence of such sets of
attitudes, especially by using the term 'image'.   Only two respondents gave six deferential responses; the most common pattern of
responses was one composed equally of deferential and non-deferential
replies: 37.2 per cent of all respondents, including 44 per cent of
manual workers, gave ambivalent responses.   Moreover, even amongst
relatively deferential workers the modal world view did not correspond completely with that expected: the majority of the deferential

believed that management was concerned only with profits, and nearly
half thought that the interests of management and workers were
opposed.   There was considerably more support for trade unions than
might have been expected, in view of the traditional deferential
acceptance of managerial authority, and management's historical
opposition to trade unions.   In short, the deferential showed some
attitudes which have been regarded as characteristic of proletarian
traditionalists.   Similarly, the relatively non-deferential at
Casterton shared some beliefs with the deferential, especially the
conception of the class structure as a multi-layered hierarchy, with
opportunities for individuals to move up the scale.

One implication of the mixed character of these views is that
some items in the original characterisation of the deferential worker
are not distinctive.   Hence not all who viewed the class structure
as a multi-layered hierarchy were deferential, although the deferential were likely to view the class structure as a hierarchy.   A
further implication is that there is a discrepancy between generalised perceptions of the social order (or, more precisely, responses
to questions concerning that order) and experience of that order in
everyday life.   Hence, the difference between the deferential and
the non-deferential was revealed less sharply in the question on
conceptions of the class structure in general than in the question
relating directly to experience of the unequal distribution of
rewards at work, that on the justice or otherwise of the distinctions between the hourly paid and the monthly paid staff.   Replies
to questions on social imagery which are framed in general terms may
reflect imperfectly assimilated ideology rather than the translation
of immediate experience into symbolic form: hence the contrast
between the apparently 'unitary' conception of hierarchy and the
immediate consciousness of conflict.

The 'mixed' character of the attitudes of the Casterton Mills
workers indicates that the social imagery of the deferential worker
is more complex than originally suggested: belief in the value of
loyalty, in the legitimacy of managerial authority, and in the open-
ness of society, can coexist with a consciousness of sharp conflict
between the interests of management and workers.   This pattern may
be common to all deferential workers;   as Blackburn and Mann stress,
there is little reason to expect workers to possess a consistent
image of society when their experience of society is so varied (see
below, Chapter 8).   However, the heightened consciousness of conflict
may simply be the result of the redundancy;   the redundancy may have
fragmented the attitudes of a previously deferential labour force,
leading to questioning of the unitary conception of the firm
fostered by paternalist capitalism.   Hence workers gave deferential
replies to questions on attitudes which were unlikely to be directly
affected by the redundancy, for example on the importance of individual initiative, but more 'proletarian' replies to the questions
directly concerned with management/worker relations.   In short, two
vocabularies coexisted alongside each other.   The first, based upon
long experience of a paternalist management, was expressed in deferential terms;   the second, based upon recent experience of economic
change and rationalisation, expressed in 'proletarian' terms.
Since our evidence derives from a case study, and there is no comparative data available, we cannot choose between the view that all

deferential workers possess 'inconsistent' attitudes, or only deferential workers experiencing rapid economic change.

DETERMINANTS OF DEFERENCE

One of the major merits of Lockwood's paper was the critique of a
simple association between occupational status and specific images
of society, and the emphasis upon the need for a more finely textured
analysis of social milieux. The need for this critique of an automatic linking of occupational status and imagery was confirmed by
our own investigation: there was no simple association between
occupational status and deferential attitudes (Table 6.16).

TABLE 6.16 Deference and occupational status

	Manual %	Non-manual %	All %
Non-deferential	33.6	37.4	35.3
Ambivalent	44.0	28.6	37.2
Deferential	22.4	34.1	27.3
Total	100.0	100.1	99.8
N	116	91	207

The most striking contrast is between the ambivalence of the manual
workers and the relative clarity of the responses of non-manual
workers: non-manual workers were more likely than manual workers
to be deferential or non-deferential - they were less likely to be
ambivalent. This comparative lack of ambivalence amongst non-
manual workers may indicate that they possessed more coherent value-
systems than manual workers - or simply greater facility in recognising the drift of related questions sprinkled throughout a long
questionnaire - or that the non-manual group contained a more heterogeneous collection of occupations than the manual, and therefore a
more dispersed distribution of occupationally derived attitudes.
It was impossible to decide between these two explanations on the
evidence available. But the major conclusion to be drawn from
the comparison between non-manual and manual groups is that deferential workers are found in both: the difference in proportions
could be a substantively insignificant artefact of the point at
which the distinction was made between the deferential and the
ambivalent. The relative similarity in proportions may have been
due to the inclusion of a substantial number of former manual workers
in the non-manual category (but not to the inclusion of any former
non-manual workers in the manual category): a small minority of
supervisory non-manual workers had worked on the shopfloor, and some
still worked amongst manual workers. Unfortunately, there were too
few non-manual respondents, distributed over too wide a range of
occupations, to assess the significance of social origins and occupational differences within the non-manual group. Moreover, it is

not clear how one would expect social origins and deference to be
related.   For example, would supervisory staff who had risen from
the ranks be less deferential, because of their origins?   Or more
deferential because of the need to conform to the norms of the
destination group?   Lockwood suggests tentatively that administrative, managerial, technical and professional personnel are likely
to show many of the same attitudes as deferential workers, whilst
clerical workers are 'in many respects similar to the privatized
worker' (Chapter 2).   There was no confirmation for this view
amongst Casterton workers: supervisory personnel were not deferential, and clerical workers non-deferential - rather the reverse.
But the numbers involved are too small for us to do more than
suggest that we know very little about the social imagery of non-
manual workers, and further research is obviously necessary.

TABLE 6.17 Age and deference

	-34 %	35-49 %	50+ %	All %
Non-deferential	45.5	39.0	24.4	35.3
Ambivalent	30.3	44.1	37.8	37.2
Deferential	24.2	16.9	37.8	27.5
Total	100.0	100.0	100.0	100.o
N	66	59	82	207

The link between age and deference was closer than that between
occupational status and deference.   Deferential imagery was commoner
amongst older than amongst younger workers, as Table 6.17 shows.
Hence, whilst only 24.2 per cent of workers aged under 35 were deferential, 37.8 per cent of the over 50 were.   The contrast between
the young and the old is stronger if expressed negatively: young
workers were only infrequently deferential, whilst old workers were
only infrequently non-deferential.   However, the relationship
between age and deference is not a clear one, for only 16.9 per cent
of middle-aged workers (35-49) gave deferential responses.   This
may have been due to the impact of the redundancy upon workers at
the most vulnerable stage of the life-cycle.   Younger workers were
not seriously worried by the redundancy, whilst workers aged 50 or
more did not have young families, had lower financial commitments,
and received more redundancy pay than the middle-aged.   Experience
of the redundancy may thus have transformed middle-aged deferentials
into ambivalents.
   Deference is associated with age, but not explained by it, for
there is a small minority of deferentials amongst the young.   Moreover, deferential attitudes may be related to age because of location in a specific social situation, and the reinforcement of
structurally derived attitudes by long socialisation, because of
specific generational historical experiences, or because of attitudinal adjustment to typical life-cycle problems.   McKenzie and
Silver comment: 'it must be kept in mind that we do not know how or

when the older deferentials acquired their "deference" ... most -
perhaps all - may have acquired a cluster of deferential opinions
early in life, perhaps through parental or other early environmental influences' (McKenzie and Silver, 1968, p.184).   But this
suggestion is inadequate.   Parental influence may explain why
specific individuals are deferential, but not the link between age
and deference.   Explaining the link between age and deference
involves explaining the structural sources of deference, and we
must now turn to this wider question.

Two aspects of the social situation of the deferential worker
have been seen as decisive: the work situation, especially the
relation between employer and employee, and the character of the
community status system.

Lockwood sees the major source of deference in the nature of the
relationship between employer and employee: deference is likely
where work relations are 'personal and particularistic', and where
'the worker has a unique position in a functional job hierarchy and
where he is tied to his employer by a "special relationship" between
them and not only by considerations of economic gain' (Chapter 2).
These relationships are regarded as more common in small than in
large firms.

There is some evidence that interaction between management and
workers fosters affective ties, but also some evidence that it does
not (Ingham, 1970, Chapter 2; Wedderburn and Crompton, 1972, p.42).
Nordlinger, for example, argued that his data 'intimates that the
closer the workers' relations with the boss, the less likely they
are to attribute desirable qualities to their employers' (Nordlinger,
1967, p.194).   There is no evidence that interaction fosters deference. (Ingham comments:

In the questions on worker-owner interaction very few responses
(12 per cent) revealed the presence of a deferential attitude on
the part of the workers - but the following statements show that
this type of attitude is, in fact, present.   'Yes, it's a good
thing that we see the directors regularly, but they are not
treated with proper respect by everyone - there's too much
familiarity.'   'He's a real gentleman: but we use first names
you know.' (Ingham, 1970, p.105)

The reasons for rejecting the negative implications of the questionnaire responses remain unclear.)   Moreover, there is an obvious
difference between interaction necessitated by the work task and
sociability.   Nor is the evidence linking size of firm and deference convincing.   Large firms, like Pilkingtons and Cadburys, can
foster deference by adopting an appropriate corporate ideology and
managerial role definitions (Lane and Roberts, 1971).

The amount of personal contact between employer and employee, and
size of firm, are less important than actors' expectations and the
extent to which management fulfils them.   The extent to which
interaction fosters deference is likely to depend upon actors'
expectations, and the context of the interaction.   Deference is
fostered by behaviour regarded as appropriate, not by familiarity:
the gentry are expected to behave as gentry, not like the people
next door.   Hence the respect for the Casterton family, the foremost family in the area and the previous owners of the Mills, shown
by the workers in Casterton was based upon the fulfilment of a

traditional paternalist role, not frequent contact.   Casterton
Mills, Pilkingtons, and other large firms with paternalist
management styles may recruit workers pre-disposed towards accept-
int a deferential view of the world, who find further confirmation
for their interpretation of the situation in their work experience.

The first 'environmental' influence likely to affect the deference of the deferential worker is his experience of the actions and
attitudes of others, especially 'superiors', in the work situation.
Community factors were seen by Lockwood as reinforcing the effects
of the work situation: 'In the making of the deferential traditionalist certain features of community life will also play an important
part in fixing and sharpening the sense of hierarchy that he acquires
in his role as worker' (Chapter 2).   Communities with a differentiated occupational structure and an interactional status system
were seen as fostering deference.   Unfortunately we were unable to
investigate the extent to which Casterton possessed an 'interactional status system' - and indeed doubt the viability of large-
scale assessment of such a system - and in the absence of such an
investigation it is unfortunately necessary to argue a priori.   But
it is difficult to see why the simple existence of differentiation
should automatically produce deference, a specific attitude towards
that differentiation.   To assume that it does is to accept a very
mechanical view of the relationship between social structures and
attitudes.   The major feature of an interactional status system
is that individuals within it can place others on the basis of 'a
detailed knowledge of each other's personal qualities', and
'relatively complex criteria', which lead to 'widespread consensus
about the rank order of status groups in the community' (Chapter
2).   In small stable communities consensus is likely.   However,
the existence of multiple criteria in itself is more likely to
produce confusion than consensus;   consensus is easier where
knowledge is superficial and criteria are made, perhaps unrealistic-
ally, simple.   Moreover, it is easy to see why such communities
should be traditional, for social behaviour is highly visible,
opportunities for deviant behaviour limited, and sanctions against
deviance strong: but it is not obvious why they should be
deferential.

In short, the postulated mechanisms linking work and community
social structures with deferential imagery are too simple and
consequently unconvincing, based upon a mechanical conception of
the relationship between social structure and imagery.

Experience of the social structure is mediated through the
individual's attitudes and expectations, based upon his own historical experience.   Explanations of deference in a-historical
structural terms, whether the structure of the work-place or of
the community, are inadequate.   Images of society are not only a
product of present milieux, but of present milieux interpreted in
the light of past experience and expectations for the future,
individual and collective.   As Elizabeth Bott commented, '... when
an individual talks about class he is trying to say something, in a
symbolic form, about his experiences of power and prestige in his
actual membership groups and social relationships, both past and
present' (Bott, 1957, p.163).   Images of society are the product
of individual experience in specific historical circumstances, too

complex to be encapsulated in anti-historical sociological
constructs.

   (The original paper by Lockwood is confusing on the precise
status of the concept of the deferential traditionalist:
   'The traditional worker is, of course, a sociological rather
   than an historical concept; a concept relating to workers who
   are located in particular kinds of work situations and community
   structures rather than one purporting to give a description of
   the working class as a whole at some particular point in time'
   (Chapter 2).
This contrast between sociological and historical is problematic.
Does it mean that the deferential worker does not exist in 'pure'
form?   If the type does exist, in what sense is the concept not
'historical'?   Lockwood's subsequent discussion indicates that
deferential workers are regarded as existing 'at some point in time'
and therefore presumably as having an historical existence.)
   Social imagery is thus moulded by past events, individual and
collective, present experiences, and expectations of the future.
This complex interaction was responsible for the deferential imagery,
and the deviations from that imagery, of the workers whom we interviewed.   The paternalist values of a pre-industrial era were
preserved by dominant groups within the community, and their interpretation of the situation was endorsed, partly because 'it had
always been', partly because of a lack of alternatives (due to
geographical isolation and the ability of dominant groups to exclude
alternative interpretations), and partly because of economic
dependence.   This view of the world was reinforced by experience
at work, where management tempered autocracy with indulgence.
Older workers had experienced economic dependence in its most acute
form, during the inter-war years, and had, of course, been exposed
to the values of the community longer than younger workers: they
were thus more thoroughly socialised into them (for a fuller
discussion see Martin and Fryer, 1973, especially Chapter 4).

CONCLUSION

Analysis of data gathered in the course of research into redundancy
provided supporting evidence for Lockwood's characterisation of the
deferential traditionalist.   A minority of workers (37.8 per cent
of workers aged 50 or more), accepted a multi-layered view of the
class structure, the equity of the distinction between hourly paid
and monthly staff, and the existence of an ascriptive or merito-
cratic elite, were individualists rather than collectivists, and
believed in the virtues of obedience.   But deference did not imply
a unitary conception of the firm: deferential workers were only
slightly less likely than others to believe that the interests of
management and workers were opposed and that managers were only
interested in profits.   Attitudes towards trade unions were also
more sympathetic than implied in Lockwood's characterisation.
Three factors probably account for this divergence between the
Casterton deferentials and Lockwood's characterisation: the
relative lack of consideration given to employer-employee relations
in the original discussion (especially the lack of discussion of

trade unionism); the impact of the redundancy on the workers whom we interviewed, bringing a heightened consciousness of conflicting interests; and the erroneousness of the initial assumption that deference and absence of conflict were associated. Acceptance of the legitimacy of a structure of inequality does not mean acceptance of the view that there are no antagonistic interests within it.

Deference cannot be seen as the direct and inevitable product of specific work and community milieux. But emphasis upon the significance of workers' definitions of appropriate behaviour raises as many questions as it answers. What determines those interpretations? What determines the degree of managerial behaviour in accordance with them? The latter question is beyond the scope of this paper. Worker interpretations are obviously based upon past experience, present pre-occupations, and expectations of the future. Past experience provides the most important determinant, unless relevant circumstances are perceived as changing, or new interpretations of the same circumstances become available. Hence deferential traditionalism can survive in industrialised communities where the social structure, especially the demographic and economic structure, remains stable, and where new interpretations are excluded, either because of geographical isolation or because of the success of dominant groups in excluding alternative definitions. We would hypothesise, in general terms, that deference is likely where the labour force required for industrialisation is recruited through natural increase rather than immigration, or from rural areas, or where the ratio of natives to immigrants is sufficiently high to permit incorporation. Propitious economic circumstances include domination by a single employer, or small group of employers working in concert, and gradual, continuous, economic growth. But these remain speculative hypotheses.

In summary, Lockwood's speculative delineation of the deferential traditionalist is confirmed by the evidence gathered at Casterton. But deference is not a direct product of current experience within a given type of social milieux; it is based upon accord between workers' definitions and managerial behaviour. And these definitions are the joint product of past experience, present social location, and expectations of the future.

Chapter 7

DEFERENCE AND THE ETHOS OF SMALL-TOWN CAPITALISM

Eric Batstone

It has long been argued that those employed in small plants, especially in small, stable communities, are less class aware than those whose pattern of life is more open to 'national industrial and urban development'. Lockwood has developed this theme in his paper Sources of Variation in Working-class Images of Society (Chapter 2). In this paper he attempts to link the idea of deference to both a more rigorous discussion of class imagery and to various aspects of social structure.

He distinguishes an 'extreme' type of worker - the 'deferential traditionalist' - whose personal experiences of power are such as to lead him to envisage a four-fold class structure, based upon two cross-cutting factors. The first of these is a distinction between leaders and led, the second a contrast between legitimate and illegitimate bases of leadership and subordination. The criteria of legitimacy will be of a 'hereditary or quasi-hereditary' nature, such that there will exist in the worker's mind a 'high and unapproachable status group of leaders, his "betters", the people who "know how to run things", those whose performance is guaranteed by "breeding".' The deferential traditionalist, while seeing himself as nothing grander than working class, may be expected to distinguish a class of 'undeferential' workers beneath himself within the class structure.

Lockwood states not merely that such a worker is an 'extreme' type, but also that we know remarkably little about this 'elusive political animal' except in terms of his individual socio-economic characteristics. Accordingly much of what he says is 'speculative' even if it is 'not unreasonable'. However, two key elements of the deferential traditionalist's class image are clear: first, that it will be a 'prestige' or 'hierarchical' image; and, second, that he will defer to a (quasi-) hereditary elite. From the first point, Lockwood, following Bott (1957, pp.177-8) and others, (e.g. Popitz et al., 1957, pp.237, 242) argues that such a worker must distinguish a relatively large number of classes, and that he will not place himself in the lowest class he distinguishes. This, combined with the idea of a 'natural' leadership, suggests a model which appears to involve not merely criteria of status but also of power (Runciman, 1966, p.44; Ossowski, 1963, p.21) and, furthermore, a conflict between different systems of power.   However, for the purposes of this paper, we will accept Lockwood's statement that the deferential traditionalist has a 'prestige' model of class.

There has been remarkably little work done upon the deferential worker, even though he is used as a major explanation of voting behaviour (Nordlinger, 1967; McKenzie and Silver, 1968).   Lockwood was particularly dependent upon Margaret Stacey's study of Banbury (1960) which he describes as 'probably the best description of the deferential traditionalist and his social context'.   The research on which this paper is based was also conducted in Banbury, although it was not specifically directed at investigating deference.   Its primary focus was upon the relationship between plant size and class imagery.   The data derives from three main sources: first, a random sample of male manual workers stratified by size of plant; second, a series of studies of particular firms within the town; and third, observation over a two-year period whilst I was working on the re-study of the town (Stacey et al., 1975).   The data used in this article derives mainly from 38 interviews with workers from plants employing less than 100 workers, and 41 interviews with workers from those employing more than 100 workers (these plants mainly employed well over 250 workers).

The first sections of this paper concern themselves with a comparison between the deferential traditionalist and those from small plants who were interviewed.   Reference will also be made to the attitudes of those in large plants, since these provide a useful, empirical contrast.   First, particular aspects of political atti-tudes and class imagery are looked at, and a number of significant differences from the ideal type are found.   In an attempt to understand the differences noted, attention is turned to the various aspects of the work situation which Lockwood lists as importantly associated with deference.   No apparent differences are found. The community structure is then considered.   The situation of the small plant respondents is different in important respects and this might well explain certain of the differences in class imagery noted.   But it does not explain all the differences from the deferential traditionalist, particularly the conceptions of legitimate leadership held by those from small plants.   The final sections consider more fully the imagery of certain of these workers and a number of factors which help to 'explain' this picture of class structure.

While the findings of this study are in agreement with Lockwood's ideal type in so far as those employed in small plants were typically less class aware and did not have power models, they did not demonstrate any greater tendency to be deferential to a (quasi-) hereditary elite.   It will be argued here that, while this differ-ence from the ideal type may in part be explained by the nature of the 'community structure' in which these workers were located, at the same time it suggests certain criticisms of Lockwood's paper. First, that he fails to sufficiently specify the conditions for a conception of society which is essentially feudalistic (Martin, 1965; Littlejohn, 1963; Perkin, 1969).   Second, that this is in part due to his failure to consider fully the exact sources of workers' imagery (in particular, the role of 'middle-class influentials'); and, third, the complexity of class imagery,

particularly the relationship between ideas of the 'proper' structure
of society and reality as it is perceived.

POLITICAL SUPPORT

The deferential worker has received most attention in the area of
voting behaviour.   It is he who helps to keep the Conservatives in
power.   Lockwood also argues that his ideal-type worker supports
the party of his 'betters', the party of the 'national interest'.
Those in small establishments (e.g. Lipset, 1963; Nordlinger, 1967)
are also thought to vote in a similar manner.   Such an argument
receives only partial support from this study.   In the 1966 General
Election 37 per cent of those in small plants said they voted
Conservative or Liberal compared to only 15 per cent of those in
large plants.   But while those in small plants showed a greater
tendency to vote Conservative or Liberal than those in large plants,
it is nevertheless the case that even more of them voted Labour
(44 per cent).   This pattern disappeared when respondents were
asked which party they thought would be best to govern the country
at the time of interview.   This was in early 1968 at the time of
the Back Britain Movement, the plea for a Coalition Government and
the rekindling of the 'Dunkirk spirit' (Tomalin, 1968).   In this
situation the largest single category of small plant respondents
was those who rejected all the major political parties, and either
wished for a coalition or simply declared a loss of faith in
political parties - 42 per cent expressed such views, while the
number supporting the Conservative or Liberal parties fell to 29
per cent (Lipset, 1963, p.250 notes a similar tendency).   In this
context, therefore, their concern with the national interest did
not lead those in small plants to support 'the party of their
betters'.   Further, it is worthy of note that many respondents
expressed a concern for the use of business expertise in Government -
for example, by having a group of businessmen run the country -
while none of them expressed a desire for the return of the gentry
from their grouse moors to 'put things right'.   While, therefore,
those in small plants showed a lower tendency to support the Labour
party than those in large plants, it is not the case that this
meant necessarily greater support for other political parties.
Their concern with a unitary image of society did not automatically
imply support for the Conservatives.

CLASS IMAGERY

Such partial similarities to Lockwood's ideal type are also found
in terms of respondents' class imagery.   Four areas will be
considered here: the level of class awareness and the perceived
level of class conflict; the determinants of class; the number of
classes distinguished and self-placement in terms of class; the
possibility of, and desire for, social and occupational mobility.

Class awareness and conflict

It is generally argued that those with a prestige model, in contrast to those with a power model, will be less class aware and will
deny the existence of conflict between classes (Dahrendorf, 1959,
pp.280-9; Goldthorpe and Lockwood, 1963).   Very few of those
interviewed demonstrated a high degree of class awareness, but this
was especially remarkable among those in small plants.   Four
indicators of this may be taken.   First, while only 7 per cent of
those in large plants denied the existence of class, almost one-
third of those in small plants did so (for similar findings, see
Svalastoga, 1959, p.175; Gross, 1953; Haer, 1957).   Second, two
in five of those from small plants stated that class conflict was
not at all important, compared to only 10 per cent of those from
large plants.   Third, when asked about the sorts of people who
voted for the two main political parties, only 40 per cent of the
former (compared to 70 per cent of the latter) made any references
of a class nature.   These three sets of questions relate primarily
to the level of society as a whole.   But the same pattern was also
found at the interactional level.   This was investigated by means
of Kelly's repertory grid, which indicates the degree of association
between concepts (see Bannister and Mair, 1968).   The scores from
those tested shows that those in small plants felt less hostility
and more friendliness towards those whom they considered to be
middle-class than did those from large plants.   Similarly, they
felt less attachment to those they defined to be working-class.
Consistently therefore, those in small plants were less conscious
of conflict between, or even the very existence of, classes.

The bases of class

We have already questioned whether the class image of the deferential
traditionalist really is a prestige model, and have suggested that
in many respects it rests upon a power or authority base.   But in
terms of Lockwood's discussion of ideal types, we would expect that
those in small plants would place less stress upon economic or
occupational factors which here will be seen as indicative of power,
and more upon 'prestige' factors.
   Half of those in large plants identified with the working class
and said that occupational or economic factors were the crucial
determinants of class position; in contrast only 19 per cent of
those in small plants did so, (although a further 16 per cent
identified with the middle class and saw such factors as most
important in determining class position).   However, a third of both
categories stressed the importance of prestige factors (and only a
third of these identified with the working class).   While, therefore, the ratio of prestige to occupational and economic determinants of class was twice as high among large plant respondents (2:1
as compared to 1:1), in absolute terms as many large plant as small
plant respondents made reference to prestige factors.   When
respondents' descriptions of classes are considered, the same
pattern is found; while about 30 per cent of both those from small
and large plants made reference to factors classified as 'prestige'

in nature, 40 per cent of those from small as compared to 62 per cent of those in large plants refer to occupational or economic factors.   Again, a crucial point is the relatively high proportion of those in small plants who denied the existence of class.

Number of classes and self-placement

If the deferential traditionalist has a prestige model, Lockwood argues, then it is probable that he 'thinks in terms of at least a four-fold division of society'.   Further, he will not place himself in the lowest class.   The small plant respondents do not conform to this picture; none of them (nor any of those in large plants), distinguished more than three classes and only 42 per cent compared to 69 per cent of those in large plants did even this.   Moreover, only a quarter of the small plant respondents failed to place themselves in the lowest class which they distinguished.   Those who did place themselves in an intermediate class defined it, in all cases, as a middle class, typically made up of those who received a certain level of income and were 'respectable and good citizens'. The 'lower class' was typically seen as made up of 'no goods', those 'who live off the welfare state', or 'those who live off the backs of the rest of us'.   (For comparable findings see Martin, 1954; Zweig, 1961; Williams, 1965).   While this might be seen as approximating Lockwood's ideal type in that they distinguish a class beneath themselves, it is certainly not a deferential image.   Among those respondents with this type of image, the upper class was generally seen as made up of 'playboys', or 'those with more money than sense'.

Mobility

It is in terms of attitudes to mobility that Lockwood's deferential worker differs most from the conventional prestige model.   The typical stereotype of the prestige model is that mobility is seen as possible, and perhaps desirable (Dahrendorf, 1959, pp.280-9; Bott, 1957, pp.159-91); but the deferential traditionalist appears to deny the possibility of mobility, or at least not to wish for it himself.   It is interesting, however, to note that Stacey argues that the 'traditional' worker does not necessarily reject the idea of mobility (1960, p.47), and this is also true of the small plant respondents studied here.   Only one in ten thought class position was determined by birth.   Within the occupational sphere, a quarter of the small plant respondents thought that a manual worker could 'get to the top' (compared to less than one in ten of those from large plants), and, while only just over one-third of those in large plants expressed a desire for promotion, nearly two-thirds of those in small plants did so.   In addition, it is known that a number of workers wished to set up in business on their own account.

Class models as wholes

The differences in class imagery between those in small and large
plants can be seen most clearly by distinguishing two types of class
imagery; the first of these I will term consensual, the second
accommodative.   The consensual model minimises the importance of
class - it is seen either as non-existent or of no importance;
where classes are discerned they are described in prestige terms and
respondents rate themselves as working-class.   The majority of
respondents with this type of model denied the existence of class.
Those who distinguished a number of classes did so in prestige
terms - for example, the upper class drank at home, the middle class
always went into the lounge bar, and the working class into the
public bar.   The accommodative model approximates that described
by Parkin (1971, p.81) and is essentially a weak form of trade union
consciousness in Lenin's terms.   There is a stress upon occupational
or economic factors, a significant degree of class conflict is
perceived and respondents again identify with the working class.
The theme of the difficult position of the working class is common
among these respondents; the upper class is made up of 'people
who want everything you've got, have everything they want, and still
want more', while the working class 'have to work for everything
they've got and look after it'; 'the working class have to work
their way for everything'.   Those in small plants tend to hold
consensual models - 48 per cent of them did so, compared to only
22 per cent of those from large plants.   In contrast, while 54 per
cent of the latter held accommodative models, only 26 per cent of
those from small plants did so.   While, therefore, they approximate
the ideal type of the deferential traditionalist in certain respects -
in terms of their low level of class awareness, their denial of
class conflict, their relative stress upon prestige factors, and
their stress upon 'the national interest' - they are also significantly different from the ideal type in other respects.   They do
not build up complex class images, for example, and tend instead to
deny the existence of class.

DEFERENCE AND LEADERSHIP

One crucial question demands further consideration - their
definitions of legitimate leadership; in other words, are those
from small plants deferential?   It has already been seen that they
do not consistently support 'the party of their betters', even
though they appear to be especially concerned with the interests
of the society as a whole.
   One problem is what exactly is meant by deference; Lockwood
speaks of deference to an hereditary or quasi-hereditary elite,
'natural leaders'.   In this country, the idea of such natural
leaders is generally taken to mean the aristocracy or gentry,
although it should be added that Lockwood himself does not state
this explicitly.   For the purpose of this paper I will assume that
he also thinks in terms of deference to an aristocracy.   Respondents were asked a more realistic form of the question recently
employed by Nordlinger and McKenzie and Silver - 'who would you

rather see as Prime Minister - the son of a peer, the son of an
accountant, or the son of an electrician?'   The responses suggest
that those in small plants were not deferential to an aristocratic
elite - only 13 per cent chose the son of a peer, as small a proportion as did so in large plants.   Twice as many selected the son of
an electrician - marginally more than did so among the large plant
respondents.   However, the single most common choice was the son of
an accountant, while a quarter of both categories declined to make a
choice because background was not a good enough criterion by which
to choose.

We find, therefore, that not merely did those in small plants or
those with consensual models not demonstrate strong support for the
Conservative or Liberal parties, but in addition they demonstrated
no strong or even greater tendency to defer to an aristocratic
leadership.   A third indication of this is their notable lack of
reference to an hereditary elite in their class descriptions.   Of
the two-thirds of small plant respondents who recognised the existence of an upper class only 11 per cent (or 8 per cent of all small
plant respondents) described its members as aristocratic or 'gentry',
compared to one-third of those from large plants.

In terms of their class imagery, therefore, both those in small
plants, and those with consensual models, approximate Lockwood's
ideal type only to a limited degree.   Rather, they compare with
what has been more generally found, or assumed about, those working
in small firms - that they are simply less class aware.   However,
while these marked differences exist in terms of their conceptions
of class and society, there are similarities in their work situations.   This will now be considered more fully; in particular,
the sorts of firms in which they work; their involvement with
management, with their workmates and in their jobs.

WORK SITUATION

In terms of their work situation, the small plant respondents are
remarkably similar to the ideal type.   Lockwood states that the
deferential traditionalist will be found in small family firms, in
service and pre-industrial craft jobs, and in agriculture.   Eighty
per cent of the small plant respondents were employed in one-plant
family firms where the owner was actively involved in the day-to-
day management of the company.   They tended to be concentrated in
construction and other 'traditional' industries such as printing
and local distributive trades.   In contrast, those in large plants
typically worked in metal manufacture, or nationalised undertakings
such as the railways or the Post Office.   Finally, those in small
plants were employed in particular types of jobs - only 8 per cent
of them were employed in jobs of an essentially machine-minding
nature; many of them were not in factory employment, for example
bricklayers and their labourers, and a number were in jobs where
they were mobile and had a good deal of contact with customers or
clients.   (However, differences in industry, technology and nature
of the work task were not found to be associated with variations in
class imagery.)

Relationships with management

The small plant respondents were also comparable to the deferential
traditionalist in terms of their relationships with management.
Not merely did they have contact with, in terms of the company, more
powerful members of management, but also they had more frequent
contact - almost three-quarters had seen a manager (typically the
'gaffer') in the last twenty-four hours, compared to significantly
less than half of those in large plants.   Such contact was not
merely more frequent, but also tended to be of a more diffuse and
particularistic nature and in some cases was not confined to the
workplace.   Almost 60 per cent said they got on with management
'very well' compared to 24 per cent of large plant respondents
(see Ingham, 1970; Indik, 1963; but equally important are the
values of employers themselves - Birch, 1959; Stacey, 1960, p.28).
It was precisely because of this contact with management that
those in small plants, and especially those with consensual models,
rated their firms as good to work for; two-thirds of them did so,
while only 18 per cent referred to economic rewards as a reason for
favourably rating their employers.   Such relationships were valued
more generally by workers in small plants - when asked, three-
quarters of them stated that they would prefer to work in a small
firm, and 90 per cent of their reasons concerned personal contact
with management, the 'friendliness' and the 'family atmosphere'
which they thought typical of the small firm - 'in a small firm
you don't just become a cog in a wheel'; 'there's more personal
contact'; 'you're treated as one of the family in a small firm and
you're well looked after'.

Job involvement

While Lockwood says nothing specifically about the job involvement
of the deferential traditionalist, in Table 2.1 he lists him as
being intrinsically involved in his work.   Between 50 per cent and
60 per cent of both those in small and large plants (particularly
skilled workers) valued intrinsically interesting and varied work
tasks and felt that they gained such satisfaction from their present
jobs.   But whereas over a third of those in large plants said they
placed primacy upon the economic rewards of work (including job
security) only 8 per cent of those in small plants did so.   In
contrast, a quarter of the latter again stressed the importance of
good relations either with workmates or management as a source of
job satisfaction.   (Twenty per cent of those in small plants said
they had thought of leaving their present jobs, but these did not
typically have consensual models.   Sixty per cent of those with
consensual models liked their jobs for intrinsic reasons, compared
to only 23 per cent of those with accommodative models.)

Relationships with workmates and the occupational community

The deferential traditionalist does not, according to Lockwood,
identify with his workmates either outside or inside the workplace.

He is not a member of an occupational community.   Those in small
plants in overall terms, indicated only a marginally lower level
of involvement and identification with their colleagues than did
those in large plants - for example, 43 per cent compared to 54
per cent of those in large plants said they would be very or fairly
sorry to leave their present workmates;   only just over half of
each category considered any of their workmates as close friends;
33 per cent of those in small plants compared to 44 per cent of
those from large plants said they saw a fair amount of their workmates outside of work.

However, while this broad similarity between those in small and
large plants was found, those with consensual models appeared to be
especially isolated from their workmates - for example, only 31 per
cent of them compared to 67 per cent of those with accommodative
models said they would be very or fairly sorry to leave their
present workmates;   on other questions a similar low pattern of
attachment and interaction was found.   Furthermore, those with
consensual models tend to be employed in jobs which require a low
level of interaction with other workers in the performance of work
tasks - 63 per cent compared to 31 per cent of those with accommodative models.

While such a low level of involvement with their colleagues at
work is clearly in part due to the nature of the work situation,
what appears to be equally important is contact with workmates
outside of the workplace which cannot be purely attributable to
feelings of attachment developed at work.   For example, having
workmates as neighbours cannot be seen as solely or even mainly due
to the existence of high attachment to workmates, if only because
residential location frequently predates working for a particular
firm.   Those with workmates as neighbours were more likely both to
say that they got on well with their neighbours and to express a
high degree of attachment to their workmates;   the same pattern
seems to exist where respondents work with kin.   Those in small
plants were less likely to have such overlapping relationships with
their workmates.

Not only, then, do those small plant respondents correspond to the
deferential traditionalist in terms of the type of jobs in which they
are employed, but they do so also in terms of the nature of their
work situation - both horizontal and vertical relationships, and job
involvement.   How, then, are we to explain their contrasting class
imagery?   Two, possibly complementary, explanations suggest themselves.   The first, that the community structure is sufficiently
different to lead to the variations noted;   the second, that Lockwood's delineation of the characteristics of the deferential
traditionalist is incomplete.

Before considering these, a word should be added concerning the
nature of the association between size and imagery.   It has been
argued by some that the real factor is technology - but no relationship was found in this study between the dominant plant technology,
or the nature of the work task, and imagery.   What was crucial was
the system of values, as Hamilton's work also suggests (1967).
Briefly, the following seems the most plausible explanation.   Most
important is the general ethos linked to the traditions, myths and
history of the groups involved;   this is itself maintained by - or

(if it is to continue) receives only a limited challenge from - the product and labour markets.   But what, then, is the significance of size?   First, it facilitates the working out of this ethos, and in Banbury at least, size has been identified by the actors themselves as important.   Second, those entrepreneurs who most espouse this system of values - local businessmen - tend to be involved in small-scale enterprises for two reasons: the sorts of expertise which they tend to have, including local knowledge, means, generally, a limited scale of operation; and such businesses can be run on limited capital.   It is in this respect that a link exists between size and technology (at least for our purposes) - different technologies require different minimum capitals (studies which fail to find such a link have not looked at the full size range nor the full range of industrial activity and 'technologies').   Further, if this argument is correct, it follows that within the category of small plants, one would not expect a relationship between technology and imagery.

THE COMMUNITY STRUCTURE

Stacey concluded that Banbury in 1950 could no longer be considered a community in any meaningful sense (1960, pp.176-7), although a 'traditional social status system' could still be discerned.   The 'decline of the community' since that date has continued and indeed accelerated.   While the town is still relatively small (25,000 population in 1967) it has expanded rapidly since 1959 when an Overspill Agreement was signed with the GLC (Stacey et al., 1970). The town as a whole, therefore, contrasts with the localities in which Lockwood suggests the deferential traditionalist is to be found - while it is small, it cannot be seen as a stable community.
     Nor can it be seen as economically autonomous.   While local businesses still exist, and local businessmen play an important role in the political life of the town, their economic importance is limited - major employers are large, international companies, buying and selling in international markets.   Relatively few of the local businessmen, even, limit themselves to the locality in terms of buying or selling.   The decline of economic autonomy has also occurred in another important respect - a wide range of functions formerly controlled by the Borough Council and voluntary agencies have been lost.   But while such changes have perhaps been especial-ly noticeable in Banbury, they are by no means peculiar to it.
In other words, while it is likely that localities differ in the degree to which they are economically dependent upon the wider society, it is improbable that any locality is economically auton-omous to any significant degree.
     Within the small, stable and economically autonomous community in which the deferential traditionalist is to be found, four factors are stressed by Lockwood: the existence of an interactional status system; occupational differentiation; leadership positions being held by the worker's gaffer or similar middle-class influentials; and the deferential worker's non-membership of an occupational community.   The last of these has already been briefly discussed - the worker holding a consensual model is typically relatively isolated from his workmates outside as well as inside the place of work.   The three other aspects will now be considered.

Occupational differentiation

Banbury is far from being a one-class or an occupationally homogenous town; compared to England and Wales as a whole, only slightly
fewer economically active males within the Borough are managerial
or self-employed, and rather more are semi- and unskilled workers;
but this variation virtually disappears once the surrounding rural
area is taken into account (Stacey et al., 1975).   While there are
three major employers in the town they are in different sorts of
industries, and, while their combined contribution to local employment is significant, they are by no means dominant.
     Nor is it the case that those in small plants were more likely
to live in occupationally homogeneous areas or have social networks
made up primarily of workers in similar occupations to themselves.

Interactional status system

The size of the town, the number of recent immigrants, the associated mutual anonymity of many residents and the importance for
many people of non-Banbury-based relationships have all led to the
decline of an interactional status system throughout the locality.
The main Banbury re-study argues that while it has not completely
disappeared - for it still exists within small groups - the
estimation of status is no longer 'total' in most situations, and,
furthermore, there is little sign of a consensus upon status
placement (Stacey et al., 1975).   In addition, there is no reason
to assume that those employed in small plants are more involved in
such interactional status systems - their level of contacts is no
greater than was found among large plant respondents; there is no
tendency for them to be Banburians or to have lived in the town for
a long period of time; nor do they tend to be concentrated in older,
more stable parts of the town.   It is in this respect that the
small plant respondents most differ from the deferential traditionalist.

Middle-class influentials

The leadership positions within the community of the deferential
traditionalist will be occupied by his gaffer and/or those who are
similar to him - that is, small local businessmen and employers.
The tendency for such people to hold key positions in small towns
has been widely noted (Watson, 1964; Friedman, 1972) and Banbury
in 1967, as in 1950, is no exception.   While the rise of the Labour
party in the borough means that there are a number of working-class
councillors, the Conservative and Liberal parties are still
dominated by local businessmen or managers from small firms.   Moreover, it is such persons who figure prominently in other key associations of a business or quasi-political nature.   The more cosmopolitan manager typically plays little active part in the town.
     In certain important respects - most notably in terms of their
non-involvement, or limited involvement, in an international status
system - those in small plants differ from the deferential tradition-

alist. But is this really sufficient to explain their significantly
different class imagery? I would argue that it is not.   The differences in the community structure may serve to explain certain differences, particularly their failure to develop a complex, multi-class
image, but there is no reason to believe that it explains another,
possibly more crucial, aspect - namely, their failure to defer to an
aristocratic elite.

THE ETHOS OF SMALL TOWN CAPITALISM

Those in small plants did not adhere to what might be described as
a feudalistic conception of society; the ideology underlying their
model of society is one which belongs to the laissez-faire era of
capitalism; essentially such an ideology stresses three themes -
the harmony of interests of all groups; the possibility of mobility;
the importance of individualism and independence.
  In terms of their attitudes towards who should hold key positions
in society, deference does exist, but is of a significantly different kind to that of the deferential traditionalist.   Those with
ability can 'get on'; therefore, those who hold key positions must
have ability and are accordingly granted status.   To some degree,
therefore, deference is conferred on achieved rather than ascribed
criteria.   But in fact it is rather more complex than this, because
there appears to be a tendency to feel that those who hold particular positions must have earned them and are therefore worthy of
deference, although this is somewhat modified by other factors as
will be shown below.   (A similar argument has been put forward by
Banks (1964) in a rather different context.)
  Gouldner further argues that the rise to power of the middle
class meant an emphasis upon different criteria:
    the middle class standard of utility implied that rewards should
    be proportioned according to man's personal work and contri-
    bution.   The usefulness of men, it was now held, should control
    the station to which they might rise or the work and authority
    they might have, rather than that their station should govern
    and admit them to employment and privileges (1971, pp.62-3).
That deference is paid to a business elite and that mobility is
stressed are consistent with the nature of local leadership within
the town.   Not only is Banbury dominated, in terms of local
affairs, by local businessmen rather than the gentry, but conflicts
between businessmen and the local aristocracy are of some importance
in the history of Oxfordshire.   The nineteenth century was a story
of conflict between town and country, and between farming, and
commerce and industry (Lee, 1963).   Many workers identified with
the local businessmen rather than the aristocracy.   Such conflicts
can still be observed, not merely within the county's various
political bodies, but also in other associational activities.
There is, then, some degree of conflict between the local gentry
and the local middle class, as well as their basic value systems
being significantly different.   In their relationships with workers
there is also a significant variation.   While the social distance
between lord and servant is great (Perkin, 1969, p.25; Martin, 1965,
p.73) the social distance between 'gaffer' and man in small firms in

Banbury is considerably less.   In some of the very small plants
the owner actually works alongside the men and is simply 'primus
inter pares'.   But even in the larger of the small plants the
social distance is not very great; the relationship between boss
and worker is frequently informal - a 'back slapping' rather than a
'cap-doffing' one.

The background of many managers and owners of small firms is not
of the kind to encourage the belief in a class born to rule.   Many
of them, or their fathers before them, have been occupationally
mobile, starting their lives in manual occupations.   These facts
and more importantly, the myths, are often well known within the
town, and help to encourage the aspirations of those in small firms
to become self-employed themselves.   Further, even those managers
or owners who inherited their positions have frequently had some
sort of shopfloor training prior to taking up their birthright.   To
the extent, then, that class imagery is a reflection of immediate
patterns of experience it seems reasonable to suppose that those in
small firms will not believe in a distant elite who rule because of
inherent qualities associated with birth.

Finally, it is necessary to take into account the ideology of
the small businessmen themselves.   It is difficult to know the
exact significance of this for workers' imagery, but it seems
plausible to suggest that workers will be influenced by the attitudes of employers with whom they identify.   At the least their
attitudes are likely to be consistent with those of their superiors.
Lockwood fails to take any account of this fact in his discussion of
the deferential traditionalist - if their employers with whom they
identify and have close contact fail to support the right of an
aristocracy to rule, it would be amazing to find that the workers
themselves do so.

Clearly, there are variations in the ideology of local businessmen; one, for example, is a staunch supporter of the Labour party
(and there are many Labour party supporters among his employees!).
But two years' observation and discussion suggests that they are
typically strong adherents of the ethos of small town capitalism.
Not only does this ideology stress the themes mentioned earlier,
but it also includes a right and duty for local businessmen to
lead the community.   Since businessmen have proved their ability
and have certain skills, and since they gain from the locality in
terms of the success of their companies, they have a duty to look
after the town.   In addition, because they are local and know
the town, they should be free to run it without interference from
'outsiders' (see Stacey et al., 1970).

The social experiences of workers in small plants, and the values
and attitudes of those to whom they defer, are not of the kind to
foster an imagery that there is 'a high and unapproachable status
group of leaders ... people who "know how to run things", those
whose performance is guaranteed by "breeding"'.

THE CLASH BETWEEN IDEOLOGY AND REALITY

While it is somewhat artificial to make a distinction between
ideology and perception of reality, it is nevertheless useful in

that it serves to emphasise the ambiguities within class imagery which may lead to change within the existing model or the embracing of a different ideology.   In the case of those with consensual models there is an awareness that social reality challenges their conception of what is 'right' and 'proper'.   Changes occurring both nationally and in the locality serve to rock their basic system of values.   (A number of studies of right-wing movements have found that it is this sort of ideology which is important. For example, Trow (cited in Lipset, 1960, p.169) found that the 'nineteenth-century Liberals' - opposed to trade unions and large corporations, and those most similar to those with consensual models and the ethos of small town capitalism - were the strongest supporters of McCarthy in the USA.)   Many of these challenges relate to the decline of community - the loss of local power in terms of local government and the increasing role which large companies play within the town.   But equally there are more general societal changes which conflict with their ideology, most notably, the increasing importance of the large-scale bureaucracy in all spheres which limit the room for manoeuvre of the independent spirit.   That 'things have grown too big, complex and distant' perhaps best sums up these feelings, and the complexity of events nationally at the time of interview served merely to confirm such feelings.   Three indicators of this can be taken.   The first of these concerns their political support.   They had lost faith in politics and felt that the parties themselves had become large, impersonal bureaucracies;   a number of local businessmen also felt this strongly - the Conservative party was no longer the party of freedom and local independence.   This, associated with the declining autonomy of the town, which was further impressed upon them by the debate on expansion, added to their feelings of confusion.

A second indicator of such attitudes concerns respondents' answers to a question on whether any groups in this country had too much power.   Not only did almost half of those in small plants refer to the power of trade unions, but the same proportion made reference to the power of various business groups.   At first sight this appears particularly surprising;   but what is significant is that all these references are to big business - the large bureaucracies which are killing the small, family firm and which inhibit the exercise of individual initiative and ability.

Finally, this ambivalence is perhaps indicated most clearly by respondents' answers to a question on the nature of industrial relations;   while the majority of those in small plants stated that management and workers were a 'team', almost a quarter of those with consensual models thought that the relationship 'varies'. What was meant by this is most clearly indicated by a respondent who explained that he had left a job in a large plant because of the 'class antagonism you get in large firms' and had chosen the 'family atmosphere' of a small, family firm.   In other words, it seems possible that some workers in small firms are aware of two systems of industrial relations, the consensual and the conflictual. But what the studies of Gouldner (1955) and Stacey (1960) suggest is that if their expectations of the small firm are not met, then they may well adopt the approach which they see as more suited to the conflict which typically exists within the large plant.   In this sense, therefore, their imagery may be highly volatile between situations and over time.   Such change has been evident in the process of a strike situation which occurred during the research presently being undertaken by L. Boraston, S. Frenkel and myself.

But one may also raise a further question from the above discussion.   Is it really the case that social imagery derives mainly from personal experience?   Is it really the case that national crises, what is seen in the mass media, what is seen to happen in other situations, has no effect upon people's perception? Such a major question cannot be answered here - but it does seem at least worthy of attention; might it be that the class imagery discussed here was in part affected by the national economic crisis of the time?

Chapter 8

IDEOLOGY IN THE NON-SKILLED WORKING CLASS

R.M. Blackburn and Michael Mann

The aim of this paper is to explore variations in the industrial ideologies (or 'images of industry') of a major section of the working class, drawing on the results of our empirical research. (1) The importance of ideology is so generally accepted as to need no justification here, yet there has never been a large-scale survey of workers' industrial ideologies. In Britain much of industrial sociology has been based on specific limited samples where the influences of occupation, employer and community have been merged. Hence our knowledge of workers' ideologies is based on adding together a number of fairly homogeneous groups of workers from the Ashtons, Gosforths and Lutons studied.

It is not surprising that this methodology leads to an emphasis on overall diversity but sub-cultural homogeneity of workers' images of society. Lockwood (Chapter 2) suggests that we may conceive of overall working-class consciousness as composed of distinct and internally cohesive 'deferential', 'privatised' and 'proletarian' sub-cultures. Yet in recent years this approach, which informs the 'Affluent Workers' study, has come under attack. Westergaard (1970) and Mann (1973) have both noted that the consciousness of the Luton sample was actually rather ambivalent, not to say contradictory. They have further argued that almost all workers within capitalism are placed in such a contradictory real situation that it is unlikely they can develop insulated and cohesive sub-cultures of the kind posited by Lockwood. The argument can be extended to a methodological level - are the Weberian 'ideal-types' underlying the Lockwood scheme too static to aid the understanding of the essentially dialectical relationship between capital and labour?

The social context of most workers is highly diverse in terms of the occupations and backgrounds of those they meet and the types of employment available in the area. At the same time they may be subject to similar structural constraints of their class position. Therefore, our sampling attempted to reproduce both the internal diversity and the structural uniformity of the working class. In 1970-1 we interviewed at their place of work 951 non-skilled, male, manual workers spread through nine organisations in the town of Peterborough (a response rate of 87 per cent). We should point out that our category of 'non-skilled' is a wide one, including many

highly specialised jobs like engine tester and train driver, as well
as a number which are labelled by both management and unions as
'skilled' but are filled by men without apprentice training
('dilutees').   Our intention was to sample from the whole labour
market available to men without formal apprentice qualifications.
This may be broadly conceived of as the lower three-fifths of the
working class.   As men having only their labour to sell, they are
the people Marx had in mind in discussing the proletariat, and they
have remained the basic sector of the working class.   If there is
to be a cohesive proletarian class movement, then it must at least
embrace, if not actually be built on these members of the working
class.

Our choice of Peterborough - from six short-listed towns - was
dictated by its unusual employment variety and low unemployment.
The sampling procedure was highly stratified in order to obtain
coverage of the wide range of different employment types.   The
industries covered include the major ones of the town - engineering,
bricks and the railways, together with several other important
fields of local employment - food manufacturing, building, plastics,
milk delivery and local government.   This wide industrial coverage
means the firms studied differ greatly in the nature of the work and
conditions of employment.   At the same time we cover a variety of
jobs in each firm, giving 275 different jobs in the sample which we
intensively observed (see Blackburn and Mann, 1973).   It will be
seen, then, that our sample is occupationally highly diverse - from
dustmen to dilutee drillers, from brick burners to belt attendants.

In view of the methods used and the great diversity of our
sample, we cannot claim it is 'representative' of the national lower
working class;   nor would we claim 'representativeness' at the local
level.   What we do have is coverage of a wide range of the different people who, in broad terms, are located in this section of the
class structure.

The debate on workers' images has been largely based on secondary
analysis of surveys, in which attitudes of different samples have
been related together.   Here we are pursuing survey research more
rigorously, and so making clear its limits (about which we will
comment later).

MEASURING IDEOLOGY

Ideology was measured by responses to nine items designed to reveal
the worker's position on a left-right ideological dimension.   They
were as follows, though asked in the order 1, 5, 2, 6, 7, 3, 8, 4,
9 so as to mix up 'left' and 'right' items.
 1 Most decisions taken by foremen and supervisors would be better
    if they were taken by the workers themselves. (Agree = left;
    henceforth referred to as the 'workers' decisions' question.)
 2 Full teamwork in firms is impossible because workers and
    management are really on opposite sides. (Agree = left;
    'teamwork'.)
 3 All managements will try to put one over on the workers if they
    get the chance. (Agree = left; 'deception'.)

4   Industry should pay its profits to workers and not to share-
    holders. (Agree = left; 'redistribution'.)
5   Most managements have the welfare of their workers at heart.
    (Agree = right; 'welfare'.)
6   Managers know what's best for the firm, and workers should do
    just what they're told. (Agree = right; 'obedience'.)
7   Most major conflicts between managements and workers are caused
    by agitators and extremists. (Agree = right; 'agitators'.)
8   Giving workers more say in running their firms would only make
    things worse. (Agree = right; 'workers' control'.)
9   The worker should always be loyal to his firm even if this means
    putting himself out quite a bit. (Agree = right; 'loyalty'.)

The questions were political in the sense that they were designed
to tap alternative images of society, ranging from the proletarian
radical left to the deferential conservative right.   However, the
statements were clearly set in an industrial context, in preference
to political questions of an abstract or party-political nature.
The intention was to make the questions relevant to the workers'
experience and to reduce standard responses to familiar political
cues.

The worker was asked to record his agreement or disagreement with
each statement by marking a cross on a scale of the following form:

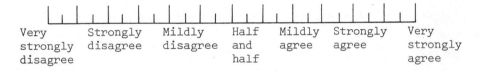

Very   Strongly   Mildly   Half   Mildly   Strongly   Very
strongly   disagree   disagree   and   agree   agree   strongly
disagree   half   agree

We devised this scaling system, after much experimentation, to
measure attitudes as precisely and continuously as the workers'
actual ideologies permitted.   Those who felt able to do so could
place their responses on a continuous scale or use the 25 scale
points (which is what we actually coded); failing that, they could
still use the seven worded points as cues; and in the last resort,
they might be able to tell us simply whether they agreed or dis-
agreed.   Technically, this is a marked improvement on a simple
choice between verbal cues, since it gives a fairly precise indication of the relative weight of each cue and allows the resolution of
dissatisfaction with the fixed choices by choosing a position between
cues.   Whether it is legitimate to treat ideology responses as
continuous variables in this way is less clear, and we will return
to this question later on.

For consistency the five 'right' items (i.e. those with which
agreement is taken to indicate a right-wing ideology) were scored in
reverse direction.   These are interval scales, not absolute
measures; they measure relative differences within the sample.   We
attempted to find wordings which would spread the responses over the
scales with means around the mid-points (0), which may then be taken
as neutral points with respect to the sample, but not as points of
zero ideology.   In fact the means ranged from -5.16 to 2.10.

We are not particularly interested in the individual items but in
their combination in a single dimension.   However, we must first

decide if such a combination is meaningful.   If they are all
indicators of the same ideology variable they should be positively
related to each other.   Accordingly we intercorrelated respondents'
scores on the nine items.   The results are shown in Table 8.1.

TABLE 8.1   Correlations between ideology items (observed scores)

		Left				Right			
	1	2	3	4	5	6	7	8	9
Left									
1 Workers' decisions	1.00								
2 Teamwork	.16	1.00							
3 Deception	.21	.24	1.00						
4 Redistribution	.27	.12	.20	1.00					
Right									
5 Welfare	.09	.12	.12	.02	1.00				
6 Obedience	.03	.01	.06	.03	.25	1.00			
7 Agitators	-.01	.01	-.06	.01	.15	.07	1.00		
8 Workers' control	.02	-.04	-.12	-.08	.14	.25	.14	1.00	
9 Loyalty	.06	.08	-.01	-.04	.31	.24	.17	.14	1.00

In general the items are positively related;   29 of the 36 correlations are positive and 22 of these are significant at the 5 per
cent level. (2)   However, two things in this table are particularly
striking;   one is the general low level of the correlation coefficients, the other is the difference in level between the set of
correlations of 'right' items with 'left' ones and those of 'right'
with 'right' or 'left' with 'left'.   Let us consider the latter
point first.

The 'left-right' correlations are all very low and seven are
negative;   the mean is less than 0.02 and only 6 out of 20 are significant at the 5 per cent level while 3 of the negative ones are
also significant at this level.   On the other hand the 'left-left'
and 'right-right' correlations are all positive and relatively high
(and so significant), with a mean of 0.19.   There is no theoretical
reason for this systematic difference, which suggests it must be a
consequence of our method and the workers' reactions to our scales.
In fact workers tended to use only a portion of the scale, distrib-
uting their answers not around the mid-point but around a mean of
their own choosing.   This may be due in part to their first
answers constraining the relevant range for other items.   Probably
more important is the well known tendency for people to agree with
all questions, though in differing degrees.   Our sample tended to
agree with both 'right' and 'left' questions, the overall mean of
all items scored in the direction asked (weighted to adjust for only

4 'left' against 5 'right' items) being +1.5.   Now, inter-item
correlations are not affected by the common tendency of the whole
sample to agree, but they are affected by individual differences in
this tendency.   Since the 'right' items are scored in reverse
direction an individual's tendency to agree leads to increases in
his 'left' item scores and corresponding decreases in the 'right'
item scores, and vice versa.   So the expected effect is to decrease
'left-right' correlations and increase the others.   This appears to
be what happened with the ideology scores recorded by our sample.

Accordingly, we subtracted a correction factor, which we
estimated at one-quarter of the apparent tendency to agree.   Thus
we took as each individual's zero point on each item a point one-
quarter of the way between the original scale zero and his weighted
mean for all items scored in the direction of agreement.   The
resulting correlations are shown in Table 8.2.   The mean correlation on 'left-right' items is now 0.11 matched by 0.12 on the
others.   Although other values were checked in analysis the
following discussion is based on the scores adjusted by this factor.
The range of means is now narrowed to -4.69 to 1.76.

TABLE 8.2   Ideology correlations: adjusted scores

| | Left | | | | Right | | | | | |
	1	2	3	4	5	6	7	8	9	T
Left										
1 Workers' decisions	1.00									
2 Teamwork	.09	1.00								
3 Deception	.14	.20	1.00							
4 Redistribution	.18	.04	.17	1.00						
Right										
5 Welfare	.19	.20	.28	.08	1.00					
6 Obedience	.12	.09	.06	.07	.16	1.00				
7 Agitators	.06	.07	.09	.08	.07	.01	1.00			
8 Workers' control	.10	.03	.03	.03	.03	.18	.04	1.00		
9 Loyalty	.14	.15	.17	.05	.23	.18	.08	.03	1.00	
T Total ideology score	.50	.44	.51	.40	.53	.47	.36	.35	.45	1.00
T - x*	.27	.22	.28	.16	.32	.22	.12	.11	.25	.97*

*   x is the score on the item (from 1 to 9) with which T - x is
     correlated.   Where the correlation is with the total T, then the
     figure given is the mean of the correlations for all values of
     T - x.

The inter-item correlations for the adjusted scores are still small, the overall mean being 0.11 compared with 0.09 on the raw data.   The crudeness of the adjustment of scores and general measurement error may both have led to underestimates but even allowing for these the coefficients would remain small (see Horst, 1966, on effects of measurement error).   This raises the question of whether the items can be regarded as indicators of a single ideology dimension.

In the first place we should note that all the inter-item correlations are positive and 28 are significant.   Also, as shown in Table 8.2, all are positively related, at a modest level, with a composite ideology score T obtained by adding the 9 items.   Since these figures contain an element of auto-correlation the bottom line of Table 8.2 shows each item (x) correlated with the total score less that item (T - x).   The correlations are all fairly low, but large enough to regard each item as an indicator of the underlying variable.   Items 7 (agitators) and 8 (workers' control) are rather poorly related and we considered dropping them but, in keeping with the logic of Likert scaling, since all the relationships are low we decided to keep all the available indicators.   With only one exception the correlation of each of these items (7 and 8) with T - x is higher than with the other eight items, which is as we should expect (and the pattern is similar for the other seven items). The inclusion or omission of any item does not make a lot of differ-ence, the correlation of T with T - x ranging from 0.96 to 0.98, so the decision whether or not to drop an item is not greatly import-ant. (3)

Another way of testing for an ideology dimension is using factor analysis.   Three significant factors were obtained with factor weights as shown in Table 8.3.

TABLE 8.3   Ideology factor weights

		Factor	
	1	2	3
1 Workers' decisions	.36	-.02	.14
2 Teamwork	.33	-.08	-.17
3 Deception	.46	-.25	-.07
4 Redistribution	.31	-.20	.44
5 Welfare	.53	-.06	-.21
6 Obedience	.39	.45	.05
7 Agitators	.16	-.09	.03
8 Workers' control	.17	.23	.11
9 Loyalty	.40	.05	-.14
Proportion of total variance	.13	.04	.04
Validity	.79	.59	.55

Clearly the first factor is the most important, (the proportions of the explained variance accounted for by these factors are respectively 63 per cent, 20 per cent, 17 per cent).   No item dominates and all contribute positively, though again the contribu-tion of items 7 and 8 are rather low.   There is, therefore, good

reason to interpret this as the basic underlying ideology factor.
This is supported by the fact that this first factor F correlates
0.97 with the unweighted total ideology T and that the second and
third factors are not readily interpretable.

CORRELATES OF IDEOLOGY

It seems that in spite of the unpromising data of Table 8.1, we do
have a measure of ideology.   If so, we may expect it to be related
to other variables.   We have explored such relationships extensive-
ly, and will report on some of the more interesting findings. (4)
In the first place we will consider four variables which we would
expect to be related to ideology: age, trade union commitment, job
satisfaction and generalised demands, this last being a composite
measure of nine items expressing criticism of aspects of their
general employment situation.   In Table 8.4 we show the correlation
of these variables with factor weighted, F, and unweighted, T, total
ideology scores.

TABLE 8.4   Ideology and related variables: correlations

	Trade union commitment	Generalised demands	Job Satis-faction	Age
Ideology T	-.14	.46	-.26	-.24
F	-.13	.50	-.29	-.25

All correlations are in the expected direction, and though not
large they are highly significant.   These relationships do seem to
indicate the validity of the ideology measures.   We have considered
the two alternative measures of ideology as a check.   On the whole
it seems the weighted measure, F, relates better to other variables,
though the difference is not enough to be important.   Since we
would also expect it to be a slightly more accurate measure, we have
used it in what follows.

It may, of course, be objected that we have selected here only
those variables which fit the argument.   In fact there are a few
other variables comparably related in the expected direction (e.g.
dissatisfaction with management, 0.39 or 0.40) while only in one or
two low correlations were the signs in the contrary direction.   The
position will become clearer as we examine more closely the relation
of ideology to other variables.

The association with trade unionism may appear weak.   However,
the measure of commitment, while taking account of office holding,
turned mainly on membership, so it is rather restricted. (5)   The
pattern may be seen more clearly by observing that 38 per cent of
non-members compared with 49 per cent of members and 67 per cent of
stewards expressed relatively left-wing ideologies (i.e. they scored
above the mean).   Since membership was more or less compulsory in
some places the effect of ideology on membership was necessarily
limited.   To be sure, membership could still have a socialisation

effect on ideology and the fact that the proportion of left-wing members is as high where there is a closed shop suggests this may happen a little, though it also shows that the highly unionised social environment does not have much effect in creating an ideological sub-culture.   Further doubt is cast on the importance of unionism as a basis of radical socialisation by the complete lack of relationship between ideology and the number of unionists in a worker's family.   Furthermore, contact with unionism, at home or work, does not increase consistency (i.e. is not associated with a lower standard deviation on ideology items), which, we shall argue, is an indication that ideology is not more salient among such workers.   It seems that contact with unionism has only limited effect in increasing radicalism above that of other workers in a similar class position.

In view of the general measurement problems, the correlation with 'generalised demands' is remarkably high and stands out among the great number of correlations we performed - of ideology with other variables and between these variables.   The link between left-wing ideology and general discontent with the workers' lot emerges clearly.   Similarly, low job satisfaction is linked with being left-wing, but as the frame of reference is narrower than with 'demands' it is not surprising that the relation with ideology is weaker.   Questions on job satisfaction tend to tap evaluations of a job within the constraints of what the worker can realistically expect to do, while 'generalised demands' tap criticisms of the constraints on the types of job available.

The tendency for conservatism to increase with age is quite strong and well known.   There are a number of hypotheses which may be advanced to explain this relationship.
1 It is not that people become more conservative with age but that their ideologies remain constant while the whole society is moving leftward.   The analogy is with voting behaviour: because most people maintain their first vote throughout their life, social change and the rise of the Labour party creates 'political generations' where each age-group is more radical than the last.
2 (a) Life has got better as they have grown older due to progressive changes in the society - they 'have never had it so good'.
(b) Or the improvement might be more narrowly related to their work experience.   With time they get promoted to better jobs, or they change jobs till they hit on the one that suits them relatively well.   Consequently in both cases they become more satisfied and so more conservative, as their experience changes within a stable frame of expectations and aspirations.
3 (a) They adjust with age; gradually beaten down by the experience of an unyielding stratification structure they reduce their aspirations and become passively conservative and satisfied, not believing in the possibility of any alternative structure.
(b) Again, this might be related specifically to the unyielding realities of work experience (cf. Kornhauser, 1965).   In both cases what changes is the frame of reference for expectations and aspirations rather than experience itself, which remains constant.

Two general factors are involved here; the relation between ideology and satisfaction and the relative importance of work and non-work life.   Before going on to consider the hypotheses it will be useful to look at the patterns of relationships.   To do this we

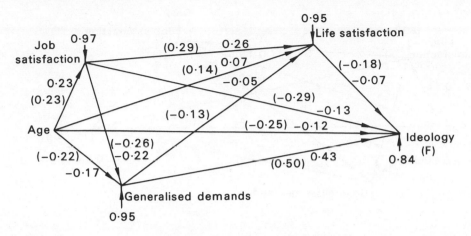

Correlation coefficients are shown in parentheses, e.g. (0.29)

FIGURE 8.1   Ideology, age and satisfaction paths

have used path analysis, and Figure 8.1 shows the intercorrelations
and path coefficients on a hypothesised causal structure.   We have
introduced 'life satisfaction' into this figure.   This is based on
a question about 'life in general' using the same cue and the same
scale as job satisfaction.

There is no way to choose rigorously between the causal model
presented and possible alternatives.   However, given that age must
be regarded as causally prior to the other variables, and assuming
ideology is dependent on all the four other variables (which is
inherent in our theoretical model) there is little scope.   Omitting
or reversing paths between the three intervening variables has
little effect on the strength of relation between them (path coefficient or residual correlation) or on the remaining paths.   In
particular the four paths to ideology are unaffected.

We see that the magnitude of some of the correlations could be
misleading.   No paths can be regarded as disappearing but some are
pretty small. (6)   By far the most important influence on ideology
is generalised demands, and through this operates one of the most
important influences of age.   The direct effect of age (just under
half its total influence) is marginally less than that of job satisfaction and rather more than that of life satisfaction.   Age has a
much greater direct effect on job satisfaction than on life satisfaction, and the influence on ideology through the latter appears
negligible.

The causal model is based on the assumption of the particular
influencing the more general, so that satisfaction/dissatisfaction
with a particular current job is causally prior to generalised
evaluations of the world of work which, in turn, are prior to the
level of satisfaction with life in general.   The greatest change
in the model would entail the assumption of causality from general
to particular: the level of satisfaction/dissatisfaction with life
in general influencing feelings about work in general, and these
influencing attitudes to the actual job. (7)   In other words the

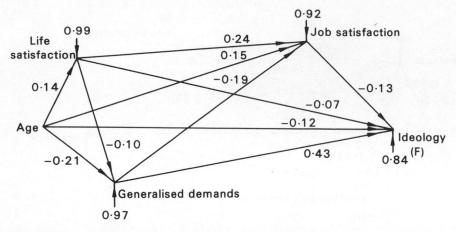

FIGURE 8.2 Alternative model of ideology paths

causal relations between the three intervening variables would be
reversed.   This would maximise the importance of life satisfaction
in the model but the path from age would still be a little lower
than from age to job satisfaction, while the influence on ideology
would remain low.   Figure 8.2 gives the path coefficients of this
model.

It seems clear that, however we look at it, generalised demands
are the most important influence, followed by job satisfaction with
life satisfaction having rather little effect.   But before we jump
to any conclusions we should recall that the content of the ideology
items related to work, and this might be partly responsible for the
low importance of life satisfaction in the models (though it could
have no bearing upon, for example, the low relationship with age).
In any case we find all four variables significantly related to
ideology, with age having a further important influence through
work experience.

What can we now make of the hypotheses?   Our evidence is inconclusive but does suggest some points.   In so far as age acts
directly on ideology the first, 'generational' hypothesis is
possible.   However, it seems somewhat implausible for two reasons.
First, age differences in job satisfaction studies have been
reported so consistently, for workers entering employment between
well before the twentieth century until the present time, that such
a secular upward trend in worker aspirations should really have
produced a proletarian revolution by now.   Second, it is one thing
to argue that the younger adult is more likely to vote Labour now
because he came of age at a time when Labour was dominant.   It is
quite another to transfer the argument to the industrial sphere
over the same period.   For this would mean that young men introduced to working-class consciousness in the turbulent 1920s and
1930s would be more conservative in their industrial ideologies
than those entering the stable, prosperous world of the 1950s and
early 1960s.   Yet our data indicate that work experience is
important in determining ideology.   This also leaves the problem
of explaining why those entering employment now should be more

radical.   It seems more probable that the 'direct' effect of age
actually operates through other aspects of experience not measured
in the model, for example in previous jobs.

The remaining hypotheses incorporate two sets of alternatives:
work or non-work influences, and improved conditions or beaten down
through powerlessness.   We have seen that both work and non-work
influences operate, though work influences were much more important
in our data.   We cannot choose between the two non-work hypotheses
but we do have some relevant data concerning the possible work
influences.

There is no tendency in our sample for older workers to have
better jobs.   Age is unrelated to present job level and also to job
characteristics.   Of course, there are undoubtedly occupational sub-
worlds where age-related career structures exist, but there is no
such tendency overall.   Therefore older workers are not more
contented because they have objectively better jobs.   Furthermore,
they do not appear to have subjectively better jobs either, in that
our data show no consistent tendency for older workers to have jobs
more in accord with their orientations (though this is a tentative
conclusion pending further analysis).

Considering involuntary job changes (redundancy, etc.) and unemployment lends some support for the 'beaten down' hypothesis
though again the data are inconclusive.   It is a little surprising
to find that the relationship with ideology is negligible in each
case, and the number of involuntary moves is actually associated
with conservatism.   Since both variables increase with age (due to
greater time at risk and also to past circumstances) this is part
of the explanation.   Controlling for age the relation of involuntary moves to conservatism disappears while unemployment appears
marginally more related to radicalism.   These are important
elements in working-class experience; two-thirds had experienced
unwanted changes (one-half if we exclude war-time direction and
conscription) and a quarter had been unemployed 'for longer than a
few days at a time'.   The lack of relation to ideology is, therefore, striking.   The explanation in terms of 'things are better
now' is not particularly persuasive when we see that these men tend
to have lower-level jobs and poorer pay than the other workers.
What we might expect to be radicalising experience seems to have
been offset by the hopelessness of the situation, by being 'beaten
down'.

As experience of work does appear to be of considerable importance in developing ideology, we will look at their present and past
employment.   In the first place we find there is some variation
between firms, with a tendency for radicalism of workers to increase
with the size of the firm. (8)   This is in keeping with the findings of previous research, though the actual mechanisms relating
ideology to size remain problematic - is it an effect of worker-
management relations, closeness of the control system, relations
with fellow workers, or what?   We are not in a position to solve
this complex problem but our data are relevant to some of the issues
involved.   Dissatisfaction with management is relatively highly
correlated with left ideology (r = 0.40) but as we have no objective
measure of the relations between workers and managers the causal
nature of this association is unclear.   We did attempt to get

TABLE 8.5 Correlations of job scores with ideology, general demands and job satisfaction (a positive correlation would denote that workers with a higher job score were more left-wing, more demanding, and more satisfied).

Job characteristic	Ideology	Generalised demands	Job satis- faction
A Skill components			
Ability to determine pace of work	-.15	-.09	.14
Manual dexterity	.09	.06	-.02
Reading, writing and linguistic ability	-.11	-.10	.02
Mathematical calcula- tions	-.10	-.06	.02
Length of necessary learning period	-.09	-.05	.05
Autonomy of decision- making	-.08	-.07	.08
Length of work-cycle	-.07	-.06	.09
Memory for rules and routines	-.08	-.11	.04
Object variety	-.06	-.07	-.03
Complexity of decision- making	-.04	-.09	.04
Visualisation of shapes and relationships	-.03	-.06	.01
B Degree of effort required			
Concentration	.15	.08	-.07
Pace of physical effort	.11	.08	-.07
Quantity of physical effort	.07	.02	-.07
C Work Environment			
Noise	.10	.03	-.07
Fumes, dirt, heat	.09	.08	-.04
Exposure	-.04	.00	.08
D Social interaction with			
Supervision	.10	.09	-.13
Co-workers and customers	-.08	-.06	.01
Required teamwork with co-workers	.03	.04	-.01
E Recruitment and promotion			
Extent to which higher grade recruits from below	-.11	-.09	.02
Present promotion chances	.00	.01	-.02
Past promotion experience	-.02	-.04	.06

relatively objective data on aspects of the job itself (by intensive observation of jobs we scored them as 30 five-point scales of characteristics) so we turn now to an examination of job characteristics.

We correlated all the job characteristics which are scaleable with ideology, generalised demands and job satisfaction.   The results are shown in Table 8.5.   The levels of association are low throughout, but there is some definite patterning.   The relations of job characteristics to generalised demands follow closely those with ideology while those with job satisfaction are in the opposite direction, as we would expect.

The more frequently a worker interacts at work with his supervisors, the more radical, demanding and dissatisfied he is.   This might seem to be at odds with one orthodox interpretation of the 'size effect' in which it is argued that frequent interaction with management in small firms tends to make workers more conservative. But we must be very careful to distinguish between the 'social' and the 'control' aspects of hierarchical interaction.   A voluntary relationship based on affective ties between manager and worker may lead to conservatism (though Nordlinger, 1967, disputes this). But where it is compulsory and part of a system of managerial control, then it will lead to resentment.   As in our sample the correlation between autonomy of decision-making and supervision interaction was -0.60, there is little doubt that this was a disliked control relationship.   It is also interesting to note that such interaction was greater in the larger 'impersonal' work organisations.

Of the skill components only manual dexterity is positively related to ideology - that is, those jobs allowing the worker to exercise more dexterity are occupied by more radical workers.   All the other skill components are wielded disproportionately by the more conservative workers.   On the other hand, the harder the physical burden and the more unpleasant the environment, the more radical, demanding and unsatisfied the workers.   The general point is clear; the worse the job, the more its occupants exhibit a generalised sense of grievance.   This may not seem surprising, but it is important to bear in mind that aspects of a job need not be viewed the same way by all workers.   For instance, the relations with exposure to the weather appear to contradict the general point, but our research shows many regard out-door work as a major attraction of a job.   Not all share this view so we see that reactions to this job characteristic depend on individual orientations; on other characteristics there is such a degree of consensus that jobs may be regarded as hierarchically arranged on the characteristics. (9)

In the absence of any precise measure which we could use for positions in a job hierarchy, we have used a rather rough sevenfold classification. (10)   We used this in considering the levels of the workers' present, past and possible future jobs, and the jobs of their friends and relations.   We also used it to measure the gap between the respondents' present job and these other levels. Some of the results are included in Table 8.6.

The correlation between present job level and ideology is negligible.   One possible reason for this, we suggest, is the narrow range in job level in comparison to the whole class structure, giving little scope for variation in relation to ideology.   We shall return to this point presently.   An interesting point is that the low semi-skilled group is more left-wing than either the groups above or the group below.   This stratum was also more radical when we looked at the respondent's best job level, at the average level of his friends' jobs, and at his expected future job.   It may be that the relative conservatism of the lowest, unskilled group is due to this stratum being the locus of a 'lumpenproletariat', the ageing, the unfit, the marginal.   The jobs are those without even the minimal specialised functions of, say, routine machine-minding.

TABLE 8.6 Job level and downward mobility correlated with ideology and satisfaction

All workers (N = 951)	Job level		Gap between level and present job level	
	Ideology	Job Satis-faction	Ideology	Job Satis-faction
Fathers	.07	.03	.04	.05
Highest	.14	-.01	.11	.03
Best	.02	.11	.00	.09
Last	.04	.04	.02	.05
Present	.03	-.03	-	-
Friends	.07	.03		
Relations	.11	.01	Not calculated	

Positive correlations denote: 1 The higher the job level, the more right-wing and dissatisfied.
                              2 The higher the gap, i.e. the downward mobility, the more right-wing and dissatisfied.

   Apart from this we find a general trend: the higher the jobs in his personal experience, the more conservative the worker.   This is particularly true with respect to the jobs of his father and other relatives, and also his own highest job.   Where the worker has control in the form of evaluation or choice, as with best job or friends' jobs (unlike family, friends are chosen) the relationship is slight.   It seems that those aspects of the workers' frames of reference which are beyond their control discriminate them ideologically in a way which their preferences do not.
   In considering job levels, we find that the pattern of association for job satisfaction is roughly the reverse of what we observed in relation to other variables.   No longer do right-wing ideology and satisfaction occur together.   On the contrary, contact with higher job levels goes with conservatism but also with more dissatisfaction.   To understand this we must look not at the levels but the gaps between the respondent's present job and the levels of others in his frame of reference.   Then we find, in keeping with previous

research, (11) that the greater the relative downward mobility
the more the dissatisfaction with present position.   The interesting point is that this does not also operate with ideology.   In
fact downward mobility is associated with being right-wing (and also
making less generalised demands) (12) but greater job dissatisfaction.
Since dissatisfaction tends to produce radical ideology, the effect
of past contact with higher levels tends to have a more conservative
effect than is apparent.

When we control for the effects of previous experience we find
that present job satisfaction is much more clearly related to the
level of the job than appears from the zero order correlation,
making the pattern of relationships more intelligible.   On the
other hand the effects on ideology seem to be slight but cumulative:
in past and present experience higher levels are associated with
conservatism.

To explain the contrary effects exerted by occupational level we
must distinguish between the worker's view of industrial structure
and of his place within it.   Experience of, and contact with,
higher social levels appears to exert a general conservative effect
which is relatively persistent.   This may be through socialisation
but it seems likely that, in view of the persistence, it also
results from widening the worker's frame of reference and thereby
lessening the experience of constraint.   But at the same time, it
enlarges the worker's personal expectations within the structure;
and if these are inadequately met relative to prior experience or
present reference groups, then dissatisfaction results.   So in
any assessment of the potentialities for working class consciousness,
we must take into account this dissatisfied yet conservative group,
discontented with their own individual achievement within an
accepted overall structure.   It is a weakness of any radical
working-class movement that it cannot easily capitalise on the work
discontent of this section of the manual labour force.

Let us now look briefly at aspects of the workers' background
which we might expect to be related to ideology.   On the whole we
find here a fairly striking lack of relationship.   Considering
connections with agriculture, we find no direct relationship between
ideology and previous agricultural employment or rural birth, while
those who live at present in rural areas are slightly more radical.
These findings appear to run against the expected association of
conservatism with agriculture.   Moreover, the 83 respondents in our
sample who had ever worked in the supposedly 'proletarian' industries of mining and shipbuilding were slightly more conservative than
the remainder of the sample.   But, of course, selective turnover
might be operating, so that the most radical farm workers and the
most conservative miners leave their industries (and appear in our
sample).   If this is so, then the 'traditional' industries might
be retaining labour forces with an homogeneous 'image of society'
(cf. Lockwood, Chapter 2) only because they are steadily losing
manpower.   As most writers in this area stress the stability of
industries associated with 'traditional' images of society, it
should not surprise them that such images are not found in the more
dynamic urban/industrial sector of the economy.

The large number of ex-agricultural and ex-mining workers points
to the heterogeneity of the sample.   So too do the birthplaces of

the sample, for only 38 per cent were born within 10 miles of
Peterborough, while 21 per cent were born outside of the United
Kingdom.   There is little variation in ideology among the different regional and national groups.   The Commonwealth immigrants
(from India, Pakistan and the West Indies) are marginally the most
radical, while the groups from Italy and Eastern Europe, while no
more radical, are more homogeneous than the British Isles groups,
(13) possibly indicating the existence of sub-cultures.   Religion
overlaps slightly with birthplace in that the Moslems fall exclusively within the 'Commonwealth' regional group and Italians are
almost all Catholics (the remainder are atheists).   The Moslems
emerge as the most radical, followed by the atheists and Protestant
'sects', while the Catholics, Church of England and other Protestant
'churches' tend to be relatively conservative.   Again the differences are not great, however.
     Home ownership might be expected to relate to ideology, and
indeed owners are slightly more conservative than council renters
and clearly more conservative than those paying board and lodging.
But these differences are largely a product of age.   The youngest
workers (who are most radical) are more likely to be paying board
and lodging while older workers are disproportionately conservative
home-owners.   If we control for age, then type of tenure actually
discriminates according to age: it makes no difference at all among
the youngest, creates slight effects in middle age, and only becomes
marked among those aged over 55. (14)   Perhaps the right-wing young
workers will become house-owners when they become older; or perhaps
with around 40 per cent of manual workers now owning their own homes,
property ownership is less of a discriminator than hitherto.

CONSISTENCY

So far we have established that a left-right ideological dimension
does exist in the workers' consciousness, and that it does relate to
certain other aspects of the workers' lives.   However, it can
hardly be described as dominant.   Correlations of ideology with
other variables are consistently low, and so are they also with the
nine ideology indicators (see Table 8.2).   Let us now look a little
further at the pattern of responses in these components of our
ideology measure.
     For each worker we calculated the standard deviation of his
scores on the nine items.   This may be regarded as a measure of his
ideological consistency or rather inconsistency; the higher the
standard deviation, the more variation in the ideological positions
taken up on the various items. (15)   The mean value is 5.7, which
is not particularly large compared with the standard deviation of
2.94 for the distribution of mean ideology scores (T/9) over the
sample. (16)   On the other hand it does suggest a high degree of
individual inconsistency.   As the range on each item is only 24,
three standard deviations is more than half the range.
     The ideology items do not logically interrelate, so it is quite
possible for a worker to hold compatible views on different items,
which are ideologically inconsistent.   For example he may seriously
hold a 'left' view on workers' rights to profits and a 'right' view

on workers' control.   The question then arises whether he is
giving greater importance to the particular issues than the underlying ideological dimensions or whether he is just confused.   The
former suggests coherent images of society in which the left-right
ideological dimension has low salience, while confusion suggests an
absence of any clear ideological perception (or a failure to understand the question).

To sort out confusion from what we may call the 'pragmatic'
images, we must introduce questions of the specific meaning of the
items.   Though this is a difficult and somewhat subjective venture,
it seems to us that some pairs of items are closer or more contradictory in their meanings.   Perhaps the most directly contradictory
are item 3, 'All managements will try to put one over on the workers
if they get the chance' and item 5, 'Most managements have the
welfare of their workers at heart'.   To agree with both does seem
to indicate some confusion, though we should not overlook the
possibility that they answer with different frames of reference -
the managers mean well but it is part of the managerial role to
'put one over' (see Beynon and Blackburn, 1972).   Then item 6,
'Managers know what's best for the firm, and workers should do just
what they're told' and item 8, 'Giving workers more say in running
their firms would only make things worse', clearly overlap.   Also
item 8 appears to contradict 1, 'Most decisions taken by foremen and
supervisors would be better if they were taken by the workers themselves', though it would be just consistent to approve of workers'
control at the shopfloor level while denying control at the level
of the 'firm' (or vice versa).   Finally, item 6, regarded this
time in terms of its emphasis on obedience, may be considered to
overlap with 9, 'loyalty', at least in everyday usage.   If workers
are not confused these groups of items should be particularly well
related so, bearing in mind our adjustment to the directions of
measurement, the correlations should be relatively high and positive
in each case.   On the whole this is what we find (see Table 8.2);
'welfare' and 'deception' do produce the highest correlation of all;
'obedience' is relatively highly correlated with 'workers' control'
and 'loyalty'; but the correlation between 'workers' control' and
'workers' decisions' is just below average.   The 'pragmatic'
relations of responses can perhaps best be seen from a factor analysis with varimax rotation.   The first factor is dominated by
'welfare' and 'deception' together with 'loyalty' and 'teamwork'
and to a lesser extent 'obedience'.   The items relate in a general
'support for management' syndrome.   The second factor concerns
management/workers control, bringing together 6, 8 and 1 - 'obedience' (though here, presumably, under the aspect 'management know
best'), 'workers' control' and 'workers' decisions'.   However,
the last is more clearly associated in a third factor with 'more
profits to the workers' which makes little sense other than both
items demand more for the workers. (17)   Finally 'agitators' is,
not unreasonably, the basis of a separate factor.   Altogether the
pattern is too clear to support an hypothesis of general confusion.
On the other hand, with the highest correlation of 0.28 there is a
high degree of inconsistency.   To be sure, consistent pragmatic
answers do not require everyone seeing a pair of similar items in
quite the same way, so we should not expect too high correlations.

Nevertheless, it seems clear that pragmatism, in the sense of response to the specific substance of an item (possibly intermixed with confusion) far outweighs ideology, for our sample.

It seems clear that in the consciousness of our sample as a whole, ideology plays little part.   Of course, it may be argued that we have chosen a sample which is so diverse as to ensure variety in ideology.   Coming from different ethnic and social backgrounds and employed in different work situations, we should expect them to differ also in their images of society.   It is possible that there exist distinct sub-cultures within the non-skilled working class, such as, for example, occupational communities.   If this is so, our generally inconsistent picture may be made up either of distinct groups, each with coherent but different images of society, or a majority with low ideology and a few committed groups who may serve as a source of ideological leadership.   The first possibility hardly seems tenable in view of the high inconsistency scores of many of the sample, and further doubt will be cast on it in considering the second.   We shall, therefore, direct our attention to looking for one or more ideologically consistent groups.

It has frequently been argued that in isolated working-class communities sub-cultures develop in which radicalism flourishes. This we cannot test with our data, but if the sub-culture remains isolated it cannot provide ideological leadership.   Such leadership must reach the mass of the workers.   Hence it is an important question whether there are groups in a section of the working class such as we have studied within which there is a strong consistent ideology.

We have, therefore, examined the correlations of ideology with other variables for a sub-sample of the more ideologically consis-tent workers, as measured by their standard deviations.   If they belong to ideological sub-cultures we may expect appreciably higher correlations, but in fact there is no significant difference. However, the more consistent tend to be more right-wing, which supports the view that right-wing values are the orthodox dominant ideology and radicalism is opposition to the established norms - 'deviant' as Parkin (1967) expresses it.   Those whose views are continually reinforced by the dominant values, i.e. the right, are more consistent.   Now the question that arises is under what conditions the left-wing 'deviance' can flourish, and the usual answer directs us back to sub-cultures, particularly in occupational communities.

The search for sub-cultures is one for discontinuities in our data, and it may be argued that seeking for correlations, even over the relatively consistent sub-sample, is still searching for linear-ity.   We must look for definable groups or sections of the popula-tion who share a common ideological position.   The ideological coherence of such groups may be assessed by the standard deviations of the scores within it.

Participation in trade unionism might be expected to provide the basis of a radical sub-culture, but we have already noted there is reason to doubt the socialisation effect of contact with unionism. To be sure, members are more radical on the average but they are no more coherent (in the sense of sharing similar ideological positions) than non-members.   We might well expect to find the activists who

hold office to provide the basis of ideological leadership and they
certainly do tend to be more radical, though individually no more
consistent.   They also tend to be more homogeneous but it is doubtful if they interact sufficiently to be regarded as forming a sub-
culture.

Ethnic and religious background are two factors which might lead
to distinctive ideological groupings, and we have already noted
slightly differing ideological positions.   However they are not
internally cohesive except where the two combine in the group of
Moslems.   These workers were more radical and more homogeneous than
any other group.   For reasons of language, culture and racial
prejudice they were probably the most socially isolated of all the
workers, and so the most insulated from the dominant values.   For
the same reasons they were also those least able to provide ideological leadership for the mass of workers.

Occupational communities are probably the most important potential source of coherent images of society.   As a first step we may
consider the various firms of our sample.   Workers tended to have
friends and sometimes relations who worked for the same employer,
so we might have expected greater consistency within firms than
across the whole sample but, as Table 8.7 shows, there was little
trend in this direction.   The exceptions were two of the smaller
firms.   In Bettles, a building firm, the sample was small, so the
difference from the rest is not significant.   The milk roundsmen
of Horrells are exceptional in being fairly consistently right-wing,
which may seem to indicate a distinctive sub-culture.   However, a
basic feature of their common occupation is the low interaction
with each other (and high interaction with the public).   They are
not so much a group with shared ideology as individuals with similar
work situations attracting men with, or causing them to have,
similar ideological perceptions.

The brickworkers probably come closest to fitting the model of a
'traditional proletarian' occupational community and we see that
they did score above average on radicalism and consistency, but
they were not markedly different from the rest.   Railway workers
might also be regarded as approximating an occupational community
but they were little different from the average.   The most radical
firm is Perkins, though there is fairly high variation in the workforce.   Here the work resembles the stereotype of a car plant,
dominated by the production line, while the firm is recognised
throughout the area as providing the best pay for the least hours.
This is just where we might expect the workers to be most instrumental.

If workers form an occupational community we would expect many of
them to have friends and relations in the occupations.   We do not
have information for the whole area but the larger employers tend to
cover the whole of their own occupation anyway.   Furthermore, if
an occupational community includes more than one firm its coherence
should be at least as great in each firm.   Accordingly we have
considered those with relations (brothers, fathers, father-in-law)
working in the same firm.   For friends we have taken a stronger
measure, the number of friends with whom he actually works.   Altogether, 34 per cent of the sample name at least one workmate among
their closest friends, and 25 per cent have a brother or father

TABLE 8.7   Ideology and size of firm

	Perkins	London Brick	Baker Perkins	British Rail	P'boro' Corp.	Farrows	Bettles	Combex	Horrells	All
Size	6000	3000	2000	1500	250	120	80	75	50	—
Mean F-score	0.9	-0.3	-4.3	-1.8	-1.3	-1.4	-2.2	-1.5	-7.1	-1.5
Standard deviation*	10.5	9.1	10.7	9.4	9.0	10.6	6.9	11.5	8.0	10.0
N	190	172	155	159	121	49	16	32	32	926

* As the mean F - scores do not differ greatly when compared to the whole range of possible scores, it was considered unnecessary to standardise for the mean by calculating coefficients of variability.

(in-law) working in the same firm.   These percentages vary by firm
and the highest are at London Brick with 45 per cent naming a workmate as a friend and 40 per cent with relations in the firm, British
Rail where 43 per cent had relations working, and Baker Perkins with
40 per cent who had friends as workmates.   This supports the idea
of brickworkers forming an occupational community, and to a lesser
extent the argument applies to railwaymen.   At Baker Perkins this
characteristic goes with relatively varied right-wing ideology.

At what point we can begin to talk of 'occupational communities'
when dealing with such variables is uncertain.   Yet the relatively
tightly knit groups should have more similar attitudes than the
others if the concept has empirical utility.   Hence we separated
within each firm those who claimed a friend or relative there from
those who did not.   If occupational community factors were
influencing ideology, then the standard deviation of the former
groups' ideology scores should be smaller than the latter.   However, no such trend is to be found.   There are as many differences
in the unexpected direction as in the expected.   In all firms,
those with relations there (though not those with friends) tend to
be more radical than those without, but the differences are fairly
low.

Our consideration of sub-cultures and occupational communities
has revealed some evidence of their relevance, but not much.   There
are no major sections of the labour force with strong sub-cultural
ideologies.

WORKING-CLASS IDEOLOGY

Our analysis so far seems to suggest a low importance for ideology,
with only weak relationships with other variables and a general
absence of consistent radical ideology.   However, it would be
wrong to infer from this that the workers have images of society
devoid of ideological content.   We propose a rather different
interpretation, but first we must consider another possible explanation - that our measures are ineffective for technical reasons.

There can be no absolute assurance on this, but the explanation
seems unlikely.   It may be claimed the method of asking the
ideology questions or their contents are inappropriate, though they
are of a sort used in other studies, so that if we have fallen down
here a lot of previous research falls with us.   Anyway, workers
will respond very readily to the kind of individual cue we gave
them;   it is merely that their responses do not necessarily add up
to a structured whole.   Many studies have demonstrated that
respondents give meaningful answers within the frame of reference
of their own interpretation.   Only if the salient features of two
questions are seen in the same frame of reference should we expect
consistency from a respondent.   We may also note that the low
levels of association discussed in this paper are not so unusual
as it may seem.   What is unusual is that we have deliberately
made explicit the strengths of relationships.   Our strategy
stands in contrast to the conventional procedures of leaving
measurement assumptions implicit so that the strength of relationships cannot be tested, or of using statistical significance as a
sufficient basis for an argument.

   Probably the most potent criticism is that we have inadvisedly
attempted to use continuous scales on each item.   Those with
coherent ideological views might operate with dichotomous images,
rather than see things in terms of continua.   But this argument
is not supported by our data.   When we grouped the responses
around the seven worded points on the scale, the average inter-
item correlation fell from 0.11 to 0.08 and fell still further to
0.05 with the three-point scale (Agree, Unsure, Disagree).   Some
workers may have encountered difficulty with our continuous scale,
but on the whole it seems to be superior to the more conventional
use of a limited set of alternatives.
   Also we must repeat that the method has been successful.   We
have found a meaningful ideological dimension.   It may, nevertheless, be objected that we have been measuring the wrong thing, and
in one specific sense we would not entirely disagree.   The contradictions, or apparent contradictions in responses to ideology items
indicate that the left-right ideological aspect was in no way
dominant in their responses.   If this ideological dimension were
the dominant frame of reference, they would tend to be consistent
on all items.   Similarly their inconsistency, as measured by the
relatively high standard deviations of their scores, points to the
same thing.   Ideology is of low salience in their consciousness.
But if the left-right dimension has little importance, do other
ideological components, which we have not measured, enter into
their images of society?   To some extent we would answer in the
affirmative, and we will return to this point presently.   At this
stage we must stress that low salience is not to be confused with
absence of ideology or holding a neutral position.
   The crucial issue is our understanding of the workers' perceptions of society.   The first point to make is that, paradoxically,
the apparent inconsistency of ideological positions is really an
indication of uniformity in the sample.   We are looking at variance
around a point on an ideological dimension which distinguishes our
respondents from other parts of the British population but produces
little real differentiation within the section of the working class
from which the sample was drawn.   In other words, our sample is
relatively homogeneous in ideology.   The nine ideology items are
indicators of the workers' 'true' ideological positions, but on
each item the whole sample tend to have the same expected value,
with deviations from this value randomly distributed.   Since each
item is essentially an indication of the same ideological position
for everyone, there is little relationship between items, i.e. the
correlations are low.   Perhaps this point is most clearly seen in
terms of latent structure analysis.   If our sample are ideologically homogeneous they may be regarded as forming a 'latent class'
and hence in keeping with the axiom of local independence, the
answers of each respondent on the various items are independent.
Members of another 'latent class', which would here be occupants of
a different class position (in a sociological sense) would have a
different set of expected values on each indicator, but within that
class also there would be no relation between indicators.   Furthermore the ideological homogeneity of our sample leads to the low
relationships with the various independent variables.   It is
probable that if a sample were drawn with ideology scores over the

whole range to be found in the country, then correlations with
other variables would be high, but because we cover only a narrow
range of ideology the 'errors' become disproportionatly important
and correlations fall.

We must not overstress the homogeneity of the sample. There are
ideological differences, reflected in the persistent, if low
correlations.   In fact the differences between the extremes of our
sample are quite substantial, and a sub-sample of workers at these
extremes gives appreciably higher associations between ideology and
other variables.   However, the workers are mostly clustered in a
rather narrow range, so that 'errors' contribute substantially to
the distribution of scores.   In saying this it should be clearly
understood that 'errors' refers not so much to mistakes in measurement (though these will exist) as to contributions to the score
arising from elements in the workers' answers due to influences
independent of the ideology dimension being measured.   In sociology,
as distinct from statistics, 'error' is usually of this type.

We have argued that in our sample there is both homogeneity and
low salience of ideology.   Since either could produce low correlations between the nine ideology items, how can we separate their
effects?   First, the highly individual variance and apparent
contradictions can only be attributed·to low salience of ideology.
Second, both the variance between workers and the correlations of
ideology with other variables are low, which points to homogeneity.
However, to clinch the matter, and rule out the possibility of
explanation in terms of bad measures, we need some external criterion of the workers' homogeneity.

We would like to make direct comparison with other studies of
manual workers and of other social strata.   The position of fully
skilled workers is of especial interest in delineating the unity or
diversity of the working class.   This is not yet possible, however,
because of the paucity of other studies, and because identical
questions to ours have not been used (other studies have generally
used the fixed-choice questions which we have criticised).   While
awaiting further research, we can merely point to the general
tendency revealed in most studies for significantly different left-
right ideological position to be found in different levels of the
social stratification system (for a review, see Mann, 1970).

So if our sample share a common ideological position distinct
from other sections of the population, we would expect them to
share a common class position. (18)   In a broad sense we know this
is so, since our sample is restricted to non-skilled manual workers.
On the other hand, the sample was chosen to encompass a wide variety
of work and market situations, within the range available to such
workers.   We therefore needed to test whether the broad position is
relevant to their consciousness (bearing in mind that variations
within the broad class position may still relate to the variations
in ideology which do exist).   To do this we used the Cambridge
measure of class status.   The theory and form of this measure is
described elsewhere (Stewart et al., 1973), and we need only note
here that it is a relational measure, using smallest space multi-
dimensional scaling of the occupations of respondents and their
friends.   Whereas there is one clear class-status dimension for
occupations drawn from the whole population, it was barely discern-

ible within our sample.   Interaction was predominantly with other
non-skilled manual workers, and such differentiation as there was
within this stratum reflected residence and place of work rather
than any internal stratification.   In relational terms, therefore,
our sample do share a common class position.

CONCLUSION

It seems clear that the majority of our sample of non-skilled
workers occupy very similar ideological positions.   In spite of
the diversity of their work and market situations, their fundamental
similarity of class position has led to similarity on the ideological dimension.   At the same time this ideological dimension is of
low salience in their images of society.
     The study is based on one locality, the town of Peterborough and
it may be objected that we have lighted on an unusual situation.
There are regional variations and if our research were conducted
elsewhere we might find strong ideological images.   Yet a recent
study by Cotgrove and Vamplew (1972) which finds strong regional
differences, does not run as contrary to our model as might be
supposed.   The differences they find vary according to two factors:
the number of white-collar affiliations of the workers, and the
industrial relations record of each firm (the latter counteracting
the effects of the former in the case of their South Wales and
Manchester samples).   The latter is somewhat unsatisfactory without
further analysis, in that it might be attributable to the workers'
prior images of society or to other in-plant factors, such as the
managerial control system, which are not held constant in the study.
But the former is in line with the findings reported here.   The
distinctively working-class image of society is radical, or
'proletarian', and the greater the contact with the working class,
the more radical the worker.   Of course there are variations,
including working-class communities with strong radical ideologies,
but there is nothing in our analysis to suggest that Peterborough
workers differ greatly from those in similar class positions elsewhere.   Nor is this so surprising.   There never has been and
there is not now a working-class movement with the support of the
great majority of workers.   It is then hardly remarkable that there
is no great unifying proletarian ideology.
     As explained, Peterborough is socially highly heterogeneous.   So
if ideology is not dominant throughout we might nevertheless expect
ideological sub-cultures.   Yet there is little evidence of this
either.   In fact, a priori, the heterogeneity might be seen as a
help or hindrance to the existence of distinctive ideological
beliefs.   The industries, ethnic groups, and residential groups
might be relatively well insulated from each other, so that 'sub-
culture' could flourish;   or they might rub off on each other and
cancel out the idiosyncracies.   The temptation is to jump to the
latter interpretation of our results.   But it is worth asking just
how likely it is that Pakistanis, Italians and United Kingdom
citizens of various kinds are to 'rub off on each other' in the
context of modern Britain.   And in what circumstances different
industrial cultures will not rub off on each other, if industries

as diverse as the ones in our sample do so?   And where can inter-
acting urban and rural cultures remain separate, if industrial
Peterborough and the East Anglian fenlands cannot?   The answer is
clear: that sub-cultures are the product of isolation, and can only
exist in settings where the individual is excluded from membership
in the wider society.   That is why they are the property of
exploited classes and geographically and economically isolated
communities.   It is significant that the workers who come closest
to an ideological community are the Asian Moslems.   Yet all of our
workers, even those whose wives live in Purdah, live in the same
economic society.   When the economy falters, they are all threat-
ened - in the two years subsequent to our interviewing, redundancies
were announced in six of the organisations in the study and rumoured
in another two.   They are also in touch with rival interpretations
of their common reality.   Through the mass media and workplace
interaction they learn that 'strikes are caused by agitators and
extremists', that 'loyalty' is a much-prized virtue but also that
men should work for their living (and shareholders clearly do not),
and that management 'think only of profits'.   There is only one
ideological sub-culture to which workers can adhere, the working-
class 'proletarian' ideology, and very few are positively committed
to it.   Most remain confused by the clash between conservatism and
proletarianism, but touched by both.   Which workers are not in this
situation?   There are no other systematic images possible for the
worker who is actually a part of industrial society.

We do not wish to appear to end on a slightly patronising tone.
If the workers in our sample are 'confused' then they have every
right to be, for that is an accurate reflection of the reality that
confronts them.   What are they to make of normal affluence and
sensible industrial relations on the one hand, and intermittent
redundancy and authoritarianism on the other?   For that matter,
what are we - practising sociologists, paid to contemplate such
problems - to make of them?   If we must admit that sociology provides no coherent theory of society, or of capitalist society, then
our own images are also 'confused'.   Yet it is perhaps possible to
make a virtue out of this defect, by moving away from the usual
Durkheimian or vulgar Marxian conception of society as a structured
whole, to one that views society as structured around a fundamental
contradiction.   Society is co-operation in pursuit of scarcity,
and from this stems its unstable dialectic.   This may not take us
far towards a theory of society, but it does enable us to make more
sense of workers' images.   For instead of viewing them as approxim-
ations to consistent and coherent images, we should regard them as
attempts to grapple with the real contradictions of the worker's
situation.   In fact, the 'images' described in this paper are
attempts by the workers to compound the two possible (and contradictory) world views in this society: Mannheim's (1936) 'ideology'
of the ruling class, and 'utopia' of the proletariat.

Despite the contradictions, however, one further principle of
unity characterised the consciousness of these workers, reflecting
their own powerlessness.   They tend to accept but not legitimate
their present position, and so do not see the relevance of a
political ideology concerned with social changes in areas more
remote than the structures they know and accept.   They are well

aware that things might be better, yet they tend to express 'satisfaction' with their work;   they find little in their experience to
suggest that fundamental changes are possible. Their discontent is
expressed more clearly in their 'generalised demands'.   The items
of this question tapped views of the inevitable unfairness of the
world of work - an unjust situation which has to be put up with.
It is very revealing that this question above all others was closely
related to our ideology measure.   Their ideological perceptions
relate to the reality of their own lives, lived within the apparently inevitable constraints of an existing social structure, and not
to intellectual political ideas.   Only when they become conscious
of a possibility to change society are they likely to encompass it
intellectually and adopt a coherent utopia.

Finally, we would like to point the way for further research
into 'images of society'.   In a sense, our methodology has successfully made itself obsolete.   Our demonstration that coherent, consistent ideologies in the conventional sense do not exist now
renders inadequate our kind of attitude survey data.   However, we
should very clearly reject the charge that attitude surveys could
not even in principle illuminate this field.   It is only by using
this method that we have tested (to the extent that sociology ever
'tests') and found wanting the hypothesis that workers possessed,
either as a class or in sub-cultures, consistent and coherent
images of society.   It is now necessary to move on to other methods
because of our demonstration.   The way forward does not lie with
the traditional critic of the survey method, the omniscient narrator
of most qualitative studies.   We may suspect that the coherence
of the story lies in the narrator's art rather than in empirical
reality.   At the very least, we should know - as the ethnomethodol-
ogists observe - how writers like Goffman, or in the field of
ideology Robert Lane, got their dope.   Hence the research we now
favour would make as clear as does the survey method the nature
of the investigator's stimulus as well as the worker's response,
and would add to that more persistent and explicit probing of
possible structures of response.   We need to know not simply the
final result of whether workers are able to synthesise ideological
contradictions, but also the process by which they attempt to do
this.   One method would be an intensive, though structured, set of
discussions with individual workers, actually challenging them about
contradictory lines of thought.   Another would be discussions among
groups of workers in which argument is encouraged.   Complementing
these would be projective techniques using hypothetical situations
of ideological significance.   Alongside these approaches there
remains a need for more methodologically conscious studies of
workers' responses to actual contradictory situations, not only the
occasional dramatic strike but also more mundane day to day
processes of accommodation.   Whatever the approach, the methods
should be integrated to the theory, and be seen to be integrated.

NOTES

1 This work arises out of a larger research project supported by
   the SSRC.   The strategy of data collection was not specifically

designed for the present purpose.   We should also like to acknowledge help and advice from our colleagues in the Department of Applied Economics at Cambridge, Ken Prandy, Sandy Stewart and Joyce Wheeler.

2 A correlation of just over 0.06 is significant at the 5 per cent level for a sample of this size, or applying a one tail test, since we clearly predicted positive correlations in this case, the relevant coefficient is just over 0.05.   This is a very small correlation, because of the large size of our sample, and more attention will be paid to the levels of correlations and the consistency between them than to their significance levels.

3 Though the more items there are, the less any one can influence the total.

4 Table 8.8 shows the correlations between variables discussed. The key to Table 8.8 is as follows:
   1 Ideology (radicalism) F
   2 Ideology (radicalism) T
   3 Inconsistency of ideology
   4 Generalised demands
   5 Job satisfaction
   6 Life satisfaction
   7 Age
   8 Number of times unemployed
   9 Involuntary moves, per cent
   10 Wages per week
   11 Highest job held
   12 Present job
   13 Father's job
   14 Union commitment
   15 Family union membership
   16 Rurality of birthplace
   17 Rurality of present home
   18 Jobs in agriculture, per cent

5 Several of our measures are only at the ordinal level, but for convenience they have been treated as though they were interval measures, and product moment correlations calculated between all variables.   When the ordinal categories are few, as with unionism, the relationship is liable to be underestimated.   Such checks as are possible indicate similar results, e.g. calculating phi.   However, when correlating ordinal data with an interval level variable (e.g. ideology) there is always uncertainty about appropriate cutting points.

6 The path from generalised demands to life satisfaction is only significant at the 10 per cent level provided we are willing to accept a one tail test, on the ground that the sign is in keeping with the hypothesised causal model.   All other paths are significant at the 5 per cent level at least, for one or two tail tests.

7 This sounds plausible but it leaves a problem of how more general attitudes can be formed.   Perhaps an interaction model would be best, but it would not change the general argument.

8 Correlating ranking by size with ranking by mean ideology score of employees gives Kendall's tau = 0.5.

TABLE 8.8 Ideology and selected variables : correlations

	1	2	3	4	5	6	7	8	9	10	11	12	13	14	15	16	17	18
1	1.00																	
2	.97	1.00																
3	.11	.14	1.00															
4	.50	.46	.07	1.00														
5	-.29	-.26	-.04	-.26	1.00													
6	-.18	-.16	-.06	-.13	.29	1.00												
7	-.25	-.24	-.10	-.22	.23	.14	1.00											
8	.02	.01	.02	.04	-.04	-.05	.06	1.00										
9	-.04	-.04	.00	-.02	-.01	.00	.12	.20	1.00									
10	.04	.05	.03	.01	.04	.04	-.06	-.14	-.07	1.00								
11	-.14	-.13	-.01	-.09	.01	.00	.02	-.08	.01	.01	1.00							
12	-.03	-.03	.02	.03	.03	.03	.02	-.16	-.08	.15	.21	1.00						
13	-.07	-.09	-.10	-.03	-.03	-.03	.01	-.07	.00	.08	.15	.03	1.00					
14	.13	.14	.08	.11	-.03	.05	.05	-.08	-.09	.18	.00	.10	-.06	1.00				
15	-.02	.01	.09	.01	.11	.07	.05	-.04	-.03	.08	-.01	.12	-.25	.10	1.00			
16	.00	.00	-.06	.03	-.03	.01	.04	-.03	.02	.06	-.10	-.11	-.10	-.04	-.07	1.00		
17	.06	.03	.07	.04	-.05	-.04	-.11	-.06	.04	-.03	.03	.01	-.13	.04	-.02	.17	1.00	
18	.01	.01	-.11	-.03	.02	.07	.14	.00	1.02	-.02	-.22	-.12	-.09	-.03	-.08	.36	.19	1.00

9   See the data reported in Blackburn and Mann, 1973.
10 Comprising seven categories of which numbers 3-7 are divided
    according to a preliminary scrutiny of our job scores data;
    1 = High non-manual (Registrar-General's social class I and II,
        excluding technicians).
    2 = Low non-manual (R.G.'s social class III, plus technicians,
        foremen).
    3 = Skilled (all trades for which apprenticeship or extensive
        qualifying period - e.g. railway engine crews - is
        necessary).
    4 = High semi-skilled (engine testers, furnace operators,
        store-keepers, highly specialised workers).
    5 = Medium semi-skilled (oilers and similar maintenance workers,
        complex machining, specialised railwaymen, drivers, store-
        men with clerical duties).
    6 = Low semi-skilled (mates, assemblers, routine machining,
        specialised labouring).
    7 = Unskilled (machine-minders, cleaners, labourers, warehouse-
        men).
11 See, for example, Form and Geschwender, 1962; Laslet, 1971, in
    examining inter-generational mobility, suggests that the effect
    on job satisfaction is essentially due to present job since
    father's occupation has little effect and there is no need to
    introduce an interaction term for mobility experience, in the
    explanation.   Our data do not seem to support this view.   As
    Bohrnstedt (1969), points out, the correlation of the gap
    between two variables with a third variable (here satisfaction)
    is a function of the separate correlations of the two original
    variables with the third.   In this sense there is no inter-
    action term needed.   Bohrnstedt also demonstrates the inappro-
    priateness of a gap as a measure of change.   The problem here
    is that it confounds the effect of the worker's present job.
    If we partially correlate the gap with satisfaction controlling
    for present job, this is equivalent to the partial correlation
    of previous level alone (father's level, highest, etc.) control-
    ling for present job, as recommended by Bohrnstedt.   The rela-
    tive effect of previous levels (i.e. the effect of mobility) is
    then rather greater than that implied by zero order correlation.
12 Generalised demands closely follow ideology in all job level and
    'gap' measures.
13 Homogeneity measured by lower variance of ideology scores.
14 Also age differences wholly account for the fact that single men
    are more left-wing than married men.
15 To allow for the fact that the items themselves may scale, as
    reflected by their different mean scores, we measured from these
    item means in calculating standard deviations.
16 As we would expect, variance between individuals is significantly
    greater than variance 'within' individuals, (F = 2.1). This may
    be regarded as another check on the validity of the ideology
    score.   However, the strength of the association is not partic-
    ularly great; the proportion of variation on the item scores
    explained by the mean scores of individuals is given by $E^2 = 0.21$.

17 The result of the 'profits to the workers' question is suffic-
    iently interesting in its own right: 50 per cent agreed while
    only 27 per cent disagreed (the rest being unsure).   This is
    easily the most radical response from our sample.   It may
    indicate that whereas, as the other questions revealed, manage-
    ments are viewed ambivalently by the workers, shareholders are
    viewed with hostility (an acceptance of bureaucracy but not of
    capitalism?)
18 The possible explanation in terms of a distinctive socialisation
    in the same town falls down because of the diverse regional and
    cultural backgrounds of the workers.

Part three

THEORY AND METHODOLOGY

Chapter 9

SOME PROBLEMS OF RESEARCH INTO CLASS IMAGERY

Martin Bulmer

A major lacuna in the recent literature on class imagery is the absence of detailed methodological discussion (in both its more general and more specific senses) of some of the problems associated with its study.   Several of these issues are raised and considered in the papers in this third section.   What is the nature of images? What is the status of ideal types? What is the empirical support for implicit historical comparisons? What is the status of the concept occupational community? What is the nature of sociability and of communal solidarity?   What is the relationship between the abstract categories of the sociologist and the flux and change of the real world?   Since a number of these issues are germane to future research upon class imagery, some of the questions which they raise are perhaps worth sketching in outline by way of introduction. (1)

THE NATURE OF SOCIAL IMAGERY

Sociologists spend much time establishing the status of concepts which they use to organise the study of social reality.   The analytical concepts 'social class' and 'status group', for example, are abstractions from the real world which are not necessarily direct representations of reality.   At the other extreme, concepts used to denote empirical entities raise questions about those entities. Does, for example, the Mafia exist? What is the nature of glossolalia (Speaking with Tongues)?   What are the origins of witchcraft beliefs and accusations?   Are the concepts 'Mafia', 'glossolalia', 'witchcraft', unambiguous and immediately intelligible?   Problems of both an analytic and empirical kind are posed by the use of the concept of social 'images'.   What is the status of the concept, and does it denote anything real?

These very complex questions are tackled in Willener's paper in this section and run through the majority of the earlier contributions.   In particular, the consistency, stability and content of social images are all discussed at length.   On the consistency of social images, an issue of both analytic and empirical significance, there is strong disagreement.   Early work on social imagery suggested that it was possible to identify consistent and cohesive images of society (e.g. Willener, 1957, p.213), a view recently restated by Goldthorpe (1970a, pp.334-6) with modifications in respect of the range of respondents' social experience.   Blackburn and Mann, on the other hand (in Chapter 8), argue both that the images elicited by empirical research are confused and contradictory, and that this is what one would expect; it is a reflection of the contradictions with which a worker is faced in a capitalist society.   Consistent images of society are only to be found in situations of exceptional social stability (as in geographically isolated settlements with an immobile population, associated with particular heavy industries).   Cousins and Brown (in Chapter 4) argue for an intermediate position, where out of confusion it is possible nevertheless to discern patterns of responses.   The issue is not easily resolvable, and is likely to remain an open one.   In part it turns upon whether one expects to find consistent images of society (a conceptual issue).   In part it turns on whether one does appear to find consistent images (an empirical issue).   In part it depends on how one approaches empirical investigation of images (a methodological issue).   It is at least possible that the 'brisk interview' in a social survey is not the ideal means of eliciting actors' perceptions of the world (a point developed below).   Studies using alternative approaches, such as extended interviews with a small number of respondents (e.g. Lane, 1962), have suggested that there may be a greater degree of consistency than is apparent in the analysis of survey results.   How far does the consistency of images depend upon the research situation and the means by which actors' images are elicited?

On the stability of images there is more agreement.   The stable and timeless images of the ideal type, when compared to the flux of the images held in the real world, stand in the same relation as an abstract pen-and-ink drawing of a situation or object and a cine film of the same situation or object.   The issue is rendered more complex by the variety of social forces impinging upon an individual actor, so that the presumption of his image of society remaining stable over a lifetime appears rather unlikely.   In addition to the work and community milieux which Lockwood identified as being associated with the formation of certain types of images, there are the influences of the wider society, of the macrostructure, which Willener (Chapter 10) and Westergaard (Chapter 15) both point to. And as Willener suggests, the value of studying crisis situations (such as strikes or political conflicts) is crucially relevant to the issue of how stable images of society are held to be.   The isolated single-industry community, as embodied in the ideal type, appears very much as a limiting case in the analysis of the sources of stability and instability of social imagery over time.

As far as the content of imagery is concerned, conceptual considerations are not unimportant.   Is one concerned with the descriptive or the normative elements in imagery?   Is one concerned with the Gestalt of a particular individual, or the 'deposit of ideas' of an occupational group or sub-culture?   Is one concerned with patterns, perspectives, imagery or visions (to use the distinctions suggested by Willener)?   Empirical aspects of content, however, come to the fore.   The predominant element in the empir-

ical research is the heterogeneity and diversity of images elicited,
in comparison to the clear simplicity of the ideal type.   As
Cousins and Brown suggest, one should allow for a greater degree of
indeterminacy in the relationship between structural position and
imagery held than the ideal type suggests.   In part, the identification of certain work and community milieux with certain types of
imagery does not fit perfectly with the emphasis, in Bott's original
hypothesis, upon an individual's 'experience of power and prestige
in his actual membership groups and social relationships past and
present' (Bott, 1957, p.163).   One would expect there to be a good
deal of actual variation in social imagery, even in a single-
industry community with a geographically isolated immobile population.   In part, too, the conceptual specification of an actor's
'orientation' to work, to community, to society, to class implies a
consistency which is an abstraction from the diversity which is
found in practice.   In relating images to social structure, the
most immediately realisable aim is to show congruences between
particular social characteristics and particular types of imagery,
rather than to demonstrate necessary causal relationships between
the one and the other.

   Indeed, the problems associated with the nature of imagery are
generalisable to the study of culture more generally.   The variety,
diffuseness and lack of precision evident in the study of imagery
does not mean that the investigation of the social sources of their
variation is misconceived.   Rather it underlines the point that
subjective aspects of social action and social relations are by
definition idiosyncratic, particularistic and relatively formless.
One does not therefore abandon the sociological study of culture,
however.   For the central question remains: what is the relationship between structure and culture, between the relatively exact
indicators of structural position in society and the diffuse or
elusive meanings and interpretations which men hold about their
own society? (2)   It is often remarked that the sociological study
of culture is in its infancy.   Perhaps the sociological study of
imagery is a case in point.

PROBLEMS OF RESEARCH PROCEDURE

The study of social imagery does not raise only conceptual and
substantive issues.   It has also thrown up a series of methodological problems which centre around how an action frame of reference
can be operationalised in carrying out empirical research.   'Opera-
tionalise' is not used in its strict positivistic sense, but rather
to indicate the problem of how to bridge the gulf between the
sociologist's theoretical constructs and the actual operations
(research design, data collection, analysis) which are necessitated
by any attempt to confront theory with data.   The papers in this
volume present a wide range of findings, varying in their form in
terms of size of sample interviewed, kinds and degree of structuring of questions asked, mode of coding the results so obtained, and
rigour of analysing the numerical results.   They share, however,
a quite striking reliance upon interview data gathered by a social
survey, the method used almost universally to date in the sociologi-

cal study of social imagery.   Moore's paper is the only report of
empirical research not relying mainly upon social survey data.
This tendency in the reporting of results in partly belied by the
actual conduct of research.   All of the research projects reported
in Part Two involved one or more of the authors in extended periods
of observation in the work or community milieux with which they were
concerned.   Yet this experience is not directly reflected in the
research reports on class imagery which they present, relying as
they do very largely upon social survey analysis.   The use of a
combination of methods is a well established and fruitful sociological strategy.   Is it perhaps time that some other research
strategies be used to study class imagery?

One obvious approach, partially used by several authors, is
that of participation in and observation of the way of life of those
whose imagery is being studied.   Participant observation research
is, of course, the hallmark of social anthropology (rather in the
way that the social survey is the most widely used method in sociology), and its use has obvious relevance in the present context.

> Anthropologists have long realised - if not always clearly -
> that the transitory interview, held with respondents who do not
> share their view of the encounter, is an unreliable source of
> information in itself.   It is not until they have been in the
> society long enough to fit into one of its better-defined roles
> that they can 'tap' a valid communication system and hear the
> kinds of messages that others in the culture hear (Benney and
> Hughes, 1956, p.142).

Several studies of the social situation and social imagery of farm-
workers have been carried out using these methods (e.g. Emmett,
1964;   Littlejohn, 1963), and there is no doubt that they could be
adapted more widely, as numerous American studies of particular
occupational groups demonstrate (e.g. Becker, 1963, Chapters 5 and
6;   Gold, 1964;   Polsky, 1971, pp.43-114).   Nor need the traditional detachment of the ethnographer be emulated.   The study of
industrial and political conflict in particular would seem to
provide opportunities for 'active' research such as that taken by
Lane and Roberts (1971).   Moreover, although the industrial sociologist has traditionally taken either a managerial or a neutral
stance, there are good research reasons, as Roy has recently argued,
for deliberate identification with the workers' point of view and
with union organisations, particularly in investigating more
sensitive issues such as imagery and consciousness (Roy, 1970),
provided that 'over-rapport' can be guarded against (Miller, 1952).
A recent study of car workers shows that this type of identification
can be used as a research strategy successfully (Beynon, 1973).

A related development of interest is what has come to be known
as cognitive anthropology, in which a serious attempt is made to
appreciate the meanings which the members of a particular culture
hold about the world, and the ways in which they interpret the
social experiences in which they are involved (cf. Spradley, 1970).
This has obvious affinities with mainstream anthropology, but
perhaps represents a more systematic attempt to grapple with the
ways in which language may structure our understanding of the world,
by focusing upon the terminology which members of a sub-culture use
in communication with each other.

Yet ultimately, to make sharp distinctions between different
types of research strategy is unhelpful, since either different
strategies are combined in one investigation, or one strategy encap-
sulates elements of another.   In the study of imagery, it may be
more useful to consider, as well as alternative strategies, the
particular problems associated with interviewing and the methodological problems to which it gives rise.   A whole range of discrete
technical issues have been discussed in the literature, (3) but
certain more general strategic questions are perhaps of greater
import.   The limitations of the social survey relate not so much
to the interview as an instrument of data collection;   for its
practitioners, at least, seem satisfied that it yeilds valid data.
(4)
    The nub of the issue is the appropriateness of different modes of
interviewing, since there is clearly scope for considerable variability.   Given the complexity of social images, the 'brisk interview', typically carried out by a paid interviewer in one (and only
one) meeting with the respondent, is not the only and may not be the
best way of eliciting images of society.   Checks and safeguards
may of course be built in, and interviewers carefully trained, but
the transitoriness and impersonality of the encounter, as well as
extraneous influences derived from the social characteristics of
the interviewer, have led some to suggest that other modes of
interviewing may be more appropriate (cf. Deutscher, 1969; Phillips,
1971).
    Bott, of course, interviewed her respondents on several extended
occasions, returning with fresh questions and establishing a more
personal acquaintanceship than is usual in social survey research.
It is perhaps surprising that this mode of conversational interviewing has not been more practiced, particularly in view of the
gain which seems to accrue in terms of the coherence of the accounts
of social imagery which it may produce.   A somewhat similar emphasis
upon an open-ended and unstructured approach to interviewing is
given by Cicourel and Kituse in their study of educational decision-
makers, where they argue that 'questions about how personnel in the
educational system conceive of their students and how routine
organisational decisions are made require a flexible methodology and
must reflect the ways in which persons in everyday life generally
conceive of objects and events' (Cicourel and Kituse, 1963, p.149).
    Robert Lane's study of political ideology (1962), referred to by
Lockwood in Chapter 14, is an unusual attempt to use a similar
approach.   Lane describes his procedure, following Reik, as
'listening with the third ear', in a relaxed and conversational
situation.   The raw material of his study consists of several
hundred pages of verbatim transcript for each respondent.   The main
features of the interviews were that they were discursive (not
following any set pattern), dialectical (involving an exchange of
views rather than a one-way process), and contextual (opinions,
beliefs and attitudes being set in the context of other opinions,
beliefs and attitudes).   This last point is particularly significant.   Beliefs and images were treated in the context of other
beliefs and images, rather than as isolated artefacts. (5)   Such
contextual analysis, Lane admits, is not easy.   His respondents
tended to keep concepts narrow and close to personal experience.

There is the danger of confusing respondents' and sociologists' categories in the analysis of meaning.   And the method is extremely time-consuming;   Lane was only able to interview fifteen respondents. Nevertheless this kind of approach would seem potentially fruitful for the analysis of social imagery, and indeed for the study of cultural belief-systems more generally.

A related, though distinct, approach to the study of complex beliefs and values lies in using stories or written material as a stimulus to get respondents talking about the subject of interest. A simple version of this is the well known question used in surveys about the firm as a football team. (6)   However, more complex procedures can be used.   Jones, for example, in his pioneering study 'Life, Liberty and Property', wanted to tap ideas of respond- ents about corporate property.   To this end, he constructed a number of short stories or anecdotes about industrial situations and industrial conflict, based upon real events which had taken place. At the end of each story, respondents were asked to say whether they approved or disapproved of the action described.   Moreover the questions evoked quite strong and extended responses from some interviewees, even though the answer required was merely a yes or no (Jones, 1941, pp.20-2, 357-70).   Such a procedure seems to have been little followed, other than the use of much more truncated questions in survey research.

The possibility of using material based upon current events or literary sources as a stimulus in investigating class imagery and beliefs remains.   For example, Cohen and Taylor in their study of long-term imprisonment used literary identification as one of their research methods.   Building on the fact that their captive evening- class spent much of the time reading, novels and plays were used as a way of discussing attitudes and behaviour which were difficult to approach directly.   Comparisons between different accounts enabled prisoners to comment on the accuracy or authenticity of particular views of a subject (Cohen and Taylor, 1972, pp.36-7).   The use of such a technique in the study of class imagery would obviously be more difficult to arrange, but there is no reason in principle why this approach could not be followed.   The presentation of written interpretations - whether of events such as a strike, or of personal experiences such as being a servant in an upper-class household - could provide an entree into the subject of investigation which a relatively short and elliptical survey question - however well phrased and however skilfull the interviewer - cannot easily achieve.

The possibilities do not end there.   The procedure of group interviewing has been relatively little used in research on class imagery, yet might repay the work it needs to set up.   In such a situation, the presence of the sociologist is less intrusive than when face to face with a single respondent, and the possibility of the exchange of ideas (and of direct comparison and contrast) between respondents, much greater.   Interviewing participants in the heat of the action has also been little used (though cf. Willener, 1970; Lane and Roberts, 1971).   Attempting to obtain reflexive accounts from workers about past events which would relate to class imagery and class beliefs is another possible line of approach.   In principle other methods, such as those of historical reconstruction (used by Moore) or the gathering of personal documents, may also be valuable.

In discussing these procedures, the emphasis has been deliberately placed upon methods which seem likely to yield valid knowledge about class images.   Most of them are of an intensive and
qualitative kind, and necessarily involve a loss of representativeness, a criterion which should not necessarily override all others
in the design of sociological research.   Nor are these methods
necessarily as reliable as those involving a standardised interview
schedule, since a larger element of personal variability will enter
in to the research situation.   Yet given the problems associated
with the study of class imagery, and the need for new approaches
(which Blackburn and Mann explicitly advocate at the end of Chapter
8), it seems reasonable to suggest that the validity of data on
images is a greater difficulty than either its representativeness
or reliability.   In an ideal world one would seek to maximise all
three, but sociological research rarely approximates to the ideal.
    This brief discussion of research technique has skated around
the underlying problem, in investigations of class imagery, which
is one of interpretation.   As Allcorn and Marsh point out in
Chapter 12, interpretation is difficult enough when the material
to be interpreted consists of published texts.   Sociologists,
however, often have to construct the very texts which are to be
interpreted, and this construction itself consists of interpretations.   The intellectual framing of research into class imagery
is therefore of particular importance, and several different lines
of approach have been suggested.   Willener's paper provides some
useful distinctions to make between different kinds of imagery, as
a ground-clearing operation.   Others have suggested the usefulness
of analysing situations rather than samples, in order to attempt
to contextualise imagery by relating it directly to the situations
in which it is produced (cf. Douglas, 1967, p.339).   Some regard
the study of vocabularies of motive as a promising line of approach,
focusing upon the social structuring of meaning and the ways in
which men select verbal alternatives in the light of their social
situation (Mills, 1940;   Taylor, 1972).   Analytically, insufficient
attention has been paid to the concept of depth levels in the study
of imagery (cf. Gurvitch, 1950;   K.A. Thompson, 1971), though this
has frequently been discussed in work on class consciousness (cf.
Mann, 1973, p.13;   Giddens, 1973, pp.111-7).
    Interpretive problems may also be tackled indirectly through the
organisation of research.   Cross-cultural comparative research is
one obvious strategy. (7)   Another is what Willener has called
cross-analysis, in which research groups who do not agree on how to
interpret particular phenomena could exchange data and explicitly
give those in the other groups the right to interpret data the way
that they want.   In this way the effects of perspective or frame
of reference in interpretation may to some extent be controlled.
Third, Willener has suggested the value of several pieces of
research being planned collaboratively in advance.   If there could
be co-ordinated discussion of research before it was undertaken in
a particular field, there would be a greater chance of cumulation
and one would not always have to discuss issues ex post facto. (8)
    These are, however, unlikely to be definitive solutions, and
interpretive problems will continue to perplex students of class
imagery, just as they present the most challenging problems in the

adoption of an action frame of reference.   The present set of
working papers can not be regarded as having done more than high-
light these particular issues.

THE PROBLEM OF HISTORY

The paper in this section by Davis and Cousins usefully draws
attention to a double dilemma posed by the debate stemming from the
Lockwood article.   What is the past situation with regard to class
imagery, in comparison to the present?   Were, for example, 'traditional proletarian' images of society more widely held in the past
than they are in the present?   And second, what is the relationship
between the components of the ideal type and historical reality,
between the 'ideal' and the 'actual'?
     Sociologists are singularly poorly placed to answer this first
question.   What J.A. Banks (1970, p.62) has termed the 'trained
incapacity' of sociologists with regard to historical studies is all
too evident.   The very few studies available have mostly been
carried out by historians, as, for example, E.P. Thompson's massive
study of the development of class consciousness during the industrial revolution (1963) or John Foster's more detailed studies of
particular towns undergoing industrial growth (1968).   More
recently Razzell (1973) has re-analysed some of the 'Morning Chronicle' material of Henry Mayhew in the light of Lockwood's 1966
article, the only attempt (apart from Moore's paper here) known to
the writer to apply it directly to historical sources.   This is
not to ignore the formidable body of historical material about the
growth of trade unionism in Britain.   However, even if this
provides data on the growth of organised class consciousness, it is
predominantly the history of union organisation and the union
leadership.   There is relatively little data on the class consciousness or class imagery of the rank-and-file union member.   If the
main characteristic of the discussion of the nature of imagery is
disagreement and contradiction, that of the historical dimension
is emptiness, in the sense of how little there is to go on in
discussing this field.   There is therefore very great scope for
sociologically informed historical research into class imagery,
perhaps by way of the history of particular occupations or particular localities.   It is, however, fraught with methodological
difficulties, both in the collection and analysis of data, and the
rigours and difficulties facing the historical sociologist of
imagery should not be underestimated (cf. Anderson, 1972, pp.77-81).
     The lack of fit between ideal type and historical reality is an
analytical problem, suggesting to some the limitations of static
ideal types.   As Davis and Cousins suggest, there is at least
ambiguity in the treatment of the historical comparative dimension
in Chapter 5 of 'The Affluent Worker in the Class Structure'.
Perhaps this ambiguity lies in the minds of the reader rather than
elsewhere, but there is no doubt that ideal type analysis of this
kind has difficulty in bridging the analytical gap between ideal
construct and actual historical processes.   If the typology in
that chapter is treated as developmental (from dichotomous to
pecuniary model of society), substantial empirical objections can

be levelled at such a procrustean treatment of the course of working-
class social development.   If, on the other hand, the ideal type
is merely an ideal type (i.e. a heuristic device), it is not clear
how it illuminates the course of historical development, if it does
so at all.   The ideal type may, of course, be used as a reference
point at particular points in time, in a series of (as it were)
snapshots.. The criticism stands that the use of ideal types in
the study of class imagery is in its nature ahistorical.   Do ideal
types necessarily involve a loss of analytic power in relation to
change and development?

THE USEFULNESS OF IDEAL-TYPE ANALYSIS

More sweeping criticisms of the use of ideal types have also been
made, suggesting either that their use in the study of class imagery
forces data into pre-existing categories or that they fail to
provide a sufficient range of theoretical alternatives.   Both
criticisms represent a complete misunderstanding of the status and
purpose of ideal-type analysis.   As Bell and Newby correctly
emphasise in Chapter 5, the typology's use is heuristic rather than
explanatory, and the types represent reference points or extremes
around which or between which variation may be expected to occur.
Far from being pre-existing categories or boxes into which data is
to be fitted, ideal types are constructs to be compared with the
empirical data, in the expectation that significant differences
will be apparent.   Nor are ideal types intended to provide a specification of the whole range of theoretical alternatives available,
as a comparison of the empirical papers with the original Lockwood
article will make clear.   Again, their purpose is to act as
reference points for theoretical analysis, from which it starts out
but from which it will be expected to diverge.
    The use of ideal types in sociological work has had a chequered
history (cf. Martindale, 1959; Rex, 1971), characterised by
persistent misunderstanding of what they are intended to do.   As
a methodological device for instituting comparisons, the test of
an ideal type's worth is not its truth or falsity, but its fruitfulness.   In the context of the present symposium, for example,
it is possible to compare Lockwood's three-fold typology with the
more simplified two-part typology in Chapter 5 of 'The Affluent
Worker in the Class Structure', contrasting the ideal type of a
'traditional working-class perspective' with a 'middle-class
perspective' (Goldthorpe et al., 1969, pp.118-21).   The 'traditional working-class perspective' is in fact close to Lockwood's
proletarian traditionalism, and omits the traditional deferential
type.   The papers by Bell and Newby, Martin and Fryer and Batstone
above suggest that the inclusion of this third element in the 1966
article was a fruitful one, and its omission in the book is to be
regretted.
    At a different level, one may compare Lockwood's typology with
the three different modal types of class consciousness suggested
by Parkin (1971, pp.81-2), the 'meaning systems' of, first, the
dominant value system; second, the subordinate value system, and
third, the radical value system.   In accord with the argument

earlier, it may be suggested that this typology is more concerned
with class consciousness (as distinguished from class imagery) or
with the development of 'meaning-systems' at a societal level
through the normative ordering of society (as opposed to the
location of the sources of class imagery in actors' primary social
experiences at work and in the community).   Clearly one might
choose between Lockwood's and Parkin's ideal types in terms of
either theoretical focus (class imagery or class consciousness) or
methodological interest (the normative integration of society
versus the importance of micro-structural factors).   In either
case, however, the choice is by no means an arbitrary one, for it
rests upon reasoned theoretical premises.

The availability of competing ideal types merely underlines,
moreover, their heuristic purpose.   Critics of ideal type analysis
usually attribute to them other characteristics which do not
properly belong to them.   In evaluating the papers in Part Two,
centred around Lockwood's ideal types of 'traditional proletarian'
and 'traditional deferential' worker, keep in mind that
> the construction of ideal types recommends itself not as an end
> but as a means ... it is no hypothesis but if offers guidance
> to the construction of hypotheses.   It is not a description of
> reality but it aims to give unambiguous means of expression to
> such a description ... the ideal-type is an attempt to analyse
> historically unique configurations or their individual compon-
> ents by means of genetic concepts' (Max Weber, 1949, pp.92, 90,
> 93).

THE SOCIAL BONDS OF THE WORKING CLASS

One field in which ideal-types have been over-used is in the analysis of close-knit, multiplex, small-scale, geographically confined
patterns of social relations.   Status, community, 'mechanical'
solidarity, the 'folk' society, have all been proposed as charac-
terisations of the social relations of Gemeinschaft, and all have
been found wanting when attempts have been made to use them to
analyse the course of social development away from such a pattern
of social relations.

Nevertheless, the nature of the affective, diffuse and particularistic social relations between members of the same occupation or
between those who live in the same locality is of basic relevance
to the theoretical argument of Lockwood's original paper.   If in
that article these features are summarised rather too elliptically
in the terms 'community' and 'occupational community', yet they are
clearly central parts of his argument, relating as they do to the
social bonds of particular segments of the working class, and hence
to the formation of particular types of imagery.   The importance
of these concepts is substantive, and does not depend on their
embodiment in an ideal type.   For Lockwood is concerned to treat
occupation as a variable intervening between market and work
situation on the one hand, and class imagery on the other, in
contrast to its common use as an indicator of social class.   This
in turn recalls Blauner's earlier attempt (1960) to explain gross
differences in work attitudes between different occupations and

industries, one factor in which was the development of occupational communities.   The papers by Salaman and by Allcorn and Marsh in this section both consider this subject, and suggest rather different lines of theoretical attack, Salaman in terms of occupational identity, Allcorn and Marsh in terms of the distinction between sociability and solidarity among those who work together.

Does the concept 'occupational community' retain any usefulness in the analysis of social imagery?   Salaman's paper represents a very interesting attempt to change the meaning of the term and to enter a plea for a more serious sociology of occupations, but it does not bear directly on the use of the term in the recent literature.   Allcorn and Marsh point out that a distinctive occupational community is characteristic of quite a wide range of occupations - miners, dockers, fishermen, printers, steelworkers, lorry-drivers, railwaymen, shipbuilding workers - but that variation in kind of occupational community has not been much considered.   This is an important point, since the prototype of the occupational community has been taken to be the geographically isolated mining community. In fact, this is quite a-typical as a pattern of work and residence, justifying the designation 'quasi-occupational community' (Salaman, 1971a, p.55).   The grouping together of mining with docking and shipbuilding in this respect in the ideal type glosses over the kinds of variation which may occur between different industries. For example, the characterisation of shipbuilding workers as sharing in an occupational community requires considerable modification, since social relations at work may be a more important source of identification (and imagery) than social relations outside work between fellow shipbuilding workers (Brown et al., 1973).   At the other extreme, the absence of occupational community as a condition promoting deference was pointed to by Lockwood.   The study of groups such as domestic servants, in relative occupational isolation, may also throw light on the relative importance of a common work situation in generating social imagery (cf. Davidoff, 1973).

The trend of current research into occupational communities is away from the enumeration of the structural features of different occupations (particularly in terms of the extent to which members socialise together in their off-hours), towards a broader and more theoretically adventurous consideration of the nature of occupational identification.   Salaman's paper represents one line of inquiry. Brown and others (1973) suggest a different approach which seems equally promising, in terms of the concept of 'occupational culture'. This emphasis upon the culture of work and occupation perhaps represents a shift to studying the content of social relations at work and outside rather than their form, and the meaning which belonging to a particular occupation has for those involved in it. Such an approach to the study of subjective aspects of stratification is not new (cf. Miller and Reissman, 1961;   Parkin, 1967), and draws on the larger literature on the sociology of sub-cultures (cf. Arnold, 1970).   Instances of illuminating empirical studies of particular occupational groups from this point of view include Liebow's account of the work experience of lower-class American negro males (1967), Miller's comparative survey of the dockworker sub-culture (1969), and Brown and others' study of shipbuilding workers (1973).   This kind of research has obvious affinities with

the sociology of occupations developed by Everett Hughes and his
students (cf. Hughes, 1958), a link which Salaman seeks to re-
establish.   It underlines the extent to which the study of social
imagery becomes a study in the sociology of culture, although none
of the studies cited fall into the pitfalls besetting those who
have written about the culture of poverty (cf. Valentine, 1968).

This continuing concern with the nature of social relations in
traditional working class communities also connects with Allcorn
and Marsh's important distinction between sociability and solidarity.
There is no doubt that a failure to make this distinction has marred
a number of pieces of work on changing working-class patterns of
life, and Lockwood's ideal types embody at least a tendency to run
on from one to the other without sharply distinguishing them.   Moreover, Allcorn and Marsh make a further distinction between solidarity
based upon action stemming from a common perception of a group's
position in the division of labour, as distinct from solidarity
based on a common perception of sharing a similar position in the
class structure.   Such a distinction is of course basic to the
discussion of 'instrumentalism' among affluent workers, but is of
relevance in considering the traditional worker as well.   The
distinction between sociability, solidarity based upon common
interests derived from an occupation or industry, and class-conscious
political action, reinforces the extent to which the study of social
imagery is not merely a study of class consciousness.   Certainly
the debate has been dominated by the exceptional case - it seems
probable that the mining community, so frequently cited as the locus
of a traditional proletarian world-view, is in fact one of the very
few milieux in which patterns of sociability and work-based solidarity completely overlap.   Even there, the further identification
of mining communities with class-based political action is not a
universally tenable generalisation, as Moore's paper emphasises.
In fact there has been very considerable variation in degree of
radicalism between different mining communities and different mining
areas in Britain, both historically (cf. Gregory, 1968) and at the
present time.

Moreover as Westergaard emphasises in Part Four and has done so
previously (1965, pp.104-8; 1970, pp.128-9), solidarity of a class-
based political kind is at least partially antithetical to the
particularistic solidarity and localism of the traditional homogeneous working-class community.   This has led some sociologists to
argue that the concept of 'traditional proletarian' is a contradiction in terms, and others to suggest that there is a need for a
further ideal type embracing universalistic class consciousness
(by analogy with Parkin's type of radical meaning-system, involving
an oppositional interpretation of class inequalities).   Lockwood
considers these arguments in Chapter 16.

The trend of the argument, therefore, is to suggest the inadequacy of 'occupational community' as a simple explanatory principle
in the understanding of class imagery, and the need to break down
the nature of occupational identification, occupational culture,
and social relations among those who work together, more finely
than this simple concept allows.   The complexity of the analysis
of the social sources of class imagery is suggested once again.
Social relations outside of work clearly play an important part in

the formation of imagery, but the ways in which this influence
operates requires subtle and complex theoretical analysis, in which
the notion of an occupational culture plays an important part.

CONSCIOUSNESS, SOCIAL STRUCTURE AND SOCIAL ACTION

An important theme, implicit in the whole symposium and explicitly
confronted in Part Four, is the nature of the relationship between
the study of images of society and the understanding of social
action of a radical or revolutionary kind.   It is touched on in
the conclusion to Cousins and Brown's paper on shipbuilding workers
and in Blackburn and Mann's discussion of their Peterborough
research.   Willener raises it again in discussing the nature of
imagery and its articulation.   It is implied in criticism of ideal
type analysis as ahistorical and static.
     The present volume does not perhaps proceed very far toward an
analysis of class consciousness in industrial and political organisations, although it provides some pointers to it.   Willener's
discussion below of 'active' types of imagery is germane, as is
Westergaard's focus on the structural conditions underlying universalistic class consciousness.   Within the framework of the original
article, he attempts to specify the conditions under which radical
class consciousness may appear.   Cousins and Brown make several
similar suggestive points in discussing their material on shipbuilding workers.
     How might the study of industrial and political class conscious-
ness develop, and what would distinguish it from the research
reported here on class imagery?   One fruitful line of approach
would seem to be to study 'active' situations, and the development
of consciousness in such situations.   The most immediately access-
ible kind of situation is of course in industrial relations, and
an illuminating recent study by Beynon (1973) exemplifies how the
study of industrial class consciousness may be carried forward.
Such a focus may result in narrowing the scope - Beynon's study
emphasises the significance of consciousness of the firm as distinct
from the wider social and political situation - but has the advantage of relating subjective orientations to a tightly structured set
of social relationships, those between management and workers.
     The study of images and consciousness in the course of industrial
and political crises of different kinds is also possible.   Very
little work of this kind has been done, but it is clearly a promising area.   Willener's research into the events of May 1968 in
France, for example, was carried out from just this standpoint
(Willener, 1970).   The sociology of strikes and other industrial
disputes (cf. Eldridge, 1968; Hyman, 1972) provides opportunities
for such research, as a recent study by Lane and Roberts carried
out in the course of the Pilkington strike demonstrates (1971).
     It would also be worth exploring some of the issues thrown up
by the present volume.   One of the most salient of these is related
to the absence of class consciousness and to the social conditions
producing deferential attitudes and behaviour.   Runciman's work
(1966) represents one attempt to explain the construction of world
views which are not of an antagonistic, class-based, kind.   A

different strategy would be to study the sources of structured ignorance, the conditions which prevent the emergence of class consciousness among workers in an objectively weak class situation (such as agricultural workers - cf. Newby 1972a and b).   And this would be likely to lead to the study of the images of society of those in dominant class positions (such as managers, proprietors and other employers) in order to explain the imagery or consciousness of those over whom they exercise domination.

This in turn suggests the need for a greater emphasis upon the reciprocal relationship between social structure and imagery which Lockwood built into his ideal types.   This view has recently been stated by Hyman, who argues for a 'structural dialectic of social structure and social consciousness'.

There is ... a complex two-way process in which men's goals, ideas and beliefs influence and are influenced by the social structure.   To do justice to its complexity, industrial sociologists must be attuned to this dynamic interaction between structure and consciousness.   A static or a one-way analysis necessarily distorts social reality, and is therefore an inadequate basis for understanding industrial behaviour or predicting its development.   The greatest potential for further progress ... must lie in the elaboration of a dialectical approach (Hyman, 1972, p.73).

What a dialectical approach would look like when applied to the study of social imagery remains, however, unclear for the time being.

Fruitful as these lines of approach may possibly be, the problematic nature of the relationship between class imagery and political and industrial class consciousness should be emphasised.   The study of class consciousness is the study of collective class action. The study of images of society is the study of (predominantly) verbal expressions, in different research contexts, of men's normative orientations to behaviour and of their predispositions to act. Major events such as the UCS work-in or minor outbreaks such as the Vauxhall strike of 1966 (Blackburn, 1967, pp.48-51) are clearly of a different order to verbal responses elicited usually in interview situations.   The disjunction between sentiments and acts identified by sociologists from La Piere in 1934 onwards renders any straightforward linkage between verbal utterances and overt behaviour too simplistic.   Irwin Deutscher indeed has argued, in two essays with disturbing methodological implications (1972, 1973) that there need be no necessary connection between sentiments and acts.   Or there may in some situations be an inverse relationship; for example, strong collective action may take place without a strong shared consciousness of common interests or class solidarity.   Again, a note of caution may usefully be sounded as a reminder of the fact that academic inquiry necessarily involves a certain distancing from action in the world.   The study of social imagery does not provide the key to a new radical 'Weltanschauung', even though the pursuit is not without wider ethical and political significance.

CONCLUSION

Several new lines of development are suggested by the papers in
the present volume.   One is the need to balance the emphasis here
upon micro-structural factors in the genesis and sustenance of
class imagery with more detailed attention to macro-structural
factors such as the economy and polity.   The influence of the mass
media upon the formation of imagery is also important.   Second,
studies of imagery should not be confined to the working class, but
should be extended to middle-class and elite populations.   Little
attention is given here to the image creators and sustainers, or
even to those who exercise power in day-to-day industrial situations
such as managers and supervisors, though Bell and Newby are currently engaged upon a study of capitalist farmers in the class structure,
following on from their research on agricultural workers.   Third,
more specific historical research into imagery and class relations
is required, difficult though this is to carry out.   The most
important single weakness of the ideal typical approach to the study
of imagery is its failure to treat the historical dimension in an
unambiguous fashion.
   Several subsidiary areas of further research are also indicated.
All the papers refer to the images of society of men; when is
someone going to do research on women's images of society?   The
value of a thoroughgoing sociology of occupations is suggested,
treating occupation as something more than an indicator of social
class position.   The possible fruitfulness of the analysis of
industrial and political situations and of active research, is also
brought out.   The need to examine the structural contradictions
faced by workers in a capitalist society is indicated.
   The papers in this volume do not aim to provide a cut-and-dried
account of the state of knowledge about social imagery, but to
explore some of the issues involved.   The contributions to this
section are working papers intended to point the way to further
research, by means of theoretical and methodological discussion.
Such discussion is not carried out in abstracto.   Indeed, one of
the notable features of work on class imagery as a whole is the
way in which research problems, theoretical approaches, and methodology are bound up together.   Theories alone, and methods or
techniques alone, are not sufficient; their significance lies in
their relationship to each other and to the substantive research
problems which are the focus of attention.

NOTES

1   An editor is particularly dependent on others, and I should like
    to acknowledge here the extent to which in preparing this
    methodological note I have drawn on the Durham conference
    proceedings (SSRC, 1973), and have benefited from the contri-
    butions of the conference participants in discussion.   More
    especially, I am grateful to Richard Brown, Jim Cousins, David
    Lockwood and Alfred Willener for their comments on an earlier
    draft of this paper.
2   To pose the question in this way assumes that it is meaningful to

talk of 'social structure' and of 'relatively exact indicators of structural position in society'.   In other words, the study of society entails something more than the confrontation of the sociologists' and the actors' views of the world;   there is in some sense an 'objective reality'.

3   These include the tendency to conformity in replies to questions (Jones, 1941, p.330), the ways and means of coding answers to open-ended questions on class (Runciman, 1966, pp.317-20; Goldthorpe et al., 1969, pp.200-2), the tendency for respondents to give different answers to general as opposed to specific questions about their propensity to take collective political or industrial action (Mann, 1970, pp.429, 432), and variations in answers to different questions on perceptions of class (Platt, 1971).   Other issues have been raised by Blauner (1960, pp.354-6), Bott (1957, Chapter 6), Goldthorpe (1970a, pp.334-8) and others, and the discussions at the conference on which this symposium is based provide another source (SSRC, 1973).

4   'Interview data, when obtained by well-qualified personnel and carefully interpreted, can provide valid information on social behaviour and relationships as well as attitudes....   In our own interviews, we were strongly impressed by the open manner in which questions were generally answered and issues discussed, and by respondents' preparedness to show themselves in what, to them at least, appeared as an unfavourable light.   Where it was possible to check on the response to interrelated questions, no serious degree of inconsistency was found in the answers that individuals gave' (Goldthorpe et al., 1969, p.50).

5   As Lane puts it, 'one of the features of what is sometimes called "understanding" is to grasp the context of an event, that is, temporally to know what went before and what is likely to follow, spatially to know the terrain, in human terms to see the play of the many motives involved.   To understand an event in this way is to contextualise it;   not to do this is to morselise it, to see it isolated from the surrounding features that give it additional "meanings"....   Contextual political thinking ... reflects a configurational and reflective turn of mind - in several ways.   One way is to picture an event as part of a stream of events;   that is, it is historical.   Another is to compare and contrast events so as to group them in some way that sheds light on their common characteristics.   Still another is to bring the event into contact with a conceptual framework such that it may be seen to illustrate or modify or rebut some part of that framework' (R. Lane, 1962, pp.350, 353).

6   For example: 'Here are two opposing views about industry generally.   I'd like you to tell me which you agree with more. Some people say that a firm is like a football side - because good teamwork means success and is to everyone's advantage. Others say that teamwork in industry is impossible - because employers and men are really on opposing sides.   Which view do you agree with more?' (Goldthorpe et al., 1969, p.207).

7   For example, Professor V. Allen of the School of Economic Studies at the University of Leeds is currently engaged upon a comparative study of the social consequences of declining industries, with SSRC support.   This study is concerned with the impact of

a decline in employment in selected industries in Britain and France on the social behaviour of their workforces.   It is being conducted in collaboration with a research team from the Centre National de la Recherche Scientifique, Aix-en-Provence. The selected industries are coalmining, the port industry, and woollen textiles.   The first stage of the project deals with the coalmining industry.   In Britain this involves a comparison between three mining areas with contrasting qualities.   The purpose is to seek an understanding of the sources of consciousness of miners in an unstable work environment.

8   There is, however, the need to balance the gains from co-ordination with the dangers of a kind of domination over individual research projects which might result.

Chapter 10

IMAGES, ACTION, 'US' AND 'THEM'

Alfred Willener

Among the surprises which await the continental sociologist when
he comes among his British colleagues are the vigour of argument
(behind a polite front) and particularly the patience with which
the theses of a notable article (on this occasion by David Lockwood) are not only discussed logically or ideologically, but are
thoroughly considered in terms of detailed empirical researches,
even though these researches were not planned or carried out as
replications.   For all that there is, in the papers of this symposium, a serious professional purpose, this does not exclude, but
in part explains, a certain degree of detachment also found in the
previous discussion of these issues in French, German and other
industrial contexts and sociological debates, as well as in the
British material about the 'new working class' and 'embourgeoisement'.   It is both an advantage and a drawback.   To the extent
that the analytic approach compartmentalises, and thus involves
detachment, it is disconnected from the living reality and dimin-
ishes the suggestiveness of certain terms (images of society) and
of great issues (structures, change, consciousness).   Most of us
are too familiar with this paradox and end up by choosing either the
bracketing of problems or involvement in the complexities and life
of the real social world, when one should try and keep a sense of
the necessary dialectics between the two.

From now on I see my role, faced with so much careful and de-
limited research work, as that of the outsider who should be permitted to stir things up a little. (1)   The debates which I took part
in during the conference have reassured me subsequently of the
presence of temperaments who confront one another much more sharply
orally than seemed possible after reading the papers (or is it I
who doesn't know how to read between the lines?).

How can one be a professional researcher and teacher and avoid
sociological self-bureaucratisation (of the instrumentalist or
other kinds)?

I do not know how to reply to such a question in a simple way.
Perhaps the answer lies in choosing one's research projects in
terms of society's problems, of reality external to the academic
world.   Perhaps also in playing with notions which are both from
society and from sociology, in order to recall those aspects left

on one side.   It is purely an intellectual exercise.   Of course,
in this exercise the sociologists ('us') are part of the field they
are studying and the population ('them') is practising a kind of
'spontaneous sociology' (to use Bourdieu's word);   the only difference between 'them' and 'us' being our own attempt at 'scientific
sociology'.

FROM IMAGES TO IMAGES

There exist very nicely produced children's books, inspired by
great minds (as, for example, a recent book based on Piaget).
Perhaps there should be published books of images for adults, or
more to the point, for adult sociologists, asking talented designers
to make less analytic (i.e. more analogic) the classical thoughts
which were not all that analytic but appeared to be so in their
original, written form.

  Here is how a sociologist could start such a book, in the form of
a miniature fairy-tale (mine not Piaget's):

  Once upon a time there were people looking around them, at
  reality, and at images, exploring both, more or less in comparison.   Having performed long enough the relevant perceptual
  operations, a system of 'operative structures' developed in their
  heads.   Subsequently they saw reality, even once reality had
  changed, in terms of these structures, since they had formed
  persistent images of this reality.   From then on, and forever
  after, these images remained inside their heads.

  What is wrong with this, I think, is the premiss of a starting-
point ('In the beginning there was man and reality').   We are all
talking about a less clear-cut situation: recent populations find
themselves in a process in which there is, certainly, a confrontation with the (or a) reality, but a reality more and more obviously
made up of images, in the sense of picture-images.   One must bear
this ever-present factor in mind, because it is given little attention in some of the other papers.

An image is an image is an image (2)

We are surrounded with pictorial images.   It is a banal truism.
We are overloaded with images: TV, photography, publicity, etc.
And I would ask a naive question of the researchers;   if it is true
that there exist very encapsulated communities of workers in Britain,
what part does television play in forming their image(s) of society?

  Theoretically a delicate problem is posed to bother us.   What
should be considered a pictorial image?   Should it be called, to be
more exact, a 'material image', in order to distinguish it from
mental images?   It is useful therefore to distinguish the photo-
graphic image, the painted image, the electronic image, from the
image which is in a sculpted, architectural or urban form, and this
in turn from more abstract printed images which are nonetheless
objectified?

  The next category is then the non-pictorial image, let us call it
a mental image.   And it is perhaps worth delineating its characteristics, even if this is rather elementary.

The concept of image as static

This is modelled on the idea of a still photograph, perhaps an
automatic portrait, or better still an X-ray (the skeleton of
society).   Many conceptions of an image of society suggest an
idea of fixity, often of permanence, at least of crystallisation
for a quite considerable period.   This is not necessarily produced
in too visible a manner, since one can still present a variety of
quasiphotographs, such as an evolutionary series (as in a family
photograph album).   It involves a longitudinal approach.
   Let us ask a slightly embarrassing, but necessary, question.
If it is true that populations have 'one' image of society - we
shall come back to the extent of its structuring and coherence
later - why should it necessarily be static?   Should one not
develop a sense of flux?   Psychologists talk of the flux of consciousness, should we not explore the 'cinema' of our social
representations - even if, admittedly, the speed of the film would
be very slow in certain groups, notably those termed traditional?
   And when we say 'our' social representations, we should keep in
mind what Levi-Strauss said about the difference between anthro-
pologists and sociologists: that the latter cannot be identified
with the former because they are part of the society which they
study.

They and/or we are part of the images

If we see pictures, for example, on TV, they are about 'them', but
this 'them' is sometimes us ('people like us'), it is seldom ourselves directly.   Therefore, the meaning we are experiencing is
the product of a complex made up by, first, a picture-image;
second, an image of the society; third, our own position in the
society.   We therefore come to pose the following questions.   How
is it that the channels of mass communication represent so rarely
'us' and so often 'them'?   Why is it that the papers here refer so
rarely to this source of images, notably television?   And - on the
same theme - how is it that the sociologist does not distinguish
more between his self-image and the image of society? (3)   (These
can be of a different nature, for example, the whole society being
seen in terms of prestige strata and one's own position in it in
terms of socio-economic categories.)   Finally, how can we, as
sociologists, talk of 'them' (workers, power) without revealing our
image of ourselves, and of society?
   This prepares us for the abandonment of the categories (unfortunately always current) of mirror-consciousness (as perceived
through a supposed direct confrontation with 'objective reality'),
and of false-consciousness, which are based on a dichotomised
(either/or) view of the world.   Perhaps the sociologist of images
should reach beyond the comfortable simplicity of a straightforward
causal chain, and look more closely at the processes which involve
various interdependencies.   And one path towards progress would,
I suggest, be to find ways of conceptualising 'reciprocal inclu-
sions' (see Figure 10.1).

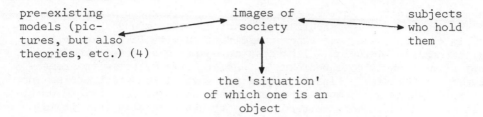

FIGURE 10.1

Thus the 'situation' of which one is the object contains already, beside elements termed 'objective' (economic factors, the power structure) the image of society which interprets them.   In the same way for the other boxes, 'subjects who hold them', or 'models', one finds that they contain, beyond the interpretations included in these images, objective elements which structure them, which enter (so to speak) into their incarnation.

There are images and images

Nearly any kind of sociological data can be used to investigate an image of society.   It is true that only some of these data contain an explicit spontaneous formulation, by the actors themselves, of an image of themselves or of an image of society.   The most one can say is that our reflections come up against boundary problems.   It is in fact necessary to develop a typology of images not just in terms of content, but in terms of extent and durability of images.
    I can only try and sketch certain categories here.   To start one can make an analogy with the work of the photographer.   Like the sociologist or the social actor himself, the photographer must choose a point of view from which he will look at reality (a point of view).   He must decide in which direction, north, south, etc., he is going to look (perspective).   He will choose a more or less wide-ranging objective, and will focus upon a figure from a lesser or greater distance - he will frame it.   Finally, if he is a photographer, he will choose one or several moments at which to actually shoot a photograph;   if he is a film-maker, he will take a lesser or greater sequence (selecting the right time).   And of course afterwards there is all the processing to be done (various selective decisions during the processing).
    I would distinguish, among social imagery, between (i) those images whose essential features are their global structure (dichotomies, hierarchies);   one is interested there in patterns and eventually in content (power or other divisions such as in-group/ out-group, (NB us/non-us is not the same as us/them);   prestige scales);   (ii) those images which are perspectives, for example approaches in terms of work, or approaches in terms of community, or in terms of age-groups.   In each of these two cases, one should define whether it is a question of simple boxes or of points of departure for long elaborations.   In other words, people or the sociologist can use them reductively or can insert them into long

arguments (in this latter case, it is obviously the content of these arguments which should be presented and examined).

7 In certain cases, one finds oneself faced with (iii) imagery, with complete histories, elaborated not just in a stereotyped manner, but with strongly coloured expressions, to some extent with stereotyped caricatures.   Finally, there are (iv) vistas which strike one by their range and scope; they encompass history, the cosmos, work, literature, education, culture.   One thinks naturally that it is the Germans who have such visions most frequently, since they have invented the word 'Weltanschauung'.

It goes without saying that one can find many examples and even mixtures in various pieces of research.   It is worthwhile, for example, comparing the recent work of Scheuch (1968) on the social imagery of the German 'new left' as a vision or vista of the world, and its type of imagery and analysis, with the classic work of Popitz (1957) who discovered among the workers he and others studied what was perhaps a kind of imagery.   Dahrendorf (1959) discussed images of society treating them largely as patterns (mainly in terms of authority).   Touraine tends to conceive of the same subject-matter in terms of perspectives (images in terms of work, i.e. creation).

There can be scarcely any doubt that the papers in the present colloquy are differentiated very greatly from one another in terms of the nature of the images of society being considered.   One finds the consideration of patterns ('distinctive patterns, which can with only slight exaggeration be called images of society', Martin and Fryer, Chapter 6), as well as visions of the world, sometimes by the same authors ('the modal view of the world did not correspond completely with that expected', Martin and Fryer, Chapter 6).   In entirely the opposite direction, some papers conceive of measures of ideology ('measurement of ideology in three different ways, on 25-, 7-, and 3-point scales', Blackburn and Mann, Chapter 8), putting in the forefront discussion of the research instrument which is an instrument of reference from which one derives something that is in the realm of images.

Non-images?

If we have the right to derive images from a mass of data - and several authors construe thus the patterns, the perspectives or the vistas - why not admit the reality and importance of the non-image? Only those who hold an imagery of which they are conscious can be considered as 'equipped' with an image (i.e. a structured image). The others tend either not to be conscious of their image, or to have more than one type of image.   And therefore those who reply to questionnaires, or talk in free interview situations, without necessarily ceasing to be concise or coherent, find themselves in a state of non-opinion, to which it is of the utmost importance to make reference here.   For the sake of clarity one can say that they have a non-image which, in a sense which is only slightly more abstract than all the other uses of the word 'image', is the limiting case (i.e. it is still a kind of image = confusion, complete lack of structure, total pragmatism, etc.).   Why should only a structured, permanent or lucid image deserve the label 'image'?

One is confronted again here once again with the now classical problem of the 'end of ideology'. A non-ideology is an extreme case, a particularly insidious limiting case, of ideology. If there is no such thing as a mental figure which helps to orient someone on the complex ground of his daily life, what is happening? Perhaps the lack of a structured image expresses that the individual is prey to a father figure (his boss, the state, etc.)? Perhaps the individual who finds himself in this situation is so completely alienated that he waits for others to structure his understanding of the world? ('It seems clear that pragmatism, in the sense of response to the specific substance of an item (possibly intermixed with confusion) far outweighs ideology, for our sample', Blackburn and Mann, Chapter 8).'Workers will respond very readily to the kind of individual cue we gave them; it is merely that their responses do not necessarily add up to a structured whole', Blackburn and Mann, Chapter 8). 'They do not build up complex class images, for example, and tend instead to deny the existence of class', Batstone, Chapter 7).

FROM IMAGES TO ACTION

Image-ination

The fact that images contain an element of imagination is more than a simple truth. It reminds us that actors are not only the products of a situation, but that they contribute to producing that situation. There we have the beginning of an overlap between image and action. Images are more or less static faced with a situation which, in fact, is in the course of evolving. Or else they are more or less in the course of changing when faced with a situation which is, itself, blocked. Even a sequence of static images, different from each other, can represent a sort of reproduction of movement or imaginary movement of considerable significance at the level of action. Even relatively slight changes in one's self-image, faced with an unchanging external situation, can be strategic, indicative or revealing.

Although the British studies, as far as I know, only refer rarely to images other than mirror-images - which presuppose a fundamentally receptive attitude on the part of actors - it seems to me important to add two other kinds of image to the four preceding categories: those which have to do more particularly with conception (as opposed to reception). They should be considered, moreover, despite the French context in which some of us have developed them, (5) as peaceful projects or even as simple nostalgic images, as much as plans of violent action or active 'life projects'. (6)

(v) The image as a project transcending, in effect, straightforward perception. The project includes a strong element of conception (or, if you like, of explanation) of what is and this implies what ought to be. It is obviously not irrelevant whether an action accompanies, follows, or never occurs in aid of the realisation of the project. But consider also the case of lack of

action; very often the judgment that a social actor comes up with
in a situation, and in his position at a particular point in time,
implies a project, even if there is no action to carry it out.

(vi) In the case of the action-image, on the other hand, the
two levels of reality are directly mixed, in one process: the
action as an image-producing situation; the image as an action-
producing (or continuing) situation; either of these two sides
can be predominant. This notion seems most appropriate to those
cases where action precedes or accompanies the conception of an
image, this image being either an image of the existing society or
an image of an alternative society (to be established in the future).
The role of imagination seems to become even greater, as the situation 'hots up' and implies more upheaval in the future. (7)

Ambivalence and action

For various reasons a social actor may seek to avoid the necessity
of acting, or may find himself unable to act, in the strong sense
of the word (to behave in such a way that a social change is
produced).

If one wants to discuss the approach of a sociology of images
and its relation to action, it seems to me that the three sorts of
image present in the studies in this symposium: the structured
image, the non-image, and the multiplicity of images or ambivalent
image held by an actor, are all representative of what one might
call schizoid social imagery. An image clarifies and obscures at
the same time, it is a medium by which one may launch an offensive,
or conceal oneself. The schizoid state of affairs stems from the
fact that there is not always congruence between the offensive
orientation of the image and action; or that even a defence
mechanism, intended to protect the image, can have an effect strate-
gically which is offensive; and so on. Without going into all
the cases which it would be useful to distinguish, suffice it
to suggest that, each time one studies an image, it would be worthwhile to specify if it is one or other of the elements which
predominates (defensive-offensive). In any case, ambivalence can
take one of several forms; a non-image (vague in outline; presence
of more or less contradictory elements); two or more images held
by the same actor; or contradiction between the structured image
of an actor and his mode of action.

Returning to the notion of 'normality', this leads one to pose
the question - and perhaps even in relation to a population described as 'traditional' such as the one studied here, which is not
entirely untouched by changes that occurred in the rest of society -
whether schizoid social imagery is not, from now on, 'normal'. (8)
Is it not the entirely coherent respondents (in terms of the
correspondence between an image and a way of acting) who are the
exception?

We would ... use the term ambivalence. Our own research has
shown that workers in these situations hold a multiplicity of
class images or meaning-systems from which they will draw upon
the one most appropriate to explain a particular situation with
which they are confronted (Bell and Newby, Chapter 5).

The problem is not eased when respondents appear to have given
many very varied answers to questions about classes and class
differences.... A social situation which gives rise to a coherent image of society may well be the exception rather than
the rule (Brown and Cousins, Chapter 4).
Situations where those who work together also spend their
leisure time together so that social relations at work are
reinforced and overlaid by relations outside work (Brown et al.,
1973, p.97).

Beyond artefacts?

Certain images are less 'real' than others.   It goes without saying
that the intention of the sociologist is to distance himself from
artefacts;   first of all, from those which he creates himself, if
only by coding data in a certain way from questionnaire responses;
then from those which alienating social conditions produce in
society, 'conditioning' actors to misread the situation and misread
their own position in society.

Unfortunately the papers in this collection, like other experiences, show that the efforts toward 'depassement' of these two
levels - to obtain 'hard facts' and to collect them in violent
situations which are conducive to maximum 'depth' - tend to be
contradictory.   One is once again in a dilemma.   We undertake
systematic research, in such a way as to yield an adequate body of
data, fairly complete and analysable, which is carried out in a
technically serious way;   but we do not know whether these data on
images of society are meaningful.   Or else we find ourselves in a
violent situation, in the heat of the action, in the course of
which events we try to gather data, probably with little system,
probably the data is difficult to analyse.   The result is technically imperfect, but quite probably more meaningful.

This symposium has as its theme Lockwood's excellent paper of
1966.   Elsewhere our colleague has expressed, informally, an
interest in the study of 'hard facts' and at other times, an
interest in the study of violence.   The above dilemma can perhaps
be illuminated by reference to a theoretical paper by the same
writer (Lockwood, 1964).

Problems having to do with action are obviously framed in terms
of actors.   Lockwood defines the level of 'social integration' as
a source of social meaning.   And naturally this is the level at
which violence takes place, since in general violence is carried
out by an actor (against a thing, or directly against another
actor).   Less obviously, and more rarely defined, the level of
'system integration' is the source of sociological relevance and
meaning.   It is at this level that full and systematic data are
normally collected.   One can thus distinguish two kinds of trend
in the studies on social imagery: (a) those who tend to focus on
the degree of social integration, normally considering in the
course of intensive studies the problem of violence (overt, covert,
direct or indirect);   (b) those who tend to focus on the degree of
system integration, by means of extensive data permitting comparisons between different segments of the population.

At the second of these levels one notices that conflicting images or simply dissonant images can go along with system integration.   We seem to enter here an interesting but paradoxical field for reflexion: that which is centrifugal at the level of social integration (images in polar opposition) can at the same time be centripetal at the level of system integration (images, the same ones, being complementary, etc.).

Ideal and 'ideal' types

We have all read a lot about real and ideal types.   This does not make it much easier to cope with the fact that a trans-situational (ideal-typical) image of society - and we know this is more 'real', i.e. a more adequate analogue of the underlying socio-logic - is hard to get at.   What we have at hand are discrete situational data.   So how do we get from the latter to the former?

There is, of course, an easy way out of this problem.   A pseudo-solution is, as we all in principle know, to create a kind of theoretical frame of reference.   This can produce any number of 'ideal-types'.   But this only pushes the whole question a little farther away, through more cenceptual complexity, towards the 'academic'.   We must still ask, after that, which are real and which are not so real ideal types?

As if this were not enough of a problem we then come across the second classical, but much less recognised, trap: how 'ideal', in terms of a social value judgment, is a specific real type; how 'ideal' is a specific (real) ideal type?

Maybe this will seem to some to be simply a play on words.   To be sure, this is an area of problems where the 'us' (sociologists) and the 'them' (populations) comes in.   This is perhaps one of the main reasons why this is such an irritating problem.   But there is more to it than that: how 'ideal' is the population's situation?   That far many beginner's analyses go anyway.   But (level 2): how active is the population's image towards a situation more likely to be 'ideal'?   And (level 3): how active is the sociologist's image of the population's image towards a situation more likely to be 'ideal' (as experienced by the population, or as supposed, by the sociologist, to be an ideal in the future experience of the population)?

On top of this, an 'ideal' can be projected onto the past (as in communitarian golden age imageries).   If that was 'ideal', what about the present state of affairs as described by us (sociologists) on the basis of what they (populations) feel?   Is it an idealised ideal-type we want to demonstrate as real, or not?

Since the value of these typologies is essentially a heuristic one, it would be inappropriate to criticise them on the grounds that in each and every case they do not coincide with empirical reality (Bell and Newby, Chapter 5).	ideal real?
The complexity of class imagery, particularly the relationship between ideas of the 'proper' structure of society and reality as it is perceived (Batstone, Chapter 7).	'ideal'

The typical stereotype of the prestige
model is that mobility is seen as possible, and perhaps desirable (Batstone,
Chapter 7).

It is difficult to avoid encountering
the idea of the 'new working class'
since the former has been used as a
benchmark from which to measure the
distinctiveness of the latter (Davis
and Cousins, Chapter 11).

image of
'now'

Because the ideal-type of the 'traditional worker' actually hid from the sociologist the historical past, he was able to
say this being 'old', therefore this must
be 'new' (Davis and Cousins, Chapter 11).

image of
'then'

'Us' and 'them': from images to consciousness

Without going too much into the discussion of the differences
between images and consciousness (images involving some degree of
reflexiveness: what is the situation looked at from what position
of 'us'), let us end this paper with a few additional questions on
what Goldmann called 'possible' consciousness.

In some posthumously published essays (Goldmann, 1971) it appears
that he pursued his interest in virtuality - once expressed through
his suggestion that one should use provocative and conflictual
interviewing techniques, in order to see how far people's opinions
actually go, and how far respondents can stand pressure.   This
time he tackles one of the problems of this symposium: who
eventually defines the image of society we are talking about re any
sort of class or social category?

Possible consciousness (1971, p.10) is to be expressed as 'the
changes that may be produced in (a group's) consciousness, without
modifying the essential nature of the group'.   And he calls this
'zugerechnetes Bewusstsein' (9) - which, to my understanding, means
this is the image of itself beyond the one it actually has, a class
of people can stand, (i) as far as the calculation of the observer
goes (zu-'rechnen'), and (ii) this is based on the horizon of these
people as it is (present description), and shall be (predictive
description), in other words, one is talking about their consciousness, as a (future) attribute ('zu'-rechnen).

This, in those terms I would like to adopt here to make my final
point, can be expressed very simply: 'us' sociologists are defining
the 'us' workers (or other population) while not losing sight of
what we, as specialists, know about past, present and future trends
of society, but also by not losing sight of what the actual position
of workers is and shall be.   Therefore, that consciousness which
people can possibly hold without getting to feel they are losing
their identity, is a highly superior construct.   It places itself
at the intersection between (i) what is; what could be, (ii) what
is; what should be, (iii) what 'us' - sociologists - think about
'us' workers - population; what 'us' workers think about society,
and (iv) more generally, what is objective and what subjective,

since the 'calculation' and the attribution ('Zu'-rechnen) cannot
be dissociated.

The boundary problem between images and consciousness is a much
more intriguing one, I think, than just one concerned with people's
minds, since people studying people are people.   Just how much of
our own images of society and our own consciousness come into our
understanding and evaluation of data, images and consciousness as
expressed by 'them' (people studied) is never irrelevant, nor easily
specified.

Whether we are considering images of society or consciousness,
both of these are, to various degrees of intensity, mediations
between introjection and projection, between what is and projects
for what someone thinks should and/or could be.   We can look at
them from both points of view.   We are in a double double-bind.
There are two conflicting injunctions, themselves conflicting
injunctions: (a) the observer must understand, i.e. use his own
images and conciousness; he must not go beyond the real images or
consciousness of the population; (b) the observer must look at
people as they actually are; (10) he cannot be satisfied by taking
things at their face value.

Once the image, or consciousness, has been presented we are
still faced with the possible action these products, or their
holders, may eventually (11) contribute to progressive change.   We
may look at them pessimistically for what they are not; or optim-
istically, for what they are and can be used for - and some of the
images may be considered as 'negatives' (to use once again a
photographer's term).

What, today, is in the realm of 'actuellement' and 'eventuellement', may, tomorrow, be the ground of 'actually' and of 'eventually'.

NOTES

1 This paper is a re-written version of one presented orally in
   September 1972, not only to open a conference but to re-open
   consideration of a subject which has for a long time seemed to
   the author a very exciting one.   The paper was translated from
   the French by the editor and the author.   The responsibility
   for any imperfections or errors in translation lies with the
   editor.
2 A washing machine is a washing machine is a washing machine was
   Lockwood's way of saying something my colleagues and I also
   formulated about cars; a worker who has a car has a car, i.e.
   not necessarily a prestige object or anything as abstract as
   this.
3 In relation to this, see H.P. Dreitzel (1962).
4 Moore (above, Chapter 3) 'independently derived beliefs about
   society may have influenced the miners' interpretation of their
   social experience'.   'Lockwood seems to have underestimated the
   importance of ideas as such in forming images of society.'
5 Cf. Willener (1970).
6 For examples of this type of project, see Touraine and Ragazzi
   (1961).

7 This is the reason for suggesting, to keep the verbal analogy
   for a condensation observable in reality, the neologism image-
   ination, or even, as we suggested 'imageinaction'.
8 From this viewpoint, the contribution of the sociology of
   images is not grounded on simple and stable conceptions, but
   on those of a variety of worlds and contradictions to be
   explored (images v. actors) - by which I do not mean that one
   can not (or ought not) use the notion of 'false consciousness'.
9 Goldmann claims this to be a standard term used by Marx in
   'Die Heilige Familie' where, as far as I can see, it cannot
   be found.
10 Note the interesting mismatch of the French and English here:
   actually = reellement, actuellement = now.
11 Eventuellement = possibly; eventually = finalement.

Chapter 11

THE 'NEW WORKING CLASS' AND THE OLD

R.L. Davis and Jim Cousins

At the same time, however, one should note that the perspectives of the 'classic' sociologist are far wider than those of sociologists who would define the scope of their subject in terms of modern methods of field research.   Because of the limitations of the techniques to which they are wedded, the latter are forced to restrict themselves largely to the study of social milieux (communities, work situations, local associations, etc.) considered statically or over very short-term periods.   Without forsaking their techniques, they are thus unable to appreciate or to explain how these social milieux have emerged from, and are conditioned by, the structure of the wider society in which they are set, or how ongoing changes at the level of the milieux are related to changes at a societal level.   To do this would entail a shift precisely to the classic mode of sociological analysis. It would mean thinking in terms of societies as developing structures, or, in other words, it would call for the introduction of a historical dimension.... In pursuit of aims of this kind, the special relevance of historical data is not difficult to appreciate.   In the first place, any attempt at a developmental approach will obviously require such data.   For example, when we speak of the transition from 'traditional' to 'industrial' society, or from the 'folk' to the 'urban' community, or from 'familial' to 'bureaucratic' business enterprises, we are in effect using conceptions the validity of which can only be derived from historical study... As I see it, then, the tradition of historically oriented study must continue to form the core of sociology.   If such a view is prejudicial to the scientific status of the discipline, then so much the worse for that (John H. Goldthorpe, 1962, p.28).

To emphasize the continuity of this theme, (1) which is being raised anew today, is not, of course, to disavow its contemporary relevance.   It is to suggest however, that what is seen to be 'new' about the present day working class must not be discovered by a distortion of the immediate past, by an over-simplified view of the 'traditional' working class (David Lockwood, 1960, p.249).

THE HISTORICAL NATURE OF THE 'TRADITIONAL WORKING CLASS'

Although this symposium (2) is dealing specifically with the 'traditional' worker as characterised by Lockwood, it is difficult to avoid encountering the idea of the 'new working class' since the former has been used as a benchmark from which to measure the distinctiveness of the latter (Goldthorpe et al., 1969, especially p.118); indeed Lockwood's fully fledged concept of the former arose out of a concern with the latter. The ideal-type of the 'tradition-al worker' is developed alongside the debate as to what 'new' characteristics the working class was taking on, so that the compari-son can be drawn (Lockwood, 1960; Goldthorpe and Lockwood, 1963; Lockwood, Chapter 2).

Without engaging in a debate as to Weber's meaning of 'ideal-types' - whether they are aids to discovery and as such disposable, or the core - constructive elements of an abstract science of society - one can still assess the contribution such a methodology has made in recent debates on the working class. It has to be concluded that it has led discussants, try as they may to avoid it, to fall into the trap which Lockwood himself, in a passage quoted above, warned against in 1960. The inadequacy of the methodology is exposed when attempts are made to typify trends and directions within a segment of society which are only trends and directions and not structural units. To avoid recognising and confronting this, the typifier has to claim a special significance for the period of history which receives his detailed attention, turning it into a 'break' or 'departure'. In this latter connection, it is interesting to note how the 'new' working class, held at arm's length in inverted commas by Lockwood in 1960, has by 1969 actually become the new working class - that which was questionable has emerged as fact (Goldthorpe et al., 1969, especially pp.116, 164, 185, 187, 190).

That the difficulties and pitfalls of continuing debates of this nature were apparent to Lockwood is evidenced by his 1960 paper, and he would no doubt agree with E.J. Hobsbawm that the unchanging past presented in stereotyped 'traditionalism' is 'a myth of vulgar social science' (Hobsbawm, 1972). That the subsequent research papers and reports failed to avoid some of them might charitably be a function of the lack of 'distance' between researcher and subject, the necessity to produce 'findings', etc., i.e. features of the research situation. Be that as it may, whereas the working class in 1960 had a history, by 1966 the 'traditional worker' had become 'a sociological, not an historical concept' - an ideal-type (Lockwood, Chapter 2).And again, in Goldthorpe et al., 1969, the point is made that

it is at this juncture perhaps worth underlining ... that such concepts as the 'traditional worker' or 'traditional working class community' must be understood as tools of sociological and not historical analysis. Their use, for example, contains no implication that at some period of time all or even most of the members of the working class displayed social characteristics, or lived in communities with characteristics, of the kind that are labelled as 'traditional' (p.86, note 1).

Yet it is clear that in many ways the 'traditional worker' in

Lockwood, and subsequently in Goldthorpe and Lockwood, is as much
an historical concept as a sociological one (if we permit ourselves
to draw the distinction).   From even a casual reading, it is clear
that Lockwood's own 1966 'types', and the previous outline of them
in 1963, have a direct reference to the nineteenth- and twentieth-
century history that he showed such awareness of.   In 1969, it is
not only past sociological literature but also 'empirical evidence'
that is 'reflected' in the ideal-types (Goldthorpe et al., 1969,
especially p.121).   If sociological literature does not exist in
time, presumably 'empirical evidence' does!   Again, in 1966, 'both
types (of traditionalists) are to be found ... (in industries and
communities which, to an ever-increasing extent, are backwaters of
national industrial and urban development)' (Lockwood, Chapter 2).
That is, 'to be found' in time and space, one must assume.   In the
same article, the development of the 'privatised worker' ideal-
type is stated as stemming from the Luton research project - as
'leaning heavily' on a then forthcoming paper by Goldthorpe expressing some preliminary findings (Lockwood, Chapter 2, note 3).   This
ideal-type is, then, directly derived from research at a particular
time and place.   It has the same status in the scheme as the others;
thus they too must be historically derived or else the typology has
questionable meaning since its components are on the one hand real
and on the other imaginary.
    The developmental framework employed by Goldthorpe and Lockwood,
despite their own criticisms of other such perspectives (Goldthorpe
et al., 1969, especially Introduction and Conclusion) only compounds
this.   Thus the end of Lockwood's article:
    A purely pecuniary ideology is, of course, just as much of a
    limiting case as a purely class or purely status model of
    society.   But it may be that it is at least as relevant as the
    other two in understanding the social and political outlook of
    the increasingly large section of the working class that is
    emerging from traditionalism' (Chapter 2).
And in 1969, 'our own research indicates clearly enough how
increasing affluence and its correlates can have many far reaching
consequences - both in undermining the viability or desirability of
established life-styles and in encouraging or requiring the development of new patterns of attitudes, behaviour and relationships'
(Goldthorpe et al., 1969, p.163), and 'at one level of analysis, the
new working class (sic) must obviously be seen as a product of
economic and social structural changes of a long term kind' (Goldthorpe et al., 1969, p.190).   So, in 1969, 'some proportion' of
the Luton workers were thought to have 'had no doubt experience of
community life of a kind which approximated to this pattern ...'
(the traditional kind) but that 'traditional working class influences on these men and their families were likely to be at a
minimal level.   Whatever their previous community experience may
have been, they were now largely free from the continuous and
essentially conservative social pressures exerted by the extended
family and by established neighbourhood custom' (Goldthorpe et al.,
1969, p.86).   Thus their discussion recognises a process as
existing, and seems clearly to identify 'traditionalism' with the
historical past, and the 'new' working class as 'emerging' from
this.   If this were not so, then the language of 'convergence' and

'prototypicality' could not be used.   (For detailed argument on these lines, see Cousins, 1971). As another commentator has said, 'a perspective on present social experience is gained by postulating a tendentious relationship between what is observed now and a structural type associated firmly but unspecifically with the "past"' (Abrams, 1972, p.20).   To claim that the 'traditional worker' is a sociological concept, or that the typology only represented an heuristic device, as such incapable of verification, is too convenient a solution and sidesteps the problem of confronting 'what actually happened'.   If sociology is to be grounded in history, as both Goldthorpe and Lockwood once claimed, the construction of ideal-types which purport to be 'non-historical' is not helpful; and if one is using them in a debate essentially concerned with developments in working class life, their unhelpfulness is extreme.   Because the ideal-type of the 'traditional worker' actually hid from the sociologist the historical past, he was able to say this being 'old', therefore this must be 'new'; instead of 'this is how things are at the moment; how did they get to be like it'. (3)   In other words the employment of the typology has led to rather more confusion than enlightenment.   This is really only emerging now as 'images of society' are shown to be as diverse as the social situation in which they are located; and indeed as the sociologist looks to history to see what kind of a working class existed in times gone by.   If this was a standard sociological practice, and if Goldthorpe and Lockwood had employed it (as perhaps their earlier writings led us to expect that they would), then we might well have had a much wider-ranging debate about the affluent worker of the Luton studies.   This is finally only attempted in the Introduction and Conclusion to the third volume of 'The Affluent Worker'.   One particular important confusion might never have occurred had that research been fully grounded in history - and that is the apparent confusion of oppositional politics with 'traditional proletarianism'.   That industries like docking, mining and shipbuilding (Lockwood, Chapter 2) can be identified as (in particular) having those industrial and community structures likely to engender 'traditional proletarianism' must be a result of an inadequate grounding in the histories of those industries; a grounding which, as we hope to suggest, ought to have led to a rather different analysis.

   Similarly, the identification of 'instrumentalism' as a new departure ignores the kind of bond between a man and his job that has long existed as a basic feature of capitalist society.   As Westergaard points out, Goldthorpe and Lockwood have merely 're-discovered the cash-nexus' (Westergaard, 1970, p.111).   (The fact of 're-discovery', too, points up Goldthorpe and Lockwood's - and contemporary sociology's - lack of appreciation of the historical past.)   Westergaard goes on to point to the ambiguity of the world views which the Luton researchers uncover, and claims that because the Luton workers' commitment to work is a brittle one that possibilities of class action arise - 'the cash-nexus may snap just because it is only a cash-nexus - because it is single-stranded' (Westergaard, 1970, p.120).   Such 'possibilism' is only recognised in the concluding volume of the 'Affluent Worker' series.   Again, this 'closed-ness' of the debate can be traced to the ideal-type

methodology and the attribution of sets of characteristics to
individuals based on their answers to questions at a particular time
and place, and the elaboration of these answers to a human type -
'this is them' - without the qualifying 'this is not necessarily
them for all time'. This despite the action perspective!

Indeed, this methodological procedure and consequent misreading
of the historical position of the working class produces unintended
deformities in the interpretation of the whole 'affluent worker'
debate.   What began as an attack on the revisionism of the
embourgeoisement thesis ends by lending support to a new and subtler
kind of revisionism.   This possibility is recognised by 'The
Affluent Worker' team themselves (Goldthorpe et al., 1969, p.165;
the argument should be compared to the almost identical alternative
possibilities of working class social development envisaged by
G.D.H. Cole in Cole, 1948, p.160).   In the conclusion to 'The
Affluent Worker' great efforts are made to suggest that the idea
of the 'new worker' should be given a radical rather than one of
several conservative interpretations (Goldthorpe et al., 1969,
pp.164-87).   This is in line with what may have been the original
desire to see in the 'new worker' a new source of political radicalism rather than the reverse (Goldthorpe and Lockwood, 1963, p.156).
But the nature of the 'traditional working class' that is outlined;
the greatness of the differences between the 'new workers' and the
'old'; and the identification of the declining 'traditional worker'
with class consciousness and proletarianism necessarily drag the
arguments the opposite way.   The association of affluence, political
and social calculativeness, and mobility with radical politics and
radical collective action could be much better seen if the association had not been made with reference solely to a particular,
contemporary (and reified) social formation: the 'new worker';
and if the assumed opposite of the 'new worker' - the 'traditional
worker' - had not also been pre-eminently associated with class
consciousness, class action and the left tradition in politics.
The false contrast of 'old' and 'new' almost inevitably leads to
conservative interpretations of the affluent worker.   And these
conservative interpretations are little different from the originally
counterposed idea of embourgeoisement except that they are, sociologically, more complex and convincing.

REVISIONISM AND 'NEW' WORKERS

As Lockwood himself makes clear 'the theme of working-class
bourgeoisification is almost as old as that of its proletarianisa-
tion' (Lockwood, 1960, p.248). (4)   What he does not point out is
that affluent 'new' workers have appeared in several distinct types
of revisionist argument.   Indeed there is even a tendency for the
'new workers' of one generation to appear as the 'old workers' of
the next.   What is perhaps most interesting about the successive
phases of revisionist argument are the changing models of the
middle class in which the working class is to be assimilated.   The
history of 'bourgeoisifications' is the history of the decline and
finally, by 'convergence', the possible disappearance of bourgeois
social formations.

As early as the 1850s commentators were welcoming the existence
of a 'new' working class - respectable, temperate, a member of
Co-op and Penny Banks (Ludlow and Lloyd Jones, 1867;   Giffen, 1883),
who would eventually become a class of worker-capitalists who would
eliminate the employer by co-operation through the limited liability
companies (Mill, 1848 (1965 edition pp.758-96);   Ludlow, 1852).
Later, as the unreality of the idea of capitalist producer co-operatives became apparent, the 'new model' worker was seen as associating with, rather than eliminating, the employer in systems of piece-
work sub-contracting, profit sharing, and price-based wage sliding
scales (Brassey, 1879;   Price, 1887;   Ashley, 1903;   Marshall, 1925).
These ideas were able to flourish during the period of the so-called
Great Depression (1873-96) as, though wages fell, food costs fell
much faster and real wages therefore continued to improve.   It was
during this period that smallholdings were seen as the solution to
seasonal unemployment, notably in mining areas producing house coal
(de Rousiers, 1896, pp.232-7).   In an early article the Webbs saw
the instability of associative collective bargaining in profit-
sharing, sliding-scales and Conciliation Boards without mass trade
union organisations (S. and B. Webb, 1896, pp.1-29).   Therefore
the 'new worker' was to be organised in a 'new' unionism - national
and industrial rather than sectional and local.   These would be
capable through a body of professional bureaucrats of making proper
collective bargains with the employers and enforcing them;   and
capable of supporting their membership in periods of sickness and
unemployment by their own properly administered welfare schemes
(S. and B. Webb, 1897).   These organisations would be able to
contribute to national order and efficiency;   and the new unions
with their 'new workers' were thus caught up in the intoxicating
turn of the century combination of 'imperialism and social reform'
(Semmel, 1960, pp.53-83).

   In his classic work of revisionism Bernstein draws on this
British tradition of the 'new worker' (Bernstein, 1909).   He makes
use of British thinking on wider shareholding (pp.44-5);   the
survival of petty capitalism in industry (pp.54-6);   the retail
co-operatives (pp.120-6);   the use of smallholdings (pp.130-3); and
the Webbsian idea of collective bargaining as a 'Labour Partnership'
(pp.140-1);   he also supports imperial development as a source of
cheap food (pp.177-9). (5)

   These older versions of revisionism like the present ones did not
claim to analyse the whole of a society with reference to its past.
They take particular tendencies or possibilities and anticipate the
results of these tendencies being generalised over the whole of the
working class.   In this sense the notion of 'prototypicality'
(Goldthorpe et al., 1968a, p.136) is common to them all.   But if
any change is generalised over the whole, then society as a whole
must change and so must the relationship between societies.   In
this way, the best-established directionalities must encounter
rivals, and suffer the results of their own success.   The cheap
food that underpins the association of capital and labour in sliding
scales requires the expropriation of the Irish peasantry;   the
'Labour Partnership' supports the conflict of empires;   the 'instrumental worker' may cause declining profitability and competitiveness
in a national capitalism (Glyn and Sutcliffe, 1972).

In comparing older revisionisms with the new ones differences
do emerge.   Earlier revisionisms were much more focused on the
relationship of capital to labour.   The revisionism based on
life-style and patterns of consumption does not emerge clearly
until later (Cole, 1934).   This in itself is suggestive of changes
inside the bourgeoisie.   The bourgeoisie with whom the earlier
revisionists sought to associate or integrate the working class
was a bourgeoisie of entrepreneurs or semi-autonomous plant managers
who exercised economic power.   This social formation has in modern
revisionism now disappeared or been reduced in status.   Consequently
the 'new' working class is parallelled by a 'new' bourgeoisie - no
longer economically dominant over the working class, perhaps even
equivalent to the workers in economic rewards;   different from
them perhaps, only in 'normative' and 'relational' ways (Goldthorpe
and Lockwood, 1963, p.136).   'Class doesn't matter any more.   They
are as well off as we are' (doctor's wife at a coffee morning
quoted in the 'Newcastle Journal').   Economic conflict has been
replaced by social comparison.   But this assumes a decline in the
bourgeoisie perhaps even more drastic than the decline of an
alleged traditionalism in the workers.   Now, it can hardly be
assumed that the functions of the bourgeoisie as the older revisionists saw them - economic domination over the working class by the
provision of employment and wages - have disappeared along with the
social groups that formerly exercised them.   It is the failure to
consider this dimension of the 'instrumental, affluent worker's'
situation that makes the 'new worker', despite protestations, a
revisionist concept.   The assumption of continual economic growth
plays the same part in this modern revisionism as the assumption
of continually falling food prices played in the old.   Indeed
because modern revisionism has strayed further from the idea of
labour as a commodity than the old by its concentration on norms
and relations, it is much less relevant to the idea of the proletariat and consequently, as a revisionism, much less convincing.
The idea of the earlier revisionists that mass unionisation of the
working class would serve to associate labour and capital rather
than divide them is of permanent significance.   Modern revisionism,
in overlooking this in its conceptualisation of the 'traditional
worker', makes one of its basic mistakes.   Yet another warning
sign might have been found for modern revisionism by an examination
of the old.   The old was ready to recognise many-sided differentiations amongst the working class;   the old saw in the 'traditional proletarian' industries of mining and steel the best modern
examples of mass trade unionism supporting the mutual interdepend-
ence of capital and labour.

THE WORKING-CLASS COMMUNITY AND THE SOCIAL ORDER

As suggested in the first part, one source of confusion in Lockwood's typology and its subsequent usage is the apparent linking of
'opposition' to 'traditional proletarianism', particularly in those
communities with distinctive characteristics which are said to be a
feature of industries such as mining, docking and shipbuilding.
Although Lockwood hints that he is primarily concerned with their

'pre-war' history (Lockwood, 1960, p.249), these are industries
which developed into maturity in the previous century and early
part of this century, and likewise then laid the basis for those
'distinctive communities' associated with them.   The long-term
history of such industrial workers is uneven - as Lockwood recognises in 1960, the story of the British working class has many
twists and strands.   However, a reading of the history of the
workers in such industries is much more likely to bring us to
appreciate the arguments of John Westergaard (Westergaard, 1965
and 1970), and more recently Frank Parkin (Parkin, 1971), than to
allow us to sympathise to any great degree with the idea of the
'traditional proletarian'.   In his earlier paper, Westergaard
is critical of the assumption that 'the kind of working class unity
which finds expression in industrial, or more especially in political, action, draws its nourishment from the simpler and more intimate loyalties of neighbourhood and kin'; and the implication that
'the solidarity of class ... is rooted in the kind of parochial
solidarity which is its very antithesis'. So, 'the "particularistic" ties of neighbourhood, kin and regional culture provide no
adequate basis for the maintenance of the "universalistic"
loyalties involved in class political action' (Westergaard, 1965,
pp.107-8).   While not being specifically critical of Goldthorpe
and Lockwood here, Lockwood noted this argument in discussing class
imagery though did not seem to recognise its import for his
characterisation of the 'traditional working class community'
(Chapter 2, note 25). (6)   These kinds of strands of criticism
have been elaborated recently by Parkin (Parkin, 1971).   Westergaard's questions, 'can radicalism be effectively measured by the
strength of support for the Labour party and the unions?' and
'are not universalistic labour movements the antithesis of solidary
collectivism?' (Westergaard, 1970, p.126 - neither direct quotations)
are elements discussed in Parkin's analysis of the 'meaning systems'
of capitalist social structures.   The value-system historically
shared by the working class has been and is an essentially 'subordinate' one, an adaptation to the 'dominant' one.   The 'power-model'
of society (which Goldthorpe and Lockwood identify with 'traditional proletarianism') should not be seen as 'exemplifying class
consciousness or political radicalism'; and the 'pervasive sense
of communal solidarity typically found in the underclass milieu'
must not be assume to embody it either.   The meaning system of
working class community is parochial, whereas 'becoming class
conscious' is essentially a learning process.   The Labour party,
the unions, are all elements deriving their meaning from this
subordinate value system - they are all adaptive to the dominant
one, and accept its rules.   'Oppositional values are the creation
of political agencies based on society rather than on community and
are not derivative from the subordinate value system' (Parkin, 1971,
pp.88-96).
    With these trenchant criticisms in mind, what then do we make
of Lockwood's 'mining, docking and shipbuilding'?   The histories
of these industries would probably show that he has misinterpreted
certain phenomena as evidence of 'opposition' whereas they are
better interpreted in terms of Parkin's 'subordinate value system'.
Whereas at times and in certain places a kind of class consciousness

has been achieved, this is rare and not characteristic of the history of such industries; and where it has broken through, it might be argued, has been when the stability and order which Lockwood associates with those industries and their communities has been lacking.   The possibilities of similar circumstances arising again are not totally negligible, if historical parallels carry any weight or suggestion.

THE MINERS OF SOUTH-EAST NORTHUMBERLAND (7)

An observer in 1855 remarked:
> The (Northumberland) pitmen are in every sense a peculiar race, and strange indeed is their manner of life, passed, as it is,in the bowels of the earth, shut out from the light of day.   From early boyhood to old age their thoughts and occupations are with coal - consequently, their knowledge of the world, beyond the colliery district, is very limited and an occasional journey to any place beyond Newcastle, is quite an event in their monotonous lives (Whellan, 1855, p.133).

If there were institutions which embodied values rising above the limitations of the colliery village these were the various Methodist chapels, perpetuating an essentially 'accommodative' set of values rather than an oppositional one, although at the same time providing the opportunity for self-determination for a certain sector of the population in limited spheres of their social lives. J.T. Taylor, owner of Earsdon colliery in S.E. Northumberland, told J.R. Leifchild, (8) the Northumberland and North Durham Commissioner for the Employment of Children Commission, that
> the pitmen owe so much of religious knowledge as they possess to certain sects of Dissenters, especially the Wesleyan Methodists. The Church should have done her duty better towards them.   They are fond of becoming preachers, class-leaders, etc., themselves, and this opens the door to a vast deal of vanity and conceit; inasmuch that I suspect there is more of vain glory and hypocrisy than of any sounder feeling amongst such of them as have become attentive to matters of religion (Royal Commission on Employment of Children, 1842, no.198, p.608).

This part of the Northumberland coal-field had begun to be exploited in full in the 1820s, as the pits on the side of the Tyne became exhausted and the industry moved towards the deeper reserves; from this time on, and up to the mid-century, the area north of the Tyne between Newcastle and the coast and up towards Blyth became populated.   In those villages and townships developed in the 1820s and 1830s, the chapels began to appear in the mid-1840s and after; and it was the Methodists, notably the Primitives, also known as the 'Ranters', who came to be the formal leaders of such communities as they stabilised and matured, and who more than any other sect or organisation, provided the link between Methodism, Unionism and co-operation (e.g. Fynes, 1923, pp.282-3).   Their values, however, were never oppositional; although they recognised the existence of classes in society, they sought a harmonious functional solution - the integration of the interests of labour and capital.   The story of unions in Northumberland, mainly under their influence, is an adequate illustration of what Parkin calls 'union-consciousness'.   Prior to the 1844 strike in Northumberland, Martin Jude's 'Miners Association of Great Britain and Northern Ireland' (aims - 'to lessen hours, get fair wages, and agitate for government interference') sent a circular out addressed to the coal-owners and talking of the desire to amicably settle grievances, the essential harmony of interests of capital and labour, and the damage that strike action brought to both sides of industry.   The slogan of the eventual strike (the mine-owners ignored the circular) was 'a fair day's wage for a fair day's work' (Fynes, 1923, pp.49-51). Defensiveness and desire for conciliation mark these nineteenth century organisations;   some union-type bodies were really, in the main, straightforward benefit societies.   The Miners' Permanent Relief Fund of the late 1860s looked forward to a day when 'masters and men would shake hands with each other and recognize each other as members of one human society' (Fynes, 1923, p.215).   Many strikes have a defensive quality about them, as the owners accelerated their onslaught on wages, deeming them to be determined, according to the harsh laws of nineteenth-century capitalist logic, by prices.   The miners' appeal is often to the wider society - the petitions to Parliament always stress the loyalty of these subjects to the crown and their desire to live in peace (Fynes, 1923, pp.52-3). The message essentially is 'we are part of this society;   let us share in what it has to offer'.   So defensive at times did the formal union leadership become that rank-and-file strikers were severely censured at Cramlington in the 1860s (Fynes, 1923, p.251); as early as this in its history, the union had come to see one of its functions as being the prevention of any serious disturbances between capital and labour.

David Douglass has recently put forward a similar analysis of the miners' unions (with special reference to Durham) with the added contention that the leadership of the unions has prevented the development of class-consciousness and has acted against the interests of the rank-and-file (Douglass, 1971).   As he shows, rank-and-file militancy has always been a feature of some of the lodges, though in varying degree.   This much, too, emerges from a reading of Fynes and of Welbourne's history of the unions (Fynes, 1923;   Welbourne, 1923).   It has never been more than piecemeal, however.   It would be illuminating to analyse the conditions both in the industry and the community, under which it has occurred. The little evidence that exists suggests that it is not in those kinds of situations that Lockwood suggests breed 'proletarian traditionalism'.   Rather, it is when flux, not stability, is a dominant feature, both in terms of the industry and the community - at the time of the development of new pits, for instance, before the 'solidary community' has evolved.

In the newly developed areas the pitmen were less an accepted part of the social order and an increasing number of them were new to life in the colliery rows.   Lead-miners who had left their exhausted workings to bind themselves at the coal-pits, colliers from Scotland, Wales and the Midland counties, Irish peasants, and small-country labourers, knew little of the hereditary claim to steady employment and of the traditional high standard of life.   They were expected to conform more

closely to the other inhabitants, the farm hands whom they
displaced and the cokemen and furnace-men who came to live in
the iron towns which grew up near the pit-heads.   They had no
reason to claim the privilege of the old pitmen, 'undisturbed
quarters, respectful distance, and freedom from arrest'.   They
had no pride in their calling.   It was a means to a living, not
a station in society....   In every account of labour troubles it
is plain that the centres of unrest were the new pits.   The men
had lately come, they were as ready to go (Welbourne, 1923,
pp.46-7).

This kind of 'instrumentalism', then, was the precursor of the early
challenges to the coal-owners and ordered society (the one representing the other in the earlier part of the century in the coalfield).

Although excessive waves of migration occurred throughout the
century (both in- and out-migration), and at times of labour troubles
'blackleg' labour was imported from other regions of Britain (e.g.
tin-miners from Cornwall - Welbourne, 1923, p.129) keeping the
mining area in some degree of 'turnover', elements of the 'distinctive community' did begin to appear in mid-century and later -
the chapels from the mid-forties, the co-operatives from the 1860s.
(9)   These shared in the same subordinate value system as the
unions, and were basically organised by the same people. (10)   As
such, they blurred any possibilities of achieving a class consciousness and substituted, perhaps imposed, their own kind of 'accommodation'.   Although in the later stages of the century, visiting
London dockers found some welcome for their Marxist socialism
(Welbourne, 1923, pp.203-4), and rank-and-file activity increased
before the First World War, these formal characteristics and these
governing institutions, were never defeated.   When the transition
came, too, allegiances were mainly transferred from one set of
accommodating agencies to another, the latter including the Labour
party and the workingmen's clubs. (11)

CONCLUSION

There are several historical parallels here that have implications
which Goldthorpe and Lockwood only finally, and rather begrudgingly,
acknowledge.   First, 'Affluence' can be reified into a state of
near permanence;   as we have been recently reminded once again,
such permanence cannot be assumed (Glyn and Sutcliffe, 1972).   The
possibilities of class action once this is clear (coupled with the
exposure of the 'cash-nexus') are a reality.   (Recent strikes
might well be instanced as demonstrating this - e.g. those of the
miners and the dockers.)   Second, the 'new' industries and associated communities do provide arenas in which class conflict can
arise since they are not 'encumbered' with those community structures which inhibit the development of consciousness.   However,
that they might become 'encumbered' is a possibility too.   As
Westergaard says, referring to Luton:

if conditions 'favourable' to the simple 'embourgeoisment'
thesis were deliberately chosen, in order the more firmly to
refute that thesis if it should fail to hold water, just the
same conditions happen also to be 'favourable' to the 'privat-

ization' hypothesis which the authors put in its place (Wester-gaard, 1970, p.119).
The evidence in south-east Northumberland points to a lag in the development of community institutions and structures; as does evidence from the Yorkshire coalfield, where 'only since 1870 has an identifiable mining community come into existence in Yorkshire' and the distinctive community took until the First World War to emerge there - i.e. a thirty-year lapse between settlement and identity (Storm Clark, 1971). (12)

The linkage of prosperity and affluence; labour mobility and economic growth with aggressive wage bargaining and political radicalism is not a new departure in the analysis of the British working class. The 'new' worker is nothing new. In the early 1700s commentators were pointing out the connection between the availability of smart-looking cotton dresses and the impudence of maidservants. The real argument against the embourgeoisement thesis is not to posit a 'new' working class. The so-called 'old' working class areas have in the past been boom areas like Luton and have shown much the same kind of characteristics. Not only this, but they too were regarded as locations of a new working class in their day. The argument against the embourgeoisement thesis is a theoretical one. To be a proletarian is not to be pauperised but to be a commodity. The so-called 'new' working classes by their very privatisation and instrumentality have been some of the most proletarian sections of the British working class; and possessing, because they were affluent, much more confidence and capability in its organisation. Militancy in pre-war Britain was found on building sites and in aircraft factories, not in mines and shipyards. The so-called traditional community should be assoc-iated not with class consciousness and militancy but with political isolation and defeat. Those very aspects which Lockwood saw as accompanying the new worker and affecting an ever larger part of the working class, were in fact threatening the differentiation of the working class, the sectionalism of its organisation, and the sectoralism of its experience. These are the true supports of working class conservatism and, in the traditional working class community, find, certainly not their only, but perhaps one of their chief, expressions.

We contend, finally, that the contrasts between 'new' and 'old' that have been drawn both in the past and contemporaneously have obscured rather more than they have made clear. Since, in the most recent case, the contrast has been drawn with the use of an ideal-typificatory method, one must subject such a method to intense scrutiny. To avoid the misleading effects of that method, one solution might be sought in making the resultant typology ever more sophisticated - to include newly-discovered factors and dimensions, or ones which ought to have been included in the first place. Our own conclusion, however, is that to veer away from such intellectual jig-saw puzzling is necessary, and that a greater concern with what people are (were) actually doing and the situa-tional and historical circumstances they are (were) doing it in is the proper concern of sociology. Should such a concern be 'prejudicial to the scientific status of the discipline', then indeed 'so much the worse for that'.

NOTES

1 The 'continuing theme' is, of course, the one of working-class
   embourgeoisement.
2 This paper was written in the summer of 1972 for the conference
   in September of that year, and has here been slightly modified
   for publication.   However, there have been no major alterations
   in the arguments presented to the conference.   None the less,
   subsequent research on our part has led us to a revision of some
   of these ideas, principally those dealing with the idea of
   dominant and subordinate value systems and working-class action
   (specifically in relation to the miners of south-east Northumberland).   For this, see Cousins and Davis (1973).   Both
   papers arise out of a programme of regional and community
   studies in north-east England supported by the Joseph Rowntree
   Memorial Trust.
3 The somewhat saddening feature of these criticisms of Lockwood,
   and of Goldthorpe, is that as the quotes from their earlier
   work amply demonstrate, the historical perspective was originally
   firmly held, but over the process of the research seems to have
   become submerged.   Perhaps, as we suggest, this is partly as
   a result of the employment of the typificatory method, but also
   perhaps the significance for other researchers is the danger
   inherent in the whole research situation of the mechanisms
   (data collection, analysis, the necessity to present 'findings')
   using up resources which might be better employed developing
   the original ideas.   Maybe this is evidenced by the return,
   when all the 'findings' have been presented, to the historical
   debate in the third volume of the Luton study, in particular in
   the Introduction and Conclusion.
4 Lockwood goes on to quote a series of commentators which
   includes Engels, Michels and Evan Durbin.
5 Rosa Luxemburg, Berstein's great opponent in the German Social-
   Democratic Party, also pointed to the critical part played by
   colonies in supplying ever cheaper food and raw materials and
   thus postponing the confrontation of capital and labour (Luxemburg, 1951).
6 Lockwood in fact responds to Westergaard's point by providing a
   counter to associated arguments (in Anderson and Blackburn,
   1965) of the kind that the growth of instrumentalism could
   heighten class consciousness as workers become engaged in wages
   struggles;   Lockwood's contention is that instrumentalism could
   itself produce a narrow and parochial kind of radicalism -
   purely and simply, workplace bargaining for higher wages in
   order to maintain consumption standards.   That Westergaard's
   point, if valid, tends to undermine the idea of the traditional
   working class community as the fount of 'opposition', he does
   not consider.
7 For the case of shipbuilding, see Cousins and Brown (1970) and
   Brown et al. (1972).
8 Leifchild might well stake a claim to a place amongst the early
   British sociologists, as he painstakingly collected evidence and
   conducted interviews with young mineworkers in every part of the
   coalfield.   Many of these interviews he reported in more or

less verbatim form; to conduct them, too, he acquainted himself
with the local dialects.

9   Cramlington Co-operative was the first in the region, in 1861
(Cramlington District Co-operative Society Ltd, 1912).

10 The Rev. D. Rutherford, Chairman of the Co-operative Mining
Society argued in 1873 that 'the application of our principles
over any considerable area of our coalfields would soon put an
end to the coal famine, to all its sad consequences, and would
introduce harmony between the conflicting interests of capital,
labour and trade' (Fynes, 1923, pp.192-3).

11 For a run-down of the history of workingmen's clubs in the
North-East, see Elkins (1970).

12 In this connection, it is of some interest to note Welbourne's
description of the Cornish tin-miners, who, on arrival in
south-east Northumberland, exhibited some degree of 'privatisation' and 'complementarity' in their conjugal role-relationship.
'The men set to work to whitewash the houses, that they might
a little resemble the cottages they had left behind. They had
none of that feeling, still strong in the north, that a man has
amply performed his share of the marriage compact when he has
handed over to his wife the bulk of his earnings. They did
not shame to help their wives to wash, or even to cook'
(Welbourne, 1923, p.130). Was this a relationship transported
from Cornwall? Or a function of the migrant situation (albeit
exaggerated by a hostile 'host' population)?

Chapter 12

OCCUPATIONAL COMMUNITIES - COMMUNITIES OF WHAT?

D.H. Allcorn and C.M. Marsh

INTRODUCTION

The processes which constitute industrial societies and which commonly provide the starting point of sociological inquiry exhibit two opposing tendencies. The very term industrial society suggests that the organisation of work is inextricably involved in the ordering of society, even that the ways in which work is organised are the ways in which society is ordered. At the same time it is a sociological commonplace that, for most people in industrial society, the activities and relationships of the work-place are separated from the other activities and relationships of everyday life. (1) Thus in general there are no institutionalised connections between pursuing a particular occupation and living in a particular locality. More specifically, residence in a partic-ular place or association with workmates and colleagues outside working hours are rarely explicit and enforceable conditions of recruitment and employment. The employment relationship is ostensibly a market relationship and industry is thereby institu-tionally isolated from the rest of social life (see especially Dahrendorf, 1959). Where people live and who they associate with outside the workplace are thus rendered contingent on other circum-stances. This is necessarily so if the employment relationship consists solely in the sale of labour-power as a commodity and all other considerations are excluded. Indeed, the exclusion of all other considerations in constructing an ideal labour market produces 'a very Eden of the innate rights of man. There alone rule Freedom, Equality, Property, and Bentham' (K. Marx, 'Capital', 1, p.176). (2)

Sociologists, unlike political economists, or for that matter Marx, have rarely been prepared to idealise the labour market, the employment relationship and the organisation of work in this way. Proceeding from observations of what happens in everyday life and seldom concerned with the analysis of capitalist production as a whole, although some such analysis is often assumed, sociologists have far more often set out to investigate in greater or less detail the possible connections between what happens at work and what happens elsewhere, and to discover possible patterns and

regularities of what, on the initial definition, are contingent
circumstances.   Thus for many sociological purposes the outcomes
of the processes which Marx and others treat as problematic are
taken as given.   Conversely, some of the outcomes of processes
which Marx, at least in his analysis of the capitalist mode of
production as a whole, was prepared to treat as given or predict-
able, notably the increasing uniformity in the circumstances of
the proletariat, (3) remain problems for sociological investigation.   Variability in the circumstances of everyday life is
commonly an initial assumption in sociological inquiry and one for
which the evidence from published studies provides considerable
support.   Thereafter, although different investigations have
sometimes gone in very different directions, attempts and sometimes
sustained attempts are made to relate the observations of a particular situation to more general and wider-ranging processes and
structures in society.   These attempts and the assumptions and
interpretations which they engender provide the context in which
we have attempted to examine a single sub-set of the possible
connections between work and social stratification in an industrial
society, namely the connections which Lockwood has postulated
between the intermediate categories and concepts of occupational
community, and images or models of society (see Chapter 2).

    For our own very limited purposes, and also for expository
convenience, it is convenient to formulate three problems for
further consideration:
  (a) The circumstances in which activities and relationships
      sustained outside the workplace are crucial to the constitu-
      tion and definition of occupational community.
  (b) The conditions under which images and models of social life
      and more especially of social inequality may be supposed to
      apply to the entire society.
  (c) The conditions under which images of social inequality are
      consistently distinguishable from images of the organisation
      of work and the division of labour in society.

TYPES OF OCCUPATIONAL COMMUNITY

In his examination of possible correlates of work satisfaction,
Blauner remarks that 'levels of work satisfaction are higher in
those industries and in those kinds of jobs in which workers make
up an occupational community' and proposes three criteria for
recognising such communities:
  1 'The essential feature of an occupational community is that
    workers in their off-hours socialize more with persons in
    their own line of work than with a cross section of occupa-
    tional types.'
  2 'Participants "talk shop" in their off-hours.'
  3 'Occupational communities are little worlds in themselves.
    For its members the occupation itself is the reference group;
    its standards of behaviour, its system of status and rank,
    guide conduct.'
Blauner further identifies two sets of circumstances in which occupational communities are likely to develop, spatial isolation and

peculiar hours of work, and one in which they are not: 'occupational communities rarely exist among urban factory workers'
(Blauner, 1960, pp.350-2; see also Blauner, 1964).

These criteria are, it seems, applicable either singly or in
various combinations.   The first appears most readily adapted for
empirical social research, especially survey research, and to
quantitative treatment.   Questions corresponding to Blauner's
first criterion which are usually asked contain either or both of
two possibly significant modifications, a reference to 'friends'
or 'close friends', and a specification of where the interaction
takes place (cf. Goldthorpe et al., 1969; Brown et al., 1973).

The second criterion, 'shop talk', has less often been used,
possibly because it is less readily convertible to questions
suitable for survey research.   Information on this issue does,
however, appear in studies which draw on direct observation and
participation (Dennis et al., 1956; Tunstall, 1962; Duncan, 1963;
Hollowell, 1968).   The third criterion is more complex, and possibly
combines a number of elements, not all of which need necessarily be
present simultaneously.   Thus it would seem entirely possible for
sets of occupations to have a well defined 'system of status and
rank' - this is presumably true by definition in bureaucratised
settings - without thereby constituting 'little worlds in themselves'.   It is also not entirely clear if Blauner supposes these
'little worlds' to extend beyond the limits of the workplace.   In
the absence of an explicit statement that they do, we shall assume
that they may but need not. (4)

Studies of a variety of industrial settings in Britain have
suggested the presence of distinctive occupational cultures,
notably among miners, dockers, fishermen, printers and steelworkers,
and also among lorry drivers, railwaymen and shipbuilding workers
(Dennis et al., 1956; Scott et al., 1963; University of Liverpool,
1954; Horobin, 1957; Cannon, 1967; Sykes, 1967; Scott et al.,
1956; Hollowell, 1968; Salaman, 1971b; Brown et al., 1973).
These studies meet Blauner's criteria to varying degrees.   Dennis,
Henriques and Slaughter's study of miners in 'Ashton' and the
studies of Hull fishermen by Duncan, Horobin and Tunstall match
the criteria exactly, and if it is supposed that to qualify as an
occupational community the social relations among workers must meet
all three criteria unequivocally, coalmining and trawl-fishing may
be unique. (5)   However, for most purposes workers in four other
industrial settings also meet the three criteria: dockworkers,
railwaymen, shipbuilding workers, and steelworkers. (6)

Cannon's study of compositors and Sykes's study of trade union
organisation in the printing trades suggest that social relations
among printers meet Blauner's third criterion so exactly that if
it was the sole criterion they would constitute the example of an
occupational community par excellence.   It seems entirely possible,
however, that printers do not meet either of the other two criteria.
Both Cannon and Sykes provide detailed analyses of the social
relations of the workplace.   Cannon also examines the extent to
which the influence of the occupational community extends beyond
the ambit of the workplace.   However, apart from a passing reference which Cannon makes to the possibilities of meeting workmates
outside the workplace, the evidence in these two studies that

printers commonly engage in the kinds of activity and relationships
which meet the first two of Blauner's criteria is slight and
equivocal.   There is no evidence from these or other sources of
any marked tendencies among printers towards residential propinquity,
nor of any pronounced overlap between the activities and relationships of the workplace and those undertaken outside.   On the other
hand, Cannon does provide evidence of a substantial congruity
between norms and values at the workplace and outside, and also
draws attention to expressions of solidarity with the working class
and the labour movement generally (Cannon, 1967, p.178). (7)   It is
possible therefore that the printing industry provides an example of
a distinct type of occupational community which consists of the
occupations and institutions peculiar to the industry, which is
largely concerned with the technical and social organisation of work
and with the maintenance of the custom and practice which this
organisation embodies, but which, qua community, is manifest only
at the workplace.

In contrast to the situation which may obtain in printing,
Hollowell's study suggests that social relations among lorry drivers
may meet all Blauner's criteria and to that extent constitute an
occupational community (Hollowell, 1968).   However, this may be an
occupational community which, qua community, is less likely to
affect the other activities and relationships of its members outside
the immediate ambit of the occupation and the workplace.   It may
also be an occupational community which is less likely to give rise
to images and ideologies which would facilitate and justify
concerted attempts to maintain any existing advantages which an
occupation enjoys or make good the disadvantages from which the
occupation is thought to suffer.   If so, it is possible that lorry
drivers provide an example of another distinct type of occupational
community, one which exhibits recognisable patterns of sociability,
shop talk, and of differentiation within the occupation, but which
is largely ineffective in exercising any collective measure of
control over the organisation of work or in affecting the overall
situation of the particular occupation in question.

A cursory examination of other studies of workplaces in Britain
suggests the possibility that occupational communities vary in
other respects which appear relevant to the investigation of the
connections between occupation and social stratification.   For
instance, the social relations of the workers in the waterproof
garment industry which Cunnison and Lupton describe appear to meet
all three of Blauner's criteria, but some of the most important
values and standards of comparison which go to make up the occupational reference groups appear to originate and to be sustained
outside the workplace and then as it were projected upon the social
relations of work (Cunnison, 1966, especially Chapter 3; Lupton,
1963, especially pp.91-3; and more generally, Goldthorpe et al.,
1969).

Put more generally, differences in the conditions to be found
in local labour markets alone are sufficient to suggest that even
if the various industrial settings in which occupational communities
have been observed resemble one another in some respects, they will
differ markedly in others.   These variations may also be found
within the industries concerned, although it is often easier to make

surmises about this problem than to bring published evidence to
bear on it.   The circumstances of dockworkers in the Manchester
docks or of miners in 'Ashton' in the early 1950s were not
necessarily identical with those of other dockers or miners, nor
do they necessarily obtain unchanged in the 1970s. (8) Inspection
of these resemblances and variations may however draw attention to
important differences between these and other kinds of industrial
settings not so far considered which are also relevant to the study
of images and models of society.

With the possible exception of road transport, the industries
in which occupational communities have been observed were established in something like their present form during the nineteenth
century, and in the case of printing, appreciably earlier.   Many
of the elements of the technical and social organisation of work
observed in these industries in the second half of the twentieth
century, including the workplaces themselves and even some of the
machinery in use, are identical with those of a century before.
It is thus possible for several generations of men to have been
employed in the same industry, if not necessarily the same occupation, and in most of these industries a high proportion of new
recruits have been sons of those already employed, or previously
employed in the industry.   (The likely exception is road
transport.)   This may facilitate, though not necessitate, the
transmission of a variety of traditions and the formation of a
core of workers who have undergone some kind of anticipatory
socialisation in the elements of an occupational culture and are
therefore somewhat more likely to remain the bearers of such a
culture. (9)   It is plausible that such circumstances are more
likely to engender occupational community than those which bring
together for the first time a heterogeneous labour force which
lacks a core of workers who have already undergone some form of
anticipatory socialisation. (10)

These industries also provide the possibility of spending an
entire working life in the same occupation or sub-set of inter-
related occupations.   At the same time, with the notable exception
of printing and shipbuilding, the acquisition of the specialised
knowledge and skills often required in these occupations has not
been accompanied by apprenticeship or other generally recognised
forms of training.   Consequently skills, knowledge, and seniority
are rarely transferable from one industry to another, or in some
industries from one workplace to another.   Where these circumstances
are accompanied by high levels of earnings and more especially by
earnings appreciably higher than those which could be obtained by
leaving the industry, it seems likely that a fairly stable labour
force will emerge, itself one of the possible preconditions of the
development of occupational communities.

Between and very possibly within the industrial settings which
we are considering, there are appreciable variations in the extent
of state control and intervention, in the size of economic enterprises and of operational units, and in methods of payment, levels
of earnings and security of employment.   These variations in turn
appear to be related to the extent to which the effective operational unit in the industry is a small clearly defined group or
individual responsible for deciding exactly how particular tasks

are to be performed; for instance the crew of a fishing vessel
at sea or a lorry driver on the road compared with, say, furnace
crews in a steel works.   They may also be related to variations
in opportunities for promotion, in the chances of becoming self-
employed within the same industry, and in the ways in which competition between individual workers and groups is evaluated and
regulated. (11)   In particular, it is plausible to suppose that
'shop talk' will be most frequently observed where earnings are
related to some form of individual or group piece-rates and, at
the same time, high levels of earnings depend upon a combination
of effort with skill in solving technical problems under conditions
which are not fully subject to the joint control of workers and
management and which often involve considerable risks. Coalmining
and fishing, especially when compared with, say, printing are cases
in point.

There are also pronounced differences between the various
industrial settings in the conduct of industrial relations, the
importance of trade unions, and the involvement of workers in the
labour movement.   In coalmining, the relations of miners with coal-
owners and colliery managers and more recently with the NCB have
often been marked by a degree of overt and sustained antagonism
rarely matched in other industries.   Miners have also been
especially active in sponsoring candidates for Parliamentary
elections in coal-field constituencies.   Local branches of the
NUM appear to be intricately involved in occupational communities
of miners.   In printing, it would seem that to imagine the removal
of the Chapel and the multifarious activities associated with it
would leave virtually nothing of the occupational communities
which have been described, whereas in fishing the sudden disappearance of the Fishing section of the TGWU would leave the occupational
community virtually intact.

SOCIABILITY AND SOLIDARITY

Considerations such as these suggest that it may be appropriate
to seek for variations in images and models of society not only in
the different situations of those workers who are involved in .
occupational communities, compared with those who are not, but
also in the different kinds of occupational communities which there
appear to be.   To sketch classifications of occupational communities would lie outside the scope of our present discussion.
However, some further examination of two possible components of
such classifications, both deriving from Blauner's criteria, is
relevant to our present purposes.   These are sociability, an item
to which considerable attention has been paid in a number of
studies of workers and the working class, and solidarity.

In some discussions of work and community, sociability and
solidarity are used as more or less interchangeable terms.   Alternatively it may be supposed that solidarity is a necessary consequence
of sociability.   At all events, it is a fairly common practice in
sociological investigations to ask people if they have friends or
sometimes 'good friends' at work, and also how often and where they
meet them outside the workplace (see for instance Goldthorpe et al.,
1969; Brown et al., 1973).   These kinds of questions do presumably

yield indispensable information about friendships and interpersonal relationships.   Thus such information seems wholly
appropriate to the study of life-styles and, more generally, of
who associates with whom in everyday life.   Interlocking networks
of friends and acquaintances would certainly appear to form an
important part of the life of any community, however defined.
Friends presumably play some part, and possibly a crucial part, in
the development of personal standards of comparison used in evaluating a wide range of situations and events.   Friends are likely
to share many opinions, beliefs, ideas and possibly images of
society.   Friendship ordinarily implies a willingness to associate
on equal terms, and groups of friends may thereby comprise the
primary units of status groups in a Weberian sense and social class
as Schumpeter and T.H. Marshall employ that term (Gerth and Mills,
1948; Schumpeter, 1951; Marshall, 1963).   Moreover, the closer
the approximation of social interaction to Simmel's pure sociability
and the more highly it becomes prized for its own sake, the lower
the instrumental and adaptive content of the interaction in relation
to other sets of activities (Simmel, 1949).

Solidarity, as that term has been employed not only in sociological discussion but in the social sciences and political commentary more generally, possesses a wider range of connotations than
sociability.   Among these connotations, Durkheim's employment of
the term to apply to co-operation between unlike individuals and,
more importantly, between groups which are unlike, is an established
part of sociological usage, and it is improbable that when historians and others refer to the solidarity of the working class they
should thereby pre-suppose close friendships between millions of
people.   Where sociability is often continuously manifested and
reciprocity not unduly postponed, solidarity may be intermittent
and contingent in its manifestations, a readiness to stand by and
support other individuals and groups if and when the need arises
rather than a wish to associate with them frequently.   Interpersonal solidarity at the workplace may only appear in casual
exchanges.   Nevertheless this may be sufficient to sustain fairly
effective measures for the regulation of output (Roy, 1952, 1953,
and 1954; also Lupton, 1963).   Outside the workplace, the pattern
of drinking and talking which plays so prominent a part in
descriptions of the social life of miners and of fishermen may
reflect the solidarities outside working hours of men who during
working hours pursue the same occupations, rather than the sociability of close friends.   The distinction which Goldthorpe and his
colleagues, following the cues of their respondents in Luton, draw
between friends and mates may represent fairly exactly in interpersonal terms the distinction between sociability and solidarity
(Goldthorpe et al., 1969, pp.90-1, 105).   If expressions of
solidarity may be intermittent and contingent, it follows that
intermittent attendance at trade union meetings when matters of
immediate interest arise and a certain scepticism towards the
intentions of those who immerse themselves in union affairs is by
no means incompatible with solidarity. (12)

People need not like one another greatly in order to co-operate
sufficiently to complete the tasks which the constraints of their
common employment require.   Indeed when the occasion demands,

solidarity may be exhibited among those who otherwise greatly
dislike one another.   The solidarities of the workplace do not
depend on asking friends from work round for Sunday afternoon tea.
Conversely, the more intimate forms of sociability outside the
workplace are perhaps less likely to be observed among those who
are constrained to exhibit some form of solidarity at work. (13)
The admittedly imperfect information available may with equal
plausibility be construed as supporting any one of three hypotheses:
   that the intensity of sociability varies directly with the
   intensity of solidarity;
   that the intensity of sociability varies independently of
   the intensity of solidarity;
   that the intensity of sociability varies inversely with
   the intensity of solidarity.
   Irrespective of the merits of these hypotheses, the term solidarity is commonly applied not only to interpersonal relationships
but also to activities, to individuals and to groups which fall
outside the range of direct personal acquaintance, and thereby
implies a greater emphasis upon instrumental and adaptive components
of action in relation to other groups.   Especially in the political
and ideological senses of the term, the solidarity of a group is
manifest in its opposition to another group, or in its support for
one group in opposition to another.   Industrial action by one
group of workers in support of others in another industry and
another part of the country is unlikely to occur because they are
good friends.
   The suggested distinction between sociability and solidarity by
no means implies that to the extent that occupational communities
exhibit solidarity at all, itself a matter for empirical investigation, they necessarily exhibit class solidarity, still less that
the conscious pursuit of common interests is a manifestation of
class consciousness as that term has been generally understood.
Indeed, much of the information relating to occupational communities
can be more readily construed as evidence of occupational solidarity
and trade union consciousness.   The development of pronounced
solidarities within occupational communities could conceivably
inhibit the emergence of class solidarities.   Certainly there
seem to be no grounds for supposing that occupational communities
necessarily engender class solidarity and the strikes of coal-miners
and of dockers in 1972, despite the support which the former
received from some other workers, appear much more like collective
action undertaken in defence of their immediate economic interests
by the workers directly concerned than like concerted action undertaken on behalf of a class.   By the same token, images of society
and more especially images of divisions in society which refer
explicitly to solidarity may be as much images of occupational
community and the division of labour as images of class and of
class divisions in society.   Furthermore, sociological interpretations of whatever descriptions of social life happen to be
designated as images and models of society may themselves depend
upon the images and models of social life which sociologists
construct, among them occupational communities, social classes and
industrial society.

IMAGES AND MODELS

The terms image and model have enjoyed increasing popularity in
sociology and social anthropology during the past two decades (see
for instance Levi-Strauss, 1968; Bott, 1957; Willener, 1957;
Dahrendorf, 1959; Ossowski, 1963; Leach, 1954; Banton ed., 1965).
Perhaps partly because of this popularity it is sometimes far from
clear just how these terms are to be understood.   Moreover, the
relationship between these and some other terms employed in the
study of social stratification, notably consciousness, culture and
ideology is often uncertain. (14)   On occasions, image appears to
serve as a convenient portmanteau term covering a variety of opinions,
views, ideas, and beliefs, and the term model may be used to refer
to what would otherwise be called ideology.   However, statements
that 'different images of the same structure do not merely express
propensities: they represent a stock of different experiences and
observations resulting from differing practical interests' and that
'images of social structure, especially those which are socially
determined, are important for us because they directly condition
social ideologies and social programmes' makes the study of images
crucial to certain kinds of sociological inquiry and at the same
time poses extremely difficult problems for such investigations,
especially problems of interpretation (Ossowski, 1963).   The
problems of interpretation are sufficiently numerous and difficult
when the information to be interpreted is in the form of published
texts; sociological inquiry often involves, in addition, the
construction of the very texts which are to be interpreted and a
construction, moreover, which itself consists of interpretations.
Even when the term image is employed in more limited and modest ways
than Ossowski proposes, it nevertheless appears that there are no
generally available let alone commonly agreed criteria in sociology
for consistently distinguishing images from the other kinds of
information which are so abundantly generated and transmitted in
everyday life. (15)
     Somewhat similar difficulties attend the use of the term model.
These difficulties, however, are less acute initially as there
exists a recognisable reference point in Bott's analysis of the
implications of the term in relation to class (Bott, 1957, Chapter
6), a starting point which Lockwood among others has subsequently
adopted.   Bott advances the hypothesis that
     when an individual talks about class he is trying to say some-
     thing, in a symbolic form, about his experiences of power and
     prestige in his actual membership groups and social relation-
     ships both past and present.   These experiences have little
     intrinsic connection with one another, especially in a large
     city,
and consequently
     the individual constructs his notions of social position and
     class from his own various and unconnected experiences of
     prestige and power and his imperfect knowledge of other
     people's....He creates his own model of the class structure and
     uses it as a rough-and-ready means of orienting himself in a
     society so complex that he cannot experience directly more than
     a very limited part of it (Bott, 1957, pp.163, 165).

Such an approach appears entirely appropriate to research in which the main concern is with individuals, their interpersonal relationships and their immediate social milieux.   It is less well suited to an investigation of the kinds of situation which give rise to similarities or differences in the categories or principles which individuals use to interpret their experiences, especially in relation to some possible form of collective action, and Bott explicitly disclaims the possibility of drawing conclusions from her data 'about the conditions under which people's class models will resemble one another' (Bott, 1957, p.174). (16)   Alternative approaches will therefore require some assumptions and preferably some information about the processes which give rise to the primary experiences which individuals use in constructing their images and models.   These processes presumably include the elements which constitute groups and situations in such a way that it is possible to have experiences of power and prestige, the means of recognising and interpreting these experiences in this kind of way and not some other, and also the means of communicating them to others.   Virtually all sociological inquiry rests upon the assumption that such communication is possible and thus, without necessarily supposing that the experiences themselves can be communicated, that the interpretations of these experiences can be communicated.   The elements of these interpretations include what are commonly called ideas and beliefs.

If the starting point of the analysis is the individual, then what is initially taken as given is the situation of the individual and what is problematic are the ways in which individuals select elements from these situations and construct a representation of them.   This is not the only feasible starting point for an analysis, and it is also possible to take the capacities of individuals for constructing representations as given and to treat as problematic the interconnections of the elements of the situation in which they find themselves, or variations in the availability of different kinds of ideas and beliefs, or, if a sufficient number of simplifying assumptions can be made, the connections between situations and the ideas that people have about these situations. Approaches of this kind appear appropriate when the object of inquiry is the possibility of some form of concerted action or the outcome of the apparent actions of other individuals or groups of whom no direct personal knowledge is possible.

These considerations suggest the desirability of distinguishing the use of the terms image and model to apply to individual constructs based upon personal experience from their use to apply to beliefs and ideas about phenomena in social life which are not the product of the imagination of a particular individual and which commonly refer to phenomena beyond the range of the individual's personal knowledge and experience.   It should then be possible in principle if not always in practice to distinguish for the purposes of sociological analysis those kinds of statement which are more appropriately handled within the kind of framework proposed by, say, Bott from those which are more appropriately placed within the kind of framework which, for instance, Ossowski proposes.   The main point of the distinction however is to pose as an empirical question the connections between personal constructs or

individual representations on the one hand and structures in the
social consciousness or collective representations on the other.
Tentatively we may suggest, without doing too much violence to
established sociological usage, that constructs of the first kind
can be interpreted as referring to categories of interpersonal
relationships, including community.   Thus a two-valued power model
may represent the exercise of power by one person or group over
another within a personal relationship or community and it need not
be assumed without further evidence that this model will be
projected upon society as a model of one class oppressing another.
By contrast, constructs of the second kind refer to larger, possibly
more heterogeneous aggregates and categories, to classes, to
nations, to societies.   But acceptance of a model of society as
consisting of, say, two large warring camps does not preclude the
recognition of numerous categories of persons and relationships in
everyday life.   There seem to be no grounds for supposing, a priori,
that the personal images or models of everyday life which individuals construct are isomorphic with other available representations
of society and variations in collective representations may thus
occur independently of one another.   The sources of variations in
the one are not necessarily the sources of variation in the other.
While the contingencies and changing conditions of the labour market,
the employment relationship, and the organisation of work may be
more rapidly and perhaps more accurately reflected in changing
individual images of social life, the recurrent processes, institutions and structures of industrial society and the divisions to
which they give rise may continue to appear in ideologies and
collective representations.

NOTES

1   This paper summarises a number of issues which have arisen in
    the course of a review of studies bearing upon the nature of
    the relationships between work and social stratification in
    industrial society.   Lockwood uses some of these studies in
    constructing an ideal proletarian traditionalist (Chapter 2),
    and Salaman has considered others in discussing some socio-
    logical determinants of occupational communities (Salaman,
    1971a).   In this paper we therefore assume without further
    elaboration much of the analysis and argument which Lockwood
    and Salaman have presented, and our own considerations are
    limited to the situations of manual workers.
2   'Freedom, because both buyer and seller of a commodity, say of
    labour power, are constrained only by their own free will.
    They contract as free agents, and the agreement they come to
    is but the form in which they give expression to their common
    will.   Equality, because each enters into relation with the
    other, as with a simple owner of commodities, and they exchange
    equivalent for equivalent.   Property, because each disposes
    only of what is his own.   And Bentham because each looks only
    to himself' (K. Marx, 'Capital', 1, p.176).
3   'The various interests and conditions of life within the ranks
    of the proletariat are more and more equalised, in proportion

as machinery obliterates all distinctions of labour, and nearly everywhere reduces wages to the same low level' (K. Marx and F. Engels, 'Manifesto of the Communist Party').

4   Elsewhere, Blauner does assert that 'the work and leisure interests of those in occupational communities are highly integrated' (Blauner, 1960, p.352).   However no additional evidence is offered in support of this assertion.

5   The nature of the relationships between work and the workplace and other activities and relationships was one of the major problems investigated in these studies and consequently there is more information to which Blauner's criteria can be applied.

6   In these studies, the collection of information relevant to Blauner's criteria was subsidiary to the other purposes of the investigation and is presented in less detail.

7   The one explicit reference to friends is in relation to voting; Labour voters were appreciably more likely to have friends in the printing trade than those who voted Conservative.   It seems likely that there are marked variations in the incidence of shift working, especially night shifts, at different printing works, depending on whether or not they are engaged in the production of daily newspapers.   This is likely to have a marked effect on opportunities for association with workmates and friends outside working hours.

8   Indeed Lockwood suggests that the industries in which occupational communities have flourished in the past are 'to an ever increasing extent ... backwaters of national industrial and urban development' (Chapter 2).

9   For a discussion of this kind of anticipatory socialisation in a very different occupational context, see Becker et al., 1961.

10   Such anticipatory socialisation may of course occur in educational establishments, and the length of time spent in such establishments as part of a preparation for a professional career may well contribute to the emergence of occupational communities within certain professions.

11   Thus the chances of a deckhand on a trawler becoming a skipper or mate are considerably greater than those of a miner or a steelworker becoming a manager with earnings comparable to those of a trawl skipper.

12   The description by Goldthorpe and his colleagues of the conduct of branch and other local union business is highly reminiscent of the description by Dennis et al. of the conduct of NUM branches in and around 'Ashton'.

13   Tunstall's description of backhanding suggests that close friends are unlikely to sail on the same vessels (see Tunstall, 1962, pp.148-9).

14   However in the concluding paragraphs of his 1966 paper, Lockwood does appear to equate model with ideology and for good measure with theory of society.   'The pecuniary model is an outcome of the social rather than the economic situation of the privatised worker;   and he is only able to hold such a theory of society in so far as his social environment supports such an interpretation.... A purely pecuniary ideology is, of course, just as much of a limiting case as a purely class or purely

status model of society' (p.26).   See also Goldthorpe et al.,
1969, especially pp.145-56;   Platt, 1971, especially pp.409-10.

15 Unless, that is,responses to certain kinds of questions are
    considered to furnish an operational definition.   Thus
    questions may be presented in the form of statements with which
    respondents are expected to express agreement or disagreement.
    This procedure undoubtedly elicits information but whether
    this is information about the respondents' own images, as
    distinct from the investigators', is another matter.

16 Bott does however surmise that 'the degree of resemblance will
    vary directly as the degree of similarity in primary social
    experience' and would 'expect to find more consensus in a mining
    village than in a mixed working-class area where experiences
    were similar but not shared'.

Chapter 13

OCCUPATIONS, COMMUNITY AND CONSCIOUSNESS

Graeme Salaman

INTRODUCTION

A discussion of the utility and importance of the concept occupational community is by no means an inappropriate inclusion in any consideration of class imagery, since it has been suggested that a radical perception of society (that is one that sees society in terms of simple, conflicting dichotomous groupings) is directly related to a form of social organisation termed an occupational community.

Traditionally, British sociological interest in the nature and determinants of class consciousness, or the sorts of attitudes and definitions that were taken to underlie such consciousness, inevitably attended to what appeared to be a close connection between traditional industries and areas and radical class attitudes. Miners and dockers were regarded as the stalwarts of the radicalism in this country, and more modern forms of work and industry were held either to attract or to develop, a more conciliatory, individualistic and self-interested view of the industrial enterprise and society at large.

At the same time, of course, it was noticed that traditional industries where radicalism was seen to flourish, or at least to grow more fruitfully than elsewhere, frequently involved a sort of closeness between work and leisure (or non-work) activities, values, relationships and events, and a sort of overall conception of homogeneity and solidarity that was called an occupational community. For this reason (and this is by no means surprising in terms of available information and acceptable theoretical frameworks) occupational community was seen in terms of the sorts of characteristics displayed by members of stable, traditional industries and areas, and was held to be significantly related to the development, or maintenance, of a 'them-us' view of the world with its associated radical implications. At first sight such a connection is indeed appealing since it argues that persons involved in what they see and experience as a solidaristic, homogeneous occupational community (which is therefore, for them, clearly delineated from the rest of society) will tend to employ this awareness of apparent social distinction in their thinking on the structure of society and the nature of the relationships and interests underlying it.

But clearly, as recent events and developments have shown, this postulated connection between 'occupational communities' (of the sort specified above) and radical views is highly problematic. For one thing radicalness, however measured, is no longer the prerogative and preserve of miners and dockers; affluent workers, workers on assembly lines and white collar workers, have all demonstrated that, at least in terms of industrial action they are aware of the existence of conflicting interests in society.   Of course it all rather depends on what is taken to be a 'radical' attitude or definition and how such considerations relate to practical actions that are directly political or can be seen to have political implications.   But is it clear that the sort of 'them-us' conception typically attributed to members of occupational communities may reveal an awareness of conflict of interest, but may define the 'us' group entirely in terms of the locality or certain work or occupational groups within it.   Such a parochialism would be, of course, entirely antipathetic to the universalism (all workers, or, at least, all members of the occupation) that a true working-class consciousness is usually held to involve.

This is emphatically not to suggest that occupations are unimportant in the development of conceptions of the structure of society and the groups and categories within it.   As will be argued later, occupation can be seen as a highly important determinant of class consciousness, or social imagery, since it is through their occupations that persons directly experience the vicissitudes and variations of the economic system, the market, the organisation of work, and working conditions; and furthermore, occupations frequently carry a body of available knowledge and evaluations of the world, the occupation and its members, which is used to articulate interests and to explain discrepancies between expectation and actualities.

What is being argued, however, is that a genuinely radical view of society as against a highly developed sense of regional-occupational interests, and the nature and distribution of interests within it, does not follow simply from (or is not a necessary aspect of) the existence of the sort of traditional, stable, work based, homogeneous community typically ascribed to such occupational groups as dockers, miners, shipbuilders and printers.   Furthermore that with reference to this definition of occupational community it should be pointed out that very few workers are members of occupational communities of this sort, and that therefore, this definition of occupational community is somewhat irrelevant to discussions of the origins and nature of class imagery in society at large.

OCCUPATIONAL COMMUNITIES

The concept 'occupational community' can, however, be useful and significant in discussions of occupational culture, relationships and identifications if the notion of such communities as geographically based and located collectivities involving a strong and close overlap of work, leisure, family and regional life is eschewed, in favour of a concern for the extent to which people see themselves as members of what they regard as an occupation and a concern for the significance of this perception in terms of relationships, culture and identity.   To the extent that such a perception has obvious and important consequences for social imagery and political consciousness, the concept occupational community, even in this non-geographical, traditional industry sense, is highly relevant to the subject matter of this symposium.

The main themes of this paper can be put very briefly: that traditionally the concept occupational community has been used to refer to certain sorts of work/non-work relationships;   namely those that occur when members of stable, traditional, geographically isolated and demarcated industries and areas live and work together; and when there consequently occurs a close inter-mingling of the usually separate worlds of work, family and leisure.   It has been argued that this sort of traditional occupational community (or 'quasi-occupational' community) is directly related to the existence or development of a view of society (as divided into 'them and us') that has been considered to be related to the development of a radical class consciousness.   But such communities are rare;   and such a social imagery may or may not contain the necessary ingredients for a truly radical consciousness.

But it would be a mistake to throw the conceptual baby out with the bath water.   If the concept is not restricted to quaint, vestigial local work-based communities the concept occupational community can, it will be argued, be of considerable utility in analyses of conceptions of society and of the distribution - and compatability - of sectional interests within it, since this concept draws attention to the ways in which occupations can become significant subjective worlds for those who define their salient group membership not in class terms, but in terms of what they see as an occupation.   And by thus drawing attention to the determinants and significance of occupational consciousness (for that is what is meant by occupational community, as suggested here, since the term is used to describe what occurs when people see themselves as people with a shared investment in an occupational world of values and interests), the concept occupational community can be of utility in analyses of the determinants and nature of conceptions of group interest, whether occupational or, finally, class based. The concept thus involves a study of occupations in terms of the nature and significance of occupational membership for those who consider themselves as members, and the definitions, expectations and identifications and interests that are aspects of this membership.

Criticism and anxiety concerning the term occupational community probably stems, in part, from certain misgivings that typically surround the concept 'community'.   In general such criticism would probably suggest that the term community is highly value-laden, is vague and abstract and is irrelevant and useless in a contemporary situation.   In order to argue that the concept is both useful and interesting it is necessary to say something about these assertions.

As Nisbet has pointed out the concept community is one of the 'unit ideas' of sociology, figuring heavily in the works of all the classic major sociological theorists as they attempted to explain and describe the relational, institutional and societal changes

caused by and stemming from, the two revolutions.   Not surprisingly,
therefore, the concept community does incorporate more than its
share of evaluative undertones, since it was originally devised to
cope with and refer to the apparent break-up and disruption of an
established social order and the emergence of a new and less stable
one, and this transition had and has major emotional and evaluative
implications for many sociologists.   Usually this evaluative
tendency involves a more or less explicit romanticising of the
'golden days' of stable, 'gemeinschaft' relationships and associations when, it is claimed, societies and their members were characterised by homogeneity and a dominant emphasis on the collective at
the expense of the individual.   This sense of community has been
nicely captured by Nisbet when he writes:

> The word ... encompasses all forms of relationship which are
> characterised by a high degree of personal intimacy, emotional
> depth, moral commitment, social cohesion and continuity in time.
> Community is founded on man conceived in his wholeness rather
> than in one or another roles, taken separately, that he may hold
> in a social order (Nisbet, 1967, p.47). (1)

Within discussions of occupational communities this sort of
nostalgia is most apparent in descriptions of traditional, geographically based working-class communities, usually those associated
with declining occupations or areas.

However, the fact that the concept community can frequently be
seen as including an evaluative element should not lead us to
reject it too readily, for a sense of moral outrage or concern
invests all the unit ideas of sociology, and a great deal of sociological theory, and this in no way necessarily inhibits their
usefulness or interest.   Indeed it would be possible to argue that
the reverse is true: that the best sociology and the most important
concepts and theories are exactly those that have some degree of
emotional evaluative commitment.

The best way of avoiding evaluative bias and distortion is to
define the concept with such specificity and empirical reference as
to eliminate, or at least reduce, the possibility of distortion by
ensuring that, should it occur it would be clearly apparent.   This
leads to the second criticism: that the concept is so vague and
confused as to be useless.   Stacey has put this view very forcibly:
'It is doubtful whether the concept community refers to a useful
abstraction.   Certainly confusion continues to reign over the use
of the term' (Stacey, 1969, p.134).   And confidence in using the
concept is not increased by the knowledge that as Hillery (1955)
has noted, the concept has been used in no fewer than ninety-four
different ways.

But the concept occupational community, as has been argued
elsewhere (Salaman, 1974), despite having been employed in various
ways at different times by different writers, can usefully be seen
to involve certain common elements.   That is, underlying the
different usages there is a concern for a social collectivity
whose members 'are affected by their work in such a way that their
non-work lives are permeated by their work relationships, interests
and values' (Salaman, 1971a, p.53).   More specifically members of
occupational communities see themselves in terms of their occupational title, orient their behaviour towards their occupational

colleagues (or some section of them) share an occupationally based
value and belief system, associate in their non-work time with
these colleagues and base their interests on their work in some way.

What is more, not only do many notions of occupational community
contain at least some reference to these elements, but also these
patterns of behaviour and attitude are in empirical fact closely
inter-related, which is why they are connected conceptually.   The
second criticism then, that the concept is vague and ill-defined,
necessarily loses its force if the definition set out above and
elsewhere is adopted, and there are good grounds, both in terms of
the historical consensus underlying the usage of the concept and
the recurring empirical relationships, for taking such a definition
seriously.

But the most important argument against the continuing utilisation of the concept occupational community is not that it is
value-loaded or confused, but that it is uninteresting and
irrelevant, a concept that is only appropriate for analyses of
declining and disappearing forms of social organisation, and that
it is altogether too gross a tool to be of any use in investigating
contemporary issues of sociological significance or the difference
between present-day occupations.   The rest of this paper will be
addressed to this argument.

The defence of the concept involves two separate arguments:
that the concept is useful for the way in which it focuses attention
on certain aspects of occupations as subjective collectivities,
and second, that these occupational processes and features are
important and significant in our understanding of extra-occupational
issues and concerns, for example, the development of forms of social
imagery, and processes of change and conflict within the stratification system.   In other words it will be maintained that the study
of occupations, through the concept occupational community, is not
some recherche sub-section of industrial sociology, but a crucial
area of sociological investigation for, as Krause has put it:
'Occupations and professions are among the main mediators between
the individual and society' (Krause, 1971, p.1).

But first it is necessary to say something about the sort of
concept occupational community is, and how it serves to direct
attention to interesting and important matters.   There are two
general ways in which the term occupation is commonly used.   One,
which can be called the census category usage, merely refers to a
man's official work title - his formal job description title.   As
such it may simply be a statement of his primary work activity.
The second more significant sense refers to occupations as a
collectivity of some sort;   this sense of the word is what Taylor is
referring to when he writes:

> Occupation, sociologically speaking, involves a degree of
> corporateness, a degree of consciousness of kind, and a recip-
> rocity between the acting individuals in the occupation and the
> recognition of these individuals in the occupation on the part
> of the larger society.   This then leads to a category of work
> that may be called 'non-occupational work', using occupation in
> this second, sociological sense (Taylor, 1968, p.9).

It is this 'sociological' sense of occupation that is involved
in extreme, or exaggerated form, in the concept occupational

community as it is defined here, for the very basis of this concept is that members of occupational communities not only share the same work title, they also, as Hughes has put it, '"live together" and develop a culture which has its subjective aspect in the personality' (Hughes, 1958, p.25).   As such the concept sensitises us to the various ways in which being a member of an occupation as a collectivity can have consequences, significances and meanings for members of the occupation such that they tend to behave towards each other, towards members of other occupations, and towards their publics in similar ways and to share definitions and experiences which are significantly related to their view of society and the distribution of interests within it.   It can thus act as a searchlight, lighting up particular and significant links between work and non-work, certain characteristics of occupations as collectivities, and certain relationships between occupations and the larger society. And in so focusing on features of the internal organisations of occupational collectivities, it draws attention to the links between occupation and the wider society.   As Goode has put it, the concept is '... concerned with a little-explored area of social theory: the structural strains and supports between a contained community and the larger society of which it is a part and on which it is dependent' (Goode, 1957, p.194).   Furthermore, it is suggested that in exploring this interface between occupation and society three main elements of an occupational community - relationships, values and identity - are highly salient. (2)

The concept occupational community is concerned with what has been called occupational organisation - that is the internal structure of occupations as social collectivities.   Such a concern, it has been noted, leads to an interest in the internal aspects of occupations whose members do 'live together' and share a culture, and thus to an analysis of the extra-occupational activities of members of the occupation.   Turner and Hodge in a recent paper have stated this view well:

> The approach via occupational organization stresses one particular aspect, namely the way in which patterns of social relationships are developed, perpetuated and discontinued between networks of persons participating in similar activities in the division of labour.   It also implies examining the ways in which such networks of persons set about identifying and pursuing what they consider to be their collective occupational interests. ... The processes by which occupational organization emerges, is perpetuated, modified and possibly dissolved are but poorly understood.... In setting out to examine the crystallization and operation of occupational organization, therefore, it is necessary to consider the form of organization, the ideologies advanced, and the activities carried out, and to attempt to relate these to the wider social structure (Turner and Hodge, 1970, p.35).

How does the concept occupational community, with its emphasis on the internal organisation of an occupation, assist an understanding of the extra-occupational behaviours and imagery of members of the occupation?   A brief look at the three main elements and their inter-connections is necessary.

OCCUPATIONAL VALUE-BELIEF SYSTEMS

The investigation of the nature of occupational value-belief systems has a long history in the sociological investigation of occupation.   The work of Hughes and his students is particularly concerned with occupational cultures or etiquettes, the factors behind their development and transmissions and their role in defining and evaluating the occupational tasks and the relationships between occupational members.   Other approaches to the study of occupational value-belief systems have, in the case of those occupations designated as professions, regarded them from the point of view of their functions for the larger society and for members of the profession.   Another approach is to consider the ideas and values held in common by members of occupations - of whatever type - in terms of their role in determining members' reaction to changing occupational or extra-occupational circumstances, their status as intervening variables between occupational situations and members' reaction to these situations.

From the point of view of this paper, interest is restricted to considering those value-belief systems held in common by members of an occupation that contain reference to, definitions and evaluations of, the nature of the occupation, its members, their work and its importance, their skills and abilities and so on.   In short such systems will be viewed as ideologies, that is as descriptions and evaluations of the occupation and the world which are clearly based on and stem from a particular social location, a particular viewpoint (in this case an occupation), and which involve and present a statement and evaluation of what constitutes reality that is clearly in the interests of members of the occupation.   It has been noted not only that 'the ideas which men have about occupations and about their own work are among the most important forces in the direction of the totality of living' (Taylor, 1968, p.431), but also that, 'occupational ideologies are for all practical purposes ubiquitous.   They have vast consequences for political behaviour, social creeds, and stereotyped attitudes concerning certain types of work' (Taylor, 1968, p.431).

This view of occupations as purveyors of ideologies has of course been frequently adopted elsewhere, especially with reference to professions.   It argues that the statements of members of occupations concerning the nature of the occupational work, the sorts of skills and expertise necessary, the necessary conditions for adequate execution of occupational tasks, the nature of the proper relationship between members of the occupation and rivals, customers, quacks and publics, should be considered not so much in their own terms (as frequently occurs, especially in discussions of the professions) but detachedly, as interest-based ideologies.   Krause has put this view nicely:

> An inevitable part of any group's action on its own behalf is an ideology which summarizes the meaning of its action and gives reasons why others should support it ... occupational ideologies are used by specific occupational groups to gain the support and action of target groups, such as the occupation's direct clientele (if there is one), other occupational groups with which the group deals, the government, the general public (Krause, 1971, pp.88-9).

Such occupational ideologies present what Krause calls an
'exaggerated' view of the occupation's expertise, and argue that
greater power, control, status and so on, for the occupation, are
in the public interest.

However, it is clear that there exist considerable differences
in occupational ideologies, and in the ability of occupations to
disseminate their views of their occupation outside the occupational
boundaries.   Such differences are closely related to the position
of the occupation in the stratification system.   As Dibble has put
it in one of the few attempts to deal systematically with the ways
in which occupation may successfully develop and transmit occupational ideologies, and have them received:

> The point is not only that the ideologies of higher ranking
> occupations are more highly developed than those of lower ranking
> occupations, but also that they are more ecumenic.... The ideolo-
> gies of higher ranking occupations would often be widely diffused
> throughout the society (Dibble, 1962, p.229).

Clearly such occupational ideologies are not only a source of
power within society (in as much as to have the occupation's
definitions and demands widely accepted is clearly in the interests
of members of the occupation, or as Krause puts it: 'to define the
public interest as the same as the interests of one's group is a
privilege of power'(Krause, 1971, p.98) but such a situation is
only likely to come about when the occupation is a high ranking one.
For an occupational ideology to be successful in the effects it
produces in the target population, it is usually necessary for the
occupation to argue that it is concerned with life and death, or
some activity that is highly dangerous, demanding, responsible,
important or sacred.   Thus it is argued that the occupation itself
must be empowered to select, train, socialise, supervise and examine
its members, or control entry to the occupation in some way.   And
this form of occupational control (with its obvious consequences
for the functional power and replaceability of occupational members)
is also a form of power.

But if it is true that the concept occupational community (if
defined as suggested above with reference to the three elements of
relationships, values and identities) does cause attention to be
paid to the sorts of ideologies held by members of occupations, it
can still be asked why is this interest important?   Why is the
investigation of occupational ideologies sociologically significant?
There are a number of answers to this.   First, occupational
ideologies are themselves intrinsically interesting objects of
study, as is demonstrated by numerous analyses of the way in which
being a member of an occupation has consequences for persons'
perception, definition and evaluation of social reality.   More
importantly the classification and description of occupational
ideologies, and the exploration of the relationship between such a
classification and other aspects of the occupation - its location
within the stratification system, its socialisation, recruitment
and training procedures and so on - are interesting matters in
their own right, apart from the light they shed on the ways in which
occupations affect those who belong to them, or on the ways in which,
as Krause puts it, the occupation mediates between the individual
and the wider society.   Interest in occupational ideologies draws

attention to the various ways in which persons see themselves as
becoming members of occupations (doctors, prostitutes, policemen)
and the subjective significance of this process for their perception and definition of their occupation and the outside world. (3)

A second reason for investigating occupational ideologies is
that it is otherwise difficult to understand the behaviour and
attitudes of members of occupations.   Numerous studies show that
persons do not react in a deterministic, mechanical way to certain
features of their work or employment situation.   They react in
terms of the meanings they ascribe to the situations they are
exposed to, in terms of their expectations and aspirations.   In
some cases these are generated by extra-work involvements and
histories, but in other cases they are developed and transmitted
within the person's occupation.   Occupational value-belief systems
are not, after all, limited to the professions;   non-professional
occupations, including working class occupations and deviant
occupations tend to involve definite views of the skills required
for their real work tasks, of the 'proper' nature of their occupational tasks, of the characteristics of a 'real' member of the
occupation, of the nature of the relationship between their
occupation and other associated occupations and the society at
large.   As Hughes has put it:

In professional, as in other lines of work, there grows up both
inside and outside some conception of what the essential work
of the occupation is, or should be.   In the occupation, people
perform a variety of tasks, some of them approaching more
closely the ideal or symbolic work of the profession than others
(Hughes, 1958, p.121).

Cannon's study of compositors (1967), the author's work on
architects and railwaymen (1971b;   1974), Sykes's study of navvies
(1969) and many other works all demonstrate the ubiquity of
occupational ideologies;   and it must be clear that members of such
occupations behave in terms of the definitions, evaluations and
perceptions involved in such ideologies when they react to their
occupational circumstances. (4)

The third reason for studying occupational ideologies, and this
follows closely from the previous one, and is inter-dependent with
it, is that such an interest leads us to an investigation of many
aspects of what in broader terms one could call stratification.
Although it has frequently and cogently been argued that the
traditional and orthodox distinction between working and middle
classes is still empirically meaningful (that is that there remain
substantial differences in work and market situation, in patterns
of association and relationship, consciousness and values, etc.)
it is also clear that there are important occupationally based
differences within these two classes, both with respect to the
'objective' aspects of the location of occupations within the
division of labour and with respect to ideologies (or, viewed
differently, occupational or class consciousness).   As Alan Dawe
has put it in an unpublished paper, 'occupations place their
occupants in different market, work and status situations;   that
different occupations give different returns over time, according
to the prevailing economic situation'.   But it is clear not only
that the middle and working class categories are differentiated

internally in terms of occupations or clusters of occupations, but also that people are not simply on the 'receiving end' of their class position; their actions are in terms of, and the result of their expectations, definitions, imagery, etc.   And these are frequently held in common by members of occupations, and transmitted within the occupation.   It is because men relate to the processes of production and the economic system through their occupation, and because membership of this occupation may involve persons in a shared value-belief system with its constituent definitions, expectations and evaluations, that class consciousness, and class action, is more frequently a characteristic of particular occupational groups than of the working class as a whole. Sometimes, of course, such consciousness and action, being restricted entirely towards improving the lot of a particular occupation (air-line pilots for example) can best be seen as occupational consciousness since it involves no questioning of the distribution of rewards and privileges in the society overall, no attempt to generalise the circumstances of the occupation to other occupations.   The relationship between occupational consciousness and class consciousness is a variable one: under some circumstances the occupationally conscious occupation merely asks for, or attempts to obtain, a larger share of the cake; at other times the disadvantaged occupation will attempt to persuade other occupational groups of their underlying similarities.

Two points then are being made here: that in investigations and discussions of class it is necessary to attend to the extent to which occupations are differentiated with reference to their location within the division of labour and all the objective variations in class situation that can follow this.   Also, that it is necessary to consider the value-belief systems held by members of these occupations if one is to gain any insight into the development of class or occupational consciousness or action. (5)   All this has been nicely put by E.P. Thompson in his book, 'The Making of the English Working Class':

> The making of the working class is a fact of political and cultural, as much as of economic, history.   It was not the spontaneous generation of the factory system.   Nor should we think of an external force - the 'industrial revolution' - working upon some nondescript undifferentiated raw material of humanity and turning it out at the other end as a 'fresh race of beings' (Thompson, 1968, p.213).

IDENTITY

Persons involved in occupational communities will, it is argued, derive some sense of personal identity, of self-image, from this involvement.   That is, they will tend to see themselves in terms of the occupational title, and as persons of particular sorts, with specific abilities, knowledge, personality characteristics and so on.   These personal descriptions will, in most cases, approximate to occupationally based definitions of the 'real' or 'good' members of the occupation, although only a few high status members will be characterised as entirely 'real', proper members.

These occupationally based self-images are then based on the value-belief systems discussed above, in that as members of occupational communities persons see themselves and their colleagues in terms of their shared values and definitions. (And, consequently, evaluate each other in these terms.) (6) Such occupationally based identities add enormously to the personal saliency of these values and definitions, in that they become part of the community member. Thus when occupational circumstances change, or when the organisation or technology of the occupation is altered so as to reduce or eliminate opportunities to practice valued occupational skills and abilities (as has occurred with the railwaymen) such alterations are experienced as personal disappointments and frustrations, as sources of anxiety.   Under such conditions the sort of occupational/class consciousness or action discussed earlier, whereby members of occupations attempt to exert some control over their destinies, to improve their circumstances, to resist the introduction of new techniques, new forms of organisation and obstruct the destruction of valued and traditional forms of relationship, involves a considerable personal significance for those persons concerned.

Indeed it could be argued that a great deal of such occupational action and consciousness is ideological not merely in the sense that it stems from a particular social location, seeks to advance the power and control of the occupation and stems from a particular interest position, but also in what Geertz has called the 'strain theory' conception of ideology (1964).   That is, that ideology is not only an aspect of men's struggle for power, their competitiveness, but also of their attempts to 'flee anxiety'.   The strain theory approach to ideology notes how social malintegration (role strain and conflict, discrepancy between aspirations and reality and so on) is experienced individually as psychological anxiety or insecurity.   Geertz notes that a number of specific types of strain theory explanation have been used: the cathartic, the morale, the solidarity and the advocatory.

Such a conception of occupational action and ideology has its main advantage in highlighting the ways in which alterations in occupational circumstances (relative to historically transmitted and generally accepted conceptions of the nature of the occupation, its importance and social contribution, the nature of occupational personnel, their characteristics and so on, in short occupational systems of definition and evaluation) have drastic consequences for members of the occupation who see and value themselves in terms of these qualities.   Such a view of occupational ideology also draws attention to the possibility that members may react to alteration in occupational circumstances not simply by attempting to change their occupational circumstances, or to improve their lot or to defend themselves against threatening changes, but also by changing their occupational definitions and evaluations.   Such a process has been clearly noted amongst certain professional and artistic occupations: a process of ideological accommodation occurs.   It was clearly evident among the railwaymen, studied by the author, who often distinguished, with very considerable bitterness, between the old fashioned conceptions of a good railwayman (that is notions which used to be generally accepted and which were not discrepant

with the actual job demands of the driver) and present day conceptions.   The old fashioned conception emphasised responsibility,
thoroughness, conscientiousness and so on;   the present day one
was cynical and instrumental, emphasising adequate job performance
and the need to 'live' outside work.

Once again it may be necessary to emphasise that occupational
identities are by no means restricted to bizarre or high-status
occupations - although it is these occupations that have attracted
most attention in this respect.   Studies of working-class occupations also reveal clear occupationally based identities: for
example, Sykes's study of navvies shows the emphasis they place,
in their talk, relationships and behaviour, on individualism (which,
as Sykes notes, is sufficiently strong as to obstruct the development of common interests or group relationships).   Furthermore,
not only did the navvies see themselves in terms of their personal
and individual autonomy and independence - of other navvies as well
as of their employers - they also accepted, although in a rather
ambivalent fashion, what they consider to be society's view of
them, at times boasting of their anti-social behaviour, at others
deploring the behaviour of navvies, but dissociating themselves
from their colleagues.   The point is, however, that navvies, like
members of many other occupations, hold occupationally based
identities.

That members of occupations see themselves in terms of their
occupational title and incorporate within their identity values
and definitions of themselves and their colleagues which are shared
by members of their occupation and derive from their shared experiences and problems has further consequences.   The most obvious
of these is that as Westley has put it, 'If one assumes with
Everett Hughes that today occupation is a major badge of identification, then one also assumes that men will act in such a way as
to protect their identity and their self-esteem' (Westley, 1970,
p.xiv).   Westley continues to argue that those behaviours of the
police which he is concerned with - their violence and their
secrecy - represent solutions to the anxieties and identity threats
posed by their occupation.   So again it is argued that occupation
not only furnishes definitions and expectations (which in this case
are incorporated into members' views of themselves), but that the
occupational experience can be at odds with these cultural, identity
elements.   Westley argues that police violence is a result of
constant threats to their self-respect (given that they consider
this self-respect in terms of their occupational title and role),
or as he puts it:

> The policeman, faced with a hostile public, given the status
> of a pariah, finds that he is constantly being degraded or
> subordinated.   This intensifies the rejection engendered by
> the public definition of him as a malicious and threatening
> intruder, and consequently intensifies his need for self-
> assertion, which becomes articulate as a need for maintaining
> respect for the police (Westley, 1970, p.150).

But the public definition of the police as corrupt and brutal is
not only partially responsible for police violence, it is also
responsible for police secrecy and in group loyalty concerning this
violence.   Anxiety about self-respect causes police violence,

Westley argues, and necessitates secrecy about such behaviour.
Finally, Westley argues that the protection of self-respect is
generally important in the behaviour of members of occupations. He
says: 'The significance of this point lies in the suggestion that
the most important goals of an occupation's membership are those
that involve the self-conceptions of the members' (Westley, 1970,
p.152).

   This discussion of occupationally based identities impinges on
the previous discussion of occupational value-belief systems in
other ways. It has been noted that occupations tend to try and
disseminate their view of their occupation, its social contribution
and importance, throughout society, and that their ability to do
this, and their success at it, is both related to the location of
the occupation within the stratification system, and is a potential
way of improving the importance and functional power of the
occupation. Furthermore, it is clear that members of occupations
will, as Hughes puts it, 'attempt to revise the conceptions which
their various publics have of the occupation and of the people in
it. In so doing, they also attempt to revise their own conception
of themselves and their work' (Hughes, 1958, p.44). In some cases
it is the formal occupational organisation - the trade union or
professional association - which carries out these conception
revising activities. (7)

RELATIONSHIPS

Members of some occupations choose their friends from their occupational colleagues. This phenomena, which has elsewhere been
termed preferential association, clearly has important consequences
for the occupational and extra-occupational behaviours of members
of occupations, since such work based relationships are bound
strongly to enhance group solidarity and the commitment of members
to the occupational value-belief system, and the associated occupational identities. At the same time, however, as many studies of
occupational communities reveal, the values shared by members of
an occupational community not only serve as a basis for evaluating
colleagues, they also operate as criteria by which to decide whether
someone is or is not, should or should not, be accepted as a
colleague; as someone who is reliable, and 'one of us'.

   Preferential association, when it occurs, is clearly related to
a common element in occupational value-belief systems, that is the
conviction, held by those who assert the significance and nature
of occupational membership (and the values that are typically
associated with this membership) of the distinctiveness and
conspicuousness of members of the occupation, or at least, of
'proper' members of the occupation. (All occupational belief
systems carry criteria for assessing the normal and deviant occupational member.) Members of occupations that have highly developed
occupational communities stress their distinctiveness and isolation
from the rest of society, in social, relational and normative ways.
Frequently, of course, this in-group feeling is buttressed by a
specific occupational argot usually based on the skills, tools and
techniques of the occupation, and an occupational mythology and

history - with its heroes and villains.   Sometimes too the in-group
element is part of a feeling of hostility towards and fear of, an
out-group, often the customers or public of the occupation.

Not surprisingly, it has been noted that participation in
relationships with occupational colleagues tends to be related to,
at the very least, an awareness of the distinctiveness, of the
separateness and isolation of the occupation which can lead to a
'them-us' view of society.   Lockwood says, for example, '... it
would seem that the tendency to adopt a power model of society is
most evident among workers who have a high degree of job involvement and strong ties with fellow workers' (Chapter 2).   And it has
been noted by Lipset et al., (1956), that among American printers,
participation in the occupational community is positively and
closely related to interest and activity in the union.

But if the concept occupational community is used not so much
to refer to the sorts of traditional, geographically based community
described by Lockwood, but more to the degree to which members of
occupations see themselves in terms of their occupational membership,
are committed to an occupational value-belief system with its
definitions and evaluations of the occupation its members and their
place in the world, and are involved in relationships with their
occupational colleagues, then the suggested relationship between
occupational community and radical consciousness becomes problematic.

Certainly, it is true that involvement in occupational communities
will involve, almost by definition, an acute awareness and evaluation
of what are held to be differentiating occupational characteristics,
attitudes and interests.   And it is true that members of occupations with highly developed occupational communities attend to
these differentiating characteristics in their social lives.   But
it is one thing for, say, policemen to have a highly developed sense
of their social distinctiveness, their being a 'race apart' and the
possible conflict between their commitment and loyalty to their
occupational colleagues and the rest of society, and quite another
to argue that this sense of separate occupational identity will
lead to, or involve, a radical view of society.

In other words the highly developed 'them-us' attitude that is
a marked characteristic of members of occupational communities is
by no means necessarily related to the development of a radical
conception of society and group interests, since this presumably
involves, as a central element, a definition of the 'us' group
which is greater than mere occupation.

Indeed it might well be that the development of an occupational
conception of 'them and us' and of a highly developed sense of
occupational interests could be an obstacle to the emergence of a
commitment to class interests as a whole.   The nature of the
relationship between occupational consciousness and class consciousness is highly complex.   Perhaps it is the case that to the extent
that occupations are successful in achieving the aspirations of
members they will have little concern for the interests or grievances of other occupational groups.   But clearly the important
determinants of class consciousness as against occupational
consciousness is the experience of exposure to the workings of a
market economy.   Under circumstances where the situation of members
of many occupations are felt to have deteriorated the previous,

possibly obstructive, occupational loyalties and demarcations will
be overlooked in favour of a new, situationally induced homogeneity.

Interestingly, however, the sorts of occupational community
mentioned by Lockwood, which are sometimes considered rather as
classic examples, may in fact be even less conducive to the sorts
of attitudes and behaviours that are usually seen as radical (8)
than occupational communities of the more general, less located
sort as described in this paper.   This possibility follows from a
difference in patterns of determination of the two types.

It has been argued elsewhere (Salaman, 1971a) that the sort of
traditional occupational community characterised by the domination
of a socially and geographically isolated area by a single industry -
such as often found with mining communities, which are often regarded
as paradigmatic examples of occupational communities - may, on the
contrary, be regarded as a 'quasi' occupational community.   This
classification may be used to draw attention to the way in which
these communities differ, in degree if not in kind, from other
occupational communities in that they are based upon men who live
together (and who may be related) and work together, rather than
men who work together deciding in some sense, to live together,
although this might sometimes simply refer to their living in the
same normative world.   Many occupational communities are the
result of various aspects of the work that men do - rather than the
geographical isolation of the area in which they live - motivating
or constraining them to involve themselves in their work tasks,
activities, values and relationships.

In an earlier paper it was suggested that these determinants
relate the three situations and are: ' ... involvement in work
tasks, marginal status and stratification situation, and the
inclusiveness of the work or organizational situation' (Salaman,
1971a, p.59).   The point about non-traditional occupational
communities is, it is suggested, that they are produced because
members are motivated, by virtue of various aspects of their work,
or the way it is organised, to commit themselves to a work based
value-belief system, or to relationships with their occupational
colleagues.   Foremost among the determinants of this sort of
occupational community is involvement in work tasks and skills,

> Members of occupational communities are emotionally involved
> in their work skills and tasks; they value their work not only
> for the extrinsic rewards it brings but also for the satisfaction
> they derive from actually doing it, and for the opportunities it
> offers them to use their work skills (Salaman, 1971a, p.60).

Differences in the typical patterns of causation between the
geographical, 'quasi' occupational community and the type of
community discussed in this paper may be relevant to the development of different types of social imagery, in such a way that the
classical community, which is so heavily oriented towards a
particular regional occupational group may be less likely to develop
a perception of occupational (or class) interests that supercede
regional parochialism, than the community which is based on the
occupation as a whole.   At least the latter type of occupational
community offers the possibility of a general occupational consciousness.

CONCLUSION

Because of the traditional salience of the concept occupational
community in considerations of the nature and determinants of
types of social imagery, this paper has attempted to consider
occupational communities in terms of their relevance to the development of conceptions of social structure and the distribution of
interest within society.   It has been argued that the concept
occupational community need not necessarily be restricted to
analyses and descriptions of what Lockwood has termed 'proletarian
traditional' occupational communities - that is those typically
found in geographically isolated areas dominated by coalmining,
shipbuilding, etc.   Rather the concept, which may usefully be
seen as involving a close relationship between work and non-work
activities, values, relationships, interests and identities, can
be used with advantage and insight in analyses of the development
of conceptions of interest, solidarity, identity among members
of any sort of occupation.
     Furthermore, it has been suggested that by focusing attention
on the value-belief systems held in common by members of occupations,
and the consequences these have for members' self images or
identities, and the ways in which these are buttressed, supported
and maintained by, and transmitted within, extra-occupational
networks of colleague-based friendship and associational relationships, the concept occupational community highlights certain
important areas of enquiry and research.   These include the
attempts of members of occupations to disseminate their occupational
ideologies (their conceptions of the nature of the occupation, its
'proper' tasks, skills, abilities, contributions and demands, the
nature of the occupational relationship with various others and of
the interests of members of the occupation, and so on).   Also the
important role played by these occupational ideologies in affecting
occupational members' reactions to and definitions of changing
occupational circumstances.   And most importantly, the definition
of occupational community set out and advocated in this paper, by
referring to the subjective significance of occupational membership,
and the associated involvement in occupational values, beliefs,
definitions and relationships, considers how occupations relate to
conceptions of society and of interests within it.
     That new members of occupational communities tend to see them-
selves in terms of their occupational title and the values, beliefs
and qualities associated with involvement in the community, and to
evaluate themselves and their colleagues in terms of these values
and beliefs, has important consequences for the nature of members'
reactions to changing occupational circumstances and to their
perception of the structure of society.   It has been argued that
occupational value-belief systems may be seen as ideological not
only in the sense that they represent statements of occupational
interest, but also in that they are solutions to the anxieties and
stresses caused to members of the community who experience a
disparity between aspiration and reality.   It has been noted that
the involvement of members of occupational communities in relationships with their colleagues will have consequences for members'
views of the world and for their concern for, and knowledge about,

their occupational interests.   Finally, it has been argued that these issues concerning the extra-occupational behaviours and attitudes of members of occupational communities are significant areas of sociological interest.

It might be felt that this argument represents something of a conceptual takeover bid: that it is being asserted in this paper that any issue of interest in the sociological analysis of occupations as collectivities can be seen as stemming from the utilisation of the concept occupational community.   In a way this is so: since it would seem preferable to consider not so much does this occupation have an occupational community or not?   But rather, how far does this occupation display one or more of the elements of an occupational community - and what consequences follow from this?   Occupational 'communitiness' could thus be seen as a question of degree, and hopefully attention could be diverted from such barren issues as to whether this or that occupation was an occupational community, to investigations of the various elements mentioned above and their effect on the behaviour and attitudes of occupational members.   But this is not to suggest that the elements mentioned are not usually strongly inter-related and inter-dependent.

NOTES

1 The suggestion that community refers to men relating to each other in some 'complete' or 'whole' way - or to forms of relationship which involve men meeting each other in a multiplicity of roles - and these are frequently used as definitions of community, clearly lends itself to a positive evaluation of this sort of relationship, or appears to in many cases.
2 It is a further strength of the concept that it ignores the usual orthodox divisions within occupational sociology, such as professions, artistic work, manual work, etc., and treats all forms of occupation together.   It is thus able to carry out what Hughes sees as the task of a sociology of occupations: 'Our aim is to penetrate more deeply into the personal and social drama of work.... Until we can find a point of view and concepts which will enable us to make comparisons between the junk peddler and the professor without intent to debunk the one and patronize the other, we cannot do our best work in this field' (Hughes, 1958, p.48)
3 Such an interest clearly subsumes what may be called the symbolic interactionist perspective on occupations, with its associated concepts of career, socialisation, reference group, labelling, etc.   It also includes the classic exploration of the meaning of work initiated by Hughes and his students.   But its pedigree is even longer than this: it can be directly traced back to Durkheim and his interest in specific professional-occupational morality ('moral particularism') in the forms of morality specific to occupations.
4 It is of course another and larger question as to what are the factors that influence the content of such ideologies.   It is clear that such ideologies are heavily influenced by men's

problems and experiences - as these are shaped by their occupational and extra-occupational histories.   It is also clear
that these experiences themselves involve the mediating effect
of shared definitions and evaluations.   Experience necessarily
involves some processes of evaluation and definition.   Thus
the importance of an historical approach to the subject is
apparent: any particular occupational ideology will be heavily
influenced not simply by the historical and current work market
and status situation, and the extra-occupational social (community) relationships of members of the occupation (or group of
occupations), but also by the cultural history of the occupations: the shared definitions, perceptions and evaluations that
have been, and are currently, transmitted within the occupation.

5   It is not being argued that this occupational focus is all that
is necessary in order to study the development of class
consciousness;   obviously attention must also be paid to the
distribution of power within society, the extent of cultural and
ideological hegemony and so on.

6   There is a rich literature on occupational conceptions of valued
characteristics and traits.   These evaluations are an aspect of
the occupational mythology and history.   In my research railwaymen respondents, when discussing the qualities of a good railwayman, would frequently refer to some named character who displayed
in extreme form, a specific and memorable occupational virtue.
Polsky notes the same tendency when he writes: 'They (hustlers)
do, of course, sometimes speak contemptuously of outsiders;   but
in developing solidarity feelings they rely much more on
emphasizing the joys of hustling, talking of its virtues (such
as autonomy and heart), rating each other, discussing its technology, telling tales of its heroes and villains and so on'
(Polsky, 1971, p.73).

7   Once again it is necessary to note that this tendency of occupations to try and enhance their public image, is by no means
restricted to high ranking occupations.   Hughes describes how
he discovered, by studying negro industrial workers, that 'even
in the lowest occupations people do develop collective preten-
sions to give their work, and consequently themselves, value in
the eyes of each other and of outsiders' (Hughes, 1958, pp.45-6).

8   It should be acknowledged that there are considerable difficulties
in isolating so-called radical attitudes and behaviour.   Union
militancy could follow from attempts to realise sectional
interests;   political passivity may reflect a global disenchant-
ment with the existing political choices.   Furthermore, as the
papers in this symposium have shown it may be extremely naive
to expect persons' attitudes concerning the nature of society,
the industrial enterprise, the relationship between managers
and managed and so on, to be discrete, 'consistent', stable
entities to be stumbled over and measured, and which will be
directly and 'logically' related to future actions and statements.

Part four

CONCLUSION

Chapter 14

IN SEARCH OF THE TRADITIONAL WORKER

David Lockwood

Social life has an obdurate complexity which can be counted upon (fortunately) to badly dent, if not demolish most sociological concepts that are unlucky enough to make contact with it. It would therefore be surprising if there were not, in the studies reported in this symposium, many empirical 'deviations' from the typologies of the deferential and proletarian traditionalists set out in my 1966 paper on working-class images of society. Indeed, considering the method by which these types were arrived at (and by now it should be all too clear that this process was by no means as complete or as explicit as it should have been) this result is inevitable. For the way in which the concepts were constructed almost condemns them to being empty boxes to which no empirical instance will approximate. The method was one of conflation (Finer, 1955), that is the assembly of a set of properties defining work and community structures which, together with certain sociological assumptions of a general kind, may be thought to constitute extreme or limiting cases of working-class milieux. The cases were of a limiting kind in the sense that all the relevant properties bearing upon the production of a given mode of social consciousness were assumed to have values which are at a maximum or minimum so that all factors work together cumulatively in one direction to create a certain, and again, limiting image of society. Thus the types of work and community structure represent an imaginable but not necessarily a probable or even possible state of affairs.

One immediate shortcoming of this procedure is that no indication of the method of ranking these properties, much less of weighting one property against another, was provided. Therefore, since it is not to be expected that all properties will be present in the empirical case, or that any one of them will be present to the degree postulated, it becomes exceedingly difficult to assess, except in a very subjective and arbitrary way, the significance of research findings which seek to relate the particularities of social milieux to social imagery. To a large extent, the problems raised by the contributors to this symposium bear directly on this problem of the lack of specification of the original analytical scheme. One paper, namely that by Salaman, on the bases of differentiation of occupational communities, addresses itself explicitly to this sort of question.

Another deficiency of the original scheme is that there is a glaring difference between the nature of the properties defining work situation and community structure.   While the latter is characterised by reference to such structural elements as degree of occupational status differentiation and degree of interactional and attributional ranking, the definition of the work situation is in terms of the social psychological attributes of workers; that is, work involvement and degree of identification with employers and workmates.   Now, quite obviously, job involvement is not something that can be considered independently of factors external to the work situation, and is in any case not a property of the industrial structure.   Again the assumption that positive or negative identi-fication with employers and workmates is directly related to degree of interaction is far too simple, and is, in respect of both its terms, sociologically ungrounded.   In short, the structural properties of work organisations underlying these orientations (such as the size and degree of bureaucratisation of the productive unit) remain to be specified in a way comparable to the differentiation of the community structure.   This is not, however, a problem on which any contributor has directly seized - indeed most have quite sensibly described the work situation in their own, better terms - and I shall not pursue the matter any further here.

Before going on to examine some of the substantive criticisms which have emerged from the various research reports, I should like to deal briefly with one rather important matter of terminology: that is, what is actually meant by 'traditional' in this context. In both the paper by Moore (Chapter 3) and that by Cousins and Brown (Chapter 4), the ambiguity of the statement that the tradition-al worker is to be conceived of as a sociological rather than an historical category is deservedly brought to our attention.   At the same time, though, neither of these two contributors manages to resolve the ambiguity they have discovered.   The brunt of their criticism is that implicitly, and despite the insistence on its being a sociological concept, the paper on working-class social imagery placed the traditional worker in the relatively recent past, by contrast with the privatised worker who is seen as representing a trend away from traditionalism.   On the whole, I think this is a fair point, although it should be said that in an earlier article on the 'new' working class I was at pains to show that the opposition of a pre-war traditional working class to a post-war modern working class was extremely 'simpliste' and under-estimated the extent to which forms of privatisation had already become widespread in the period between the two world wars (1960). Nevertheless, against the implicit notion of a movement from traditionalism to modernity in the working class, Moore, and more particularly Cousins and Brown argue that in fact the structure of work relations in ostensibly 'traditional' industries such as shipbuilding and mining has changed in such a way as to increase rather than decrease the potential for proletarian consciousness. I shall deal below with the implications of their studies for the original typology of the traditional worker; here I am only concerned with the admitted difficulty of using the concept to define both a social structure and an historical progression.   I think that the ambiguity which arises from wishing simultaneously

to refer to these two different aspects can be resolved by
reserving the term 'proletarian' to refer to the general and
(relatively) timeless properties of certain kinds of work and
community structures, and to use other more descriptive terms to
refer to the particular and historically specific forms of class
consciousness which arise in part, but only in part, from such
traditional proletarian milieux. This distinction enables one to
say that while a certain sociological configuration is conducive
to a general propensity to see the social world in a way that is
different from that produced by another set of work and community
relations, it is nevertheless also the case that the manner in
which this image of social inequality is infused by a political
ideology proper will vary according to the historical context in
which such structures occur. There is nothing particularly
profound about this, but it does help to clarify the argument to
Cousins and Brown and Moore. For although it may be possible to
identify changes which are likely to make for a greater degree of
some kind of proletarian imagery at the present among Tyneside
shipbuilders and Durham miners, the form which it takes is not
likely to bear much resemblance to say the proletarian traditionalism of the nineteenth century community described by Zola in
'Germinal' or even to that of Ruhr workers in the 1920s. Thus
the recrudescence of proletarian consciousness referred to by
these two contributions does not in itself invalidate either the
empirical generalisation that there has been a decrease in
traditionalism of the variety described by Hoggart and others, or
the hypothesis that certain types of work and community structure
are more likely than other types to support a proletarian social
imagery.

These rather basic points may be made in a rather different way
by examining another of the findings of Cousins and Brown (Chapter
4) and Moore (Chapter 3) that among the workers they studied there
was little evidence of class conscious solidarity and much of
intra-class hostility. The fact that there exists a considerable
amount of xenophobia among certain workers with respect to other
workers who do not 'belong' to their own yards, craft or skill
groups or to their own residential community is taken to be a
damaging piece of evidence as far as the original typology is
concerned. But this is based on a double misunderstanding, first
of the purpose of the typology, and secondly of what was actually
said about the nature of solidarity in traditional working-class
communities. Here the distinction between what Goldthorpe and I
termed 'communal sociability' and what various contributors have
referred to as 'class consciousness' is vital. It was never part
of the intention of the original essay to provide an account of
working-class consciousness. It would be nonsensical to try to
explain the formation of a societal and political ideology of this
kind exclusively from the vantage point of work and community
relations. The purpose was more limited: to show how certain
forms of the latter sustained communal sociability and dichotomous
class imagery. As I have already noted, the latter provide only
the most elementary matrix of sentiments out of which a political
class consciousness might be fashioned. For example, in his study
of German workers, Popitz shows that a dichotomous class image of

society is compatible with a whole range of concrete beliefs, all
the way from a fatalistic, accommodative attitude to a class
conscious, revolutionary outlook (Popitz, 1957).   In the second
place, and this was specifically mentioned in the paper I wrote
with Goldthorpe (1963), the constellation of beliefs and styles of
life which we called communal sociability contains many elements
inimical to the development of class solidarity.   Here I have in
mind not only the internal status differentiation of the community
by the criterion of respectability (which Moore seems to have overlooked in the criticism he makes in Chapter 3) but more importantly,
the parochial and generally accommodative outlook associated with
such isolated and tightly knit groups (Parkin, 1971, pp.88-90).
The dichotomous, 'us-them' view of the social world which is
determined fundamentally by belongingness to the work community is
prototypically represented as an inter-class relationship.   But
it is well known that it can be applied within the class with
varying degrees of salience.   Cousins and Brown show the structural sources of one such fracture in communal sociability;   and
in doing so they point to a set of variables in the work situation
that were not included in the original analysis.   However, while
it is the case that the concept of the traditional worker did not
postulate the existence of such marked internal differentiation and
job competition among the proletarian sub-category as they in fact
found to exist, there is nothing in the original essay that contra-
dicts, and much that supports, their conclusions about the consequences of this situation.   For whether the internal differentiation of the Tyneside workforce has diminished or not is simply a
fact;   its significance is determined by the theoretical context
in which it is set.   And in this respect, Cousins and Brown's
emphasis on the fact of differentiation is perfectly compatible
with the hypothesis that communal sociability will be most highly
developed when, among other things, the occupational community is
completely homogeneous.   In this sense, their argument is an
elaboration of the original concept of the proletarian traditionalist structure and a demonstration of the correctness of the
hypothesis relating variations in this structure to levels of
communal sociability.   To be sure, this is an ex post facto interpretation of the original scheme, but it is a logically consistent
one which involves only the introduction of a neglected variable
and not a revision of the major premises.   If internal differentiation were shown to be associated with a high degree of communal
sociability then that would be a completely different matter.
  I have dealt with these issues at some length because they seem
to exemplify a general principle which I raised at the beginning
of the paper and the recognition of it will greatly facilitate an
understanding of the comments I now wish to make on cognate issues
raised by other contributors.   That is to say, in many cases,
findings which appear to be discrepant with the original analysis
of the traditional worker can be shown to be matters relating to
the interpretation of the structural variables rather than problems
concerning the relationships between these variables and forms of
social imagery.   I now turn to several more instances of this kind
of discrepancy, leaving until the final section those criticisms
which are directed at the more fundamental assumptions of the
analysis.

The paper by Bell and Newby (Chapter 5) is, in many respects, an exemplary continuation of the analysis of the structural setting of the deferential traditionalists, and, even though their evidence for the social imagery of the various categories of worker they differentiate is rather sparse, the hypotheses they put forward are eminently worthy of investigation.   Here I shall concentrate on the question of how far their subdivisions of the deferential worker category represent an elaboration of the original model and how far the assumptions of the latter are undermined.

In Figure 5.2, which summarises their findings, they follow the logic of the original article most clearly in the differentiation of the work situation and they improve upon it by dichotomising this variable in terms of a structural rather than an attitudinal property (namely bureaucratisation).   The 'local social situation' or community dimension is also relatively familiar in so far as extreme values are concerned; but the concept of an 'encapsulated community' is I think a very special case whose relevance to original thesis is perhaps not entirely obvious.   Before dealing with this concept I should like to say something briefly about types 1, 2, 5 and 6.

The deferential traditionalist proper is now located in the box labelled 'non-bureaucratic farm situation' and represents the extreme type of which the opposite is the 'bureaucratic occupational community' situation.   The latter, however, is an extreme type only in relation to the deferential pole.   In actuality, it seems to inhabit an intermediate region between the deferential and the proletarian worker, sharing this property space with the type of 'paternalist proletarian' category with which Moore is concerned. Indeed, while Newby and Bell refer to 'proletarian' aspects of their 'bureaucratic occupational community' situation, Moore identifies strong 'deferential' components in his account of the Durham mining villages.   In both cases a major defining character-istic is the presence or lack of personal relationships between employer and employee.   These have been generally defined as absent in the limiting case of proletarian traditionalism, and although this may constitute a useful conceptual benchmark, Moore's paper is a valuable reminder that the extent to which paternalistic relations have been present, especially during the formative stages of capitalist industrialisation, is easily underestimated.   Indeed, such relations were very strongly established in heavy industry in pre-1914 Germany, to take only one well documented example.   An important conclusion follows from this consideration.   Should such historical research as Moore's show that paternalism was preponderant this would not only undermine the ideal type of the traditional proletarian worker but it would mean that at a stage of capitalist industrialisation when forces external to the local work and community milieux were highly conducive to the development of political class consciousness the immediate social relations of working-class life were ameliorative of class consciousness, whereas at a later stage, if anything, precisely the opposite combination of effects is operative so far as the local and national relations of production are concerned.   (I am referring here to the well known, and I think, basically correct, analysis of changing class relations in terms of a process of 'civic integration' that is above

all associated with the work of Marshall and Bendix.)   However
this may be, the personal interaction of employer and worker is
clearly one that brings into the conception of the traditional
proletarian situation an element which has been taken as the crucial
defining characteristic of the deferential worker; and in this case
the consequences for social imagery of this 'extraneous' factor
appear, as Moore has shown, to be considerable.

    As one would expect, in Bell and Newby's analysis of the situa-
tion of agricultural workers paternalistic influences are in one way
or another given a quite general importance as a determinant of
social imagery.   Their presence and effect are most clearly evident
in the 'non-bureaucratic farm' situation.   However, in the 'bureaucratic farm' situation there is also some degree of personal identification with the employer which cuts across those aspects of the
work situation which predispose employees to adopt a two-class
model of society; and they label the resultant orientation 'deferential autonomy'.   A similar modification of a basic boss-worker
ideology occurs in the 'non-bureaucratic occupational community'
setting as a result of the personal involvement of farmer and
worker.   Thus the 'farm' variable in the former case and the 'non-
bureaucratic' variable in the latter case have essentially the same
effect in modifying perceptions of class in a particularistic
manner, even though these variables are located on different
analytical dimensions: community and work respectively.   This
suggests that the two dimensions are perhaps not as independent of
each other as the use of such a property-space diagram would imply.
However, it is certainly the case that the factor of personal inter-
class ties is an element of underlying importance in all the major
types they distinguish, even in cell 6 (occupational community and
bureaucratic farming) where its absence accounts for a more proletarian industrial situation and a propensity for workers to hold
'radical meaning systems'.

    Much more apparently alien to the formulation of the deferential
worker is the idea of an 'encapsulated community', though on closer
examination it turns out to be a property of the local status order
which is implicit in one of the variables identified in the
original paper.   By contrast with the situations just discussed,
the presence of an encapsulated community engenders a much higher
degree of ambivalence in social imagery because of the coexistence
of 'agrarian' and 'urban' status criteria in the community, criteria
which are subscribed to by locals and newcomers respectively.   The
result is that there is no dominant status system but rather
conflicting definitions of prestige, and the ambivalence in the
social imagery of agricultural workers in such a community is taken
to be a reflection of this lack of integration in the allocation
of social worth.   This was not an eventuality which was allowed
for in dealing with the status system in the original paper, which
assumed variation only with respect to the interactional-attribu-
tional dimension of status.   But it is not difficult to show that
the limiting concept of an interactional status system entails both
consensus on status criteria and the internal consistency of the
criteria themselves.   This does not however imply that the opposite
limit of attributional status ranking has negative values in these
respects, though there are reasons for supposing that consensus and

consistency are more easily maintained in an interactional status setting.   And it may be noted that in the case discussed by Bell and Newby disequilibrium was not an internal and spontaneous development of the indigenous status system but rather a result of the importation of alien values.   Their findings, then, like those of Moore, Cousins and Brown, reveal the inadequacy of the explica- tion of a key variable in the original model; but again, as I have tried to show, this deficiency can be rectified at no cost to the logical consistency of the model.

A related problem arises from the research reported by Batstone, who makes much of the fact that workers in small industrial plants in Banbury do not adhere to a 'feudalistic' conception of society and that deference is paid instead to the local business elite.   I do not wish to go into the question of whether the group of workers he has studied more than marginally qualifies for the label of deferential traditionalists (in some ways they appear to be closer to the paternalistic proletarian situation described by Moore) or the question of whether Batstone has actually shown that among these workers deference is accorded to the business elite by virtue simply of occupational achievement as opposed to 'natural leadership' qualities. Instead my comments will focus on his assumption that under whatever circumstances deferential workers will defer to aristocratic status groups.   This assumption should be immediately suspect because it contravenes the more basic premise that workers' images of society will be constructed out of their experiences of social inequality in their immediate social milieux.   In so far as these circumstances are conducive to the development of a hierarch- ical deferential view of society the objects towards which this deference is directed will naturally vary according to their availability in the local situation.   Only in the limiting case of a fully elaborated status hierarchy including aristocratic groups at the apex of being present as a local interactional system would one assume the 'feudalistic' orientations which Batstone takes to be a necessary characteristic of deferential workers per se.   This confusion seems analogous to that evinced by Cousins and Brown in their implicit assumption that the ideal type of proletarian worker is somehow invalidated by the discovery of communal schism rather than communal solidarity.   A highly simplified model, taking extreme types, cannot be directly applied to particular instances without interpreting and elaborating the variables in the light of the underlying assumptions; and it seems to me that this is the problem that is involved in both these cases.   And, given the conceptual density of the original variables, this has been highly successful, thanks largely to the authors' own good common socio- logical sense.   Thus I entirely agree both with Batstone's argu- ment that the original paper 'fails to sufficiently specify the conditions for a conception of society which is essentially feudal- istic' and with the following assumption of his own interpretation of 'transfer of deference to a business elite' (though transfer is not exactly the correct word): 'To the extent, then, that class imagery is a reflection of immediate patterns of experience it seems reasonable to suppose that those in small firms will not believe in a distant elite who rule because of inherent qualities associated with birth' (Chapter 7).

So far, I have restricted my remarks to those issues raised by
contributors which seem to raise crucial, though not insuperable
problems of interpretation of the original set of variables.   But
some remaining criticisms relate to more fundamental matters and
to these I now turn.

I think it is necessary to distinguish between, on the one hand,
the kind of ambivalence in images of society that is, so to speak,
the natural product of deviations from and admixtures of the ideal
types of work and community structures such as have been noted by
Moore (Chapter 3), Batstone (Chapter 7) and Bell and Newby (Chapter
5), and on the other hand the more generalised ambivalence,
expressing itself in a divergence between deferential behaviour and
attitudes, which is described by Bell and Newby in the sections of
their paper entitled 'Deference' and 'Patronage'.   The latter
type of ambivalence was not considered as a general attribute of
deferential traditionalism, and this is mainly due to the fact that,
as Bell and Newby point out, the original paper failed to make
clear 'the mechanisms whereby interaction with leads to identification with those in superordinate positions' (Chapter 5).   The fact
that such ambivalence is well documented (especially among such
groups as household domestic workers who may, by virtue of their
employment relationships, be regarded as archetypal of the deferential traditionalist) means that such a reaction cannot be
dismissed as an incidental feature but that it must be regarded as
a systematic aspect of hierarchical status systems.   This thesis
has been advanced in some detail by Tumin who argues that this type
of response is a 'defence mechanism' of the lowest status groups
against the insupportable self-depreciation imposed upon them by
the dominant criteria of social worth:

> Wherever we examine the responses of subordinate members of
> hierarchical systems, we find some systematic, though often
> informal, arrangements by which the impact of the subordinate
> status is reduced; even if this is done feebly, by gesture and
> jokes, the scope of subordination and hence of inferiority is
> always kept to the severest minimum possible (Tumin, 1961, p.480).

That such an element of ambivalence is not specific to the situation
of the deferential worker is also very likely.   Even traditional
proletarian communities are not entirely oblivious of or immune from
the definitions of social status of the wider society and this is
shown by the tendency to elaborate sub-cultures based on values
which are accorded greater importance than they have in the official
hierarchy of the society and which may in some cases represent an
inversion of the dominant ranking: for example among the 'upside-
downers' of the traditional working-class community of Bethnal
Green described by Young and Willmott.   These considerations suggest
that as far as status images of society are concerned, the original
paper presented a type of deferential orientation which, even in the
limiting, ideal case, was not based upon a valid sociological
premise.

To recognise this fact does not mean however that workers in
traditional deferential situations will be any the less predisposed
to accept a basically hierarchical view of the social order; and
to this extent it is a less fundamental criticism than the one
advanced by Blackburn and Mann in their paper in this symposium.   In

a previous publication (1970), Mann has endeavoured to show that
among lower classes in Britain and the USA there is a discrepancy
between their apperceptions of the more remote and abstract features
of society and of those more proximate and concrete issues which
affect their everyday lives.   There is a clear continuity of this
argument in the present paper, where Blackburn and Mann reiterate
the thesis that the working class in general neither possess nor
need to have coherent images of society because ideologies are only
articulated by those who are concerned with the preservation or the
change of the status quo;   that is, by elites or working-class
political activists.   This line of reasoning is now deployed to
explain the finding that among Peterborough workers there is no
evidence of well integrated industrial-political attitudes.   Now
it should be said at once that the lack of a coherent image of
society is not the only explanation which might be given of the low
correlations between the various measures of ideology which were
used in this study.   As Blackburn and Mann admit, we are dealing
here with an extremely heterogeneous population which is not
easily classifiable, either as a whole or by subgroups, in sociological as opposed to 'demographic' terms.   More importantly,
there is the point made by Cousins and Brown in paraphrasing one
of the conclusions of Mann's own previous writings that 'replies
to general questions may reflect the dominant ideology whereas
questions with more concrete reference may be answered in an
apparently contradictory way which reflects more closely the day
to day interest of the respondents' (Chapter 8).   Following from
this it has to be asked whether respondents do not sometimes reply
to such general questions in terms of their own particular
industrial experiences.   If this were the case, it might explain
why in the Peterborough sample replies to questions ostensibly
relating to workers' 'attitudes to industry in general' exhibit
the degree of inconsistency of lack of ideological salience that
they do.

Quite apart from this, however, it should be noted that the
supposed incoherence relates more to political beliefs than to
social imagery, the questions being designed to 'reveal the worker's
position on a "left-right" ideological dimension' (Chapter 8).
This, I think, is a distinction worth stressing.   Earlier on I
argued that the existence of communal sociability and a dichotomous
class image of society were not sufficient conditions of political
class consciousness.   Here the reverse is in need of emphasis:
namely, that evidence of a lack of a coherent industrial-political
ideology is not necessarily a demonstration that respondents do
not hold definite images of society.   This is not an ad hoc
revision of the position taken in the original paper and other
related publications.   In particular, it was stressed that deferential Tory voters are not to be regarded as identical with deferential workers;   and it is by no means surprising to find that
under certain circumstances some groups of workers who possess a
hierarchical image of society are not Conservative but Labour voters.
Batstone's research is a good example of this possibility.   Again,
in the case of the affluent, privatised worker my colleagues and
I have always maintained that political affiliation is relatively
indeterminate so far as class imagery is concerned, particularly

among groups espousing a 'money model' of society.   In our research
we found that within a group characterised by work and community
relations favouring such a social imagery the variable of the
respondents' white-collar affiliations proved to be of most importance in explaining variations in party loyalty.   Cotgrove and
Vamplew have provided confirmation of this finding in their study
of process production workers (1972), and Blackburn and Mann report
that their conclusions in this respect are 'in line' with their own
results (Chapter 8).

The significance of the connection between the social class
composition of immediate kin (1) and the subject's party loyalty
has to be seen in the context of research into political socialisation which indicates that party loyalties are established early on
in life by family influences and that the 'appropriate' political
beliefs are acquired later on, and are, moreover, sufficiently
flexible to allow for the persistence of party loyalties through
the vicissitudes of particular party policies.   In other words,
political ideology is not easily subject to modification by experience and is not primarily a basis on which an individual decides
to support one party rather than another.   On the contrary, such
beliefs function to protect and rationalise a party commitment
which has already been entered into and which is difficult to
displace by appeal to the discrepancy between ideology and events.
Now there is no inherent reason why such an ideology which is made
up of a fairly limited, abstract and 'ascribed' beliefs should be
identical with a social class imagery which is much more diffuse
and inchoate, and more spontaneously acquired by the individual's
experience of his immediate work and leisure environment.   At any
rate, there is room for a considerable 'looseness of fit' between
political ideology as it is measured by means of responses to items
on a questionnaire and social imagery which is ascertained by open-
ended interviews.

I would argue, then, that while the evidence from the study by
Blackburn and Mann may be compatible with the interpretation that
no clear-cut ideologies exist among their sample of Peterborough
workers, this is not conclusive proof that these workers lack well
defined class images.   I have said that the latter cannot be
investigated by means of questionnaires and I suspect that the same
is true for political beliefs;   that is to say, if one wishes to
study the coherence of political ideologies from the point of view
of the person's intellectual ordering of the world and not from the
point of view of the statistical correlations between his graphic-
ally recorded replies to nine questions.   The fact that the
respondent's answers to the investigator's questions do not exhibit
the consistency which the investigators believe should obtain does
not preclude the possibility that the respondent could provide a
rationale for this apparent inconsistency if he were given the
opportunity of relating his replies to his own construct of social
and political life.   Of course, this begs the question of whether
ordinary people have and need to have coherent beliefs of this kind.
But on the evidence available there is yet no compelling reason to
think that the Leninist view of Mann is to be preferred to the
Gramscian one which holds that the category of intellectuals is not
to be confined to those who write books and make speeches;   a view

incidentally which has been excellently exemplified by Lane's
biographical interviews with fifteen blue- and white-collar
workers in Connecticut (1962).

Yet the question which Blackburn and Mann have posed is important
and must remain an open one.   And in making problematic the assumption that distinctive images of society are at all widespread have
raised a further issue which several other contributors have also
commented on: that is, whether the formation of working class
images of society can be studied only from the view point of immediate work and community relations, especially when changes in these
relations seem on the whole to be breaking down the closed and
isolated local societies of the traditional working class, and at
the same time exposing them increasingly to the often countervailing
ideological influences of the mass media, mass organisations and
national economic forces.   Such a criticism is echoed by Batstone
when he asks: 'Is it really the case that social imagery derives
mainly from personal experience? Is it really the case that national
crises, what is seen in the mass media, what is seen to happen in
other situations, has no effect upon people's perception?' (Chapter
7).   And Moore makes a similar sort of point in arguing that the
original paper 'underestimated the importance of ideas as such in
forming images of society' and that it ignored the role of political
parties 'in deliberately promoting or suppressing certain views of
the social order' (Chapter 3).

I can deal with these extremely important questions in only the
most summary fashion.   To some extent they were anticipated in the
original paper.   The conception of' the privatised worker was an
attempt to consider the consequences for class images of the
dissolution of the relatively closed types of local structures
which harboured the traditional worker.   Moreover, in the context
of such changes in work and community milieux, I did explicitly
consider the possibility that not only would privatised workers be
more open to the mass media but also that the kind of 'classless'
social imagery purveyed by the latter would be congruent with the
'desocialised' conceptions of inequality that these workers are led
to construct from (and able to maintain in) the social settings in
which they work and spend their leisure.   This is simply one
instance of the sociological rule that the ideological products of
the mass media and political parties and churches have an effect,
a generally reinforcing one, in so far as they correspond to the
preconceptions of the audience at which they are directed.   Or to
use Weber's terminology there must be an 'elective affinity' between
ideas and 'interests' (both ideal and material) if ideologies are
to be able to articulate and direct these latent, sub-ideological
predispositions.   Moore's own account of the role of Methodism in
creating a moral bond between employer and worker is a good example
of this: the precondition of such religious beliefs performing
this function was their homologous relationship to the paternalistic
work structure that existed in the mining villages.   As he himself
points out: 'The Liberal-Methodist view of class structure would
not have stood up if the coal owners had not in some way conformed
to the expectations arising from the Methodist model' (Chapter 3).
Of course, this is not to say that such a particular ideology could
be predicted as a universal concomitant of this type of social

structure.   I have already argued at some length earlier on in this paper that it is a misunderstanding of the intention of the original work to expect that it should enable one to explain the specific forms of class consciousness which obtain in different historical settings.   But the thesis would be entirely invalid if there were not always some definite relationship between the structures of work and community, social imagery and of received ideology proper.   More than this has never been claimed for the original analysis. (2)

Finally, the question of whether the concept of the traditional worker is any longer viable is not for me to answer.   Its disinterment from the pages of the 'Sociological Review' has put me under a certain obligation to adopt at least an avuncular interest in its resuscitation in this symposium.   Perhaps it has been revived only long enough to enable us to return the official verdict that it has after all succumbed to facts; and that is not inconsiderable.

NOTES

1 It may be noted that the degree to which 'white-collar affiliations' are present in a worker's social network is not to be regarded as an 'extraneous' and ad hoc variable in the typology of deferential, proletarian and privatised workers.   Although it was only dealt within a footnote of the original article, it was treated as being systematically related to the industrial and community milieux in which such workers are to be found.

2 While the concepts of 'theodicy' and 'soteriology' may appear inappropriate concepts for the analysis of secular ideologies, a full understanding of the humbler, everyday solutions of the problems of suffering and injustice is probably only to be arrived at in such terms.   In this respect, the original essay, by treating images of society simply as ideal cognitive replications of the social milieux, leaves much to be desired.

Chapter 15

RADICAL CLASS CONSCIOUSNESS: A COMMENT

J.H. Westergaard

I shall not make a point by point commentary on Professor Lockwood's
paper on the traditional worker.   Nor do I want to disinter his
earlier paper yet again in detail: he himself confessed to an
avuncular rather than a paternal interest in that.   But I do want
to take up a few general issues that arise partly from several of
the contributions to the symposium, partly from David Lockwood's
commentary; and to start from some of the points in his original
paper and his remarks about it above.

I take a good deal of his partial defence of the 1966 paper.
But there is, first, one matter on which he seems to protest too
much.   He was concerned in the 1966 paper, he says, with the
question of 'communal sociability' as it affects class imagery;
not with class consciousness.   To my mind the distinction is
spurious.   It is a distinction, of course, which he relates to the
presence or absence of explicit political elements in 'stratification consciousness'.   But it seems spurious, above all, because
any kind of class imagery has political connotations.   Class imagery
involves an image of society; or a series of perhaps contradictory,
conflicting, rather confused and ambivalent pictures of what society
is like and where the individual fits into it.   However confused,
however contradictory, there are inevitable political elements,
whether they are explicit or not.   Moreover, both he and everybody
else here have been concerned, more or less directly, with just
those political connotations.

The point is not just a terminological one.   For it ties in with
my next one.   To my mind - and I have said the same thing before -
the fundamental weakness of the 1966 typology was that it allowed
no room, no box, for 'universalistic class consciousness' (to use a
clumsy shorthand phrase) or for the elements of such consciousness.
David Lockwood refers above to 'proletarianism Mark II'.   This is
precisely what I have in mind by a universalistic class consciousness.   But he locates 'Mark II' only in the future.   In fact - and
the point is essential - strong elements of Mark II have been present
in the past as well, and are present today.   They may very well be
present in the future: I certainly hope they will be.   But one
cannot simply ignore their past and present reality, even though
they have been mixed with contradictory features.   Yet that is just

what the 1966 typology does.   It has no room for a universalistic class consciousness, or for what it may be better to call simply a radical class consciousness.   (Revolutionary, on the other hand, would be the wrong term: a revolutionary consciousness is just one particular version - or perhaps several particular versions - of a radical class consciousness.)   A radical class consciousness involves identification with, a recognition of common interests with, workers in other situations, outside the immediate locality, outside the particular conditions of an occupational community.   Hence the label universalistic.   It involves identification and recognition of common interests with wage earners in other occupations.   It is quite distinct from identification with what earlier in the symposium was called occupational culture;   distinct, too, from identification with an occupational community in the geographical sense.   It involves at least a tentative vision of an 'alternative society'. It certainly involves opposition.   The vision of an alternative society may be an implicit one;   but historically it has been more than that.   Some vision of this kind has been carried within all the Social Democratic movements, as well as in the Communist movements, of Western capitalist society: a vision, however inchoate, of a society different in character and quality from capitalism. The point (and my criticism here is not aimed at the particular type of proletarianism which David Lockwood identified in his typology of 1966, but at the general nature of the typology) is that the typology does not allow for that sort of vision as a part of class consciousness.   It cannot be accommodated within the box where proletarian traditionalism sits, as Lockwood himself has explicitly recognised.   Nor can it be accommodated in the other boxes.   But the historical reality is that the parochial boundaries of traditional proletarianism have indeed been transcended, and are still being transcended every day, by working-class opposition characterised by a sense of general class identity.   I find the failure to allow for this surprising.   To admit it as a possibility for the future only - proletarianism Mark II - is not enough to remedy the omission.

The omission is surprising not only in the historical light of the growth of labour movements;   but also in the light of the social commentary of a whole host of Victorian reformers and critics.   For they often explicitly recognised the clash (either actual or potential) between the conservative restraints of localism, on the one hand, and the radical and therefore frightening implications of any breach of those restraints, on the other.   I am always reminded on this point of Thomas Chalmers who in his book 'The Civic and Christian Economy of Large Towns' in the 1820s advocated a system of 'localism', to break down the working-class districts of the big cities into small units.   His purpose was in part to restore - or to introduce - Christianity to the working class;   but it was also to do so for one particular reason, the reason so many Victorian commentators had in mind when they wanted to Christianise the working class: that was to stifle any rebellious tendency.   His argument was precisely that if working-class interests could be turned inwards into the locality, then workers would be prevented from forming alliances and loyalties across the restraining boundaries of the locality;   and social order would be safeguarded.   Divide and rule.

So the Victorians were very conscious of this clash between the conservatism of localism and the potential radicalism of non-localism.   And it is just because the clash has been recognised long ago that I find the failure to make a place for a category of universalistic class consciousness, or for elements of it, very puzzling.   Lockwood finds, he says, Cousins and Brown's results from their study of shipbuilding workers quite compatible with his typology.   Their picture of fragmentation within the shipyards, within local communities, and among crafts, is a picture that emphasises just those parochial restraints of traditionalism which loomed large in the 1966 paper.   That is quite right.   But the point misses the main significance of the shipbuilding study, which lies in the character of present and potential changes.   These changes involve not just an erosion of internal divisions between crafts, between individual shipyards, and individual parts of ship-yards;   they point also to an increasing identification outside and beyond the parochial boundaries of shipyard and community – of workers there with workers in other situations elsewhere, in other shipyards, even in other industries.   It is just that kind of identification which the typology does not allow for.

Let me make one other point, apparently en passant though still with reference to the 1966 paper.   I have never myself been able to follow the common assumption – which is made in that paper too – that a 'power and conflict' image of society must necessarily be associated with a dichotomous view of society.   Of course there is evidence that the two often empirically go together: that people with an eye for conflict and the weight of power in society often also see society as split in two.   But that need not be so.   And a sophisticated 'power and conflict' image of society would certainly not be a simple dichotomous one.   It would have a major dichotomous element.   But it would also, to be realistic, have to recognise conflicts additional to, and sometimes cutting across, the main conflicts of interest on which a dichotomous model focuses.   Indeed, this is not a point just en passant, or a mere technical quibble.   For the assumption that power and conflict imagery must go with dichotomous imagery leads to a search in the wrong direc-tions: to much too one-eyed and simple minded a search when attempts are made to understand and classify social imagery.   It leads to a very mechanical kind of count of the number of classes, or strata, or what not, which are recognised and given tags by individual respondents in surveys.   To count up in that way is to miss the point.   The real question is not the number of categories which people distinguish;   but the nature of the relations which they recognise between them, and the basis of the differences which they see.   Counting class labels is an easy and misleading sub-stitute for the complex and sensitive analysis required.

But I want to return to my main point, the omission from the 1966 typology of any provision for universalistic class consciousness. If I am right about this, the crucial question then is: what are the circumstances which make for class identification of that universalistic kind, or for some elements of it however mixed with contradictory features?   What leads to the emergence of a vision, or the fragments of a vision, of an alternative society;   to an 'oppositionism' which goes beyond the parochial boundaries of

locality, of craft, of a particular industrial segment?   Clearly
David Lockwood is right that one very important thing is to try
to identify the structural sources of this.   And Frank Parkin in
'Class Inequality and Political Order' (1971) attempted to deal
with just this issue.   He took up the point that there have been
quite strong elements of a universalistic class identification in
the labour movements of all Western capitalist countries except
the USA; and he attempted an answer to the question of their
source.   His answer in crude outline, if I follow it correctly,
was that these universalistic elements are in a sense alien to the
working class and to working class culture.   They have no indigenous
roots there, but are imported from outside the working class:
borrowed from intellectuals and professional politicians who, whatever their individual origins, do not derive their visionary ideas
from the world of ordinary labour.   Now I am convinced that this
is not an answer, that it evades the question.   Although certainly
one needs to go through it more carefully than there is any hope
of doing here, labour history seems clear enough that a great deal
of opposition of a universalistic kind, involving a vision of an
alternative society, has its own roots within the working class.
And that in this country goes back at least to Chartism.   Take,
for instance, one or two of the essays in Asa Briggs's collection
of Chartist studies.   The point is made clearly there that there
were socialist objectives and ideas in Chartism, even though they
were pushed into the background for much of the time; and that
these were to a considerable degree a feature of working class
Chartism, rather than of the middle class reformism which formed
another wing within the movement.   It seems, then, to put it
plainly, that Parkin's answer is just wrong.   But to say that
is not to say that I have 'the answer' to the question what are
the circumstances, the conditions, the structural features which
can make for the emergence of class identity among workers otherwise
separated by locality and trade, for a common vision of an alternative society.   I would like, however, to make some very elementary
points towards an answer.
    The first (and this in partial mitigation of some of my earlier
critical comments) is that David Lockwood's identification of a
'traditional proletarian type' and of its sources in occupational
communities, has been valuable in pin-pointing part of the dilemma
which both historically, and perhaps in a different sense still now,
has confronted working class movements.   Radical class consciousness, and the organisation and action on the part of the working
class which go with it, require two basic kinds of precondition.
Both are complex, but simple labels can be attached to them.   One
is solidarity; the other is vision.   Now it may well be that the
conditions which have helped to produce the kind of everyday
solidarity characteristic of working-class life are to some degree
at war with the conditions conducive to vision.   Working-class
daily life is circumscribed in very concrete ways by parochial
limitations, by local boundaries and by boundaries of kinship, by
the pressures of immediate need.   This is a consequence of relative
poverty, insecurity and deprivation; of the business simply of
making life liveable when resources are tight.   And it poses a
dilemma for working-class movements, because if they are to be

successful they must transcend those limitations.   If they are to
arouse and maintain a consciousness of class and political purpose,
then these parochial limitations - the everyday limitations of a
life of propinquity, the blinkers of what is here and now - have to
be pushed aside.   But to point to the dilemma is not to say that
it cannot be resolved: for the dilemma historically has been - and
is continuously being - resolved, if only in part.   On the contrary,
it is to ask just what are those conditions which have helped and
still help to resolve it, and to make for a wider, non-parochial,
universalistic class identification - for the vision that has to
join with solidarity and extend its initial boundaries.   The
conditions for that must lie essentially - and here I come back to
David Lockwood's penultimate remarks - in the wider society rather
than in local circumstances.   I want to take this up in a moment.

   The second point is that the factors which helped in the initial
formation of class consciousness among workers, in the past, may
offer comparatively little guide to the relevant factors today.
One example, perhaps, is the part played by local solidarity.
Despite its parochialism the strength of that must have been
historically important in the formation of working-class organisation, working-class action, working-class consciousness.   It
provided the immediate basis for any kind of working-class organisation at all: for the realisation that action was possible; and for
at least a primitive consciousness of potential strength.   But
that is in the past; and the kind of solidarity which was necessary
at an early stage, closely dependent on its local roots, is almost
certainly much less important today.   Take an example which goes
back to the earlier discussion above about 'size effects'.   The
issue raised then was whether the size of units of production had
an independent effect on class imagery; or was the apparent effect
merely there because size was highly correlated with a number of
other important characteristics relevant to class imagery?   My
suspicion is that in the early stages of the formation of working-
class movements (and still today at the fringes of our society,
where residual non-proletarianised sections of the population are
being incorporated into the national working class), there sheer
scale of the workplace and work community was and may still be
important.   Numbers are likely to be crucial in the early stages
to give consciousness of strength, to allow some degree of anonymity
vis a vis employers and authorities.   But typically now, size is
probably much less important by itself; and its remaining importance may arise largely through its continuing association with a
number of other factors which help to make or break class organisation and identity.

   My third point goes back again to David Lockwood's 1966 paper.
It concerns the question where we look for the structural features
which either inhibit or promote class identity and opposition to the
current order.   The point of the 1966 paper was to direct attention
to the role of 'micro-structural' features - that is, of conditions
and relationships in the local community and at the workplace - in
the formation of social and class imagery.   To start by looking
there was reasonable enough.   But the result now, I think, has
been to divert attention from 'macro-structural' features.   Yet it
follows from my earlier argument, if that is right, that the import-

ance of macro-structural features has been and is increasing by
comparison with local community and workplace conditions - the
importance, that is, of large-scale market forces and of the national,
even international, socio-political context of events; of the mass
media too perhaps, though their role may be liable to exaggeration.
Indeed there is a risk that we may also ignore the large part played
in the past as well by such features, and by market circumstances
as distinct from community and workplace conditions.   On the
latter point, Asa Briggs, for example, examined the socio-economic
structure of several British cities in the nineteenth century and
tried to relate variations in their economic structure to variations
in their history of working-class politics.   He was concerned not
least with the role of market factors; and found, to take one
example, an explanation of Birmingham's long resistance to labour
politics in the persistence of small-scale enterprise there and of
associated market circumstances.   Local market circumstances then,
of course, varied much more than now.   To keep our eyes fixed on
the distinctive features of local communities is more liable to
mislead when we try to understand what goes on today.   There are
certainly plenty of examples of the importance of 'macro-structural'
features and market factors, in inhibiting or promoting class
consciousness, in the papers in this symposium itself: in those
by Cousins and Brown; on agricultural workers by Bell and Newby;
and by Moore in his discussion of the mobilisation of class
consciousness among miners.

So too today, if we look over the history of the past few years
at the signs of a growing, though still limited and ambivalent,
radicalisation of workers.   Among those signs have been, in particular, a partial breakdown of the previously tight institutional-
isation of conflict in industry, through the growth and militancy
of shopfloor organisation; a shift in the locus of class conflict,
at least temporarily, away from parliamentary and council chamber
politics to industry - and of opposition away from the Labour party
to the unions; a greater diversity of forms of industrial and
other 'direct' action; and not least a reaction of panic on the
part of the establishment, which in turn has led to a confrontation
in industrial relations - with a reluctant engagement even of the
official unions and a re-emergence of large nationwide strikes -
which is out of line with the more usual emphasis upon compromise
and tight containment of conflict in British society.   If we look
for the sources of these shifts, we have to look precisely to
large-scale factors of market and socio-political context.   To
look at conditions in local communities and individual workplaces
helps very little to explain these nationawide and even international
trends.

Chapter 16

THE RADICAL WORKER: A POSTSCRIPT

David Lockwood

I address myself here to the concept which provided the 'unofficial' theme of the conference on which this symposium is based, a concept which is invoked at several points in the discussion of research reports and which is dealt with at some length by Westergaard in his contribution above.　The views expressed in this connection may be summarized by saying that the 1966 paper foreclosed rigorous analysis of what Parkin (1971, p.97) has termed 'radical meaning systems' among the working class by its imposition of a truncated set of categories that allowed only for the comparison of a traditional proletarian worker with a new privatised worker. Neither of these types, so it is held, manages to capture the socio-economic situation and social imagery of a putative, new, radical working class which, although existing mainly as a poten- tial formation and making its presence felt only intermittently, is nevertheless an important point of reference:　and not only for political reasons but also because, theoretically considered, it represents a type of working class which is characterised by a fusion and a higher development (dare I say 'Aufhebung'!) of attributes of both the proletarian and privatised workers.

Now while it is true to say that the radical worker does not figure among the 'dramatis personae' of the 1966 paper, he is certainly implicit in the property space underlying the differen- tiation of the proletarian, deferential and privatised workers. The latter may be distinguished from one another along two dimensions:　on the one hand by the degree to which work and community relations make for particularistic as opposed to univer- salistic solidarities;　and on the other by the degree to which workers' images of society endorse or reject the dominant ideology. Thus both types of traditional worker share the property of being embedded in predominantly particularistic milieux, but differ from one another in that whereas the deferential is oriented to the existing order of (status) hierarchy there is in the case of the proletarian worker at least some primordial image of an alternative social dispensation, as Westergaard correctly insisted in his remarks on Parkin's thesis.　The thesis that 'if socialist parties ceased to present a radical, class-oriented meaning-system to their supporters, then such an outlook would not persist of its own accord

among the subordinate class' (Parkin, 1971, p.98).   This primordial
image of an alternative order is most clearly expressed in the
everyday morality of communal sociability and in the solidaristic
collectivism of trade unionism, both of 'which involve beliefs and
values which are congruent with and receptive to socialist ideology
and which further condition its development.   The social imagery
of the privatised worker shares with that of the deferential an
orientation to the existing order of (pecuniary) hierarchy, but
his work and community relationships are potentially more conducive
to universalistic solidarities if only because he is detached or
isolated from the particularistic bonds common to both deferential
and proletarian milieux.   It is then the combination of class-wide
solidarities and an oppositional consciousness that characterises
the radical worker, or what Westergaard referred to as 'an identification with workers in other situations outside the local community' and 'a tentative vision of an alternative society'.   This
type of class consciousness has been described as 'ideological
collectivism' by Anderson in the course of his critique of the
concept of instrumental collectivism, which was a term used by
Goldthorpe and I in seeking to distinguish the orientation of the
privatised worker from the solidaristic collectivism of the
proletarian traditionalist.   And largely in response to the work
of Anderson (1965) and Westergaard (1965) the 1966 paper did, albeit
all too cursorily, consider the conditions under which an ideological collectivism might emerge.   But the baseline was the concept
of the privatised, not the radical worker.
   So far I have tried to demonstrate that there is no difficulty
in locating the radical worker within the same analytical framework
as that which was used to delineate the original three types of
workers.   However the problem remains, now as it did in 1966, of
specifying the conditions under which adhesion to a 'radical
meaning-system' is likely to become at all widespread among the
working class.   And this problem resolves itself first and
foremost into the question: under what conditions does socialist
ideology articulate with workers' images of society?   For the
emergence of a radical class consciousness has its precondition
in the affinity between the theoretical consciousness of socialist
soteriology and the practical consciousness of working class life.
The problematic nature of the relationship between these two
levels of consciousness must be the starting point of any analysis
of working class radicalism.   For this reason I find it curious
that Westergaard should seek to argue that the distinction between
images of society and political (in this case radical) class
consciousness is spurious on the grounds that any kind of class
imagery has political connotations.   The question is surely how
the political connotations of holding one or another kind of
belief about the structure of social inequality affect the worker's
receptivity to ideologies which seek to present an alternative
vision of society.   Moreover, to argue that no valid distinction
of this sort is possible seems to ignore the fact that a labour
movement is itself a stratification of consciousness in which there
is a normal tension between the polished ideological products of
its intellectuals and the roughly assembled constructions of social
reality which arise from the everyday experiences of the mass

membership.   Finally, if there is no meaningful distinction between these two levels, then why is the hiatus between them perceived as a crucial one by every acute left-wing observer of the contemporary working class?   Gorz's is by no means an isolated voice in claiming that the weakness of the working class and socialist movement has been its 'inability to link the struggle for socialism to the every-day demands of the workers' (Gorz, 1967, p.5).

This is not to say that the study of the images of society that are fashioned by the immediate work and community relations of the worker is sufficient for the analysis of the conditions under which a radical meaning system might emerge.   As I have argued above, with reference to proletarian traditionalism, the specific histor-ical form of class consciousness cannot be understood simply by a sociology of working-class milieux in abstraction from the wider economic and political context.   Yet at the same time the patterns of beliefs and aspirations which stem from experiences of proximate social situations are an essential part of the analysis.   And on this matter students of the radical potential of the working class would appear to agree that the particular configuration of beliefs which is requisite for radical class consciousness (identity, opposition, totality, alternative) is far from being the axiom of shopfloor thinking (see for example Gorz, 1967; Mann, 1973; Beynon, 1973).   On the contrary, the 'spontaneous' tendency is for demands to be focused on what has come to be called 'economism and defensive control', a strategy which largely conforms to Lenin's idea of trade union consciousness.   This finding is, of course, not incompatible with the diagnosis that underlying these limited goals there are latent dissatisfactions, much more threatening to capitalist relations of production because they cannot be met within them, but which can be brought into the workers' consciousness through a moral re-education which is geared to a progressive encroachment on managerial control.   The radicalisation of the worker thus entails the manufacturing of new forms of relative deprivation by a systematic arraignment of the existing industrial order which will demonstrate the interconnect-edness of particular conflicts and at the same time provide a conception of a practicable, alternative socialist totality.   It is for this reason that the question of the points of articulation between such an ideology and workers' images of society, far from being a category mistake, acquires such an important theoretical and political significance.   However, the precise nature of the means by which consciousness can be raised to a radical level by such a strategy of producing 'positive' discontent is not a matter of agreement (for example, Gorz, 1967, pp.13-18 and Beynon, 1973, pp.230-1 appear to arrive at opposite conclusions about whether unions can operate as the key agency of radicalisation).

As to the wider institutional conditions of a possible radical-isation of the working class my remarks must be inappropriately brief.   Much stress has been placed on the consequences of recent changes in market forces for the creation of a consciousness of a community of fate among different sections of workers who have previously imagined their positions immune from and unrelated to the adversities afflicting those in other firms and industries. Without wishing to deny the significance of such new features of

the workings of the capitalist economy, their consequences for
radicalisation can easily be overrated, and, moreover, this
concentration on economic conditions may divert attention from the
conceivably equally important political sphere.   If one is looking
for sources of universalism in the structure of modern capitalist
societies, then surely an even more strategic structure than the
market is the institution of citizenship.   In its relevance to
class conflict, its major aspects are as follows: the limitations
which it imposes upon the 'naked economic power' of the marketplace;
the civic incorporation of the worker; and the institutional
separation of industrial from political conflict.   All these have
been held to militate against the development of 'radical meaning-
systems' among the working class.   And quite correctly.   For in
thinking of a recipe for radicalism, it is only necessary to
contemplate the effects of a re-establishment of a property
franchise or the transfer of social services from a citizenship
to a market method of allocation.   The unquestionably radicalising
effects of such a retrogression would be due not only to the
de facto reversion to a pure class situation but also, and mainly,
to the sense of relative deprivation created by the removal of
established status rights.   The very improbability of this kind
of change only serves to underline the crucial importance of
citizenship status for any assessment of class conflict at the
present time.   But citizenship is not entirely a one-edged weapon;
it provides a conception of equality whose logic is not inherently
confined to the political order.   And there is no guarantee that
demands for further extensions of the principles of citizenship
would have the ameliorative effects on class relations that civic
incorporation has had in the past.   One specific and now central
arena in which recourse to universalistic standards might indeed
widen and intensify class conflict is that of incomes policy, which
is itself conditioned by the fact of a universal franchise and thus
by the imperative political need to legitimise the relativities of
restraint that are called for in the face of national economic
crises.   This has been well stated by Goldthorpe (1969, pp.198-9):

> It is not simply that a 'freeze' or period of tight control over
> incomes may be followed by heightened militancy in wage demands,
> threatening greater inflationary problems than before.   There
> is a further, yet more awkward possibility: namely, that
> through increasing information about, and interest in, differ-
> ences between occupational rewards and conditions, the actual
> operation of an incomes policy will serve to broaden compara-
> tive reference groups among the mass of the population, and at
> the same time bring issues of equity and fairness into greater
> subjective salience.... To the extent that evaluations of income
> and other economic differences do become less confused and
> obscure, there is little reason to suppose that what will emerge
> will be greater consensus from one group or stratum to another:
> the far more likely outcome, given the prevailing degree of
> inequality is that conflicts will become more clearly defined
> and more widely recognised - that the anomic state of economic
> life will be made increasingly manifest.

The ex-Chairman of the Prices and Incomes Board has recently gone
further than this in arguing that wage demands are already informed

by the worker's 'attempt to extend into the economic field the
political equality to which he has become accustomed', and that
'the struggle for economic equality is to the twentieth century
what the struggle for political rights was to the nineteenth
century' (Jones, 1973, pp.22-3).   Be this as it may, the 'exploitation' of the dominant ideology is not the least important strategy
that organised labour can pursue if its goal is a radical one.   And
in this context it is again necessary to maintain the distinction
between images of society with which the 1966 paper was concerned,
and the process of ideological mobilisation for which the former
may, or may not, provide an adequate base.

BIBLIOGRAPHY

ABRAMS, M. (1961), Class and Politics, 'Encounter', 17, 39-44.
ABRAMS, M. and ROSE, R. (1960), 'Must Labour Lose?', Penguin, Harmondsworth.
ABRAMS, P. (1972), The Sense of the Past and the Origins of Sociology, 'Past and Present', 55, 18-32.
ALLEN, V. (1966), 'Militant Trade Unionism', Merlin, London.
ANDERSON, M. (1972), The Study of Family Structure, in E.A. Wrigley (ed.), 'Nineteenth Century Society', Cambridge University Press, pp.47-81.
ANDERSON, P. (1965), The Origins of the Present Crisis, in P. Anderson and R. Blackburn (eds.), (1965), pp.11-52.
ANDERSON, P. and BLACKBURN, R. (eds.), (1965), 'Towards Socialism', Fontana, London.
ANDRIEUX, A. and LIGNON, J. (1960), 'L'Ouvrier d'aujourdhui', Paris.
ANGELL, R.C. (1936), 'The Family Encounters the Depression', Scribner's, New York.
APTER, D. (ed.) (1964), 'Ideology and Discontent', Free Press, New York.
ARGYRIS, C. (1957), 'Personality and Organisation', Harper & Row, New York.
ARNOLD, D.O. (ed.) (1970), 'The Sociology of Subcultures', Glendessary Press, Berkeley.
ARNOT, R. PAGE (1949), 'The Miners, 1889-1910', Allen & Unwin, London.
ASHLEY, W.J. (1903), 'The Adjustment of Wages', Longmans, London.
BAKKE, E.W. (1933), 'The Unemployed Man', Nisbet, London.
BANKS, J.A. (1964), The Structure of Industrial Enterprise in Industrial Society, in 'The Development of Industrial Societies', Sociological Review Monograph Number 8, Keele, pp.43-61.
BANKS, J.A. (1970), 'Marxist Sociology in Action', Faber & Faber, London.
BANNISTER, D. and MAIR, J.M. (1968), 'The Evaluation of Personal Constructs', Academic Press, London.
BANTON, M. (1964), 'The Policeman in the Community', Tavistock, London.
BANTON, M. (ed.) (1965), 'The Relevance of Models for Social Anthropology', Tavistock, London.

BEALES, H.L. and LAMBERT, R.S. (eds.) (1934), 'Memoirs of the Unemployed', Gollancz, London.
BECKER, H.S. (1963), 'Outsiders', Free Press, New York.
BECKER, H.S., GREER, B., HUGHES, E.C. and STRAUSS, A. (1961), 'Boys in White', University of Chicago Press.
BEER, S.M. (1965), 'Modern British Politics', Faber & Faber, London.
BELL, C. and NEWBY, H. (1972), 'Community Studies', Allen & Unwin, London.
BELL, C. and NEWBY, H. (1973), The Sources of Variation in Agricultural Workers' Images of Society, 'Sociological Review', 21, 229-53.
BELLERBY, J.R. (1956), 'Agriculture and Industry: Relative Income', Macmillan, London.
BENDIX, R. (1963), 'Work and Authority in Industry', Harper & Row, New York.
BENNEY, M. and HUGHES, E.C. (1956), Of Sociology and the Interview, 'American Journal of Sociology', 62, 137-42.
BERGER, B.M. (1960), 'Working Class Suburb', University of California Press, Berkeley.
BERGER, P. (ed.) (1964), 'The Human Shape of Work', Macmillan, New York.
BERGER, P. and LUCKMANN, T. (1966), 'The Social Construction of Reality', Allen Lane, London.
BERGER, P. and PULLBERG, S. (1965), Reification and the Sociological Critique of Consciousness, 'History and Theory', 4, 196-211.
BERNSTEIN, E. (1909), 'Evolutionary Socialism', Independent Labour Party, London.
BEYNON, H. (1973), 'Working for Ford', Penguin, Harmondsworth.
BEYNON, H. and BLACKBURN, R.M. (1972), 'Perceptions of Work', Cambridge University Press.
BIRCH, A.H. (1959), 'Small Town Politics', Oxford University Press.
BLACKBURN, Robin (1967), The Unequal Society, in R. Blackburn and A. Cockburn (eds.), 'The Incompatibles: Trade Union Militancy and the Consensus', Penguin, Harmondsworth, pp.15-55.
BLACKBURN, Robin (ed.) (1972), 'Ideology in Social Science', Fontana, London.
BLACKBURN, R.M. and MANN, M. (1973), Constraint and Choice: Stratification and the Market for Unskilled Labour, paper given at the British Sociological Association Annual Conference, on Social Stratification, April.
BLAUNER, R. (1960), Work Satisfaction and Industrial Trends in Modern Society, in W. Galenson and S.M. Lipset (eds.), 'Labor and Trade Unionism', Wiley, New York, pp.339-60.
BLAUNER, R. (1964), 'Alienation and Freedom', University of Chicago Press.
BLONDEL, J. (1963), 'Voters, Parties and Leaders', Penguin, Harmondsworth.
BLOOM, U.H. (1963), 'Mrs. Bunthorpe's Respects: a Chronicle of Cooks', Hutchinson, London.
BLYTHE, R. (1969), 'Akenfield', Allen Lane, London.
BOHRNSTEDT, E.W. (1969), Observations on the Measurement of Change, in E.F. Borgatta (ed.), 'Sociological Methodology 1969', Jossey-Bass, San Francisco, pp.113-33.
BOTT, E. (1957), 'Family and Social Network', Tavistock, London.
BRASSEY, T. (1879), 'Foreign Work and English Wages', Longmans, London.

BRENNAN, T., COONEY, E.W. and POLLINS, H. (1954), 'Social Change in South-West Wales', Watts, London.
BRIGGS, A. and SAVILLE, J. (1960), 'Essays in Labour History, First Series', Macmillan, London.
BRIGGS, A. and SAVILLE, J. (1971), 'Essays in Labour History, Second Series', Macmillan, London.
BROWN, R.K. (1973), Sources of Objectives in Work and Employment, in J. Child (ed.), 'Man and Organisation', Allen & Unwin, London, pp.17-38.
BROWN, R.K. and BRANNEN, P. (1970), Social Relations and Social Perspectives amongst Shipbuilding Workers: a Preliminary Statement, 'Sociology', 4, 71-84 and 197-211.
BROWN, R.K., BRANNEN, P., COUSINS, J.M. and SAMPHIER, M.L. (1972), The Contours of Solidarity: Social Stratification and Industrial Relations in Shipbuilding, 'British Journal of Industrial Relations', 10, 12-41.
BROWN, R.K., BRANNEN, P., COUSINS, J.M. and SAMPHIER, M.L. (1973), Leisure in Work: the Occupational Culture of Shipbuilding Workers, in M.A. Smith et al. (eds.), (1973), pp.97-110.
BUTLER, D. and STOKES, D. (1969), 'Political Change in Britain', Macmillan, London.
CALDER, A. (1969), 'The People's War: Britain 1939-45', Cape, London.
CAMPBELL, J.K. (1964), 'Honour, Family and Patronage', Clarendon Press, Oxford.
CANNON, I.C. (1967), Ideology and Occupational Community: a Study of Compositors, 'Sociology', 1, 165-87.
CAPLOW, T. (1954), 'The Sociology of Work', University of Minnesota Press, Minneapolis.
CENTERS, R. (1949), 'The Psychology of Social Classes', Princeton University Press.
CICOUREL, A.V. and KITUSE, J.I. (1963), 'The Educational Decision-Makers', Bobbs-Merrill, Indianapolis.
CLELAND, S. (1955), 'The Influence of Plant Size on Industrial Relations', Princeton University Press.
COHEN, S. and TAYLOR, L. (1972), 'Psychological Survival', Penguin, Harmondsworth.
COLE, G.D.H. (1934), 'What Marx Really Meant', Gollancz, London.
COLE, G.D.H. (1948), 'The Meaning of Marxism', Gollancz, London.
COMMON, J. (ed.) (1937), 'Seven Shifts', Secker & Warburg, London.
CONVERSE, P.E. (1964), The Nature of Belief Systems in Mass Publics, in D.E. Apter (ed.) (1964), pp.206-61.
COTGROVE, S., DUNHAM, J. and VAMPLEW, C. (1971), 'The Nylon Spinners', Allen & Unwin, London.
COTGROVE, S. and VAMPLEW, C. (1972), Technology, Class and Politics: the Case of the Process Workers, 'Sociology', 6, 169-85.
COTTRELL, W.F. (1940), 'The Railroader', Stanford University Press.
COUSINS, J.M. (1971), Some Problems in the Concept of the 'Proletariat', 'Mens en Maatschappij', 46, 198-224.
COUSINS, J.M. and BROWN, R.K. (1970), Shipbuilding, in J.C. Dewdney (ed.), 'Durham County and City with Teesside', British Association for the Advancement of Science, Durham, pp.313-29.
COUSINS, J.M. and DAVIS, R.L. (1973), 'Working Class Incorporation' - A Historical Approach with reference to the Mining Communites of S.E. Northumberland, 1840-1890, in F. Parkin (ed.), 'The Social Analysis of Class Structure', Tavistock, London, pp.275-97.

CRAMLINGTON DISTRICT CO-OPERATIVE SOCIETY LTD (1912), A Short History of the Cramlington District Co-operative Society Ltd., 1861-1911, 'Jubilee Souvenir 1861-1911', Co-operative Wholesale Society Printing Works, Manchester.

CUNNISON, S. (1966), 'Wages and Work Allocation', Tavistock, London.

DAHRENDORF, R. (1959), 'Class and Class Conflict in Industrial Society', Routledge & Kegan Paul, London.

DANGERFIELD, G. (1936), 'The Strange Death of Liberal England', Constable, London.

DANIEL, W.W. (1969), Industrial Behaviour and Orientation to Work - a Critique, 'Journal of Management Studies', 6, 366-75.

DANIEL, W.W. (1971), Productivity Bargaining and Orientation to Work - a Rejoinder to Goldthorpe, 'Journal of Management Studies', 8, 329-35.

DAVIDOFF, L. (1973), Above and Below Stairs, 'New Society', 551, 26 April, 181-3.

DAVIES, A.F. (1967), 'Images of Class', Sydney University Press.

DAVIES, C.S. (1963), 'North Country Bred: a Working-class Family Chronicle', Routledge & Kegan Paul, London.

DAWE, A. (1970), The Two Sociologies, 'British Journal of Sociology', 21, 207-18.

DENNIS, N., HENRIQUES, F. and SLAUGHTER, C. (1956), 'Coal is our Life: a Study of a Yorkshire Mining Community', Eyre & Spottiswoode, London.

DEUTSCHER, I. (1969), Asking Questions (and Listening to Answers), 'Sociological Focus', 3, 13-32.

DEUTSCHER, I. (1972), Public and Private Opinions, in S.Z. Nagi and R.G. Corwin (eds.), 'The Social Contexts of Research', Wiley, London, pp.323-49.

DEUTSCHER, I. (1973),'What We Say/What We Do: Sentiments and Acts', Scott Foresman, Brighton.

DIBBLE, V.K. (1962), Occupations and Ideologies, 'American Journal of Sociology', 68, 229-41.

DOUGAN, D. (1968), 'The History of North East Shipbuilding', Allen & Unwin, London.

DOUGLASS, D. (1971), 'Pit Life in County Durham', Ruskin College History Workshop, Oxford.

DOUGLAS, J.D. (1967), 'The Social Meanings of Suicide', Princeton University Press.

DOUGLAS, J.D. (ed.) (1971), 'Understanding Everyday Life', Routledge & Kegan Paul, London.

DREITZEL, H.P. (1962), Selbstbild und Gesellschaftsbild, wissens- soziologische Ueberlegungen zum Image-Begriff, 'European Journal of Sociology', 3, 181-228.

DUBIN, R. (1956), Industrial Workers' Worlds: a Study of the 'Central Life Interests' of Industrial Workers, 'Social Problems', 3, 131-42.

DUBIN, R. (1958), 'The World of Work', Prentice Hall, Englewood Cliffs.

DUNABIN, J.P.D. (1963), The 'Revolt of the Field': The Agricultural Labourer's Movement in the 1880s, 'Past and Present', 26, 68-97.

DUNABIN, J.P.D. (1968), The Incidence and Organisation of Agricul- tural Trades Unionism in the 1870s, 'Agricultural History Review', 16, 114-41.

DUNCAN, P. (1963), Conflict and Co-operation among Trawlermen, 'British Journal of Industrial Relations', 1, 331-47.

DYOS, H. (ed.) (1968), 'The Study of Urban History', Edward Arnold, London.

ELDRIDGE, J.E.T. (1968), 'Industrial Disputes', Routledge & Kegan Paul, London.

ELDRIDGE, J.E.T. (1971a), 'The Sociology of Industrial Life', Michael Joseph, London.

ELDRIDGE, J.E.T. (1971b), Weber's Approach to the Sociological Study of Industrial Workers, in A. Sahay (ed.) (1971), pp.97-111.

ELKINS, S.M. (1968), 'Slavery', University of Chicago Press, second edition.

ELKINS, Ted Jnr (1970), 'So They Brewed Their Own Beer: the History of the Northern Clubs and Federation Brewery Ltd', Newcastle.

ELIAS, N. and SCOTSON, J.L. (1965), 'The Established and the Outsider', Cass, London.

EMMETT, I. (1964), 'A North Wales Parish', Routledge & Kegan Paul, London.

ETZIONI, A. (1961), 'A Comparative Analysis of Complex Organisations', Free Press, New York.

EVANS, E.W. (1961), 'The Miners of South Wales', University of Wales Press.

EVANS, G.E. (1956), 'Ask the Fellows Who Cut the Hay', Faber & Faber, London.

EVANS, G.E. (1960), 'The Horse in the Furrow', Faber & Faber, London.

EVANS, G.E. (1966), 'The Pattern Under the Plough', Faber & Faber, London.

EVANS, G.E. (1969), 'The Farm and the Village', Faber & Faber, London.

EVANS, G.E. (1970), 'Where Beards Wag All', Faber & Faber, London.

FINER, S.E. (1955), The Political Power of Private Capital, 'Sociological Review', 3, 279-94.

FORM, W.H. and Geschwender, J.A. (1962), Social Reference Basis of Job Satisfaction: the Case of Manual Workers, 'American Sociological Review', 27, 228-37.

FORM, W.H. and RYTINA, J. (1969), Ideological Beliefs on the Distribution of Power in the United States, 'American Sociological Review', 34, 19-31.

FOSTER, G.M. (1963), The Dyadic Contract in Tzintzuntzan, II: Patron-Client Relationship, 'American Anthropologist', 65, 1280-94.

FOSTER, J. (1968), Nineteenth Century Towns - a Class Dimension, in H.J. Dyos (ed.) (1968), pp.281-99.

FOX, A. (1971), 'A Sociology of Work in Industry', Collier Macmillan, London.

FRANKENBERG, R. (1966), 'Communities in Britain', Penguin, Harmondsworth.

FRASER, R. (1968), 'Work: 20 Personal Accounts', Penguin, Harmondsworth.

FRASER, R. (1969), 'Work 2: 20 Personal Accounts', Penguin, Harmondsworth.

FRIEDMAN, E.A. and HAVINGHURST, W. (1954), 'The Meaning of Work and Retirement', University of Chicago Press.

FRIEDMAN, P. (1970), Community Decision-making in the United States: A Review of Recent Research, 'New Atlantis', 1 (no.2), 133-42.

FROW, R., FROW, E. and KATANKA, M. (1971), 'Strikes: a Documentary History', Charles Knight, London.

FYNES, R.J. (1923), 'The Miners of Northumberland and Durham: a History of their Social and Political Progress', Thomas Summerbell, Sunderland.

GALTUNG, J. (1971), 'Members of Two Worlds', Columbia University Press, New York.

GARSIDE, W.R. (1971), 'The Durham Miners 1919-1960', Allen & Unwin, London.

GASSON, R. (1966), The Changing Location of Intensive Crops in England and Wales, 'Geography', 51, 16-28.

GEERTZ, C. (1964), Ideology as a Cultural System, in D. Apter (ed.) (1964), pp.15-47.

GEIGER, T. (1949), 'Die Klassengesellschaft im Schmelztiegel', Cologne & Hagen.

GEIGER, T. (1969), 'On Social Order and Mass Society: Selected Papers', Edited with an Introduction by Renate Mayntz, University of Chicago Press.

GENOVESE, E.D. (1970), 'The World the Slaveholders Made', Allen Lane, London.

GENOVESE, E.D. (1971), 'In Red and Black', Allen Lane, London.

GERSTL, J.E. (1961), Determinants of Occupational Community in High-Status Occupations, 'Sociological Quarterly', 2, 37-48.

GERTH, H. and MILLS, C.W. (1948), 'From Max Weber', Routledge & Kegan Paul, London.

GIDDENS, A. (1973), 'The Class Structure of the Advanced Societies', Hutchinson, London.

GIFFEN, R. (1883), The Progress of the Working Class in the last 50 Years, Inaugural address as President of the Statistical Society.

GLENN, N.D., ALSTON, J.P. and WEINER, D. (1970), 'Social Stratification: a Research Bibliography', The Glendessary Press, Berkeley.

GLYN, A. and SUTCLIFFE, B. (1972), 'British Capitalism, Workers and the Profits Squeeze', Penguin, Harmondsworth.

GOFFMAN, E. (1956), The Nature of Deference and Demeanor, 'American Anthropologist', 58, 473-502.

GOFFMAN, E. (1969), 'The Presentation of Self in Everyday Life', Allen Lane, London.

GOLD, R. (1964), The Janitor, in P.L. Berger (ed.) (1964).

GOLDMAN, L. (1971), 'La Creation culturelle dans la societe Moderne', Denoel/Gonthier, Paris.

GOLDTHORPE, J.H. (1962), The Relevance of History to Sociology, 'Cambridge Opinion', 28, 26-9.

GOLDTHORPE, J.H. (1966), Attitudes and Behaviour of Car Assembly Workers: a Deviant Case and a Theoretical Critique, 'British Journal of Sociology', 17, 227-44.

GOLDTHORPE, J.H. (1969), Social Inequality and Social Integration in Modern Britain, 'Advancement of Science', 26, 128, 190-202.

GOLDTHORPE, J.H. (1970a), 'L'image des classes chez les travailleurs manuels aises', 'Revue Francaise de Sociologie', 11, 311-38.

GOLDTHORPE, J.H. (1970b), The Social Action Approach to Industrial Sociology: a Reply to Daniel, 'Journal of Management Studies', 7, 199-208.

GOLDTHORPE, J.H. (1972a), Class, Status and Party in Modern Britain: Some Recent Interpretations, Marxist and Marxisant, 'European Journal of Sociology', 13, 342-72.

GOLDTHORPE, J.H. (1972b), Daniel on Orientations to Work: a Final Comment, 'Journal of Management Studies', 9, 266-73.

GOLDTHORPE, J.H. and LOCKWOOD, D. (1963), Affluence and the British Class Structure, 'Sociological Review', 11, 133-63.

GOLDTHORPE, J.H., LOCKWOOD, D., BECHHOFER, F. and PLATT, J. (1967), The Affluent Worker and the Thesis of 'Embourgeoisement': some Preliminary Research Findings, 'Sociology', 1, 11-31.

GOLDTHORPE, J.H., LOCKWOOD, D., BECHHOFER, F. and PLATT, J. (1968a), 'The Affluent Worker: Industrial Attitudes and Behaviour', Cambridge University Press.

GOLDTHORPE, J.H., LOCKWOOD, D., BECHHOFER, F. and PLATT, J. (1968b), 'The Affluent Worker: Political Attitudes and Behaviour', Cambridge University Press.

GOLDTHORPE, J.H., LOCKWOOD, D., BECHHOFER, F. and PLATT, J. (1969), 'The Affluent Worker in the Class Structure', Cambridge University Press.

GOODE, W.J. (1957), Community Within a Community: The Professions, 'American Sociological Review', 22, 194-200.

GORZ, A. (1965), Work and Consumption, in P. Anderson and R. Blackburn (eds.) (1965), pp.317-53.

GORZ, A. (1967), 'Strategy for Labour: a Radical Proposal', Beacon Press, Boston.

GOULD, T. and KENYON, J. (1972), 'Stories from the Dole Queue', Temple Smith, London.

GOULDNER, A.W. (1954), 'Patterns of Industrial Bureaucracy', Free Press, Chicago.

GOULDNER, A.W. (1955), 'Wildcat Strike', Routledge & Kegan Paul, London.

GOULDNER, A.W. (1971), 'The Coming Crisis of Western Sociology', Heinemann, London.

GREGORY, R. (1968), 'The Miners and British Politics 1906-14', Oxford University Press.

GROSS, N. (1953), Social Class Identification in an Urban Community, 'American Sociological Review', 17, 398-404.

GROVES, R. (1948), 'Sharpen the Sickle!', Porcupine Press, London.

GURVITCH, G. (1950), 'La Vocation actuelle de sociologie', Presses Universitaires de France, Paris.

HAER, J.L. (1957), An Empirical Study of Social Class Awareness, 'Social Forces', 36, 117-21.

HAMILTON, R.F. (1967), 'Affluence and the French Worker in the Fourth Republic', Princeton University Press.

HEATH, C.E. and WHITBY, M.C. (1970), 'The Changing Agricultural Labour Force', University of Newcastle, Agricultural Adjustment Unit Bulletin, no.10.

HELLER, C.S. (ed.) (1969), 'Structured Social Inequality', Macmillan, New York.

HILL, S. (1972), Dockers and their Work, 'New Society', no.516, 17 August, 338-40.

HILLERY, G. (1955), Definitions of Community: Areas of Agreement, 'Rural Sociology', 20, 111-23.

HINDESS, B. (1971), 'The Decline of Working-Class Politics', McGibbon & Kee, London.

HOBSBAWM, E.J. (1964), 'Labouring Men', Weidenfeld & Nicholson, London.

HOBSBAWM, E.J. (1972), The Social Function of the Past: Some
Questions, 'Past and Present', 55, 3-17.
HOBSBAWM, E. and RUDE, G. (1970), 'Captain Swing', Lawrence &
Wishart, London.
HOGGART, R. (1957), 'The Uses of Literacy', Chatto & Windus, London.
HOLLOWELL, P.G. (1968), 'The Lorry Driver', Routledge & Kegan Paul,
London.
HORN, P. (1971), 'Joseph Arch', Roundwood Press, Kineton.
HOROBIN, G. (1957), Community and Occupation in the Hull Fishing
Industry, 'British Journal of Sociology', 8, 343-56.
HORST, P. (1966), 'Psychological Measurement and Prediction',
Wadsworth, Belmont, California.
HUDSON, D. (1972), 'Munby, Man of Two Worlds', John Murray, London
HUGHES, E.C. (1958), 'Men and Their Work', The Free Press, Chicago.
HUGHES, E.C. (1971), 'The Sociological Eye: Selected Papers', Aldine,
Chicago.
HUGHES, H.S. (1959), 'Consciousness and Society: the Reorientation
of European Social Thought 1890-1930', McGibbon & Kee, London.
HYMAN, R. (1971), 'Marxism and the Sociology of Trade-Unionism',
Pluto Press, London.
HYMAN, R. (1972), 'Strikes', Fontana, London.
INDIK, B.P. (1963), Some Effects of Organizational Size on Member
Attitudes and Behaviour, 'Human Relations', 16, 369-84.
INGHAM, G.K. (1967), Organisational Size, Orientation to Work and
Industrial Behaviour, 'Sociology', 1, 239-58.
INGHAM, G.K. (1970), 'Size of Industrial Organization and Worker
Behaviour', Cambridge University Press.
'INTERNATIONAL JOURNAL OF COMPARATIVE SOCIOLOGY' (1969), issue
entitled The Sociology of the Blue Collar Worker, 10, numbers 1-2.
JACKSON, B. (1968), 'Working Class Community', Routledge & Kegan
Paul, London.
JAHODA, M., LAZARSFELD, P.F. and ZEISEL, H. (1972), 'Marienthal:
the Sociography of an Unemployed Community', Tavistock, London,
(first published in German 1933).
JESSOP, R.D. (1971), Civility and Traditionalism in English Political
Culture, 'British Journal of Political Science', 1, 1-24.
JONES, A. (1973), 'The New Inflation', Penguin, Harmondsworth.
JONES, A.W. (1941), 'Life, Liberty and Property: a Story of Conflict
and a Measurement of Conflicting Rights', J.P. Lippincott, Phila-
delphia.
JONES, P.d'A. (1968), 'The Christian Socialist Revival 1877-1914',
Princeton University Press.
KAHAN, M., BUTLER, D. and STOKES, D. (1966), On the Analytic
Division of Social Class, 'British Journal of Sociology', 17, 122-32.
KAVANAGH, D. (1971), The Deferential English: a Comparative Critique,
'Government and Opposition', 6, 333-60.
KENDALL, S.G. (1944), 'Farming Memoirs of a West Country Yeoman',
Faber & Faber, London.
KENNY, M. (1960), Patterns of Patronage in Spain, 'Anthropological
Quarterly', 33, 14-23.
KERR, C. and SIEGEL, A. (1954), The Inter-Industry Propensity to
Strike - an International Comparison, in A. Kornhauser et al. (eds.),
'Industrial Conflict', McGraw, New York, pp.189-212.
KITCHEN, F. (1940), 'Brother to the Ox', Dent, London.

KLEIN, J. (1965), 'Samples from English Culture', Routledge & Kegan Paul, London, two volumes.

KNIPE, E.E. and LEWIS, H.M. (1971), The Impact of Coal-Mining in the Traditional Mountain Sub-culture, in J.K. Morland (ed.), 'The Not so Solid South', University of Georgia Press, Athens.

KOLANKIEWICZ, J.M. (1973), The Working Class, in D. Lane and J.M. Kolankiewicz (eds.), 'Social Groups in Polish Society', Macmillan, London.

KOMAROVSKY, M. (1940), 'The Unemployed Man and His Family', The Dryden Press, New York.

KORNHAUSER, A. (1965), 'The Mental Health of the Industrial Worker', Wiley, New York.

KORNHAUSER, A., SHEPPHERD, H.L. and MAYER, A.J., (1956), 'When Labour Votes', University Books, New York.

KRAUSE, E. (1971), 'The Sociology of Occupations', Little, Brown, Boston.

LANE, M. (1972), Explaining Educational Choice, 'Sociology', 6, 255-66.

LANE, R. (1962), 'Political Ideology: Why the American Common Man Believes What he Does', The Free Press, New York.

LANE, T. and ROBERTS, K. (1971), 'Strike at Pilkingtons', Fontana, London.

LaPIERE, R.T. (1934), Attitudes v. Actions, 'Social Forces', 13, 230-7.

LASLETT, B. (1971), Mobility and Work Satisfaction: Discussion of the Use and Interpretation of Mobility Models, 'American Journal of Sociology', 77, 19-35.

LEACH, E. (1954), 'Political Systems of Highland Burma', LSE/Bell, London.

LEE, J.M. (1963), 'Social Leaders and Public Persons', Oxford University Press.

LEGGETT, J.C. (1964), Economic Insecurity and Working-class Consciousness, 'American Sociological Review', 29, 226-34.

LEGGETT, J.C. (1968), 'Class, Race and Labour: Working-class Consciousness in Detroit', Oxford University Press.

LENIN, V.I. (1967), 'The Development of Capitalism in Russia', Progress, Moscow.

LEVINE, S.B. (1958), 'Industrial Relations in Postwar Japan', University of Illinois, Urbana.

LEVI-STRAUSS, C. (1968), 'Structural Anthropology', Allen Lane, London.

LEWIS, L.S. (1965a), Class Consciousness and the Salience of Class, 'Sociology and Social Research', 49, 173-82.

LEWIS, L.S. (1965b), Class Consciousness and Inter-class Sentiments, 'Sociological Quarterly', 6, 325-38.

LIEBOW, E. (1967), 'Tally's Corner: a Study of Negro Street-corner Men', Routledge & Kegan Paul, London.

LIPSET, S.M. (1960), 'Political Man', Heinemann, London.

LIPSET, S.M., TROW, M.A. and COLEMAN, J.S. (1956), 'Union Democracy', Free Press, Chicago.

LITTLEJOHN, J. (1963), 'Westrigg: the Sociology of a Cheviot Parish', Routledge & Kegan Paul, London.

LOCKWOOD, D. (1958), 'The Blackcoated Worker: a Study of Class Consciousness', Allen & Unwin, London.

LOCKWOOD, D. (1960), The 'New Working Class', 'European Journal of Sociology', 1, 248-59.
LOCKWOOD, D. (1964), Social Integration and System Integration, in G.K. Zollschan and W. Hirsch (eds.), 'Explorations in Social Change', Routledge & Kegan Paul, London, pp.244-57.
LOCKWOOD, D. (1966), Sources of Variation in Working-class Images of Society, 'Sociological Review', 14, 249-67.
LOCKWOOD, D. (1971), Editorial Foreword to D. Lane, 'The End of Inequality?', Penguin, Harmondsworth.
LOVELL, J. (1969), 'Stevedores and Dockers', Macmillan, London.
LUDLOW, J.M. (1852), 'The Master Engineers and their Workmen', London.
LUDLOW, J.M. and JONES, LLOYD (1867), 'The Progress of the English Working Classes 1832-1867', London.
LUPTON, T. (1963), 'On the Shop Floor', Pergamon, Oxford.
LUXEMBURG, R. (1951), 'The Accumulation of Capital', Routledge & Kegan Paul, London.
MACINTYRE, A. (1967), 'Secularisation and Moral Change', Oxford University Press.
MACK, R.W. (1956), Occupational Determinateness, 'Social Forces', 35, 20-35.
MCKENZIE, G.G.N. (1967), The Economic Dimension of Embourgeoisement, 'British Journal of Sociology', 18, 29-44.
MCKENZIE, R.T. and SILVER, A. (1964), Conservatism, Industrialism, and the Working-class Tory in England, 'Transactions of the Fifth World Congress of Sociology', International Sociological Association, Louvain, vol.3, pp.191-202.
MCKENZIE, R.T. and SILVER, A. (1968), 'Angels in Marble: Working-class Conservatives in Urban England', Heinemann, London.
MALLET, S. (1963), 'La Nouvelle classe ouvriere', Paris.
MANIS, J.G. and MELTZER, B.N. (1954), Attitudes of Textile Workers to Class Structure, 'American Journal of Sociology', 60, 30-5.
MANN, M. (1970), The Social Cohesion of Liberal Democracy, 'American Sociological Review', 35, 423-39.
MANN, M. (1973), 'Consciousness and Action in the Western Working Class', Macmillan, London.
MANNHEIM, K. (1936), 'Ideology and Utopia', Routledge & Kegan Paul, London.
MARSHALL, A. (1925), Lecture to the Co-operative Congress of 1889, in A.C. Pigou (ed.), 'The Memorials of Alfred Marshall', Macmillan, London.
MARSHALL, T.H. (1963), 'Sociology at the Crossroads and Other Essays', Heinemann, London.
MARTIN, E.W. (1965), 'The Shearers and the Shorn', Routledge & Kegan Paul, London.
MARTIN, F.M. (1954), Some Subjective Aspects of Social Stratification', in D.V. Glass (ed.), 'Social Mobility in Britain', Routledge & Kegan Paul, London, pp.51-75.
MARTIN, R. and FRYER, R.H. (1973), 'Redundancy and Paternalist Capitalism', Allen & Unwin, London.
MARTINDALE, D. (1959), Sociological Theory and the Ideal Type, in L. Gross (ed.), 'Symposium on Sociological Theory', Harper, New York, pp.57-91.
MAYER, P. (1968), Migrancy and the Study of Africans in Towns, in R.E. Pahl, (1968a), pp.306-30.

MAYHEW, H. (1971), 'The Unknown Mayhew', edited with an Introduction by E.P. Thompson and E. Yeo, Merlin, London.
MAYNTZ, R. (1958), 'Soziale Schichtung und sozialer Wandel in einer Industriegemeinde', Stuttgart.
MESZAROS, I. (ed.) (1971), 'Aspects of History and Class Consciousness', Routledge & Kegan Paul, London.
MILL, J.S. (1965), On the Futurity of the Labouring Classes, 'Collected Works', Routledge & Kegan Paul, London.
MILLER, R.C. (1969), The Dockworker Subculture, 'Comparative Studies in Society and History', 11, 302-14.
MILLER, S.M. (1952), The Participant Observer and 'Over-Rapport', 'American Sociological Review', 17, 97-9.
MILLER, S.M. and REISSMAN, F. (1961), The Working Class Subculture: a New View, 'Social Problems', 9, 86-97.
MILLS, C.W. (1940), Situated Actions and Vocabularies of Motive, 'American Sociological Review', 5, 904-13.
MOORE, R.S. (1973), The Political Effects of Village Methodism, in M. Hill, (ed.), 'A Sociological Yearbook of Religion in Britain', no.6, S.C.M. Press, London, pp.156-82.
MOORE, R.S. (1974), 'Pitmen, Preachers and Politics', Cambridge University Press.
MORLAND, J.K. (1958), 'Millways of Kent', University of North Carolina Press, Chapel Hill.
MORSE, N. and WEISS, R. (1955), The Function and Meaning of Work and the Job, 'American Sociological Review', 20, 191-8.
MURPHY, R.J. and MORRIS, R.T. (1961), Occupational Situs, Subjective Identification and Political Affiliation, 'American Sociological Review', 26, 383-92.
NEALE, R.S. (1972), 'Class and Ideology in the Nineteenth Century', Routledge & Kegan Paul, London.
NEWBY, H. (1972a), The Low Pay of Agricultural Workers: A Sociological Approach, 'Journal of Agricultural Economics', 23, 15-24.
NEWBY, H. (1972b), Agricultural Workers in the Class Structure, 'Sociological Review', 20, 413-39.
NISBET, R. (1967), 'The Sociological Tradition', Heinemann, London.
NORDLINGER, E.A. (1967), 'The Working-class Tories: Authority, Deference and Stable Democracy', McGibbon & Kee, London.
NORTHERN REGIONAL PLANNING COUNCIL (1970), 'Sub-regional Statistics', Newcastle-upon-Tyne.
OESER, O.A. and HAMMOND, S.B. (eds.) (1954), 'Social Structure and Personality in a City', Routledge & Kegan Paul, London.
OSSOWSKI, S. (1963), 'Class Structure in the Social Consciousness', Routledge & Kegan Paul, London.
PAHL, R.E. (1965), 'Urbs in Rure', LSE Geographical Paper no.2, London.
PAHL, R.E. (1968a), 'Readings in Urban Sociology', Pergamon, Oxford.
PAHL, R.E. (1968b), The Rural-Urban Continuum, in Pahl (1968a), pp.263-97.
PAHL, R.E. (1968c), Newcomers in Town and Country, in L. Munby (ed.), 'East Anglian Studies', W. Heffer & Sons, Cambridge.
PAHL, R.E. (1970), 'Whose City?', Longman, London.
PALMER, G.L. et al. (eds.) (1963), 'The Reluctant Job-Changer: Studies in Work Attachments and Aspirations', University of Pennsylvania Press, Philadelphia.

PARKER, S.R. (1964), Type of Work, Friendship Patterns and Leisure, 'Human Relations', 3, 215-19.
PARKER, S.R. (1972), 'The Future of Work and Leisure', MacGibbon & Kee, London.
PARKIN, F. (1967), Working-class Conservatives: a Theory of Political Deviance, 'British Journal of Sociology', 18, 278-90.
PARKIN, F. (1971), 'Class Inequality and Political Order', MacGibbon & Kee, London.
PARKIN, F. (ed.) (1974), 'The Social Analysis of Class Structure', Tavistock, London.
PARSLER, R. (1970), Some Economic Aspects of Embourgeoisement in Australia, 'Sociology', 4, 165-79.
PARSONS, T. (1937), 'The Structure of Social Action: a Study in Social Theory', McGraw, New York.
PELLING, H. (1968), 'Popular Politics and Society in Late Victorian Britain', Macmillan, London.
PERKIN, H. (1969), 'The Origins of Modern English Society, 1780-1880', Routledge & Kegan Paul, London.
PHILLIPS, D.L. (1971), 'Knowledge from What?', Rand McNally, Chicago.
PIEPE, A., PRIOR, R. and BOX, A. (1969), The Location of the Proletarian and Deferential Worker, 'Sociology', 3, 239-44.
PITT-RIVERS, J.A. (1961), 'The People of the Sierra', University of Chicago Press.
PLATT, J. (1971), Variations in Answers to Different Questions on Perceptions of Class: Research Note, 'Sociological Review', 19, 409-19.
PLOWMAN, D.E.G., MINCHINGTON, W.E. and STACEY, M. (1962), Local Social Status in England and Wales, 'Sociological Review', 10, 161-202.
POLSKY, NED (1971), 'Hustlers, Beats and Others', Penguin, Harmondsworth.
POPE, L. (1942), 'Millhands and Preachers', Yale University Press, New Haven.
POPITZ, H., BAHRDT, H.P., JUERES, E.A. and KESTING, A. (1957), 'Das Gesellschaftsbild des Arbeiters', Mohr, Tubingen.
POPITZ, H., BAHRDT, H.P., JUERES, E.A. and KESTING, A. (1969), The Worker's Image of Society, in T. Burns (ed.), 'Industrial Man', Penguin, Harmondsworth, pp.281-324 (translation of Popitz et al. (1957), pp.232-47).
PORTES, A. (1971), On the Interpretation of Class Consciousness, 'American Journal of Sociology', 77, 228-44.
PORTES, A. (1972), Rationality in the Slum: an Essay in Interpretive Sociology, 'Comparative Studies in Society and History', 14, 268-86.
PRANDY, K. (1965), 'Professional Employees', Faber & Faber, London.
PRICE, L.L. (1887), 'Industrial Peace, its Advantages, Methods and Difficulties', Macmillan, London.
RAZZELL, P. (1973), Introduction to P. Razzell and R. Wainwright (eds.), 'The Victorian Working Class', Cass, London, pp.xxix-xlii.
REX, J. (1971), Typology and Objectivity: a Comment on Weber's Four Sociological Methods, in A. Sahay (ed.) (1971), pp.17-36.
RIMLINGER, G.V. (1959), International Differences in the Strike-Propensity of Coal-Miners, 'Industrial and Labour Relations Review', 12, 390-405.

ROBERTS, G. (1967), 'Démarcation Rules in Shipbuilding and Ship Repairing', Cambridge University Press.
ROBERTS, R. (1971), 'The Classic Slum: Salford Life in the First Quarter of the Twentieth Century', Manchester University Press.
ROBERTSON, D.J. (1960), 'Factory Wage Structures and National Agreements', Cambridge University Press.
ROSE, G. (1968), 'The Working Class', Longman, London.
ROUSIERS, P. de (1896), 'The Labour Question in Britain', Macmillan, London.
ROY, D. (1952), Quota Restriction and Goldbricking in a Machine Shop, 'American Journal of Sociology', 57, 427-41.
ROY, D. (1953), Work Satisfaction and Social Reward in Quota Achievement: an Analysis of Piecework Incentive, 'American Sociological Review', 18, 507-14.
ROY, D. (1954), Efficiency and the Fix: Informal Inter-group Relations in a Piecework Machine Shop, 'American Journal of Sociology', 60, 255-66.
ROY, D. (1970), The Study of Southern Labor Union Organising Campaigns, in R.W. Habenstein (ed.), 'Pathways to Data', Aldine, Chicago, pp.216-44.
ROYAL COMMISSION ON THE EMPLOYMENT OF CHILDREN (1842), 'Report'.
ROYAL COMMISSION ON LABOUR (1891), 'Minutes of Evidence', Group A, Volume 1.
RUNCIMAN, W.G. (1966), 'Relative Deprivation and Social Justice', Routledge & Kegan Paul, London.
RYTINA, J. and LOOMIS, C. (1970), Marxist Dialectic and Pragmatism; Power and Knowledge, 'American Sociological Review', 35, 308-18.
RYTINA, J., FORM, W.H. and PEASE, J. (1970), Income Stratification Ideology: Beliefs about the American Opportunity Structure, 'American Journal of Sociology', 75, 703-16.
SAHAY, A. (ed.) (1971), 'Max Weber and Modern Sociology', Routledge & Kegan Paul, London.
SALAMAN, G. (1971a), Some Sociological Determinants of Occupational Communities, 'Sociological Review', 19, 53-77.
SALAMAN, G. (1971b), Two Occupational Communities: Examples of a Remarkable Convergence of Work and Non-work, 'Sociological Review', 19, 389-407.
SALAMAN, G. (1974), 'Community and Occupation', Cambridge University Press.
SAMUEL, R. (1960), The Deference Voter, 'New Left Review', 1, 9-13.
SAMUEL, R. (ed.) (forthcoming), 'Work: Industrial Work Groups and Workers' Control in Nineteenth-Century England', Routledge & Kegan Paul, London.
SAVILLE, J. (1957), 'Rural Depopulation in England and Wales 1851-1951', Routledge & Kegan Paul, London.
SAYLES, L.R. (1958), 'Behaviour of Industrial Work Groups', Wiley, New York.
SCHEUCH, E.K. (1968), Das Gesellschaftsbild der 'neuen Linken', in ibid. (ed.), 'Die Wiedertäufer der Wohlstandsgesellschaft', Markus Verlag, Cologne, pp.104-23.
SCHUMPETER, J.A. (1951), 'Imperialism and Social Classes', Basil Blackwell, Oxford.
SCHUTZ, A. (1967), 'The Phemonenology of the Social World', Northwestern University Press, Evanston.

SCOTT, W.H., BANKS, J.A., HALSEY, A.H. and LUPTON, T. (1956), 'Technical Change and Industrial Relations', Liverpool University Press.

SCOTT, W.H. MUMFORD, E. MCGIVERING, I.C. and KIRKBY, J.M. (1963), 'Coal and Conflict', Liverpool University Press.

SEABROOK, J. (1971), 'City Close-up: a Study of Blackburn', Allen Lane, London.

SELF, P. and STORING, H. (1962), 'The State and the Farmer', Allen & Unwin, London.

SEMMEL, B. (1960), 'Imperialism and Social Reform: English Social-Imperial Thought, 1895-1914', Allen & Unwin, London.

SHILS, E. (1968), Deference, in J.A. Jackson (ed.), 'Social Stratification', Cambridge University Press, pp.104-32.

SHILS, E. (1971), Tradition, 'Comparative Studies in Society and History', 13, 122-59.

SHOSTAK, A.B. and GOMBERG, W. (eds.) (1964), 'Blue Collar Worlds: Studies of the American Worker', Prentice Hall, Englewood Cliffs.

SIMMEL, G. (1949), The Sociology of Sociability, (translated by E.C. Hughes), 'American Journal of Sociology', 55, 254-61.

SILVERMAN, D. (1968), Formal Organisations or Industrial Sociology: Toward a Social Action Analysis of Organisations, 'Sociology', 2, 221-38.

SILVERMAN, D. (1970), 'The Theory of Organisations', Heinemann, London.

SINFIELD, A. (1970), Poor and Out of Work in Shields, in P. Townsend (ed.), 'The Concept of Poverty', Heinemann, London, pp.220-35.

SMIGEL, E.O. (ed.) (1963), 'Work and Leisure', College and University Press, New Haven.

SMITH, M.A., PARKER, S.R. and SMITH, C.S. (eds.) (1973), 'Leisure and Society in Britain', Allen Lane, London.

SPRADLEY, J. (1970), 'You Owe Yourself a Drunk; an Ethnography of Urban Nomads', Little, Brown, Boston.

SSRC (1973), 'The Occupational Community of the Traditional Worker: Proceedings of Conference held in Durham, 25-27 September 1972', Department of Sociology and Social Administration, University of Durham, mimeographed. (Available on loan, through public and university libraries only, from the British Library (Conference Reports), Boston Spa, Wetherby, Yorkshire LS23 7BQ, England.)

STACEY, M. (1960), 'Tradition and Change: a Study of Banbury', Oxford University Press.

STACEY, M. (1969), The Myth of Community Studies, 'British Journal of Sociology', 20, 134-48.

STACEY, M. et al. (1970), The Rejection of a Planning Proposal, paper given at the International Sociological Association Conference at Varna.

STACEY, M., BATSTONE, E., BELL, C. and MURCOTT, A. (1975), 'Power Persistence and Change: a Second Study of Banbury', Routledge & Kegan Paul, London.

STEDMAN-JONES, G. (1971), 'Outcast London: a Study in the Relationship Between the Classes in Victorian Society', Oxford University Press.

STEWART, A., PRANDY, K. and BLACKBURN, R.M. (1973), Measuring the Class Structure, 'Nature', 26 October.

STOKES, R.S. (1949), A Shipyard from Within, 'Manchester School', 17, 88-96.

STORM-CLARK, C. (1971), The Miners 1870-1970: a Test Case for Oral History, 'Victorian Studies', 15, 49-74.

SVALASTOGA, K. (1959), 'Prestige, Class and Mobility', Gyldendal, Copenhagen.

SYKES, A.J.M. (1965), Some Differences in the Attitudes of Clerical and Manual Workers, 'Sociological Review', 13, 297-310.

SYKES, A.J.M. (1967), The Cohesion of a Trade-Union Workshop, 'Sociology', 1, 141-63.

SYKES, A.J.M. (1969), Navvies: Their Work Attitudes and Social Relations, 'Sociology', 3, 21-35 and 157-72.

TAYLOR, A.J.P. (1965), 'English History, 1914-1945', Oxford University Press.

TAYLOR, L. (1968), 'Occupational Sociology', Oxford University Press.

TAYLOR, L.J. (1972), Replies to Motivational Questions, 'Sociology', 6, 23-39.

TAYLOR, R.C. (1969), Migration and Motivation, in J.A. Jackson (ed.), 'Migration', Cambridge University Press, pp.99-133.

THOMPSON, D. (1971), 'The Early Chartists', Macmillan, London.

THOMPSON, E.P. (1963), 'The Making of the English Working Class', Gollancz, London.

THOMPSON, E.P. (1965), The Peculiarities of the English, in R. Miliband and J. Saville (eds.), 'The Socialist Register 1965', Merlin, London, pp.311-62.

THOMPSON, F.M.L. (1963), 'English Landed Society in the Nineteenth Century', Routledge & Kegan Paul, London.

THOMPSON, K.A. (1971), Introductory Essay, in G. Gurvitch, 'The Social Frameworks of Knowledge', Blackwell, Oxford, pp.ix-xxxvi.

THORNS, D.C. (1971), Work and its Definition, 'Sociological Review', 19, 543-55.

TIMPERLEY, S. (1970), A Study of a Self-Governing Work Group, 'Sociological Review', 18, 259-81.

TOMALIN, N. (1968), Backing Britain - The Inside Story of a Patriotic Idea, 'Sunday Times Weekly Review', 3 March.

TOURAINE, A. (1966), 'La Conscience ouvriere', Editions du Seuil, Paris.

TOURAINE, A. and RAGAZZI, O. (1961), 'Ouvriers d'origine agricole', Editions du Seuil, Paris.

TRESSELL, R. (1955), 'Ragged Trousered Philanthropists', Lawrence & Wishart, London (reprint).

TUMIN, M.M. (1961), 'Social Class and Social Change in Puerto Rico', Princeton University Press.

TUNSTALL, J. (1962), 'The Fisherman', MacGibbon & Kee, London.

TURNER, C. and HODGE, M.N. (1970), Occupations and Professions, in J.A. Jackson (ed.), 'Professions and Professionalization', Cambridge University Press, pp.17-51.

TURNER, E.S. (1962), 'What the Butler Saw: 250 Years of the Servant Problem', Michael Joseph, London.

TURNER, R.H. (1958), Life-situation and Sub-culture: a Comparison of Merited Prestige Judgement by Three Occupational Classes in Britain, 'British Journal of Sociology', 9, 299-320.

UNIVERSITY OF LIVERPOOL (1954), 'The Dock Worker', Liverpool University Press.

URE, A. (1835), 'The Philosophy of Manufactures', (reprinted Cass, London, 1967).

VALENTINE, C. (1968), 'Culture and Poverty', University of Chicago Press.

WALKER, C.R. (1950), 'Steeltown', Harper & Row, New York.

WARNER, W.L. and LOW, J.O. (1947), 'The Social System of a Modern Factory', Yale University Press, New Haven.

WATSON, W. (1964), Social Mobility and Social Class in Industrial Communities, in M. Gluckman (ed.) 'Closed Systems and Open Minds', Oliver & Boyd, Edinburgh, pp.129-57.

WEBB, S. and B. (1896), The Method of Collective Bargaining, 'Economic Journal', 6, 1-29.

WEBB, S. and B. (1897), 'Industrial Democracy', Longmans, London, 2 vols.

WEBB, S. and B. (1920), 'Industrial Democracy', Longmans, London.

WEBER, M. (1949), 'The Methodology of the Social Sciences', Free Press, Chicago.

WEDDERBURN, D. and CROMPTON, R. (1972), 'Workers' Attitudes and Technology', Cambridge University Press.

WEISS, R.S. and Kahn, R.L. (1960), Definitions of Work and Occupations, 'Social Problems', 8, 142-51.

WELBOURNE, E. (1923), 'The Miners' Unions of Northumberland and Durham', Cambridge University Press.

WESTERGAARD, J.H. (1965), The Withering Away of Class: a Contemporary Myth, in P. Anderson and R. Blackburn (eds.) (1965), pp.77-113. (Reprinted in Westergaard, 1972.)

WESTERGAARD, J.H. (1970), The Rediscovery of the Cash Nexus, in R. Miliband and J. Saville (eds.), 'The Socialist Register 1970', Merlin, London, pp.111-38.

WESTERGAARD, J.H. (1972), Sociology: the Myth of Classlessness, in R. Blackburn (ed.) 1972), pp.119-63. (Reprint, with postscript, of Westergaard, 1965).

WESTLEY, W.A. (1970), 'Violence and the Police: A Sociological Study of Law, Custom and Morality', MIT Press, Cambridge.

WHELLAN, W. & Co. (1855), 'History, Topography and Directory of Northumberland'.

WILLENER, A. (1957), 'Images de la societe et classes sociales', Imprimerie Staempfli, Berne.

WILLENER, A. (1962), L'Ouvrier et l'organisation, 'Sociologie du Travail', 4, 332-48.

WILLENER, A. (1964), Payment Systems in the French Steel and Iron-Mining Industry, in G. Zollschan and W. Hirsch (eds.), 'Explorations in Social Change', Routledge & Kegan Paul, London, pp.593-618.

WILLENER, A. (1970), 'The Action-Image of Society: On Cultural Politicisation', Tavistock, London.

WILLIAMS, J.E. (1962), 'The Derbyshire Miners', Allen & Unwin, London.

WILLIAMS, R. (1961), 'The Long Revolution', Chatto & Windus, London.

WILLIAMS, W.M. (1956), 'The Sociology of an English Village: Gosforth', Routledge & Kegan Paul, London.

WILLIAMS, W.M. (1963), 'A West Country Village: Ashworthy', Routledge & Kegan Paul, London.

YOUNG, M. and WILLMOTT, P. (1956), Social Grading by Manual Workers, 'British Journal of Sociology', 7, 337-45.

YOUNG, M. and WILLMOT, P. (1957), 'Family and Kinship in East London', Routledge & Kegan Paul, London.

YOUNG, N. (1967), Prometheans or Troglodytes? The English Working Class and the Dialectics of Incorporation, 'Berkeley Journal of Sociology', 12, 1-43.
ZWEIG, F. (1961), 'The Worker in an Affluent Society', Heinemann, London.